FELLOWSHIP:
With God and His People

The Way of Christ
Without
Denominationalism

Second Edition

Samuel G. Dawson

Gospel Themes Press
2028 S. Austin, Suite 906
Amarillo, TX 79109
www.gospelthemes.com

All italicized words in scripture quotations are emphasized by the author.

Published by:
Gospel Themes Press
2028 S. Austin, Suite 906
Amarillo, TX 79109

Published 1988. Second Edition 2004

Library of Congress Cataloging in Publications Data.

Dawson, Samuel G., 1943-
Fellowship: with God and his people.

Bibliography: p. 432
Includes index.
1. Church. 2. Christian sects. 3. Fellowship—Religious aspects—Christianity. 4. Churches of Christ—Doctrines. I. Title.
BV600.2.D34 1988 280 88-4749
ISBN 0-938855-58-1

Printed and bound in the United States of America

1 2 3 4 5 6 7 8 9 10

"Almighty God hath created the mind free. All attempts to influence it by temporal punishments or burdens...are a departure from the plan of the Holy Author of our religion...No man shall be compelled to frequent or support any religious worship or ministry or shall otherwise suffer on account of his religious opinions or belief, but all men shall be free to profess and by argument to maintain, their opinions in matters of religion. I know but one code of morality for men, whether acting singly or collectively."

(Thomas Jefferson, Jefferson Memorial, Washington, D. C.)

Foreword

This material arose from study and preaching I have done over the last three years in my continuing search for the nondenominational way of Christ. I have preached it in many congregations, and each time, those who heard it received it enthusiastically.

In addition to myself, a number of other preachers have eagerly pick up this material and taught it with similar results. It seems to strike responsive chords in many Christians wherever it is presented. Because of the response of those who have been exposed to this material, I have sought to make it available more widely.

This book is not written just to Christians, but to all who are interested in serving Christ with no allegiance to denominational creeds, doctrines, or organizations. Hopefully, it will help revitalize our plea for nondenominational service of Christ.

I'm sure this material is not flawless, but perhaps it will be helpful to you in your work. If after you read it, you are similarly provoked, perhaps you can help me improve it where needed, or convince me where I've misinterpreted completely. Your helping me to improve this material would be appreciated.

Samuel G. Dawson
Amarillo, TX

Table of Contents

Introduction:

The Nondenominational Way of Christ

All movements, whether economic, political, or religious, have people who do not realize the full implications of what they have become involved in. For example, Martin Luther, in his great efforts to reform Roman Catholicism, saw in the far distance for a man in his time and with his background, yet Luther was concerned with only reforming Roman Catholicism. He failed to look far enough to see a return all the way back to the nondenominational way of the Lord. Had we been in his position we might not have had the character, the desire for truth, and the courage to see as far as he did from what was customary in his time.

Likewise, in this country, Alexander Campbell and other restorers saw remarkably far beyond the religious environment in which they grew up. Though Campbell was well on his way out of that environment, I doubt even he thought he had completely experienced the New Testament way of truth. Whether he did or not, he died with a denominational perspective of the body of Christ.

Similarly, along with many others, I am striving to get completely free from denominational concepts of the way of Christ, yet I'm confident I too have not made it all the way. We can well wish to have the farsightedness and courage of Luther and Campbell ourselves.

To those who are interested in the non-denominational way of Christ, the way we read about in the New Testament, we hope this study will be basic to your quest. To those of us willing to allow that the restoration of that way might not be completely over in our own lives, it is hoped this study will help rid us of whatever denominational views we may still have of the body of Christ. This study examines our basic relationship to God and to other Christians through Christ.

If the basic conclusions of this study are true, they will affect drastically many important topics related to our service of Christ. For example, this study is sure to influence the way you strive to teach the gospel of Christ to people in the world. I'm more convinced than ever that nondenominational service of Christ is what countless thousands of people are after, they just don't know it's possible. Even churches who claim to be nondenominational often come across too much like a denomination to them, and not entirely without reason.

This study will probably touch your attitude toward every single Christian in the world. It will sway your attitude toward Christians you have serious doctrinal differences with, as well as the way you treat them. This study will affect your attitude toward every congregation of Christians in the world. You will probably perceive some doctrinal issues that have troubled the people of God for centuries in an entirely different light, including the covering question, the class question, the container question, the war question, divorce and remarriage issues, and institutional cooperation among congregations.

This study will touch your outlook of how doctrinal problems ought to be resolved. Your thoughts on how churches of Christ ought to cooperate with each other, as well as church discipline, will be affected. Your language concerning things important to God, Christ, and the body of Christ will be affected, as well as the questions of who can baptize and rebaptism.

Your views on how public confession of sin should be may be affected, as well as where you worship when you travel. Current controversies concerning legalities of church discipline may be resolved in this study, as well as what our goals should and should not be as we debate important doctrinal issues. Your attitude toward uncommitted Christians in a local church will be affected.

And this study will help answer the question: Do you people think you're the only ones who are going to heaven?

In short, this study affects every sticky question confronting those involved in a quest for the nondenominational New Testament way of righteousness.

Perhaps most importantly, this study will help us to not major in minors and minor in majors as did the Pharisees in Jesus' time. It also frees us to devote ourselves more to the true service of God, while squandering far less time in matters God is not greatly concerned about.

And we're sure as the years go by, this study will probably produce profound changes in attitudes and actions that we do not have the ability to foresee.

Chapter 1

What the Word "Church" Means

What Is a Church?

We begin our study by addressing the important task of determining how the word "church" is used in the Bible. However, studying the definition of this word is not just some academic exercise! Words serve as vehicles of ideas; the way we use a word depends on the idea we have of the thing in our mind. The way we use the word "church" reflects the ideas we have about it. When using words that are important to God, e.g., the word "church," it is highly important to use the word the way God himself uses it, that we might think about the concept of the church the way God does.

Surprisingly, the word "church" is not a peculiarly religious word, nor is it used that way, even in the Bible. As a matter of fact, it is not a religious word at all.

In the New Testament, which was originally written in Greek, the word "church" is given for *ekklesia*, which comes from two words, *ek*, "out," and *kaleo*, "to call out." *Ekklesia* was used of a group of people who had been called out of some place or relationship into another one. Thus, the *ekklesia* or church of Christ refers to people who have been called out of the world into Christ by the gospel.

Use of "Church" in the Old Testament

Before we speak of the church of Christ, though, let's notice how the word was used even before Christ came, in the Old

Testament. We might think since Christ's church was not established before he came into the world, the word would not have been used in the Old Testament. In fact it was, and its use in the Old Testament helps us use the word and think about the concept as God does.

Since the Old Testament was written originally in Hebrew, the Greek word *ekklesia* does not occur in the Hebrew Old Testament. However, in the Septuagint, the Greek translation of the Old Testament that was made in about 250 BC, and that Jesus and the apostles many times quoted from, the word *ekklesia* does occur, both in a religious sense and in a non-religious sense. The word "church" occurs approximately 40-50 times in this version of the Old Testament.

For example, in Dt. 9.10, Moses rehearses how God gave Israel the Law of Moses at Mt. Sinai:

> And the Lord gave me the two tablets of stone written by the finger of God; and on them were all the words which the Lord had spoken with you at the mountain from the midst of the fire on the day of *the assembly*.

The term "assembly" is from the word *ekklesia* in the Septuagint, the same word translated "church" in the New Testament.

In Dt. 4.10, 9.10, 18.16, 23.1, 2, 3, 8 and many others, the word is translated "assembly." These passages make it obvious God spoke of the assembly of Jews, i.e., the Jewish nation, whether they were assembled or not. It refers to the people of the nation of Israel.

Use of the Word "Church" in the New Testament

In the New Testament, several passages use the word church where it has nothing to do with Jesus Christ. In Ac. 19.32, Luke describes Paul's controversy with the Ephesian silversmiths:

> Some therefore cried one thing, and some another: for *the assembly* was in confusion; and the more part knew not wherefore they were come together.

Here the word *ekklesia* (assembly) describes a mob that was trying to kill Paul! It was a riot composed of silversmiths, a group of people who had been called out of the city of Ephesus because of a distinctive relationship; i.e., they were all silversmiths.

In that same chapter, in verse 39, the town clerk broke up the riot by telling the silversmiths:

> But if ye seek anything about other matters, it shall be settled in the regular *assembly.*

In this passage the word *ekklesia* (assembly) refers to the town council, again, a "church" that has nothing to do with Christ! This "church" was another group of people, called out of the town by their relationship to the council.

This word is used a third time in Ac. 19:41 in reference to the mob of silversmiths:

> And when he had thus spoken, he dismissed *the assembly.*

All three of these passages use the word to describe the same thing: a group of people, not a building, not an organization.

Its use in the next passage also has nothing to do with the church of Jesus Christ. In Ac. 7.38 Stephen, in giving his defense shortly before his death, rehearses the history of the Jews and says, speaking of Moses:

> This is he that was in *the church* in the wilderness with the angel that spake to him in the mount Sinai, and with our fathers: who received living oracles to give unto us:

Of course Moses did not deal with the New Testament church, but with a group of people, the congregation of Israel, the *ekklesia* described in the Old Testament where this same word is used.

Thus, many passages exist in the Old Testament where the word *ekklesia* is used, not of the church of Christ, but of the nation of the Jews. Four passages in the New Testament use it of various groups of people, none of them having anything to do with the church of Christ.

The "Church" of Christ

In the New Testament references to the church of Christ, the term "church" is always a collective noun. While a noun is the name of a person, place, or thing, a collective noun is a thing that is composed of a plurality of elements.

Examples of collective nouns are: covey; herd; flock; troop; jury; team; crew; family; assembly; pride; pod; school; committee; company; crowd. One covey of quail is a bunch or plurality of quail. One quail is not a covey. Likewise, one herd of cows is many cows, not just one. A flock of sheep contains many sheep; one sheep is not a flock. A troop of soldiers consists of many, but one soldier is not a troop.

A jury consists of several members; one member is not the jury. A team, crew, family, and assembly all consist of several people, and one person is not a team, crew, family, nor an assembly. A pride consists of several lions, but one lion is not a pride. A pod consists of several whales, yet one whale is not a pod. A school consists of many fish, but one fish is not a school, etc.

The Church of Christ Is a Collective of People

So it is with the term church. A church, whether the nation of Jews in the Old Testament, a mob of silversmiths, a city council in the New Testament, or the church of Christ, is a collection of people. In Mt. 16.18, when Jesus said, "Upon this rock, I will build my church," He spoke of a number of people, a collection of people. He did not speak of an organization, like a corporation. He spoke of people. He did not speak of an institution, like a university. He spoke of people.

For those readers who are interested in institutionalism and its effects on the religion of Christ (some at this point will not be), the very root of institutionalism is right here. If we view the church of Christ as an institution people get into, we are bound to be institutional in our thinking. The church is not an institution people enter—it is people!

To be sure, the church was instituted by God, and it has organization, but the church is a plurality of people. To illustrate this point, note that no one looks at a herd of cattle and thinks, "My, what a wonderful institution!" A herd of cattle is not an institution, it is simply a bunch of cattle. No one ever remarked about a covey of quail, "What a glorious organization!" No, a covey is a bunch of quail, not an organization.

Think of every passage in the Bible where the term "church" occurs, whether in the Old Testament or the New Testament. Doesn't the phrase "bunch of people" fit the context exactly? In I Cor. 1.2, when Paul spoke of "the church of God at Corinth," didn't he speak of the people of God there, a bunch or collective of people?

In Revelation 2 and 3, when Jesus addressed the seven churches of Asia, He addressed seven groups of people in that area of the world. In Eph. 1.22-23, when Paul spoke of the body of Christ being the church of Christ, wasn't he speaking of the collective of people who belong to Christ? In Ac. 20.28, when Paul speaks of "the church the Lord purchased with his own blood," was he speaking of an organization, an institution, or a collection of people? Certainly thorough investigation shows in every single passage in the Bible where the word "church" occurs, it refers to a group of people.

Some object to the use of the word "bunch" as a synonym for church on the ground it doesn't sound religious enough. That's exactly why I've chosen it: *"church" as it's used in the Bible is not a specially religious word, and yet, with our religious backgrounds, most can hardly separate the idea of religion from it.* With our exposure to denominational, institutional, and organizational religion, most can hardly think of the word "church" without those denominational, institutional, and organizational concepts coming to mind.

First of all, notice the word "church" is a collective noun: it always stands for a "bunch of people"—whether they're Christians or not, whether they're religious or not, and whether they even believe in God or not. That's the way the word is used throughout the Bible.

"Church" Is a Non-Descriptive Collective Noun

The term "church" is not only a collective noun, but it is also non-descriptive, that is, it is a collection of people who are not described by the term itself. It is precisely because the term "church" doesn't describe the nature of the people in the group that *the term "church" can be used of a variety of people; i.e., sometimes of Christians, sometimes of the Jewish nation, sometimes of a mob of silversmiths*. This usage does no violence to the word "church," because the term doesn't describe the kind of people in the group.

Other terms in the Bible describe the same group of people, that is, the people of Christ. For example, in Eph. 1.21-23, Paul speaks of the church as the body of Christ. *Body* is another collective noun: one body has many members. Sometimes when one is asked what the church is, the reply is given the church is the body. True, but what is the body? Many are hard pressed to give a reply, other than to say the body is the church. That's like one old-timer who when asked if he knew what rattlesnake meat tasted like, said, "Sure, it tastes like bull snake!" Well, what does bull snake taste like? It's obvious: rattlesnake! We really don't know much more than before.

The Bible also speaks of the church as the house or family of God, I Tim. 3.15. *Family* is another collective noun. One person is not a family, any more than one member is a body. One might say the church is the family, and the family is the church, but he still may not have an idea of what the church is.

In point of fact, *body* and *family* are two collective nouns that give flavor to the word "church." A *body* is a collective of members; a *family* is a collective of relatives. When I know the church is the *body*, I know it is a collection of people who are members of one another; they are functionally related to one another; they work together. When I know the church is the *family*, I know it is a collection of people who are related to one another.

Thus, two collective nouns with flavor, i.e., that describe the kind of people in the group, help illustrate something about the people in the *church*, a term that in itself has no flavor. A *church* can be a collective of any kind of people. Whatever the kind of people who make it up, though, the church is a bunch of people. *The church of Christ is the people who belong to Christ and are in fellowship with Him.*

Conclusion

As a conclusion to this brief word study, review some of the basic passages of Scripture that speak of the church, keeping in mind in every case, the word means a *group of people*.

In Mt. 16.18, when Jesus said, "Upon this rock I will build my church," He spoke of a *group of people*, a group He *is still* building to this day rather than an organization he completed two thousand years ago.

In Ac. 8.3, when "Paul made havoc of the church," he made havoc of a *group of people*, the people of God.

In Ac. 15.41, when Paul and Silas "went through Syria and Cilicia, confirming the churches," they confirmed *groups of people*.

In I Cor. 11.22, when Paul asked, "despise ye the church of God," he was asking whether the Corinthians despised the *people* of God.

In Gal. 1.13, when Paul "persecuted the church of God," he was speaking of what he did to the *people*, not an organization.

In Eph. 1.22, when Paul affirms "Christ is head over all things to the church," he was speaking of the *people* who are in subjection to Christ.

In Eph. 3.10, Paul affirms the manifold wisdom of God "might be made known through the church," the *people* of God. This would happen because of the gospel, that showed Jews and Gentiles how to enjoy fellowship together in Christ.

In Eph. 3.21, when Paul says, "unto Him be the glory in the church and in Christ Jesus unto all generations." He speaks of God's being glorified by his *people*, not an organization.

In Eph. 5.25, "Christ loved the church," describes how Christ always acts in the best interest of His *people*, not an organization.

In Eph. 5.32, "This mystery is great: but I speak in regard of Christ and of the church," refers to the fellowship that can exist between Christ and his *people*, in comparison to the fellowship that should exist between a husband and wife.

In I Tim. 3.15, "the church of the living God, the pillar and ground of the truth," implies the responsibility of the *people* of God, not an organization, to uphold the truth.

In Heb. 12.23, "the church of the firstborn [ones—SGD]" is speaking about *people*, not an organization.

Chapter 2

Differences Between the Universal Church and a Local Church

Having noticed in the previous chapter the word "church" always refers to a group of people, we want now to notice two distinct ways the term is used with reference to the people of Christ in the New Testament. The New Testament writers first of all used the word "church" in a general or universal sense, which we will call the universal church. This is the church Jesus speaks of in Mt. 16.18, where He says, "Upon this rock I will build my church." It is also the church the Hebrew writer speaks of in Heb. 12.18-23:

> For ye are not come unto a mount that might be touched, and that burned with fire, and unto blackness, and darkness, and tempest, and the sound of a trumpet,... but ye are come unto mount Zion, and unto the city of the living God, and the heavenly Jerusalem, and to innumerable hosts of angels, to the *general assembly* and *church of the firstborn* who are enrolled in heaven, and to God the Judge of all, and to the spirits of just men made perfect.

Obviously, these passages do not speak of any church in the local sense, but rather the collection of all people who belong to and enjoy fellowship with Christ.

On the other hand, the New Testament writers use the word "church" in another distinct, local or geographical sense. For example, in I Cor. 1.2, when Paul addressed his letter to "the church of God which is at Corinth," he was not speaking of the universal church or general assembly of everyone who is in Christ. Rather he addressed just the Christians in a specific location. For an examination of Charles Holt's position that local churches do not exist, see Appendix 8, "Should Local Churches Exist?"

This chapter investigates the usage of the term "church" in these two distinct senses. A multitude of differences exists between these two "churches," the universal and the local church.

Distinction in Fellowship

First, a distinction exists in the type of fellowship contemplated in the two churches. The universal church is concerned mainly (though not exclusively) with fellowship with God, while the local church is concerned primarily (though not exclusively) with fellowship with other Christians.

In I John 1.1-4, John speaks of our fellowship with God in the universal church when he says:

> That which was from the beginning, that which we have heard, that which we have seen with our eyes, that which we beheld, and our hands handled, concerning the Word of life (and the life was manifested, and we have seen, and bear witness, and declare unto you the life, the eternal life, which was with the Father, and was manifested unto us); that which we have seen and heard declare we unto you also, that ye also may have fellowship with us, yea, *and our fellowship is with the Father and with his Son Jesus Christ*: and these things we write, that our joy may be made full.

In these verses, the apostle John describes the function of the apostles, giving their testimony concerning Christ. By reception of their testimony, individuals have fellowship with the apostles. Of course, the only reason fellowship with the apostles would have any value is because they were sharing with the Father, and with his Son Jesus Christ.

In verse 5 John continues:

> And this is the message which we have heard from him and announce unto you, that God is light, and in him is no darkness at all. If we say that *we have fellowship with him* and walk in the darkness, we lie, and do not the truth.

The fellowship John speaks of is also with the Father. John continues in verse 7:

> but if we walk in the light, as he is in the light, *we have fellowship one with another*, and the blood of Jesus his Son cleanseth us from all sin.

At first glance, it might seem this fellowship "one with another," is the fellowship of Christians with each other. Rather, it is a reciprocal fellowship between the only ones the passage has in view—"we" and "God." This is the same fellowship he spoke of in verse 3 and again in verse 6. Likewise, in chapter 2.1, John says:

> My little children, these things write I unto you that ye may not sin. And if any man sin, we have an advocate with the Father, Jesus Christ the righteous.

Again, John says we have an advocate with the Father, i.e., one who can restore our fellowship with Him. In this context, John is mainly interested in our fellowship with the Father (v3), with Him (v6), and with the Father and Christ in 2.1. Thus, this passage mainly emphasizes fellowship with God and Christ.

On the other hand, the local church is concerned mainly with fellowship with other Christians. Note in Phil. 4.15 where Paul says:

> And ye yourselves also know, ye Philippians, that in the beginning of the gospel, when I departed from Mace-

donia, *no church had fellowship with me in the matter of giving and receiving but ye only*:

Here Paul contemplates fellowship with other Christians, not fellowship with God. The Philippian Christians and the apostle Paul would both have been in fellowship with God regardless of whether Philippi financially supported Paul. The fellowship he speaks of was a special relationship he had with Christians when he worked especially with them.

To summarize this point, *the universal church is concerned primarily with fellowship with God; the local church is concerned primarily with fellowship with others of God's people.*

Distinction in Manner of Entry

Another distinction between the universal church and a local church exists in the manner one enters each of them. A person enters the universal church by the forgiveness of sins, while he enters the local church by joining it. As a matter of fact, the forgiveness of sins makes fellowship with God possible. In I John 1.5, John says:

> God is light, and in him is no darkness at all.

Isaiah spoke along this line when he said, in Isa. 59.1-2:

> Behold, the Lord's hand is not so short that it cannot save; neither is His ear so dull that it cannot hear. But your iniquities have made a separation between you and your God, and your sins have hid His face from you, so that He does not hear.

Consequently, it is sin that separates us from God and breaks our fellowship with Him. God's nature is such that no darkness abides in Him at all. Thus, when no guilt of sin exists, either because one has never sinned, or because one's sins have been remitted through the blood of Christ, one enjoys fellowship with God in the universal church. One enters the universal church by the forgiveness of his sins. God adds such a one to the universal church (Ac. 2.47). The Bible nowhere teaches God adds one to a local church.

On the other hand, one joins a local church. Luke says concerning Paul in Ac. 9.26:

> And when he was come to Jerusalem, he assayed to join himself to the disciples; and they were all afraid of him, not believing that he was a disciple.

Paul wanted to join this local church. He was not seeking to join the universal church. He had been in it since he had obeyed the gospel, had his sins washed away, and had come into fellowship with God.

Many who long have striven for the non-denominational way of Christ will blanch at the word "join," saying, "One doesn't join the Lord's church, one must be added to it." Certainly, we don't join the universal church like someone might join a denomination. Instead, as the next point shows, we are added to the universal church by God, while we join ourselves to a local church. This is Biblical language. A later chapter shows in detail our relationship with a local church, and contemplates both how and why we join ourselves to a local church. To summarize, we enter the universal church by the forgiveness of our sins, while we join ourselves to a local church.

Distinction in Enrollment

God enrolls us in the universal church and He never makes mistakes. In Heb. 12.22-23, the Hebrew writer says:

> but ye are come...to the general assembly and *church of the firstborn who are enrolled in heaven.*

Likewise, in II Tim. 2.19 Paul says:

> Howbeit the firm foundation of God standeth, having this seal, The Lord knoweth them that are his.

Thus, as the Lord controls the enrollment in the universal sense, He never makes any mistakes. Men may be hypocritical and fool us so we think they're in the universal church when God knows they're not.

On the other hand, our fellowship with a local church involves enrollment by men. In Ac. 9.26, after Paul was already enrolled in heaven, he sought to be numbered with the saints in Jerusalem, and eventually was. This very example demonstrates how men in their enrollments make mistakes; they even refuse fellowship to individuals with whom God is in fellowship. Thus, in the universal church, God never makes mistakes in His enrollment, while in the local church, men many times do.

Distinction in Effect of Death

In Phil. 1.21-25, Paul said:

> For to me to live is Christ, and to die is gain. But if to live in the flesh, if this shall bring fruit from my work, then what I shall choose I know not. But I am in a strait betwixt the two, having the desire to depart and be with Christ; for it is very far better.

Paul understood death didn't effect his fellowship with God, and hence his membership in the universal church. David shared these sentiments in Ps. 23.4:

> Even though I walk through the valley of the shadow of death, I fear no evil; for Thou art with me...

Likewise, in Rev. 3.21, Jesus tells Christians who may be martyred:

> He that overcometh, I will give to him to sit down with me in my throne, as I also overcame, and sat down with my Father in his throne.

Thus, even if they were killed in behalf of Christ, Christians would still be in Christ; they would still be in the universal church. Death wouldn't affect their being in the universal church.

On the other hand, death does affect our membership in the local church. In Acts 8, when devout men buried Stephen, and made great lamentation over him, even they understood Stephen was no longer a member of the local church in Jerusalem. If I am faithful to Christ when I die, I will no longer be a member of a local church, but I will still be in the church universal.

Another way of stating this distinction is to say the universal church consists both of saints (those set apart to serve God) who are alive and saints who are dead. Local churches consist only of saints who are alive.

Distinction in Beginning

The universal church, the general assembly of those in fellowship with God, began with salvation. In Heb. 9.15, we read:

> And for this cause he is the mediator of a new covenant, that a death having taken place for the redemption of the transgressions that were under the first covenant, they that have been called may receive the promise of the eternal inheritance.

Thus, individuals before the Old Covenant and those under the Old Covenant enjoyed fellowship with God on the basis of the sacrifice of Christ that would be offered. In this sense John's baptism was for the remission of sins, as Mk. 1.4 states:

> John came, who baptized in the wilderness and preached the baptism of repentance unto remission of sins.

Those John baptized received the remission of their sins just like those for whom animal sacrifices were properly offered, that is, on the basis of the sacrifice that would be offered. Yet they were free from the guilt of sin, and thus were in fellowship with God before Christ was sacrificed. Such individuals, while not in the body of Christ, were in the general assembly of those enjoying fellowship with God.

It is in this sense we read in Ac. 2:47:

> Praising God, and having favour with all the people. And the Lord added to the church daily such as should be saved. (KJV)

Or, as the American Standard Version states:

> Praising God, and having favor with all the people. And the Lord added to them day by day those that were saved. (ASV)

Who were the "them" to whom these new Christians were being added? What was the church the Lord added them to? It was clearly the universal church; these new Christians were added to the roll of those already in fellowship with God.

On the other hand, a local church may have its beginning at any time since Acts 2. The local church in Jerusalem began in Acts 2, followed by churches in Judea, Antioch, and others. A local church can begin at any time. The local church I presently work with began in the mid 1950s. The local church you work with may have begun last week. Sometimes brethren take great stock in the fact they are members of a congregation that began 150 years ago, but such a congregation might not be as healthy as one that began two months ago.

When local churches put out their signs saying, "Established in 33 AD," they confuse the universal church with the local. In all likelihood, the church is in a city that didn't even exist in 33 AD. The body of Christ, His universal church, began the first Pentecost following His resurrection. All local churches other than Jerusalem began at a later time.

Distinction in Number

Only one universal church exists. Hence in Eph. 1.22-23, we read God gave Christ "to be head over all things to the church, which is his body," and in Eph. 4.4: "There is one body." When Paul says in I Cor. 12.13: "For in one Spirit were we all baptized into one body," he speaks of the universal body or church, of which only one exists.

On the other hand, many local churches exist—so many a person couldn't begin to number them. Seven are named in Revelation chapters 2-3; other examples are the churches of Galatia, the churches in Judea, etc.

Distinction in Earthly Organization

The universal church has no earthly organization, although it may have had one while Christ's apostles were on the earth. The head of the universal church is Christ (Eph. 1.22), and at one time the apostles functioned on the earth in the universal church. In II Cor. 11.28, Paul speaks of the responsibilities that befell him as an apostle when he said; "Besides those things that are without, there is that which presseth upon me daily, anxiety for all the churches." Paul, functioning in the universal church as an apostle, had a responsibility and relationship toward many local churches that no person today has. The authority Paul demonstrates in I Cor. 5 in commanding a local church to withdraw from an impenitent fornicator reveals a relationship he had to the Corinthian church. He had the same type of relationship with the other local churches he wrote to (I Cor. 16.1-3).

The universal church has no address, no telephone number, no zip code, and no area code. You cannot call the universal church, nor can you write it a letter.

On the other hand, the local church has earthly organization. We can read it in Phil. 1.1: "Paul...to all the saints in Christ Jesus that are at Philippi, with the bishops and deacons." You can write a letter to a local church, and you may be able to call it on the phone.

Distinction in Divisibility

A real distinction is seen between the universal church and the local as far as dividing them is concerned. Since the universal church has no organization or collective action, it cannot be divided. If you cannot even write the universal church a letter, nor call it on the phone, how could you possibly divide something that only God controls?

On the other hand, a local church can be divided. The Corinthian church was divided: over preachers, over suing each other, over the use of miraculous spiritual gifts, etc. A local church might have an impenitent fornicator as in I Cor. 5, a Diotrophes as in III John, who loved the preeminence and showed it by excluding people from the local church who enjoyed fellowship with God, and a few hotheads in between. The local church could be divided beyond comprehension! Not so with the universal church.

The matter of the indivisibility of the universal church is an important one to contemplate, for many often think of issues that have divided our "brotherhood." However, unless unscriptural relationships exist between local churches, there can be no division between them.

Several years ago I visited for the first time in a city where in the 1950s a local church took the lead in sponsoring church arrangements of local churches of Christ, i.e., where many churches functioned in works that were overseen by the elders of another congregation. As I looked at their large building, I contemplated how somewhere in that building the elders of that congregation had met together and made decisions many say "divided our great brotherhood." I wondered how could that happen? How could some undoubtedly well-meaning men meet in a building in a small west-Texas town and make decisions that would affect churches all across America? The answer is, they could not, unless many thought in terms of the universal church acting collectively. The Bible's concept of the universal church won't permit such collective action. The universal church cannot be divided. As the next chapter shows, *the universal church was not divided, but rather a denominational coalition of local churches.*

Distinction in Shepherds

The universal church has but one shepherd, for Jesus says, in Jn. 10.11:

> I am the good shepherd: the good shepherd layeth down his life for the sheep.

Hebrews 13.20 speaks of Jesus as "the great shepherd of the sheep, who was brought again from the dead with the blood of an eternal covenant." In I Pet. 2.25, Peter says, "For ye were going astray like sheep: but are now returned unto the Shepherd and Bishop of your souls." Jesus is the great shepherd and the only shepherd over the universal church.

However, a local church has a plurality of shepherds, bishops, or elders, as they're also called. See Ac. 14.23, Phil. 1.1, Ac. 20.17, 28, etc.

Distinction in Composition

The universal church is composed only of the saved. In fact, by definition, the universal church is going to be saved. In Eph. 5.23, Paul speaks of the universal church as follows:

> For the husband is the head of the wife, as Christ also is the head of the church, being himself the saviour of the body.

On the other hand, *local churches are composed of some individuals who are saved and other individuals who are lost.* For example, in Rev. 2.14-16, Jesus says concerning the local church in Pergamum:

> But I have a few things against thee, because thou hast there some that hold the teaching of Balaam, who taught Balak to cast a stumblingblock before the children of Israel, to eat things sacrificed to idols, and to commit fornication. So hast thou also some that hold the teaching of the Nicolaitans in like manner. Repent therefore; or else I come to thee quickly, and I will make war against them with the sword of my mouth.

Thus, the universal church consists only of the saved, both dead and alive, while a local church consists both of saved and lost.

Distinction in Necessity of Belonging

Of course, by definition, one must be in the universal church, the body of Christ, to be saved. It is the assembly of all the saved. On the other hand, one does not have to be in a local church to be saved. First of all, this means one does not have to be in a *particular* local church to be saved, and secondly, it means one does not have to be in *any* local church to be saved. As shown extensively later, God wants Christians (at least, those who are alive) to be in local churches, although local membership is not absolutely essential in order to please to God.

In Ac. 9.26, when Paul sought to join himself to the disciples in Jerusalem, he was in fellowship with God. When the Jerusalem saints would not accept him into their local fellowship, Paul still pleased God. Similarly in Acts 8, when the Ethiopian eunuch obeyed the gospel, certainly some period of time transpired when he wasn't in a local fellowship of Christians. Yet he was still in the universal fellowship of the saved. In III John 10, when Diotrophes excluded people from the local fellowship where he was, those people were not in a local fellowship, but they still enjoyed fellowship with God in the universal church. Thus, while it is an absolute necessity for one to be in the universal church in order to share fellowship with God, it is not an absolute necessity for one to be in a local fellowship.

Distinction in Assembling

A distinction also exists in the two uses of the word "church" in that the universal church does not assemble regularly, while a local church assembles regularly, Heb. 10.24-25.

Distinction in Work

The universal church, since it has no organization, is not a working unit; it has no collective action. On the other hand, the local church has organization, it has collective action, and it is a working unit.

Distinction in Founder

Of course, Jesus founded the universal church ("Upon this rock I will build my church"), while men found a local church. The local church I presently work with was founded by a group of Christians in this city some years ago. I can find out the year, and I can list their names. So it is with the local church you may labor in, and in every local church in every city. A later chapter deals extensively with the founding of a congregation.

Summary

Thus, we see the universal and the local churches are vastly different, and since God made them different, we ought to respect those differences. Basically, the universal church is concerned with one's relationship to God, while the local church deals with our relationship with other Christians.

In our efforts to teach our fellow man, we ought to respect these differences. A few minutes' reflection shows these two concepts are generally mixed. Many talk "local church" when they discuss the religion of Christ with their friends, and they ought first to tell about the universal church. We should first teach what they should do to be in fellowship with God in the universal church. Then we can teach them what their responsibilities are in working together with other Christians in a local church.

We write many articles talking about "How to Find the Right Church," yet the universal church cannot be found! It has no organization, no address, no collective work, no collective action. The only church that can be found is the local church, for it has all those things.

When we tell individuals how to find the right church, we mix these two concepts. When we speak of the name of the church, we refer to Rom. 16.16 and I Cor. 1.2, using passages that deal with local churches. When we talk about the age of the church, we're concerned with the universal church. We know we really don't care how long a specific local church has been organized. When we speak of the organization of the church, we switch to the local church again. When we speak of how to become members of the church, and talk about faith, repentance, and baptism, we're again concerned with the universal church. Those are things people do to enjoy fellowship with God. No one was ever baptized into the local church in the New Testament. When we talk about worship, and we mention prayer, singing, preaching, the Lord's Supper and giving, that is worship that takes place in the local church, not collectively in the universal church.

Mixing these two concepts together demonstrates a lack of clear thinking about these two churches as taught in God's word. Thus, we need to give the matter serious consideration.

Later in Chapter 9, "Teaching Others," we'll discuss in detail how keeping this distinction between these two churches profoundly affects how we teach our fellow man the gospel of Christ.

Chapter 3

The Relationship of the Universal Church and the Local Church

After noticing the distinction between the universal church and the local church, we are now prepared to discuss the *relationship* of these two. Our concept of the relationship between these two churches will profoundly affect us, as mentioned in the Introduction. As later chapters show, it affects our views of nearly every controversial question that we confront.

How They Are Not Related

A Church of Denominations

What is your view of the universal church? Of what is it composed? The most popular view in our time is the universal church, the body of Christ, composed of denominations, as illustrated in Figure 1.

Of course, this view is peculiar to recent centuries, for no one believes all these denominations existed in the New Testament. Certainly, no one thinks Jesus came to establish all these denominations, or that He did establish them. Likewise, no one thinks the apostles were members of any of them, or that they even existed in the time of Jesus and the apostles.

To justify the presence of denominations, people sometimes use Jn. 15.5, 6, where Jesus says:

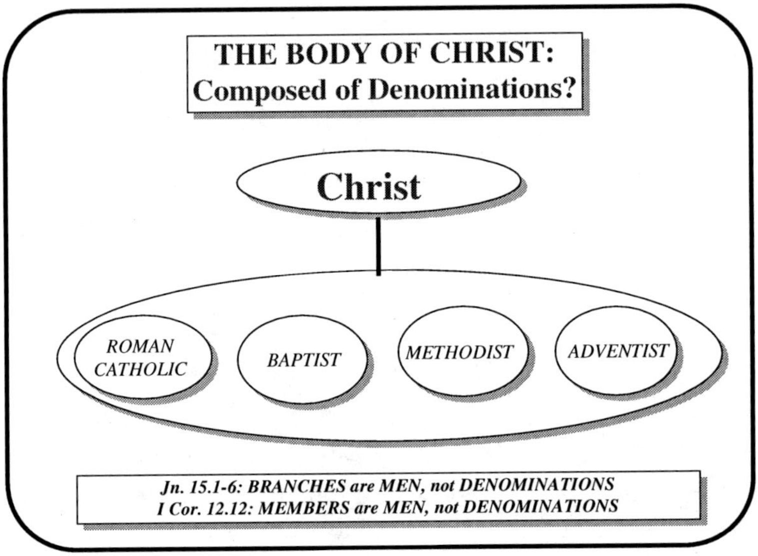

Figure 1

> I am the vine, ye are the branches: He that abideth in me, and I in him, the same beareth much fruit: for apart from me ye can do nothing. If a *man* abide not in me, he is cast forth as a branch, and is withered; and they gather them, and cast them into the fire, and they are burned.

Jesus' own words show He does not speak of a tree composed of branches that are themselves denominations, for the branches He speaks of are "men." "If a *man* abide not in me, he is cast forth as a branch." So the body of Christ, the universal church, is not composed of denominations. For a more complete discussion of denominationalism, see Appendix 1, "The Harm of Denominationalism."

A Church of Churches

Some view the body of Christ as composed of local churches, as in Figure 2:

Alexander Campbell, a leader in the restoration movement in America in the 1800s, apparently held this view of the body of Christ for quite a lengthy period of time, perhaps even dying with it. In the *Millennial Harbinger* of July 1834, he wrote:

> The church...is not one congregation or assembly, but the congregation of Christ, composed of Christ, composed of all the individual congregations on earth.

More than 20 years later, Campbell still held this view, for he said in the *Millennial Harbinger* of June 1853 (p. 303):

> Every individual church on earth stands to the whole church of Christ as one individual man to one particular church.

Such views should not surprise us. The only churches Campbell had been exposed to were churches composed of churches, i.e., denominations.

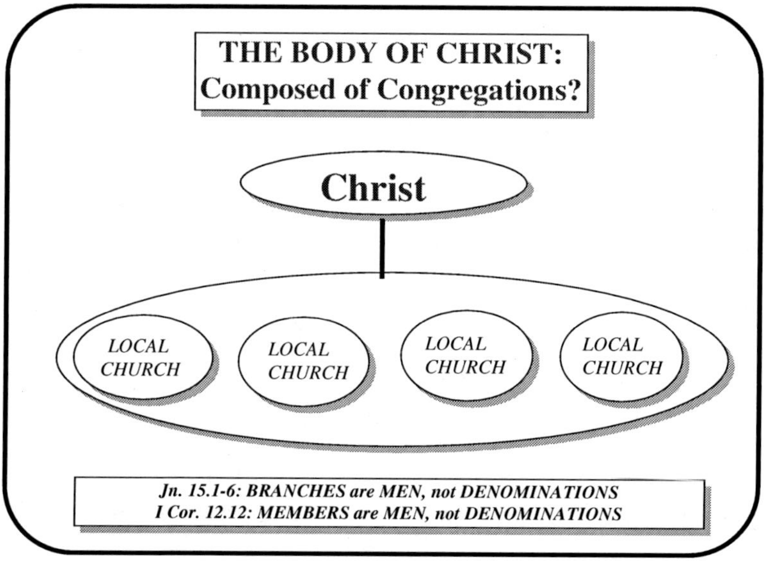

Figure 2

A Church of Churches Is a Denomination

However, is Campbell's "church of churches" view of the body of Christ any more biblical than the denominational view? Again, Jn. 15.5-6 shows the body of Christ is not composed of congregations or local churches, but rather of individual Christians. The branches in Christ are *men—not congregations, and not denominations*. The basic issue is simply this: is the universal church a church of churches, or a church of people? Is it a "bunch" of churches or a "bunch" of people?

In I Cor. 12.12-13, Paul says:

> For as the body is one, and hath many members, and all the members of the body, being many, are one body; so also is Christ. For in one Spirit were we all baptized into one body, whether Jews or Greeks, whether bond or free; and were all made to drink of one Spirit.

Evidently, Paul views the body of Christ as composed not of denominations (which were foreign to him), nor churches, but of individual Christians. In verse 27 he says:

> Now ye are the body of Christ, and severally members thereof.

Perhaps this may seem like a trivial matter. But whether the body of Christ is composed of individual Christians or of individual congregations affects many of our fundamental beliefs about the nature of the church. It also affects our foundation attitudes toward each of the people who compose it.

Before we draw the true relationship between the universal church and the local church, let's think about the different relationships in these two groups: (A) a single Christian, a plurality of Christians, a local church, and (B) a local church, a plurality of local churches, and a plurality of local churches acting collectively.

In Figure 3, we begin by illustrating the difference between a single chain link, several separate links, and a chain. The difference between several links and chain is the functional relation-

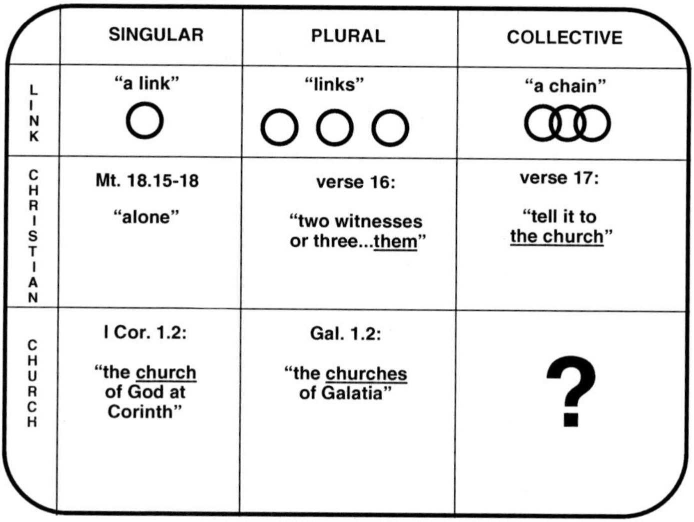

Figure 3

ship between the links. A chain is more than just several links. It is several links that function as a unit.

Some see no distinction between an individual Christian and the local church, but Jesus made the distinction. For example, in Mt. 18.15-18, He says:

> And if thy brother sin against thee, go, show him his fault between thee and him *alone*: if he hear thee, thou hast gained thy brother. But if he hear thee not, take with thee one or two more, that at the mouth of two witnesses or three every word may be established. And if he refuse to hear *them*, tell it unto *the church*:

Jesus makes clear a distinction between an individual acting, several individuals acting, and the church acting. One who says, "Anything the individual can do, the church can do," fails to recognize the distinction the Lord Himself makes. Likewise, in I Tim. 5.16, Paul says:

> If any woman that believeth hath widows, let her relieve them, and let not the church be burdened: that it may relieve them that are widows indeed.

This passage makes clear a distinction between an individual Christian acting, a plurality of Christians acting in their individual capacity, and a plurality of Christians acting collectively.

When we contemplate this concept on a local congregational level, we read of instances where a single local church acted in the New Testament. For example, in I Cor. 1.2, Paul speaks of the "church of God which is at Corinth," obviously speaking of a single local congregation. When Paul writes Galatians, he addresses it "to the churches of Galatia," *a plurality of churches, each acting independently*. After the apostles, man invented the concept of a plurality of congregations acting collectively. *A modern word describes this arrangement, although it isn't a Bible word: the word is "denomination."* This is precisely what a denomination is: a plurality of churches acting collectively. For example, the Methodist denomination consists of all the churches that function collectively in that denomination. The Episcopal denomination is a collection of local churches that function collectively to do the work of that denomination. On and on the list goes. Collective action of local churches is denominational action!

What Is a Denomination?

For an institution that has been among us for so long (approximately five hundred years), it is surprising how little many have reflected on just what a modern denomination is. Even among those who oppose the division and unbelief that denominationalism produces few have stopped to analyze exactly what it is.

A Denomination Is Not Just Something "Named"

Webster defines a denomination as "The name of a class of things; a class or kind (especially of units) having a specific name or value." Thus, we speak of currency consisting of several denominations: five-dollar bills, tens, etc. Each denomination of money consists of a category of bills.

However, a denomination then is more than something named. I have two children, both of whom have been named, but I am not the father of two denominations.

A Denomination Is an Organizational Concept

Donald G. Tinder, in the *Evangelical Dictionary of Theology* gives the following definition of a denomination in the religious sense:

> Denominations are associations of congregations—though sometimes it might be said that congregations are localized subdivisions of denominations—that have a common heritage. Moreover, a true denomination does not claim to be the only legitimate expression of the church. (Donald G. Tinder, *Evangelical Dictionary of Theology*, Ed. Walter A. Elwell, Grand Rapids: Baker Publishing House, 1984, p. 310.)

Thus, *a denomination is a collective of congregations*. When congregations function as a unit, they function denominationally. Tinder admits our naivete concerning the rise of the denominational concept:

> Even though denominations within Protestantism have come to be the largest expression of organized Christianity beyond the level of the congregation, there has never been much theological reflection on denominationalism. A look at theological textbooks or church creeds confirms this. Probably the simplest explanation for this omission is the Bible in no way envisages the organization of the church into denominations. It instead assumes the opposite, that all Christians—except those being disciplined—will be in full fellowship with all others. Any tendencies to the contrary were roundly denounced (I Cor. 1.10-13). Paul could write a letter to the Christians meeting in various places in Rome or

> Galatia with every assurance that all would receive the message. Today, for any city or country, he would have to place the letter as an advertisement in the secular media and hope. (*Ibid.*, p. 310.)

History of the Denominational Concept

In view of such widespread lack of understanding concerning the origin and rise of the denominational concept, we now want to notice its origin. It is intimate with the rise of Roman Catholicism.

Local Churches

In the New Testament, Christians joined themselves to local congregations that were self-ruling and independent (Ac. 9.26). They were overseen by elders, bishops (overseers), or shepherds whose authority was limited to that local church (Ac. 14.23, I Pet. 5.1-2). No concept existed of allegiance to another congregation, a collection of congregations, or a denomination. The New Testament speaks of the church in only two senses—(1) the universal sense, where one enjoys fellowship with all who are in fellowship with God, and (2) the local church, where one shares fellowship with other Christians in a specific locale. No concept of fellowship (a working relationship) existed larger than a local congregation.

Metropolitans

However, as the simplicity of organization of New Testament Christians deteriorated, local leaders began to exercise authority over other local congregations:

> After we cross the limit of the first century we find that with each board of elders there is a person to whom the name 'bishop' is especially applied. (George Park Fisher, *History of the Christian Church* [New York: Charles Scribner's Sons, 1827], p. 51.)

Later, Fisher says:

> The bishop of the chief city of each province was called the metropolitan. (*Ibid.*, p. 104.)

Regional Church Councils

In the second century, an inexorable movement began toward organizing the universal church. Phillip Schaff, in his celebrated *History of the Christian Church*, shows how early believers wanted some type of church government:

> A form of government (as the superiority of the bishop) so ancient and so widely adopted, can be satisfactorily accounted for only on the supposition of religious needs, namely, the need of a tangible outward representation and centralization, to illustrate and embody to the people their relation to Christ and to God, and the visible unity of the church. (Phillip Schaff, *History of the Christian Church, II* [New York: Charles Scribner's Sons, 1887], p. 133.)

Mosheim, in his *Ecclesiastical History* also points out the "Bishops" of churches in various provinces began meeting to deliberate on doctrinal issues and to coordinate provincial activities among the churches:

> These councils—of which no vestige appears before the middle of this (2nd) century—changed nearly the whole form of the church. (John Lawrence Mosheim, *Ecclesiastical History, I* [Rosemead, CA: Old Paths Book Club, 1959], pp. 116-117.)

Thus, by the end of the fourth century, metropolitans of Rome, Antioch, and Alexandria had assumed oversight of churches in several provinces. The concept of collective action of churches was now in place—a coalition of churches that constitutes a denomination. As Mosheim correctly says, the whole form of the church had been changed. This change was critical to the concept of a denomination, although *modern* denominations did not arise for at least another twelve hundred years!

Universal Church Councils

The first "universal" (Ecumenical) Council was held at the order of the Roman Emperor Constantine in Nicea in 325 AD This Council of Nicea produced the Nicene Creed. Mark it well, the Apostles of Christ and first century Christians never attended a conference of congregations, nor ever laid eyes on such a creed.

By the fourth century, the metropolitans of the four leading cities of the Roman empire, Rome, Constantinople, Antioch, and Alexandria competed for oversight of the universal collection of congregations. At the end of the sixth century, Gregory the Great, Bishop of Rome, denounced John the Faster (Patriarch of Constantinople) for his assumed title of "Universal Patriarch." In 606 AD, Boniface III was proclaimed "Universal Bishop" over all the churches.

In only five centuries, the transition from the simple organization of the autonomous local church to the universal coalition of local churches now seen in Roman Catholicism was completed. *Rather than the body of Christ consisting of Christians, the concept now was the body of Christ consisting of churches, which themselves consisted of Christians. This is the essence of denominationalism.*

The European Reformation Movement

In the reformation movement of the sixteenth century and beyond, this denominational concept was carried over into Protestantism. Leaders like Luther, Wesley, and Calvin, while they courageously fought many of the excesses of Roman Catholicism, unfortunately retained many other doctrines and concepts of Catholicism. While they rejected the Pope as the visible head of a universal collection of congregations, they kept the concept the universal church composed of congregations. Thus, the denominations that resulted from the work of these men and their followers simply added more collections of churches!

The American Restoration Movement

In the early and mid-nineteenth century, this same denominational concept was carried over into the restoration movement in America. While the restorationists of this period did a tremendous amount of work to persuade people to renounce their denominational creeds and use the Bible as their only standard, their concept of the body of Christ was still that of a church of churches, not a church of Christians. Such a concept was bound to produce still more collections of churches!

Alexander Campbell

Alexander Campbell, a leader in the restoration movement in America, apparently held this view of the body of Christ for quite a lengthy period of time. In the *Millennial Harbinger* of July 1834 (p. 315), he writes:

> The church...is not one congregation or assembly, but the congregation of Christ, composed of Christ, composed of all the individual congregations on earth. (Cited by Monroe Hawley, *Redigging the Wells* [Abilene, TX: Quality Publications, 1976], p. 61.)

Twenty years later, Campbell still held this view, for he says in the *Millennial Harbinger* of June 1853 (p. 303):

> Every individual church on earth stands to the whole church of Christ as one individual man to one particular church. (*Ibid.*)

Such views aren't surprising. As we noted earlier, the only churches Campbell knew were churches composed of churches, i.e., denominations.

Robert Milligan

Another extremely influential leader in the American Restoration Movement, Robert Milligan, apparently subscribed to this same concept:

> ...for the sake of order, convenience, and efficiency, this one body may be divided into as many churches or congregations as may be thought necessary; each one of which, when fully organized, should have its own corps of Elders and Deacons. (Robert Milligan, *Scheme of Redemption* [Nashville, TN: Gospel Advocate Co., 1868], p. 509.)

Missionary Society Controversy Wracks American Restoration Movement

We ought not be surprised that since men had labored under the denominational concept of the body of Christ for 1600 years, the American restoration movement resulted in still more collections of churches: the Christian Church, the Disciples of Christ, and the churches of Christ. In the beginning, some in these groups had the concept of independent local congregations of Christians, as was expressed by David Lipscomb, one of the most influential of their leaders:

> All meetings of churches or officers of churches to combine more power than a single church possesses are wrong...A Christian, one or more, may visit a church with or without an invitation and seek to stir them up to a more faithful discharge of their duties. But for one or more to direct what and how all the churches shall work, or to take charge of their men and money and use it, is to assume the authority God has given to each church. (David Lipscomb, *The Gospel Advocate* [Nashville, TN: Gospel Advocate Publishing Company, 1890], p. 295.)

Thus, the issue of the Missionary Society (an organization through which local churches could work collectively in evangelism) was fought on the grounds it violated the autonomy of the local church. Among most adherents to the restoration concept, the "coalition of churches" view still held sway.

Another restoration leader, W. E. Brightwell, also wrote:

> I submit this proposition: Any individual Christian, or group of individuals, smaller than a local congregation: or any group of individuals or churches larger than a local church; or any individual church itself that begins thinking in terms of what the whole brotherhood should do, and goes or sends somebody to the churches to see that they do it, and acts as an agent or agency through which the brotherhood does it, thereby constitutes itself full-grown, blown-in-the-bottle, fourteen-karat missionary society of the deepest dye! There is no way on earth to whitewash it. There is no city of refuge where he may hide from God's displeasure. To call it something else, or to leave it unnamed, is a mere technical dodge. It is not condemned because it is similar to a missionary society, but because it *violates the same fundamental principle the society violates*—namely, the initiative and autonomy of the local congregation. (W. E. Brightwell, *The Gospel Advocate*, December 20, 1934, p. 1223.)

Sponsoring Church Controversy Among Churches of Christ

To the degree these restorationists conceived of the body of Christ as a coalition of congregations, the united movement in which they were involved became increasingly splintered. Churches of Christ have been specially wracked by controversy concerning "sponsoring churches," that is a concept by which collective action of churches is realized.

What is a "sponsoring church"? It is a congregation that assumes the oversight and control of other congregations' activity in the general field of evangelism, edification, or benevolence. Being general, the work involved is not the exclusive responsibility of only one congregation, but proportionate to their ability, is the work of all the churches. The congregation assuming the oversight and control cannot sustain the work undertaken alone.

Many congregations delegate their funds and responsibilities to the overseeing and controlling congregation for their fulfillment and application or expenditure. The elders of the sponsoring church thus become the official board of a collective action of churches vested with the authority of overseeing, controlling, and prosecuting the work involved.

William S. Banowsky, author of a history of the American restoration movement from the viewpoint of the Abilene Christian College Lectures, made the following statement concerning the thrust of those lectureships, that led directly to the formation of the sponsoring church:

> The lecturers came to desire a missionary procedure which would more effectively involve the hundreds of small congregations. But they also sought a program whose scope would be more far-reaching than even the best, but isolated efforts of any one large congregation. They could not resist the temptation to shop about and contrast their plight with the obvious strong points in denominational machinery. Thus, *they sought for some practical, scriptural means of brotherhood-wide co-ordination without creating an agency for brotherhood-wide control* [emphasis mine—SGD]. (William S. Banowsky, *The Mirror of a Movement* [Dallas, TX: Christian Publishing Co., 1965], p. 313.)

Such restoration efforts were doomed to undergo denomination-type splits because they labored under a denominational concept of the body of Christ all along. It was the same concept we traced from the first quarter of the second century, and as ever, the concept produced even more coalitions of churches!

Gospel Guardian/Guardian of Truth Magazines

It is particularly ironic that at the very time the sponsoring church issue was being discussed among churches of Christ, the champions fighting against the concept were themselves embracing denominational concepts of the body of Christ. For example, the *Gospel Guardian*, a magazine published in Lufkin, Texas with Yater Tant as its editor, was highly instrumental in opposing the Herald of Truth. However, even after Tant had debated E. R. Harper and Roy Cogdill had debated Guy N. Woods on the Herald of Truth, we find the following in the Articles of Incorporation of the Gospel Guardian Foundation, which published the *Gospel Guardian:*

> ARTICLE TWO. The purpose for which it is formed is to support a religious, charitable and educational undertaking...to promote New Testament Christianity by various means, including the publication of paper and tracts pertaining only to and in support of religion, *setting forth the tenets of the Churches of Christ*...[emphasis mine—SGD]. (*Articles of Amendment to the Articles of Incorporation of Gospel Guardian Foundation*, p. 1, Filed in Office of Secretary of State of Texas, September 1, 1958, Signed by Roy E. Cogdill, Yater Tant, James W. Adams, Harry Pickup, Jr., Osby Weaver, Fred A. Hutson, and Troy C. Irwin.)

Notice the phrase "tenets of the Churches of Christ." If the churches of Christ are nondenominational, they should collectively have no tenets to be set forth. What organization larger than a local church is there to set them forth? We know who sets them forth in the Lutheran denomination, and the Jehovah's Witnesses—the denominational hierarchy. Who does it in the churches of Christ? Generally, preachers, papers, and colleges, the three things we have that are easy to be larger than a local church. Yet it is precisely this type of thinking that enabled these men to adopt such language in their Articles of Incorporation. These brethren said they were debating "institutionalism," more correctly, denominationalism (collective action of congregations). However, they couldn't condemn it as denominationalism because they had a denominational view of the body of Christ themselves, and were setting forth and defending the tenets of that view! Because of the importance of these corporate documents of the Gospel Guardian Foundation, they are reproduced photographically in Appendix 10, "Corporate Documents of the Gospel Guardian Foundation."

How extensive this thinking is among the successors to the Gospel Guardian Foundation, this author doesn't know. The Gospel Guardian Foundation, Inc., a Texas corporation, later merged with Truth Magazine, Inc., an Ohio corporation, became the Guardian of Truth Foundation, Inc., a Texas corporation, and later a Kentucky corporation. In all these transitions, the "tenets of the Churches of Christ" language was apparently never dropped, much less repudiated. It's a small step from thinking denominationally to acting denominationally. It's easy to see how such men, viewing themselves as propagating and defending the tenets of a denominational coalition of churches, can subsequently attempt to control the congregations which follow their concepts, even to the point of marking congregations in other states as unfaithful. In the New Testament, no local church had preachers, religious papers, or religious colleges to exercise that kind of influence in or over it's local work. Robert F. Turner, a clear-thinking preacher of those times said:

> ANY PROJECT OR INSTITUTION OPERATED BY OR FOR THE BENEFIT OF THE CHURCH AT LARGE, "THE BROTHERHOOD," TENDS TO DENOMINATIONALIZE THAT BROTHERHOOD. [emphasis his—SGD] (Robert F. Turner, "The Schools, and Denominationalism," *The Preceptor,* XI, No. 8 [Beaumont, TX: The Preceptor Company, June 1962], p. 124.)

For a good illustration of how propagating the tenets of a coalition of churches manifests itself as a denominational split complete with outsiders determining the course of action of local churches on controversial subjects, please see Chapter 13, "Fellowship on Marriage, Divorce & Remarriage," in the author's book *Marriage, Divorce & Remarriage: The Uniform Teaching of Moses, Jesus & Paul.*

Then Turner continues with some sobering advice in such brotherhood (really congregationhood or denomination) organizational situations:

> The institution itself may not be so much to blame as the "brotherhood" conceptions that produce and maintain the institution. Party ties are made and strengthened, opinions accepted by the majority become traditions, are crystallized into party tenets; and accepted in the second or third generation as proof of orthodoxy. When the "brotherhood" functions, there must be the acceptance of common direction and guidance; the "brotherhood voice" must be heard. And "brotherhood schools" have paved the way for denominational organizations among members of the Lord's church. No amount of denying can change this obvious historical and current fact. (Robert F. Turner, "The Schools, and Denominationalism," *The Preceptor,* XI, No. 8 [Beaumont, TX: The Preceptor Company, June 1962], p. 124.)

Restoring the Restoration Movement

Among so-called heirs of the American restoration movement, significant calls arise from time to time to re-unite the various segments of the movement. For example, the title of one prominent book with this thrust is Leroy Garrett's *The Stone-Campbell Movement, An Anecdotal History of Three Churches* (Joplin, MO: College Press Publishing Co., 1981). Garrett's use of "churches" in his title shows he's not talking about three universal churches, for he certainly doesn't believe in such. Neither is he concerned with the unity of three local churches. *Rather, he concerns himself with the unity of three coalitions of congregations*—i.e., *three denominational groups* in one grand coalition of congregations made up of the coalition of churches of Christ, Christian Churches, and Disciples of Christ congregations. Such a coalition is unknown in the New Testament; the three coalitions that arose from the restoration movement came from the denominational concept of Campbell and others. Should anyone now strive to put those many congregations back into one denominational group?

The Crossroads/Boston Movement

In the late 1970s and early 1980s, a new movement troubling churches of Christ originated from one congregation in Gainesville, Florida. In the late eighties it became dominated by a group known as the Boston Church of Christ.

Many concerns have been expressed regarding the arrangements and teachings of the "Crossroads/Boston Movement." The real issue is not whether it is scriptural to have one congregation under one eldership in a city. It is not whether a congregation can use a private home as a meeting place for worship. Nor is it whether a congregation can have only one meeting a week on Sunday. Likewise, the real concern is not whether a congregation may meet in separate groups in private homes during the week. The issue is not whether one Christian can ask another for advice about sin in his life, nor whether one Christian can ask for another to pray for him about his problem. The issue is not whether one who is older in the faith can help a new Christian in his spiritual growth, nor whether the strong is to help the weak. Likewise, the issue is not whether a Christian is to teach as many people as possible.

The real issue and concern is that the Crossroads/Boston movement still labors under a denominational view of the body of Christ. The Boston Church is, in a very real sense, the "Mother Church" of a coalition of churches who, in their literature, is composed of "Pillar Churches," "Capitol City Churches," "Small City Churches," and "Countryside Churches." Kip McKean, evangelist in the Boston Church explains in the *Boston Bulletin* of January 4, 1987:

> These are churches established in the mega-population centers of the world. These cities, and correspondingly the churches built in them, influence more than the country in which they are located. Their sphere of influence is over several countries. It is upon these "pillar" churches that the world brotherhood will be built. (Kip McKean, *Boston Bulletin*, January 4, 1987, cited by Barnett, *The Discipling Movement* [Phoenix, AZ: published by Maurice Barnett, 1987], p. 61.)

McKean, in the *Bible Discipleship Quarterly*, Spring, 1987 (cited by Barnett, p. 62) says:

> Let me begin by saying that every congregation should be involved in some way. One concept that we must stress more is that of the one brotherhood. I believe in the individuality of the local church and the local eldership over a local congregation. However, we have so overreacted to Catholicism and denominationalism that we have failed to realize that we need to be one brotherhood. What the Boston leadership has done during the 1986 seminar is to bring together all the churches which have planted another church or have church planting plans. My personal desire is to harmonize all the discipling church ministry efforts by mutual agreement to guidelines for targeting a city.

In the bulletin of the Mission Church in San Diego, California, one of the "Pillar Churches" of the movement, Gordon Ferguson writes concerning the church in the New Testament:

> A study of leader training in Acts underscores some vital issues. 1. All of the congregations were really one Body rather than highly independent segments. 2. Leaders were appointed for the purpose of maturing the Body, and not just members of one congregation. (Gordon Ferguson, *Bulletin* of the Mission Church of San Diego, CA, cited by Maurice Barnett, *Ibid.*, p. 59.)

These quotations establish that these men are not working to build a brotherhood of Christians, but rather a sisterhood of congregations, that is just another denomination. Rather than overreacting to denominationalism, the thesis of this volume is we're not quite out of it yet if we still have a denominational concept of the body of Christ. One does not have to be much of a student of the history of similar endeavors, from the second century to the present one, to confidently know this movement too is doomed to produce even more coalitions of churches. This is not because of a lack of sincerity in those involved, but because they labor under a denominational concept of the body of Christ.

Indeed, the Boston Church already practices centralized control of the congregations within the coalition. Again McKean says in the *Boston Bulletin*, November 23, 1986 (Cited by Barnett, *Ibid*., p. 63):

> We are excited to announce that the Elders of the Boston congregation have assumed oversight of the Kingston Church of Christ, a two-year old mission effort originally planted by the Miami-Gables congregation...In December, Jim and Maria Rogers will move to Jamaica to prepare to take over the leadership of the congregation in January...We believe the church in Kingston will become a pillar work.

In the *Boston Bulletin* of August 16, 1987, McKean describes how he and the elders in Boston actually started to control other congregations:

> In June, at the invitation of Tom Brown and the other evangelists of the Berkeley Church of Christ, the Elders and I sent Scott and Lynn Green to initiate the "rebuilding" of the Berkeley congregation...Sensing an even greater need for more specific teaching on discipleship, high-powered women's ministries and church plantings, Tom and the evangelists asked the Boston leadership to officially direct the work...
>
> Like the walls of Jerusalem, the Elders and I saw no need to tear down the whole structure, but to rebuild what was lacking for this part of the Christian remnant. It was decided we would not call this a "replanting" (like Atlanta or Jamaica), but to refer to this as a "reconstruction."...Firstly, the Berkeley congregation with Tom's well-built foundation and Boston's reconstruction would move to downtown San Francisco and become the San Francisco Church of Christ on September 13. Secondly, the evangelists and women's counselors would resign

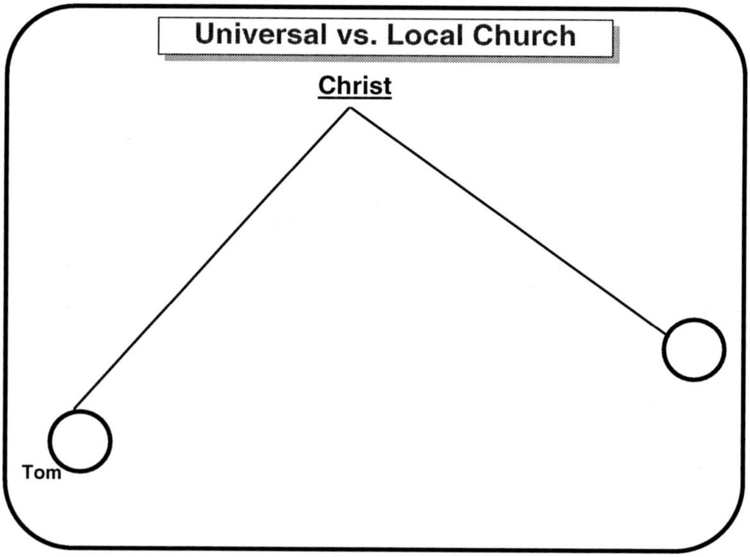

Figure 4

> and become interns. Therefore, when they are appointed in the future, they will be recognized in Boston as well as in our church plantings, such as in Bombay or New York. I foresee this to help form a uniform standard of recognition throughout the multiplying ministries. (Kip McKean, *Bulletin of Boston Church of Christ, Vol. VIII*, No. 33, August 16, 1987.)

Such collective action of congregations is denominational to the core! Thus, those interested in non-denominational congregations will flee all such collective action of congregations. The universal church is not the collection of local churches.

For a surprising doctrinal effect of the concept that the body of Christ is composed of congregations, see Appendix 9, "The Body of Christ and the Lord's Supper."

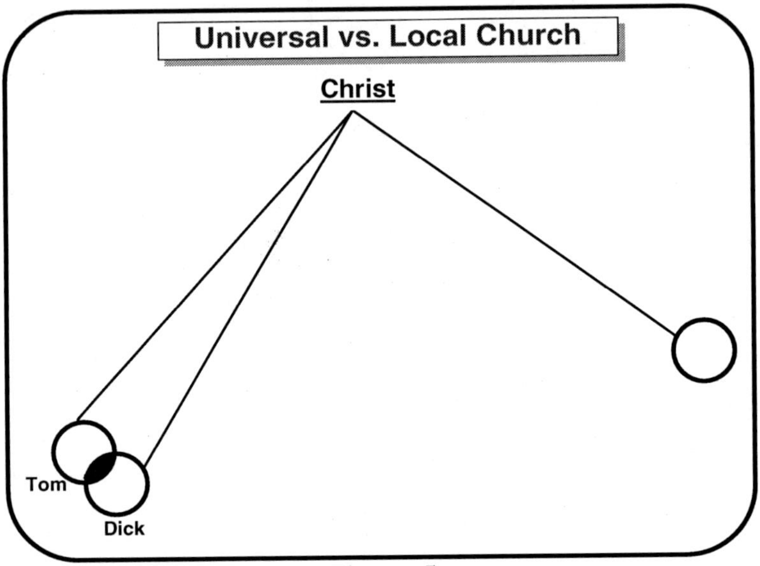

Figure 5

How They Are Related

Let's draw the relationship between the universal church, local churches, and individual Christians. We begin with two individual Christians, one named Tom, and the other is not identified yet. In Figure 4, we represent Tom by a circle to illustrate Tom's whole life as a Christian, i.e., all the duties he performs because of his allegiance to Christ. This would include his life as an employee, a citizen, a husband, a father, *and*, as a Christian working with other Christians in a local congregation. Everything Tom does as a Christian is not done as a member of a local congregation. The line going from Tom to Christ illustrates Tom's fellowship with Christ, and shows Tom is in the universal church.

Figure 5 adds another individual Christian, Dick. Like Tom, Dick enjoys fellowship with Christ, that is represented by a line connecting him with Christ.

Dick also is represented by a circle, showing Dick's entire sphere of activity as a result of his allegiance to Christ. Notice

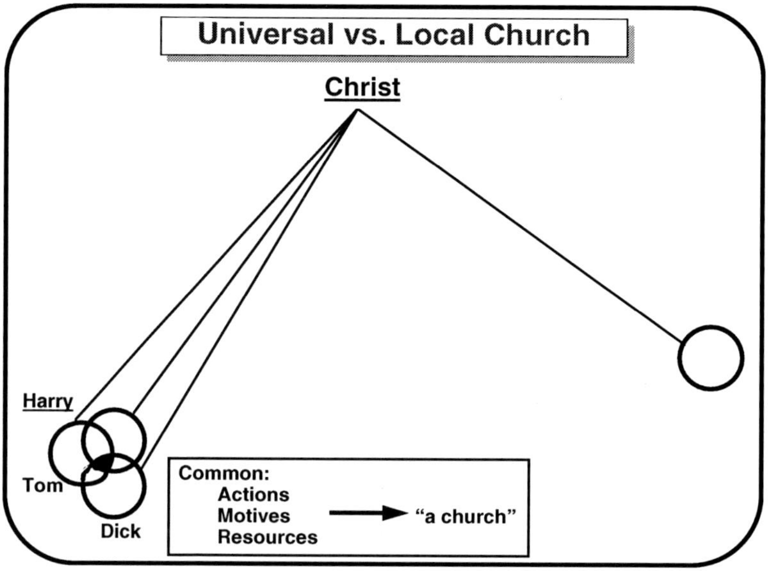

Figure 6

Dick's circle overlaps Tom's, showing these two Christians do certain things together, although no local church is involved as yet. So far, Tom and Dick may be in different cities, or different countries. Perhaps they are in business together, or labor to teach someone the gospel together. The fact the circles representing Tom and Dick do not completely overlap shows everything they do as Christians is not done together, for example, in a local congregation. Additionally, Tom and Dick are probably not in agreement on everything the Bible teaches.

Figure 6 adds another Christian, Harry. Like Tom and Dick, this new Christian is also represented by a circle. While Harry's circle shows he doesn't agree completely in beliefs and actions with Tom and Dick, all three share a common area of overlap. Let's say for now Tom, Dick, and Harry are in a local congregation of Christians. Let's say further this area of common activities is the result of common motives (allegiance to Christ), and pooling of resources (a common treasury). This is part of what makes a local congregation: It is a plurality of Christians banded together by common motives and a pooling of resources, to do

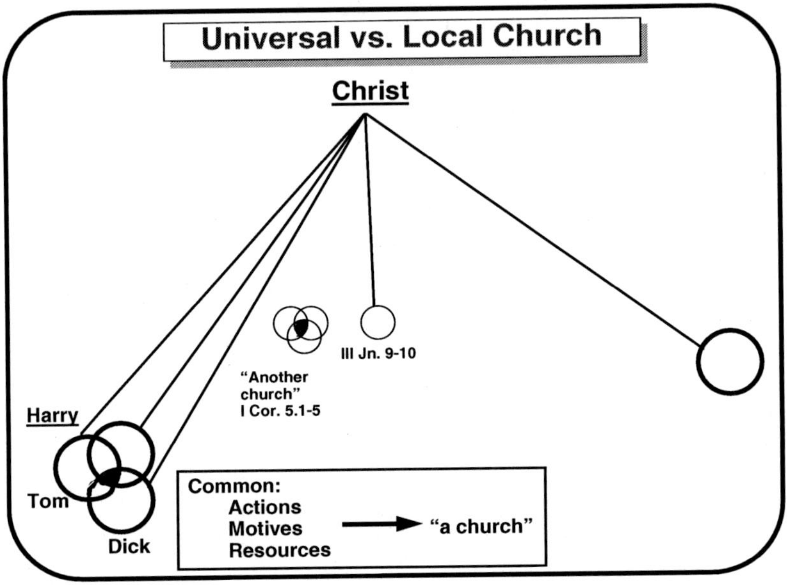

Figure 7

collectively what the members of that local church agree God wants them to do together. We will expand upon this practical definition of a local congregation later, but this will suffice for now.

In Figure 7, another local church is added. It consists of a plurality of Christians who, like those in the first congregation, do not agree on everything, but they, too, are agreed on what they do collectively, i.e., teach the gospel, partake of the Lord's Supper, make contributions into their common treasury, etc.

This second congregation, though, shows not all its members share with Christ, although they are in fellowship with each other. The Christian who enjoys fellowship with others in a local congregation, but not with Christ, might be representative of the impenitent fornicator in the church in I Corinthians 5. He was an example where a local church had made a mistake in controlling its fellowship, and had someone in its fellowship who was not a partner with God. In the case of the impenitent one at Corinth, Paul wrote the I Corinthian letter for the purpose of correcting their fellowship, and it worked. He was excluded from their

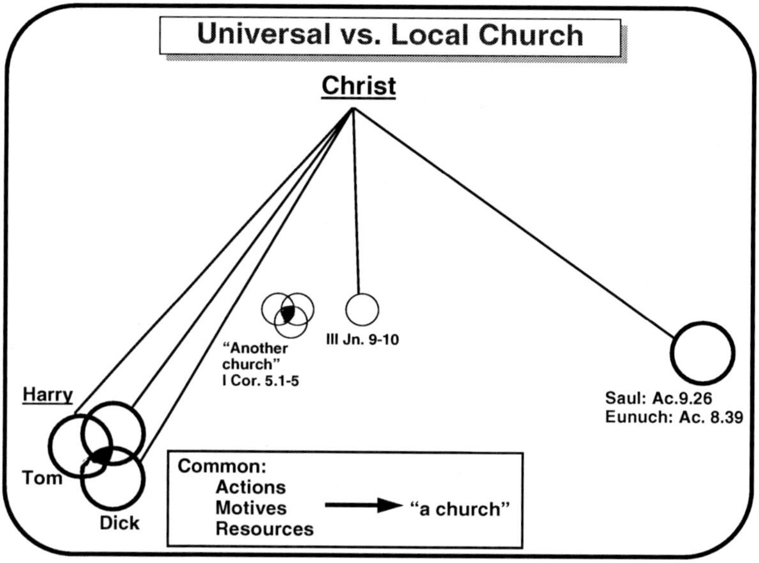

Figure 8

fellowship until he had repented, and again enjoyed fellowship with God, whence Paul again wrote the Corinthian church to accept him back into their local fellowship (II Cor. 2.5-11).

Figure 7 adds another individual Christian who is in fellowship with Christ, and yet he is not connected to any local congregation of Christians. The reference to III Jn. 9-10 indicates he might be one of those excluded from a local church by one like Diotrophes, who loved to have the preeminence, and who ejected from a local church Christians who actually enjoyed fellowship with Christ. This is an example of mistakes made in local churches, where individuals are excluded from the local fellowship who are in the universal church, while Corinth includes a Christian in its local fellowship who is no longer in fellowship with God.

The Christian unjustly excluded has no serious problem, since he is still in fellowship with Christ. On the other hand, he may think he is alright since he has local fellowship, yet he is not in fellowship with Christ. Men make mistakes in controlling their fellowship, Christ doesn't.

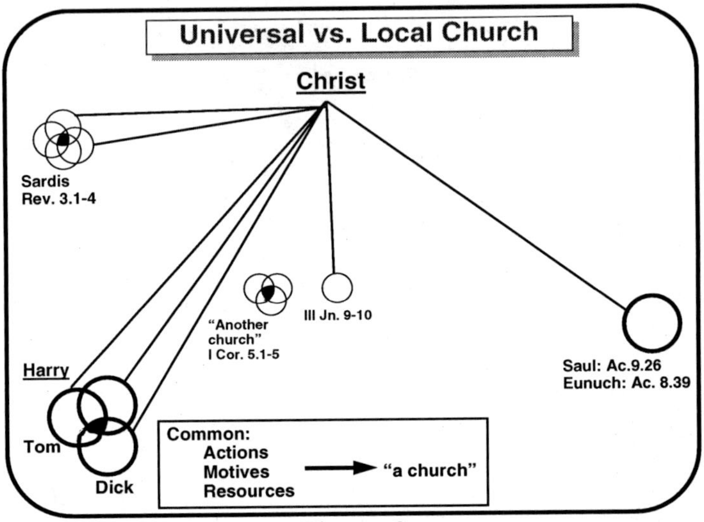

Figure 9

In Figure 8 we are ready to identify the previously unidentified Christian who shares fellowship with Christ, and yet not with a local congregation. He might be Saul in Ac. 9.26, before the fellowship in Jerusalem accepted him. He might be the Ethiopian Eunuch, Ac. 8.39, before he joined a local congregation of Christians. The cases of both Paul and the Eunuch illustrate a Christian may be in fellowship with Christ while not in a local fellowship. While the teaching of Christ certainly points out related cases as these ought to be temporary, but they existed in the New Testament, and they exist now.

Figure 9 adds still another congregation, one where the vast majority of the Christians do not enjoy fellowship with Christ, as illustrated by the absence of lines connecting them to Christ. Even though this church as a whole does not share fellowship with Christ, notice a few of the Christians do. This illustrates the church in Sardis in Rev. 3.1-4, where Jesus says:

> And to the angel of the church in Sardis write: These things saith he that hath the seven Spirits of God, and the seven stars: I know thy works, that thou hast a name that thou livest, and thou art dead. Be thou watchful, and

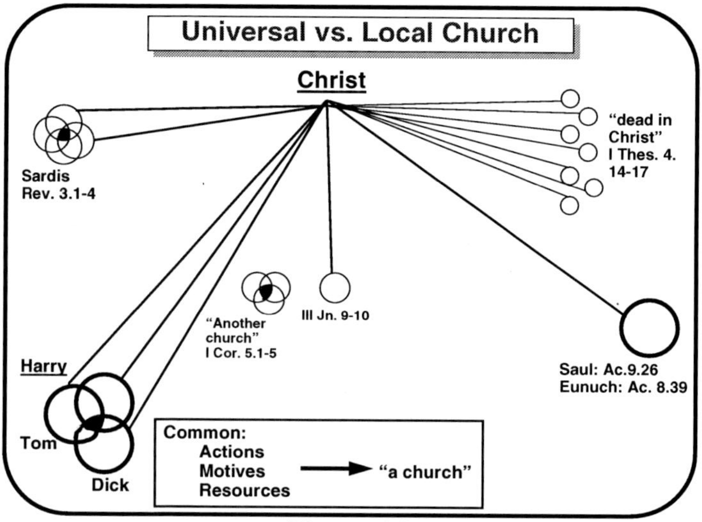

Figure 10

> establish the things that remain, which were ready to die: for I have found no works of thine perfected before my God. Remember therefore how thou hast received and didst hear; and keep it, and repent. If therefore thou shalt not watch, I will come as a thief, and thou shalt not know what hour I will come upon thee. But thou hast a few names in Sardis that did not defile their garments; and they shall walk with me in white; for they are worthy.

Since churches like this existed in the New Testament, we ought to allow that similar situations exist in our time. Many churches have a good reputation in man's eyes, but Christ doesn't recognize the vast majority of their members.

Figure 10 completes the illustration by adding a vast number of Christians who obviously are partners with Christ, but who are not in any local church. These are the dead in Christ, of whom we read in I Thes. 4.14, 17. Certainly, all of these are in fellowship with Christ, but none of them are in local congregations.

Notice that the universal church in Figure 10 is not composed of congregations, but individual Christians. It contains all Christians who are in Christ, if they are in local congregations that please Christ, if they have been unjustly ejected from a local church, if they are not presently in a local congregation, and if they are one of the "faithful few" in a congregation not pleasing to Christ. Also, the universal church is composed of all Christians, the dead as well as the living.

When we recall the classically denominational view Alexander Campbell held of the universal church, i.e., one composed of all the local congregations, we now notice such a view is unsatisfactory. It's not only not found in the Bible, but it also leaves out some of the Christians in fellowship with Christ. In other words, consider all the Christians Campbell's concept left out: (1) Those unjustly excluded from a local church by someone like Diotrophes, (2) Saul, (3) the Ethiopian Eunuch, (4) the "faithful few" in Sardis (who probably wouldn't have been listed in our list of "reputable" congregations), and (5) all the faithful dead!

What Is Not on This Figure

Figure 10 is significant not only for what it includes, but also for what it does not include. Notice that the universal church contains: (1) no denominations, (2) no working units larger than a local church, (3) no work of some congregations under the elders of another congregation, i.e, no "sponsoring churches," (4) no collective action of churches, or denominational organization, (5) no collective universal church action to split or divide, (6) no way for the universal church to be divided, (7) no collective fellowship of congregations, and (8) no address or phone number for the universal church. None of these features exist on Figure 10 simply because none of them existed among the people of God in the New Testament! This is the non-denominational way of Christ in its purist form.

Chapter 4

Fellowship with God

So far, we have shown the New Testament deals with two types of fellowship, i.e., with God in the universal church and with Christians in a local church. We have also illustrated the relationship between the two types of fellowship, and have found that the universal church is not composed of local churches (the denominational view) but of individual Christians. Some of these Christians are in local churches, and some are not; some of them are alive, and some are not. We now want to focus on the subject of fellowship with God, both what it is, and how it is established. Later chapters focus on the nature of the fellowship of Christians with one another in a local church.

Fellowship Defined

Fellowship is commonly regarded like many other Biblical terms, i.e., as a religious word, and yet it is not particularly so. Words like "love," "faith," and "grace," are frequently used and yet seldom understood. All recognize these words as pertinent to the way of Christ—they are nice words, but few use them accurately.

The term "fellowship" is generally taken to be a pleasing concept—that one pleases God, or that God looks with favor on those with whom He is in fellowship. Though these things may be true, the concept of fellowship goes far beyond this.

The word "fellowship" means "joint participation toward a common goal." This definition illustrates the three necessary ingredients before fellowship can exist: (1) action, (2) common action, and (3) common motive.

For example, *two football teams* battling it out on the playing field are not in fellowship with each other, though they have common action. Obviously, they do not have a common goal. They do not strive for the same thing, but against each other.

However, all the players on *one team* are in fellowship because they have (1) action, (2) common action, and (3) a common motive or goal. Yet common action alone doesn't imply the existence of fellowship.

People in a large traffic jam on a freeway don't consider themselves in fellowship with one another, even though they do something together. Their motives, goals, or destinations are all different. They just wait for the opportunity not to be stuck together! Again, common action doesn't imply the existence of fellowship.

An atheist and a Christian may both stop to help an injured person, and yet they are not in fellowship: the Christian helps because of his allegiance to Christ, while the atheist may help to show others one can be benevolent without even believing in God! Once more, common action alone doesn't imply fellowship.

An incident in the life of Paul illustrates this further, and even shows not all people who teach the gospel of Christ are partners with one another. In Phil. 1.12-16, Paul describes how his Roman imprisonment had turned out for him:

> Now I would have you know, brethren, that the things which happened unto me have fallen out rather unto the progress of the gospel; so that my bonds became manifest in Christ throughout the whole praetorian guard, and to all the rest; and that most of the brethren in the Lord, being confident through my bonds, are more abundantly bold to speak the word of God without fear. Some indeed preach Christ even of envy and strife; and some also of good will: the one do it of love, knowing that I am set for the defense of the gospel; but the other proclaim Christ of faction, not sincerely, thinking to raise up affliction for me in my bonds. What then? only that in every way,

> whether in pretense or in truth, Christ is proclaimed; and therein I rejoice, yea, and will rejoice.

Here Paul explains something Christians wouldn't expect, that the imprisonment of an apostle had turned out for the progress of the gospel. First of all, the gospel bore fruit because Paul evidently had been able teach some of his guards whom he would not have taught had he not been imprisoned. Also, Paul's behavior while in prison had been a good example to the Roman Christians who were now more courageous in teaching the gospel themselves.

Third, even Paul's enemies preached Christ, hoping to get him in even more trouble. These people preached the same Christ Paul preached, and yet had you asked either Paul or his enemies if they were partners with one another, both would have said, "Assuredly not!" Action occurred, preaching the gospel. It was common action, as both Paul and his enemies preached Christ. However, no fellowship existed because their motives were different. Assuredly, common action, even in preaching Christ, does not mean fellowship exists.

Since common motive is necessary to fellowship, we may not always be sure about our fellowship with some people, because we do not know the motives of everyone. Paul, in I Cor. 2.11, points out we do not know the things of a man, his desires, his motives, his goals, or his likes and dislikes unless he tells us. For that reason, while we may consider ourselves in fellowship with many apparently fine Christians, we may not be, because we do not know their motives. They may act out of pretense, as did Paul's enemies. They may be hypocrites. They may fool us, and cause us to make mistakes in our local fellowship, yet they do not fool God, who knows their hearts controls His universal fellowship without error.

Thus, fellowship consists of (1) action, (2) common action, and (3) common motive. A local fellowship of Christians consists of Christians who act together with common motives or goals. This is our elementary definition of a local church, Christians who act out of common motives to serve Christ in what they can do together. The fact that they are in fellowship with one another means they work together according to a common motive or goal.

Likewise, fellowship with God includes (1) action, (2) common action, and (3) common motive. To say one is in fellowship with God does not simply mean he approves of God, or God approves of him, but he and God act jointly with a common motive, that is, to glorify God. Most importantly, this person is a co-worker with God!

Discussion of II Corinthians 6.14-18

In II Corinthians 6.14-18, Paul uses five synonyms of fellowship that aid our understanding of the term:

> Be not unequally yoked with unbelievers: for what fellowship have righteousness and iniquity? or what communion hath light with darkness? And what concord hath Christ with Belial? or what portion hath a believer with an unbeliever? And what agreement hath a temple of God with idols?

Many times people take Paul's command, "Be not *unequally yoked* with unbelievers," as a prohibition against Christians marrying unbelievers. First of all, Paul doesn't say, "don't *become* unequally yoked," but rather "don't *be* unequally yoked." If the unequal yoke necessarily speaks of marriage, he would not be commanding Christians not to marry, but rather commanding them to sever ties that had already been made! This interpretation cannot be proper, for it contradicts I Cor. 7.10-11, where Paul had already taught these same brethren if they lived with an unbeliever and he was content to dwell with them as a faithful Christian, not to depart from him. Thus, Paul does not speak especially of marriage in this passage, although we'll see that his teaching can readily be applied to certain aspects of marriage.

Paul's use of five synonyms for fellowship aids our understanding of his teaching along with the concept of fellowship. In explaining why we shouldn't be unequally *yoked* with unbelievers, Paul asks, "for what *fellowship* have righteousness and iniquity?" This is a rhetorical question: Paul knows none exists.

Righteousness and iniquity do not participate together toward a common goal.

The same is true with Paul's next question: "or what *communion* hath light with darkness?" Again, light and darkness don't mix; they don't participate with one another toward a common goal.

Then Paul asks, "And what *concord* hath Christ with Belial?" Belial is one of the Jewish nicknames of Satan. Obviously, Christ and Satan have no concord or fellowship.

Next Paul concludes, "or what *portion* hath a believer with an unbeliever?" The term "portion" means "inheritance," and again, believers and unbelievers don't share a common inheritance.

Then Paul says, "and what *agreement* hath a temple of God with idols?" He intimates rhetorically that no agreement exists between the two.

Now, most of us have no problem understanding what the terms fellowship, communion, concord, portion, and agreement mean, but when we come to the term "unequally yoked together," we wonder. If we'll notice these six terms are used synonymously here, then we'll understand how Paul uses the term "unequally yoked." He means for Christians not to be in situations where they share fellowship, communion, concord, portion, and agreement with sin!

Paul makes the application in verse 17:

> Wherefore, Come ye out from among them, and be ye separate, saith the Lord, And touch no unclean thing; And I will be to you a Father, And ye shall be to me sons and daughters, saith the Lord Almighty.

Then in the first verse of the following chapter, he says:

> Having therefore these promises, beloved, let us cleanse ourselves from all defilement of flesh and spirit, perfecting holiness in the fear of God.

Now, can this passage be applied to the marriage relationship? Assuredly so. Christians cannot share in sin in their marriages. For example, if a believer is married to an unbeliever, and to maintain joint participation with the unbeliever, the Christian must disobey God, the solution is, "We must obey God rather than man." (Ac. 5.29) Paul states the same truth in I Corinthians 7: if an unbeliever is not content to dwell with one who lives a life of faith in Christ, and chooses to depart when the Christian won't be swayed, "let him depart." Thus, while Paul does not speak specifically of the marriage relationship, the teaching of this passage can certainly apply there.

This passage (II Cor. 6.14-18) can also apply to any relationship where joint participation with sinners in their sin involves a Christian in it. For example, in a business situation, if a Christian is a partner of an unbeliever (or an unfaithful Christian for that matter) who insists on sinning as a part of their joint business practice, i.e., cheating the government, customers, clients, etc., then the Christian must either stop the sin or stop the partnership. He can have no relationship with sinners where he is forced to be a partner (unequally yoked) in their sin. This applies to a local church as well, and it did in the New Testament, as we'll see later.

Thus, Paul's use of these six synonyms of fellowship in this passage are helpful to our grasping the concept of fellowship. Fellowship is a yoking together of partners who share agreement, concord, and portion.

Fellowship Is Teamwork

Fellowship is really much more than pleasing God, or other Christians. When one is in fellowship with God, he is on God's team; he is a co-worker with God. Likewise, when one is in fellowship with other Christians in a local church, he is on the same local team; he is a co-worker with those other Christians.

Social Eating Is Not Fellowship

Many times the term fellowship is used to describe social eating. Social eating is a poor substitute for the Bible's concept of fellowship. For instance, Paul condemns having fellowship with sinners in Eph. 5.11, where he says, "and have no fellowship with the unfruitful works of darkness, but rather even reprove them." While Jesus was on the earth, He ate common meals with sinners, Mk. 2.16, and yet we know He never sinned, Heb. 4.15. Jesus did not do what His apostle Paul later condemned, that is, while Jesus ate common meals with sinners, Jesus did not have fellowship with them; therefore, social eating is not fellowship. Of course, it may be misconstrued as fellowship, as Paul reveals in I Cor. 5.9-11.

These concepts of fellowship with other Christians are discussed more at length in later chapters. However, here fellowship is much more than social eating or pleasing someone.

Fellowship with God

Now that we grasp the basic concept of fellowship, we are ready to apply these principles to our fellowship with God. Once more, saying one is in fellowship with God doesn't merely mean one pleases God. He pleases God, but fellowship implies much more. He is a partner with God; he jointly participates with God. He and God work together in certain matters important to both. He and God operate together according to a common philosophy, the glorification of God Himself. They share a common destiny; they are no longer separate.

Fellowship Is Separated by Sin

Those of us who have sinned are properly concerned about establishing fellowship with God, because sin affects our fellowship with God. This is not just because we displease God when we sin, but because we're no longer His partners; we no longer work together with Him; we no longer share the same philosophy, and we are no longer involved in a common destiny, eternal life. This is true because of the very nature of God. In I Jn. 1.5, 6 John says:

> And this is the message which we have heard from him and announce unto you, that God is light, and in him is no darkness at all. If we say that we have fellowship with him, and walk in the darkness, we lie, and do not the truth.

Thus, God's very nature necessitates He cannot be a partner in sin: He never has been, is not now, and never will be. It's obvious that for us to be in fellowship with God, we cannot partake in sin ourselves. For this reason God told the Jews in Isa. 59.1-3:

> Behold, the Lord's hand is not so short that it cannot save; neither is His ear so dull that it cannot hear. But your iniquities have made a separation between you and your God, and your sins have hid His face from you, so that He does not hear. For your hands are defiled with blood, and your fingers with iniquity; your lips have spoken falsehood, your tongue mutters wickedness...

God explained that the sin of the Jews was the basis of the lack of fellowship which then existed, and why He no longer worked with them in answering their prayers. He did not fail to answer their prayers because He was hard of hearing, nor because He was weak, but rather because their sins had broken the fellowship that had existed between them.

Fellowship Must Be Restored Through Jesus Christ

Jesus emphasizes that the fellowship of sinners must be restored through Him. In John 14.6, He says:

> I am the way, the truth, and the life, and no man cometh to the Father, but by me.

Likewise, in Eph. 1.3, Paul says:

> Blessed be the God and Father of our Lord Jesus Christ, who hath blessed us with every spiritual blessing in the heavenly places in Christ:

If fellowship with God is a spiritual blessing, fellowship with God is found in Christ. Consequently, any attempt on our part to restore our fellowship with God cannot succeed separate and apart from Jesus Christ.

Fellowship Is Not Restored on the Basis of Complete Doctrinal Correctness

Before we notice the New Testament's teaching concerning how fellowship with God is to be established, let's notice one way it's not established, and that is by perfect or complete doctrinal correctness. Suppose that complete doctrinal purity and correctness were necessary for one to be in fellowship with God. Who would have it? Do you? Did you have it when you became a Christian? Do those you teach the gospel to have it when they become Christians? Although this writer believes doctrinal purity and correctness is of extreme importance, he also realizes he may not now be completely doctrinally correct, and certainly at the time he became a Christian he was not, nor was it necessary for him to be in order to be a partner with God.

As a matter of fact, complete doctrinal correctness was the approach to fellowship that a prominent religious group in the New Testament period used, and they failed miserably. The Pharisees, the religious conservatives of New Testament times, argued about how many laws the Law of Moses contained, and devised all kinds of human traditions to enforce strict obedience to the Law of Moses.

It's important to notice when Jesus encountered the Pharisees, he endorsed their teaching. In Mt. 23.1-3, Jesus said, concerning the Pharisees:

> The scribes and the Pharisees sit on Moses' seat: all things therefore whatsoever they bid you, these do and observe; but do not ye after their works; for they say, and do not.

In verses 23-24 of that same chapter, Jesus said:

> Woe unto you, scribes and Pharisees, hypocrites! for ye tithe mint and anise and cummin, and have left undone the weightier matters of the law, justice, and mercy, and faith: but these ye ought to have done, and not to have left the other undone. Ye blind guides, that strain out the gnat, and swallow the camel!

Note that Jesus endorsed the teaching of the Pharisees and their strict adherence to the law of God. The thing Jesus did not endorse was the practice of the Pharisees and their basic attitudes toward obeying God. They did not obey God out of confidence in God or allegiance to Him, but rather out of adherence to the traditions of their fathers. Their obedience to the law of God was not based upon faith in God. Had it been, they would have accepted the Messiah who stood in their midst.

Let not the reader take these remarks as indicative of a lax attitude on the part of the writer toward doctrinal correctness and purity. He believes in doctrinal correctness and purity, and strives for it himself. Yet doctrinal purity, while it is important, is not the basis of our fellowship with God, nor was it in the case of the Pharisees. (Please see the remarks in Appendix 4, II John 9 and the Teaching of Christ, for further comments.)

Concerning the Pharisees, one other passage we ought to notice is Lk. 18.9-14:

> And he spake also this parable unto certain who trusted in themselves that they were righteous, and set all others at nought: Two men went up into the temple to pray; the one a Pharisee, and the other a publican. The Pharisee stood and prayed thus with himself, God, I thank thee, that I am not as the rest of men, extortioners, unjust, adulterers, or even as this publican. I fast twice in the week: I give tithes of all that I get. But the publican, standing afar off, would not even lift up so much as his eyes unto heaven, but smote his breast, saying, God, be thou merciful to me a sinner. I say unto you, This man went down to his house justified rather than the other: for every one that exalteth himself shall be humbled; but he that humbleth himself shall be exalted.

Don't many often speak of the faithfulness of Christians on the mere basis of what they do? "Of course he's faithful, he's here every time the doors are open!" The Pharisees took this approach. They emphasized obedience without regard for reliance on God that should have been the source of obedience. *The Pharisees teach us it is possible to be doctrinally correct, and still be far from fellowship with God.*

Fellowship Is Restored on the Basis of Perfect Faith

While the Pharisees were not justified on the basis of their perfect doctrinal correctness, the Bible teaches actually two ways exist a person can use to be a partner with God. The first of these ways is by sinlessly obeying God, as illustrated in Figure 11A. If one perfectly understands the will of God in all matters, and then sinlessly obeys God, he is indeed righteous, just, and in fellowship with God. In Gal. 3.10, Paul says, concerning the Law of Moses:

> For as many as are of the works of the law are under a curse: for it is written, Cursed is every one who continueth not in all things that are written in the book of the law, to do them.

Similarly, in Jas. 2.10, James, in speaking of the Law of Moses, says:

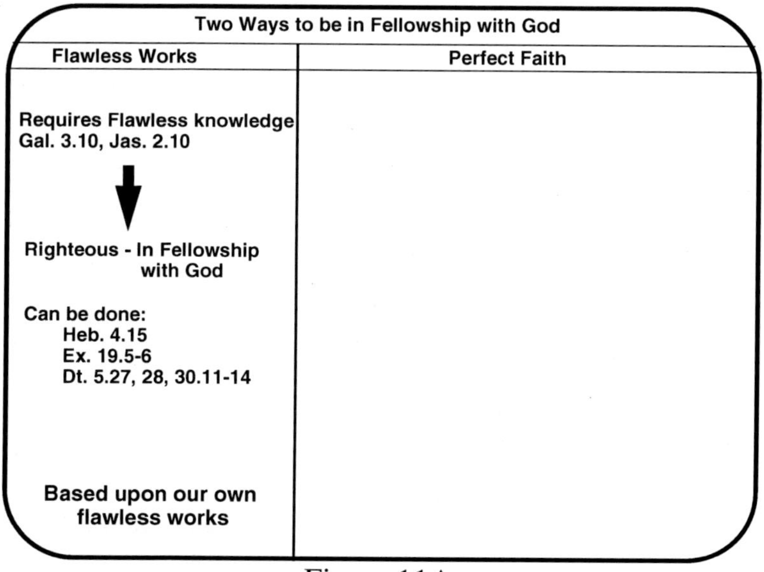

Figure 11A

> For whosoever shall keep the whole law, and yet stumble in one point, he is become guilty of all.

Thus, as long as the Jews completely understood and obeyed the law of Moses, based upon their confidence in God, they were righteous, and in no need of forgiveness of their sins. They had no sin, and did not need to be justified, for they were indeed just and righteous. However, once they fell from unblemished obedience, then they were under a curse; they were branded as lawbreakers, no longer righteous.

It is important to understand that man fully has the capacity to obey God sinlessly. When God was about to give the Mosaic covenant to the Jews at Mt. Sinai in Ex. 19.5, He told them:

> Now then, if you will indeed obey My voice and keep My covenant, then you shall be My own possession among all the peoples, for all the earth is Mine.

In verse 8, the people gave their reaction, as though they believed God did not ask too much for His fellowship with them to be based upon strict obedience to His covenant:

> And all the people answered together and said, "All that the Lord has spoken we will do!"

Of course, someone might think the Jews were naive in supposing they could keep the covenant, but consider further. In Dt. 5.27, when Moses gave them the covenant the second time, the Jews again told him:

> Go near and hear all that the Lord our God says; then speak to us all that the Lord our God will speak to you, and we will hear and do it.

Apparently, the Jews didn't think it was impossible to obey God, even though they had been acquainted with the covenant for forty years. In verse 28, God commended them for so thinking:

> And the Lord heard the voice of your word when you spoke to me, and the Lord said to me, I have heard the voice of the words of this people which they have spoken to you. They have done well in all that they have spoken.

Thus, neither did God think keeping the covenant was beyond their ability. Lastly, in Dt. 30.11-14, that took place at the end of Moses' life, God assured the Jews it was within their grasp to obey the covenant:

> For this commandment which I command you today is not too difficult for you, nor is it out of reach. It is not in heaven, that you should say, Who will go up to heaven for us to get it for us and make us hear it, that we may observe it? Nor is it beyond the sea, that you should say, Who will cross the sea for us to get it for us and make us hear it, that we may observe it? But the word is very near you, in your mouth and in your heart, that you may observe it.

Thus, God persuaded the Jews, and they understood, that keeping the Law of Moses was within their grasp. God never gave them a law that was beyond their capacity to obey. The problem wasn't that the law was too difficult for them—the problem was they just didn't keep it flawlessly.

The same thing is true with each of us and the law of God today. God never puts us in a situation where all we can do is sin. He never gives us a commandment we don't have the ability to obey. We just don't do it. Let's not slander God by accusing Him of giving us a law that is beyond our ability to keep, and then condemning us for not keeping it. We can, we just don't.

Historically, the only one who sinlessly obeyed the Law of Moses was Jesus. He was just and righteous under every circumstance. We all have the ability to do what Jesus did, as the Hebrew writer explains in Heb. 4.15:

> For we have not a high priest that cannot be touched with the feeling of our infirmities; but one that hath been in all points tempted like as we are, yet without sin.

In other words, Jesus came to this earth and lived as a human being who was subject to the same temptations as we, and yet He sinlessly obeyed God. He was righteous; He did not need to be justified, or made right. He *was* right. We all, as human beings, have the ability to do that—we just haven't done it. So here is one way the Bible teaches we can be in fellowship with God: just perfectly obey God.

The same Bible teaches another way to enjoy fellowship with God, a way those of us who haven't perfectly obeyed God will surely be interested in, a way that is different from flawless obedience. Paul presents this approach in the book of Romans, in effect the theoretical book of the Bible. He describes how men have always been justified without perfect understanding of, and obedience to, the will of God (See Figure 11B).

Paul depicts in the first three chapters of Romans the universal condemnation and consequent need of everyone for the gospel of Christ. In Romans 1, Paul establishes the universal condemnation of all Gentiles under sin, and therefore the need of all of them for the gospel. Beginning in verse 18, he rehearses their sins of a lack of gratitude toward God, vain reasoning, the corruption of idolatry, and all the sins that resulted therefrom. Finally, Paul concludes in verse 32 by saying:

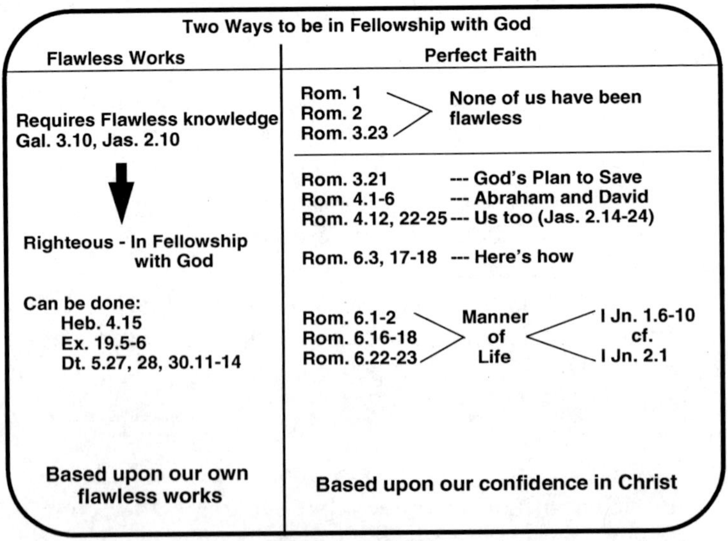

Figure 11B

> ...who, knowing the ordinance of God, that they that practise such things are worthy of death, not only do the same, but also consent with them that practise them.

Of course, Paul's Jewish listeners in Rome will think his condemnation of the Gentiles is extremely good preaching, so imagine their consternation when Paul turns to them in Chapter 2 and begins by saying:

> Wherefore thou art without excuse, O man, whosoever thou art that judgest: for wherein thou judgest another, thou condemnest thyself; for thou that judgest dost practice the same things.

Thus, Paul in Romans 2 demonstrates that when the Jews committed the same thing the Gentiles did, they also were under the condemnation of sin. In Rom. 2.17-24, Paul says:

> But if thou bearest the name of a Jew, and restest upon the law, and gloriest in God, and knowest his will, and approvest the things that are excellent, being instructed out of the law, and art confident that thou thyself art a guide of the blind, a light of them that are in darkness, a corrector of the foolish, a teacher of babes, having in the law the form of knowledge and of the truth, thou therefore that teachest another, teachest thou not thyself? thou that preachest a man should not steal, dost thou steal? thou that sayest a man should not commit adultery, dost thou commit adultery? thou that abhorrest idols, dost thou rob temples? thou who gloriest in the law, through thy transgression of the law dishonorest thou God? For the name of God is blasphemed among the Gentiles because of you, even as it is written.

Hence, Romans 2 shows the universal condemnation of the Jews, and the need of all Jews for the gospel of Christ. In Chapter 3, Paul concludes both Jews and Gentiles are universally condemned and in need of the gospel. In Romans 3.9, Paul says, concerning Jews and Greeks together:

> What then? are we better than they? No, in no wise: for we before laid to the charge both of Jews and Greeks, that they are all under sin; as it is written, There is none righteous, no, not one; There is none that understandeth, There is none that seeketh after God. They have all turned aside, They are together become unprofitable; There is none that doeth good, no, not so much as one.

Paul concludes this section in verse 23 by saying:

> For all have sinned, and fall short of the glory of God...

Here is the universal condemnation and need of everyone, both Jew and Greek, for the gospel of Christ. In verse 21, Paul introduces the solution to this universal condemnation:

> But now apart from the law a righteousness of God hath been manifested, being witnessed by the law and the prophets; even the righteousness of God through faith in Jesus Christ unto all them that believe, for there is no distinction;

After showing the universal condemnation of man, Paul begins to speak of a way God makes men righteous based upon their faith or confidence in Christ, a way that was witnessed in the law and the prophets. In Chapter 4, Paul illustrates this doctrine of justification with the cases of Abraham and David—one of whom (Abraham) did not live under the Law of Moses and yet was justified, and the other (David) who did live under the law and yet was not justified by the Law of Moses. Concerning Abraham, Paul says in Romans 4.1:

> What then shall we say that Abraham, our forefather, hath found according to the flesh? For if Abraham was justified by works, he hath whereof to glory; but not toward God.

Paul first declares that Abraham wasn't justified by works, and in this context he speaks of a certain type of works, the works of the law of 3.28. Paul affirms Abraham was not justified by flawless obedience to law works. Indeed, historically Abraham neither understood nor faultlessly obeyed the law of God. In verses 3-5, Paul says:

> For what saith the scripture? And Abraham believed God, and it was reckoned unto him for righteousness. Now to him that worketh, the reward is not reckoned as of grace, but as of debt. But to him that worketh not, but believeth on him that justifieth the ungodly, his faith is reckoned for righteousness.

Again, the works Paul speaks of are law works, meritorious works. Paul affirms Abraham was not thus justified, but rather by faith. Paul makes it clear what kind of faith it was: perfect faith, as he'll describe it.

In verses 6-8, Paul passes to David, one who lived under the Law of Moses:

> Even as David also pronounceth blessing upon the man, unto whom God reckoneth righteousness apart from works, saying, Blessed are they whose iniquities are forgiven, and whose sins are covered. Blessed is the man to whom the Lord will not reckon sin.

Of course, we know that like Abraham, David neither perfectly understood nor perfectly obeyed God. He too was justified by a certain kind of faith.

In verse 11 Paul contends Abraham is the father of all who have the same kind of faith he had:

> ...that he might be the father of all them that believe, though they be in uncircumcision, that righteousness might be reckoned unto them; and the father of circumcision to them who not only are of the circumcision, but who also walk in the steps of that faith of our father Abraham that he had in uncircumcision.

Even though Abraham did not perfectly understand the law of God, and did not sinlessly obey it, he was justified and counted righteous by God. In this way he was in fellowship with God, and became the father of all who have his kind of faith.

Notice Paul described Abraham's faith by saying it was a faith that Abraham "walked in the steps of." In other words, Abraham's faith wasn't simple mental assent. It was a working faith! This does not mean his works merited salvation, which Paul has already disclaimed, but his works were the result of Abraham's confidence in God.

Actually, Paul speaks of Abraham's faith the same way James does in Jas. 2.17-26:

> Even so faith, if it have not works, is dead in itself. Yea, a man will say, Thou hast faith, and I have works: show me thy faith apart from thy works, and I by my works will show thee my faith. Thou believest that God is one; thou doest well: the demons also believe, and shudder. But wilt thou know, O vain man, that faith apart from works is barren? Was not Abraham our father justified by works, in that he offered up Isaac his son upon the altar? Thou seest that faith wrought with his works, and by works was faith made perfect; and the scripture was fulfilled which saith, And Abraham believed God, and it was reckoned unto him for righteousness; and he was called the friend of God. Ye see that by works a man is justified, and not only by faith...For as the body apart from the spirit is dead, even so faith apart from works is dead.

Though many think Paul and James hopelessly contradict each other's teaching concerning faith and works, they actually teach the same thing. Both deny one is saved by works of the law, and both deny one is saved by mental assent. They both affirm one is saved by a certain kind of faith: "perfect faith," as James calls it, and faith that is "walked in the steps of," as Paul refers to it. Perfect faith is confidence in God that is completed by obedience that is the result of that allegiance.

Back in Romans 4.22-25, Paul concludes his teaching on our being justified in the same manner as was our father Abraham:

> Wherefore also it [Abraham's perfect faith—SGD] was reckoned unto him for righteousness. Now it was not written for his sake alone, that it was reckoned unto him; but for our sake also, unto whom it [our perfect faith—SGD] shall be reckoned, who believe on him that raised Jesus our Lord from the dead, who was delivered up for our trespasses, and was raised for our justification.

Then Paul passes into Romans 5 by saying:

> Being therefore justified by faith, we have peace with God through our Lord Jesus Christ.

Of course, he speaks of the same kind of faith that he discusses throughout Chapter 4, i.e., the faith Abraham "walked in the steps of."

Now let's see how individuals walked in the steps of that faith and became Christians in New Testament times. In Romans 5, Paul anticipates the probable Jewish argument that one act of one man (the redemption of man by Christ) couldn't possibly have that much to do with the salvation of all men. Paul counters by showing the Jews had always believed one man could do one thing that would affect all mankind. As proof, he refers to the sin Adam committed that affected us all so drastically.

In Chapter 6, Paul answers another Jewish objection to what he taught in Chapter 4, when he begins:

> What shall we say then? Shall we continue in sin, that grace may abound?

In other words, the Jews in Paul's audience would assume that since we are not justified by faultless works, they could sin all they liked. "Then, when God forgives us, that will really demonstrate the grace of God," they would think. Paul answers:

> God forbid. We who died to sin, how shall we any longer live therein?

Then Paul describes what these Roman Jews did that brought them into fellowship with God. In verses 3-11 he says:

> Or are ye ignorant that all we who were baptized into Christ Jesus were baptized into his death? We were buried therefore with him through baptism into death: that like as Christ was raised from the dead through the glory of the Father, so we also might walk in newness of life. For if we have become united with him in the likeness of his death, we shall be also in the likeness of his resurrection; knowing this, that our old man was crucified with him, that the body of sin might be done away, that we should no longer be in bondage to sin; for he that hath died is justified from sin. But if we died with Christ, we believe that we shall also live with him: knowing that Christ being raised from the dead dieth no more; death no more hath dominion over him. For the death that he died, he died unto sin once: but the life that he liveth, he liveth unto God. Even so reckon ye also yourselves to be dead unto sin, but alive unto God in Christ Jesus.

and in verses 17 and 18:

> But thanks be to God, that, whereas ye were servants of sin, ye became obedient from the heart to that form of teaching whereunto ye were delivered; and being made free from sin, ye became servants of righteousness.

The form or pattern or mold of teaching Paul refers to is the model of verses 3-6, the death, burial, and resurrection of Christ. Paul says when we obeyed the pattern from the heart, that is, upon the basis of our faith in Christ, we were made free from sin. Without the guilt of sin, we are in the new life, we are justified because of our faith, and we now share fellowship with Christ. We are in the universal church, the body of the redeemed, the collection of all who are in fellowship with God through the redemption that is available in Jesus Christ.

The main purpose of Romans 6 is to instruct concerning the manner of life Christians are to live. Rather than thinking "We can sin more so that grace might abound," Paul shows the new life we are raised to is one of service to Christ rather than continuing to sin. Newness of life implies we do not continue in sin. Being dead unto sin means we no longer walk in sin. Thus, in verses 12-13 he says:

> Let not sin therefore reign in your mortal body, that ye should obey the lusts thereof: neither present your members unto sin as instruments of unrighteousness; but present yourselves unto God, as alive from the dead, and your members as instruments of righteousness unto God.

In verses 22-23, Paul concludes his teaching on the manner of life of Christians by saying:

> But now being made free from sin and become servants to God, ye have your fruit unto sanctification, and the end eternal life. For the wages of sin is death; but the free gift of God is eternal life in Christ Jesus our Lord.

A Christian in the New Testament did not share fellowship with God because of his complete doctrinal correctness or his perfect works! He was justified on the basis of his perfect faith, his confidence in Christ that led him initially to obey the gospel by being baptized into Christ. That same confidence caused him continue to live a life of sanctified obedience to Christ, based upon his wholehearted allegiance to Him.

Historically, man has always been justified through faith in God. Before the Law of Moses, Abraham was saved by perfect faith, as already shown in Romans 4. Even before Abraham, Noah was justified in this manner, according to Heb. 11.7:

> By faith, Noah, being warned of God concerning things not seen as yet, moved with godly fear, prepared an ark to the saving of his house; through which he condemned

> the world, and became heir of the righteousness which is according to faith.

This "righteousness which is according to faith" is the same righteousness that Paul speaks of in Romans. The Jews under the Law of Moses could have been saved the same way, as Paul intimates in Rom. 9.30-32:

> What shall we say then? That the Gentiles, who followed not after righteousness, attained to righteousness, even the righteousness which is of faith: but Israel, following after a law of righteousness, did not arrive at that law. Wherefore? Because they sought it not by faith, but as it were by works.

Thus, Paul shows some of those not under the Law of Moses were justified by faith (for example, Abraham and Noah), while the majority of Jews were not justified because they sought it by flawless performance rather than perfect faith. Question: Could the Jews have sought it by faith? Certainly! David was a Jew who obtained it by faith, Rom. 4.7, and Paul demonstrates we obtain it the same way in Rom. 4.12.

Perfect Faith vs. Flawless Works: Take Your Pick

Thus, we see two ways exist for us to be in fellowship with God, to jointly participate with Him: by our flawless works, or our perfect faith. The Bible teaches both. Those of us who do not understand exactly what God wants us to do, and therefore do not sinlessly obey Him, will surely want to choose the second option. We will want to obey the gospel of Christ by being baptized into him to be made free from sin, and then living a life of allegiance to him. Our justification and our fellowship with God all depend upon our confidence in Christ, that will lead us to live lives of allegiance to Him.

Too often many base their fellowship with God upon belonging to a certain organization. What happened to the concept of confidence in Christ? Many base their fellowship upon complete doctrinal correctness. What happened to the concept of reliance on Christ? Some assume their fellowship with God comes by living pure lives. Purity of life is important, but if it's not based upon faith in Christ, it avails nothing as far as fellowship with God is concerned.

What to Do to Be in Fellowship with God in the Universal Church

Let us pause here to encourage the reader who may not have obeyed the gospel of Christ initially as these Roman Christians had done, to do just what they did to restore their fellowship with God, and be in the "general assembly and church of the firstborn who are enrolled in heaven." If you believe Jesus is the Son of God, His sonship being declared by the resurrection of Jesus from the dead (Rom. 1.4), then you need to repent. This means you determine you live a life of allegiance to Christ regardless of the cost. You will then confess your faith in Christ and be baptized into Him for the remission of your sins; you will rise to walk in newness of life, just as these Christians in Rome had done. Then you will be *just a Christian* as they were.

This will not make you a member of any denomination, any more than it made those in Rome members of a denomination. The denominations around us today didn't even exist then, none of them. Nor will you automatically become a member of a local congregation of Christians, any more than the Christians in the New Testament did. Though you will now enjoy new life in Christ, that will not end of your responsibilities in serving Him. As a disciple (student) of Christ, you will want to study further to learn what He wants you to do out of your allegiance to Him. First of all, you will want to learn about your responsibilities to associate and work with other Christians, which is the purpose of the next chapter.

What Denominations Do Not Teach

Denominations do not teach individuals how to enjoy fellowship with Christ. Preachers who tell individuals to "receive Jesus Christ as their personal Saviour" (1) preach something the Bible nowhere says, and (2) they fail to tell them what Paul told them to do, i.e., to obey from the heart that form of doctrine, to be baptized into Christ in order to enter the new life. They do not tell people how to exercise saving faith in Christ.

The issue is not the sincerity of the preachers or of the ones they teach. The issue is whether we place our trust, allegiance, and confidence in men or in Christ. We place our confidence in Christ by hearkening to what He says, not to what men say, nor to what we have always believed. This is allegiance to men, not Christ.

If preachers refuse to teach individuals how to share fellowship with Christ the way Paul did in Romans 6, then regardless of how sincere they or their followers may be, allegiance to preachers or to denominational organization will not produce fellowship with God. We must obey the gospel initially to have the new life, and we must live lives of faith to maintain fellowship with Christ.

The subject of faith is frequently talked about, but rarely understood. For that reason, Appendix 2 gives a short discussion on "Faith: The Least Understood Bible Subject."

Since Paul's emphasis on baptism may be new to some readers, Appendix 3 examines arguments against the significance of baptism. Baptism has been *de*-emphasized for some very understandable reasons in the modern religious world. This material is included to help us view the subject in a strictly scriptural perspective.

Chapter 5

Fellowship with Other Christians

Thus far in our discussion of fellowship with God, we have seen we need our fellowship restored because of our sin, and that it is restored through our obedient faith in Christ. Once we become Christians, and are in fellowship with Christ in the universal church, we still have not established fellowship with other Christians. This chapter shows how we accomplish this.

God Wants Us to Be in Fellowship with Other Christians

As we have already noticed, Christians in the New Testament were not islands unto themselves. In specific areas they associated, assembled, and worked together just as Paul joined himself to the disciples in Jerusalem in Ac. 9.26. Throughout the New Testament, we read of local churches scattered around the known world. In Heb. 10.24, the writer exhorted Hebrew Christians that they needed the benefits of associating and working together as the Lord intended:

> ...and let us consider one another to provoke unto love and good works...

As one contemplates "considering the needs of other Christians," "consider" means "to fix the mind upon," that is, to meditate and analyze how to help other Christians be faithful in their duties to Christ. The writer says we should do this to "provoke" one another to love and good works. The word "provoke" means "to call to action."

Christians have many ways to provoke one another: perhaps by visiting in their homes, by companionship on an everyday basis, solving their problems together, etc. But in the next verse the Hebrew writer implies exactly what kind of mutual consideration and provocation he has in mind when he says:

> Not forsaking our own assembling together, as the custom of some is, but exhorting one another; and so much the more, as ye see the day drawing nigh.

One way the Hebrew writer had in mind for Christians to consider one another and provoke one another unto love and good works was by associating together *in local churches*. They would assemble and work together for their individual good, and for the advantage of the gospel of Christ in their area.

Thus, in the New Testament, Christians were "joined" to local churches (Ac. 9.26). Our allegiance to Christ will produce the desire for these benefits as well.

Notice in Heb. 10.24-25 that some of these Christians were in the habit of "forsaking" or "leaving in the lurch" their assembling together, *not* because they were busy, nor because of some other activity they were engaged in. *They forsook assembling together because of physical persecution.* Verses 32-39 reveal that their Jewish neighbors and relatives violently persecuted them because they had become Christians. For that reason, some of them didn't consider their working union with other Christians all that important. The Hebrew writer exhorted them that *even in the face of physical persecution* their assembling and work together was important *for them* in their service to Christ. If it was important for them, then it ought to be just as important for us now. Consequently, we need to contemplate how to find a group of Christians we can conscientiously associate ourselves with.

Easy Ways That Won't Work

Just "Christians" Won't Do

First of all, it would be nice if we could recognize and associate and work with just anyone who claimed to be a Christian, but it isn't so easy. Unfortunately, many who claim to be Christians are not; some don't even want to be, but hypocritically pretend to be. These kinds of people existed in the New Testament period of time, and they exist now.

In addition, some who sincerely claim to be Christians are not. Out of ignorance they have not initially obeyed the gospel of Christ, as discussed in the previous chapter. They may be superb people, and we don't say we want to write them off. We simply say *if they do not enjoy fellowship with God, we shouldn't treat them as though they do.* We could well view them as disciples (learners) as were the twelve at Ephesus (Ac. 19.1-7). We can appreciate their sincerity and desire to serve the Lord without depreciating either one and without being arrogant, condescending, harsh, and unloving. We can do as Aquila and Priscilla did in Acts 18 and try "to teach them the way of the Lord more perfectly." We should do all within our power to help them get into fellowship with God, but that doesn't involve our recognizing them as part of our local fellowship. Hopefully, we will at some time be able to, but not yet! So, as we contemplate joining together with other Christians, we should keep in mind that just because someone calls himself a Christian isn't enough grounds for our recognizing him as such.

Just Preaching the Gospel Isn't Enough

Just because someone preaches the true gospel of Christ doesn't warrant our fellowship either. Phil. 1.16-17, tells of some who preached the gospel of Christ, and yet Paul did not work with them. In verse 12 Paul explains how his imprisonment in Rome turned out to be beneficial for the gospel of Christ. This surprises us because we normally don't think of apostles going to prison as advantageous to their work. In Phil. 1.16-17, Paul says:

> Now I would have you know, brethren, that the things which happened unto me have fallen out rather unto the progress of the gospel; so that my bonds became manifest in Christ throughout the whole praetorian guard, and to all the rest; and that most of the brethren in the Lord, being confident through my bonds, are more abundantly bold to speak the word of God without fear. Some indeed preach Christ even of envy and strife; and some also of good will; the one do it of love, knowing that I am set for the defence of the gospel; but the other proclaim Christ of faction, not sincerely, thinking to raise up affliction for me in my bonds. What then? only that in every way, whether in pretense or in truth, Christ is proclaimed; and therein I rejoice, yea, and will rejoice.

Notice Paul delineated some advantageous things that resulted from his imprisonment in Rome: (1) He taught some of Caesar's guards whom he would not have had the opportunity to teach had he not been imprisoned. (2) Some of the brethren in Rome became more bold to teach the gospel themselves, so the gospel was preached more from that standpoint. (3) Even Paul's enemies preached the gospel! Of course they did it insincerely, hypocritically, to try to make Paul's imprisonment even harder. However, they evidently preached the same gospel Paul preached, "Whether in pretense, or in truth, Christ is proclaimed," Paul rejoiced, because the people, who heard his enemies and obeyed that same gospel, became Christians as well.

Both Paul and his enemies preached the same gospel, i.e., they had common action. Yet because they had entirely different motives in preaching the gospel, they were not partners with one another. Paul preached the gospel to bring people into fellowship with God. Paul's enemies preached the same gospel to bring Paul harsher punishment.

Had you asked Paul whether he was in fellowship with his enemies, hc assuredly would have said, "No," and they would have answered the same as well! Thus, just because someone preaches the same gospel Paul preached doesn't warrant our fellowship with him. We certainly would not want to be partners with Paul's enemies!

Just Having a Scriptural Name Won't Do

Sometimes we look for a group of Christians who use a scriptural name to designate themselves. Just because a group of people claiming to be Christians rejects all denominational titles and selects a scriptural name applied to groups of Christians in the Bible, that doesn't mean they are Christians. Even if they are, we will see momentarily we cannot scripturally work with just any congregation of Christians.

Directories of "Faithful Churches" Won't Do

Sometimes various individuals or groups of Christians publish lists of "faithful churches." Depending on who publishes the list, the concept of "faithfulness" differs from list to list. First of all, the publication of such lists may presume some association of congregations that did not exist in New Testament times. As the chapter on the relationship of the universal church to the local church shows, the New Testament does not contain any organization larger than a local church. *Many such lists reflect an alignment of local churches that simply did not exist in the New Testament and are essentially denominational in nature.*

Secondly, such lists of faithful churches are rarely based upon "faithfulness" to Christ. Following is a letter circulated by what was probably a sincere, well-meaning Christian to create such a list of "faithful" congregations. As you read this letter, you'll probably laugh before you get to the end, but it won't be because his comments are funny. Perhaps we all can see some of ourselves in this man's desire to find a group of Christians with whom he could be in fellowship by looking in a "Directory of Faithful Churches":

> Brethren: We wish to compile and publish a list of *loyal* congregations. We want to make a directory of local congregations for the benefit of the traveling brethren who wish to worship with loyal congregations: secondly, for the benefit of brethren who are desirous of moving to a loyal congregation. To compile this directory we need the following information. Describe every act of worship

> in your assemblies. Describe your position on the communion. Do you have one or two communions on Sunday? Do you use only one cup and loaf? Do you fellowship the Sunday School or cups brethren? Do you fellowship the Old Paths Advocate? Or other digressives? Do you advocate any doctrine or act of worship that is called a hobby by most of the brotherhood? If you want to be counted among the honored few, give us correct answers to all of our questions, otherwise you will be left out of our directory...Are you living in a state of division, having pulled off from another congregation? Please answer all questions. Do you contend that the cup must have a handle on it? (quoted by W. Carl Ketcherside, "Schisms and Parties," *Mission Messenger*, November 1959, pp. 4-5.)

The concept of "loyal" in this letter has nothing to do with loyalty to Christ, at least it's not stated. Most of us can see the sectarian nature of such a document as this, and perhaps even see ourselves in it to a certain degree. Such a document seeks to produce a line-up of local churches that, in essence, is denominational itself. What will the Lord say in the judgment to questions like, "Do you contend that the cup must have a handle on it?" You may laugh, but not because there's anything funny here. Perhaps we laugh because we get tired of crying.

Thus, we're still left with the question of how to find a group of Christians we can associate, worship, and work with. In a later section, we will approach from a positive standpoint the "Fellowship of an Individual with a Congregation," but first, we want to explore a note of caution that will help us develop a scriptural set of restraints to our fellowship. It will help us understand the importance of exercising great care in establishing fellowship with a group of Christians.

"Be Not a Partaker of Other Men's Sins"

In I Timothy 5.21-22, Paul states to the young preacher Timothy words from which we take the title to this section:

> I charge thee in the sight of God, and Christ Jesus, and the elect angels, that thou observe these things without prejudice, doing nothing by partiality. Lay hands hastily on no man, neither be partaker of other men's sins...

The term "partaker" comes from the same root word for "fellowship," the subject of our study. Paul instructs Timothy not to be a partaker in other men's sins, nor to conduct himself in a way that makes him a partner in their evil deeds.

We discussed in detail in an earlier chapter another passage that gives this same type of instruction, II Cor. 6.14-7.1. We reproduce the passage here to get it before us:

> Be not unequally yoked with unbelievers: for what fellowship have righteousness and iniquity? Or what communion hath light with darkness? And what concord hath Christ with Belial? Or what portion hath a believer with an unbeliever? And what agreement hath a temple of God with idols? for we are a temple of the living God; even as God said, I will dwell in them, and walk in them; and I will be their God, and they shall be my people. Wherefore Come ye out from among them, and be ye separate, saith the Lord, and touch no unclean thing; and I will receive you, and will be to you a Father, and ye shall be to me sons and daughters, saith the Lord Almighty. Having therefore these promises, beloved, let us cleanse ourselves from all defilement of flesh and spirit, perfecting holiness in the fear of God.

The very tenor of these words instructs us not to be in fellowship with sin, to be holy and separate from it. This is a condition of fellowship with God, in Whom no darkness exists at all.

A third passage gives this same important type of instruction, Eph. 5.6-11. After discussing fleshly sins in verses 3-5, Paul says:

> Let no man deceive you with empty words; for because of these things cometh the wrath of God upon the sons of disobedience. Be not ye therefore partakers with them;

> for ye were once darkness, but are now light in the Lord: walk as children of light...proving what is well-pleasing unto the Lord; and have no fellowship with the unfruitful works of darkness, but rather even reprove them.

Again, Paul uses the words "partakers" and "fellowship" to command Christians not to be partners in others' sins. This is the nature of the cautionary note we want to discuss in this chapter. How can we associate with others in such a way as to make us a partner or "fellow" in their sins?

First of all, this is not to say we're guilty of another person's sins. In Ezekiel 18.1-20, Ezekiel discusses several cases to demonstrate God doesn't hold His people guilty for other people's sins. He discusses the case of the righteous father, who has an unrighteous son, and concludes by saying the father is not held guilty for his son's sins. Ezekiel continues by stating that a righteous son, who has a wicked father, is not held guilty of his father's sins. In verse 20, Ezekiel states the general principle:

> The person who sins will die. The son will not bear the punishment for the father's iniquity, nor will the father bear the punishment for the son's iniquity; the righteousness of the righteous will be upon himself, and the wickedness of the wicked will be upon himself.

Thus, the Bible teaches here and elsewhere we're not held guilty of another man's sins. However, the same Bible also teaches us several ways we can partake in another person's sins.

Commit the Same Sin Together

In Acts 5.1, 2, 9, we find a case of two Christians in fellowship with each other's sins by committing the same sin together. Verses 1-2 explain:

> But a certain man named Ananias, with Sapphira his wife, sold a possession, and kept back part of the price, his wife also being privy to it, and brought a certain part, and laid it at the apostles' feet.

These two Christians shared with each other in sin, by virtue of committing the same sin together. In verse 9, Peter meted out God's punishment for this sin as he says:

> How is it that ye have agreed together to try the Spirit of the Lord? Behold, the feet of them that have buried thy husband are at the door, and they shall carry thee out.

Thus, Ananias and Sapphira jointly participated in sin with a common goal. Consequently, they were partners with one another in sin and paid the price by being struck dead.

An Old Testament passage instructs us further about fellowship with sin in this manner. In Prov. 1.10-15, Solomon said:

> My son, if sinners entice you, do not consent. If they say, Come with us, let us lie in wait for blood, let us ambush the innocent without cause; let us swallow them alive like Sheol, even whole, as those who go down to the pit; we shall find all kinds of precious wealth, we shall fill our houses with spoil; throw in your lot with us, we shall all have one purse; My son, do not walk in the way with them, Keep your feet from their path...

Had Ananias and Sapphira heeded this instruction, they might not have come to their sad end. They didn't realize the seriousness of being a partner in another's sin by sinning with that person.

Commit the Same Sin Separately

In Acts 7.51-52, Stephen accused the Jews of his day of being partakers in the sins of their fathers. They were not guilty of the sins of their fathers who were already dead. Just the same, Stephen accuses them of being partners with their wicked fathers:

> Ye stiffnecked and uncircumcised in heart and ears, ye do always resist the Holy Spirit: as your fathers did, so do ye. Which of the prophets did not your fathers persecute? and they killed them that showed before of the

> coming of the Righteous One; of whom ye have now become betrayers and murderers...

In Mt. 23.29-32, Jesus had previously accused those Jews of the same thing:

> Woe unto you, scribes and Pharisees, hypocrites! For ye build the sepulchres of the prophets, and garnish the tombs of the righteous, and say, If we had been in the days of our fathers, we should not have been *partakers* with them in the blood of the prophets. Wherefore ye witness to yourselves, that ye are sons of them that slew the prophets. Fill ye up then the measure of your fathers.

Jesus' point is that even though these Jews claimed they were not in fellowship ("partakers") with their ancestors, in fact they were. By killing the Messiah the prophets had foretold, they committed the same sin their ancestors had committed by killing those very prophets. We can do the same thing with sinners today by sharing with sinners of another time or place.

Consent with Sinners

The Bible also teaches we can be in fellowship with sinners, not by committing the same sin ourselves, but merely by consenting while someone else does it. For example, in Acts 8.1, Luke tells us that as the Jews killed Stephen,

> ...Saul was consenting unto his death.

Later, after Paul became a Christian, he reflected on this sin as he begged Jesus to let him preach to the Jews in Jerusalem. In Acts 22.19-20, Paul says:

> And I said, Lord, they themselves know that I imprisoned and beat in every synagogue them that believed on thee: and when the blood of Stephen thy witness was shed, I also was standing by, and *consenting*, and keeping the garments of them that slew him.

Paul's main point in his effort to persuade Jesus to let him stay in Jerusalem was that by consenting to the death of Stephen, he was a partner in the sin of those Jews. Even the Jews themselves understood that. Paul thought that the Jews' realization of that fact would make his efforts among them more fruitful. He partook in their sin by consenting with it. Nonetheless, Jesus still didn't accept Paul's plea to stay in Jerusalem, and told Paul he had other plans for him.

In Romans 1.32, after describing the sinfulness of the Gentiles in their apostasy from God, Paul concludes:

> ...[the Gentiles—SGD] who, knowing the ordinance of God, that they that practise such things are worthy of death, not only do the same, but also *consent* with them that practise them.

These passages contain important teaching for those who are concerned about fellowship in a congregation where unscriptural things are done, activities they don't believe in themselves. *These passages teach we don't have to personally believe the unscriptural thing to be wrong, and we don't even have to practice it ourselves.* Giving consent to something that is wrong is enough for us to be in fellowship with other men's sins! We encourage its practice by financially supporting it or just merely consenting to its being done.

Know Another's Guilt But Fail to Act

A modern proverb says: "Evil triumphs when good men do nothing." This is certainly true, yet the Bible teaches when we have the ability to act and do not, then we're partners in the evil.

Ezekiel 3.17-21 substantiates this point. At the beginning of Ezekiel's teaching the Jews during their Babylonian exile, God impressed the following responsibility upon the young prophet:

> Son of man, I have appointed you a watchman to the house of Israel; whenever you hear a word from My mouth, warn them from Me. When I say to the wicked, You shall surely die; and you do not warn him or speak

> out to warn the wicked from his wicked way that he may live, that wicked man shall die in his iniquity, but his blood I will require at your hand. Yet if you have warned the wicked, and he does not turn from his wickedness or from his wicked way, he shall die in his iniquity, but you have delivered yourself. Again, when a righteous man turns away from his righteousness and commits iniquity, and I place an obstacle before him, he shall die; since you have not warned him, he shall die in his sin, and his righteous deeds which he has done shall not be remembered; but his blood I will require at your hand. However, if you have warned the righteous man that the righteous should not sin, and he does not sin, he shall surely live because he took warning; and you have delivered yourself.

Clearly, God held Ezekiel responsible for informing the people about their sin. He was not to "wait for them to bring it up"!

Eli's dealing with his wicked sons in I Sam. 2.12, 17, 31 illustrates this point:

> Now the sons of Eli were worthless men; they did not know the Lord...Thus the sin of the young men was very great before the Lord, for the men despised the offering of the Lord...

Eli's sons were wicked men, yet in verse 31 a man of God told Eli:

> Behold, the days are coming when I will break your strength and the strength of your father's house so that there will not be an old man in your house.

At first, this seems like Eli was held responsible for his sons' sins, perhaps an exception to the principle we've already noticed in Ezek. 18.20. Not so, for in I Sam. 3.12-13, God explained how Eli was in fellowship with his sons' sins:

> In that day I will carry out against Eli all that I have spoken concerning his house, from beginning to end. For I have told him that I am about to judge his house forever for the iniquity which he knew, because his sons brought a curse on themselves, and he did not rebuke them.

Eli's part in his sons' sins was that he knew their guilt, and he failed to act sufficiently to stop their sin. At least he did not fulfill his responsibility adequately not to be a partner in their wrongdoing.

These are, indeed, powerful words. More words like them are found in Ac. 20.26-27, where Paul says to the Ephesian elders:

> Wherefore I testify unto you this day, that I am pure from the blood of all men. For I shrank not from declaring unto you the whole counsel of God.

Paul makes it clear he lives under the same admonition Ezekiel lived under. When one knows the truth and fails to apply it where he can, he becomes partaker in the very sins he should restrain. Parents who keep quiet become partakers in their children's sins just like Eli. Christians who look the other way become partakers in others' sins. The man who is pure from the blood of all men is an impressive individual. He is either one who has always conducted himself properly toward others, or he has repented of his shortcomings in this regard and is striving to do better.

In summary, we become a partaker in another's sins by knowing his guilt and failing to act. May we not do so in our dealings with fellow Christians in a local church.

By Our Example and Influence

In I Corinthians 8.4-12, Paul shows another way we become a partaker in another's sins, that is by failing to consider the power of our example and influence, especially toward weaker or less knowledgeable Christians. Dealing with the conduct of a stronger Christian toward a weaker one in the matter of eating meat offered to idols, Paul says:

> Concerning therefore the eating of things sacrificed to idols, we know that no idol is anything in the world, and that there is no God but one. For though there be that are called gods, whether in heaven or on earth; as there are gods many, and lords many; yet to us there is one God, the Father, of whom are all things, and we unto him; and one Lord, Jesus Christ, through whom are all things, and we through him. Howbeit there is not in all men that knowledge: but some, being used until now to the idol, eat as of a thing sacrificed to an idol; and their conscience being weak is defiled. But food will not commend us to God: neither, if we eat not, are we the worse; nor if we eat, are we the better. But take heed lest by any means this liberty of yours become a stumblingblock to the weak. For if a man see thee who hast knowledge sitting at meat in an idol's temple, will not his conscience, if he is weak, be emboldened to eat things sacrificed to idols? For through thy knowledge he that is weak perisheth, the brother for whose sake Christ died. And thus, sinning against the brethren, and wounding their conscience when it is weak, ye sin against Christ. Wherefore, if meat causeth my brother to stumble, I will eat no flesh for evermore, that I cause not my brother to stumble.

In an age when everyone clamors for "civil rights," these, too, are strong words. Paul affirms we have the technical right to do many things, yet we may sin in so doing, because of the influence our example exerts on weaker Christians. We can sin by doing something right! *Our sin won't be what we did that was permissible, but our disregard for the weaker Christian.* In that way, Paul says, we sin against both the weak Christian and against Christ.

By Improper Association with False Doctrine

Paul makes the statement in I Cor. 15.33, "evil companionships corrupt good morals." We often hear this used as a warning that we need to take heed lest we be corrupted by the behavior of our companions. Here though, we speak of the corruption of others by false teachers! In Ezek. 13.8-10, Ezekiel condemns the false prophets of his time for this very sin:

> Therefore, thus says the Lord God, Because you have spoken falsehood and seen a lie, therefore behold, I am against you, declares the Lord God. So My hand will be against the prophets who see false visions and utter lying divinations. They will have no place in the council of My people, nor will they be written down in the register of the house of Israel, nor will they enter the land of Israel, that you may know that I am the Lord God. It is definitely because they have misled My people by saying, Peace! when there is no peace. And when anyone builds a wall, behold, they plaster it over with whitewash...

Then, concluding his condemnation of these false teachers, in verse 22 Ezekiel shows their effect on others:

> Because you disheartened the righteous with falsehood when I did not cause him grief, but have encouraged the wicked not to turn from his wicked way and preserve his life.

A little reflection enables us to see this is in reality what all false teachers do: (1) they discourage the righteous, and (2) they encourage the wicked not to turn from their wicked ways. Thus, it has always been, and it would be entirely possible now for us to partake in the teaching of a false teacher. Certainly, contemplating joining a local group of Christians should cause us to avoid improper associations.

By Financially Supporting Error

In II John 9-11, a passage discussed in detail in Appendix 4, "II John 9 and the Teaching of Christ," John says, concerning some false teachers of his time:

> Whosoever goeth onward and abideth not in the teaching of Christ, hath not God: he that abideth in the teaching,

> the same hath both the Father and the Son. If any one cometh unto you, and bringeth not this teaching, receive him not into your house, and give him no greeting: for he that giveth him greeting partaketh in his evil works."

"Partaking in another's evil works" is exactly the thing we're learning not to do in this chapter. It is important to remember that *denominational action (collective action of churches) always involves one in work over which he has no say.* John teaches we can partake in a false teacher's evil works by supporting him.

Certainly a good side exists to this principle. When we support a teacher of the truth, we partake in his good works, we are partners. In Phil. 1.3-7, Paul reveals that when the church in Philippi financially supported him (while he preached the gospel in Europe), they became his partners:

> I thank my God upon all my remembrance of you...for your fellowship in furtherance of the gospel from the first day until now...and in the defence and confirmation of the gospel, ye all are partakers with me of grace.

This relationship existed because (as Paul comments concerning earlier support from them), Philippi supported him financially, as he says in Phil. 4.14-17:

> Howbeit ye did well that ye had fellowship with my affliction. And ye yourselves also know, ye Philippians, that in the beginning of the gospel, when I departed from Macedonia, no church had fellowship with me in the matter of giving and receiving but ye only; for even in Thessalonica ye sent once and again unto my need. Not that I seek for the gift; but I seek for the fruit that increaseth to your account.

John addresses this same subject in III Jn. 5-8 when he says:

> Beloved, thou doest a faithful work in whatsoever thou doest toward them that are brethren and strangers withal; who bare witness to thy love before the church: whom

> thou wilt do well to set forward on their journey worthily of God; because that for the sake of the Name they went forth, taking nothing of the Gentiles. We therefore ought to welcome such, that we may be fellow-workers for the truth.

These passages disclose a great blessing that comes to us in supporting others to preach the gospel where we don't have the ability to do it ourselves. On the other hand, when we support one who teaches false doctrine, we are in fellowship with his evil works. We ought always to look out that we don't partake in another man's sin in this regard. When we are part of a local church, we have a God-given responsibility we cannot delegate to anyone else, of knowing what our money is spent for. That way we can make sure we're not a participant in someone else's sin.

Thus, these several principles help us determine whom we cannot be in fellowship with. Now let's complete our study on this point by determining who we *can* be in fellowship with in a local church.

Fellowship of an Individual with a Congregation

After all the notes of caution that tend to restrain our fellowship with some other Christians, we might think, "Is there anybody I can be in fellowship with?" "Must I find someone who believes one hundred percent like I do on every Bible subject to be in fellowship?"

Certainly not! But before we note areas where we can certainly differ and still be in fellowship, let's notice one fact. In this matter of an individual and a congregation of Christians being in fellowship, both the individual and the congregation share initiative and control over their mutual fellowship.

Churches Have the Right to Limit Fellowship

In Ac. 9.26-29, after Paul obeyed the gospel and became a Christian, he came to Jerusalem where Luke describes Paul's approach to the church in Jerusalem:

> And when he was come to Jerusalem, he assayed to join himself to the disciples: and they were all afraid of him, not believing that he was a disciple. But Barnabas took him, and brought him to the apostles, and declared unto them how he had seen the Lord in the way, and that he had spoken to him, and how at Damascus he had preached boldly in the name of Jesus. And he was with them going in and going out at Jerusalem, preaching boldly in the name of the Lord.

This account teaches two important lessons: (1) The individual Christian initiates the action to establish fellowship with a local congregation of Christians. (2) The local congregation has control over its fellowship; i.e., the local church doesn't have to accept just anyone into its fellowship. On this occasion, the church in Jerusalem, believing Paul was an impostor, rejected his overture for fellowship, and the case would have remained so except Barnabas brought additional evidence of Paul's conversion to the attention of Christians in Jerusalem. Upon the basis of this communication from Barnabas, the fellowship was finally established, and Paul "was with them going in and going out at Jerusalem."

A Pattern of Commendation in Apostolic Times

In Rom. 16.1-2, Paul, concluding the Roman letter, included a personal recommendation for Phoebe, a Christian lady of his acquaintance. He wrote the Roman church to commend her to them saying:

> I commend unto you Phoebe our sister, who is a servant of the church that is at Cenchrea, that ye receive her in the Lord, worthily of the saints, and that ye assist her in

whatsoever matter she may have need of you: for she herself also hath been a helper of many, and of mine own self.

In this passage, Paul did what Barnabas had done for him years before. He vouched for a Christian he knew, whom the Roman Christians did not know. It was communication in order to establish fellowship. We find much of this kind of communication in the New Testament. See I Cor. 16.3, where local churches showed approval of certain Christians by letter, and Paul approved of Timothy to local churches in I Cor. 16.10-11 and Phil. 2.19-23. In addition, Paul commended Titus to Corinth in II Cor. 8.23, Tychicus in Eph. 6.21 and Col. 4.7-9, and Epaphroditus in Phil. 2.25-30. The Apostle John did the same thing in III Jn. 12 when he approved of Demetrius.

Paul also used letters to warn of certain ones, both unfaithful Christians and outright false teachers. He warned against Alexander in I Tim. 1.19-20 and II Tim. 4.14-15; Hymenaeus in I Tim. 1.19-20; Hermogenes in II Tim. 1.15; and Phygellus in II Tim. 1.15.

Communication in order to establish fellowship was a matter of grave concern during New Testament times with their sects, Judaizers, and false teachers. It should not be less so now, with our cults, denominations, false brethren, and false teachers.

So far, we have concerned ourselves with communication from the standpoint of the congregation receiving information about a prospective member. On the other hand, it is only right for a Christian who contemplates joining himself to a local church, to know what that local church is involved in, lest he become a partaker in someone else's evil works. It seems entirely appropriate for a local congregation of Christians to inform those who are contemplating joining it in an orderly fashion. This permits those Christians to make a rational inquiry and decision concerning their local fellowship.

I recommend the course of action congregations I have labored with have taken. Let the congregation prepare a brief introduction to itself. It might be entitled, "Introduction to the _______ church," or "Getting Acquainted with the _______ Church." The purpose of this document is to describe what work the congregation is involved in, what its goals are, how they are presently striving to achieve those goals, what their financial obligations are, their procedures on discipline, benevolence, evangelism, etc. A description of the work of a congregation would go a long way in helping prospective members decide if this is a group they can conscientiously work with. This document is not a creed or a statement of *belief* of the members of the congregation, but a declaration of what that church is *doing*.

Granted, many congregations of Christians might find it difficult to write down what they're doing. For the congregation that knows what it's doing and what it's trying to do, the authority to write this information on a sheet of paper to tell others seems self-evident.

This procedure has much to commend it. For example, sometimes a visiting Christian (or prospective member) is inclined to *take advantage of* a church's desire to help the needy. If this individual sees that a local church is businesslike in realms of discipline, benevolence, etc., he will probably decide this is not a congregation where he can easily ply his deception. He will be better off, and the local congregation will be as well.

On the other hand, if a sincere Christian contemplates working with such a congregation, this businesslike approach is likely to be impressive. He will want to work with a responsible group of Christians. Again, both the prospective member and the local church will profit immensely from open communication.

In case the individual Christian does not agree with everything the congregation is doing, the channels of communication are already open. This will enable them to focus on the differences so they may be discussed scripturally and settled.

Even if a congregation chooses not to use an introduction to inform prospective members, communication still takes place somehow. In denominations, the communication that establishes local fellowship takes place in the denomination's creed.

In non-denominational groups, this communication usually takes place on an individual basis. Perhaps some pillars of the local church invite the visitor to their home, where they wait for him to "tip his hand" on some prominent religious issues. If he says the right "key words," they gladly "shake him" into the group. If he says the wrong words, they become leery of him.

The suggestion of a congregational introduction is based upon a desire for more effective communication. Appendix 5 contains a sample document for your consideration.

Does Local Fellowship Require Complete Doctrinal Agreement?

After examining the matters we must agree on to establish a local fellowship, all our scriptural restraints may make us think we must agree with everyone on everything to be in fellowship in the local sense. Yet this is not the case, either in practice or in the New Testament.

With Whom Are You in Complete Agreement?

First, on the matter of fellowship in the universal church, if you believe you must be one hundred percent in agreement with God to be in fellowship with Him, you're likely to believe the same thing in the local fellowship. We pointed out there it's unlikely any of us agree one hundred percent with God doctrinally, or with any of our brethren. Even if a congregation exists where every single Christian agrees on everything, then they would have a problem when they taught someone the gospel. The new member would not yet have been exposed to all their doctrinal positions, and therefore could not be in one hundred percent agreement. He wouldn't know what he believed on each doctrinal matter until he had time to study for himself. Thus, what do the scriptures teach we may differ on and still be in fellowship in a local church?

Matters of Expediency

God gives us a choice in matters of expediency, where all the options are scriptural. For example, in the New Testament such concerns included circumcision (Gal. 6.15), eating meat offered to idols (Rom. 14.3), observing one day above another (Rom. 14.1-6), etc. God wants us to use our best judgment about how to conduct ourselves most expeditiously in these areas. Such issues should not disrupt fellowship in a local church. Later in this chapter, we'll speak specifically about how to conduct ourselves in these matters with the requisite attitudes. In matters of judgment, differences naturally occur. As a result, both sides can even be right!

Issues Not in Realm of Expediency, But Which Do Not Affect Our Collective Action

In addition to the realm of expediency, realms exist where God did not give us choices. Yet our individual difference doesn't have to affect our collective action in a local congregation.

For example, very fine Christians take both sides of the question as to whether or not I Corinthians 11 teaches Christian women ought to wear an artificial covering in our assemblies today. The answer is unquestionably not in the realm of expediency. God does not say the women can if they want to, but they don't have to if they don't want to. He nowhere says, "Covering is nothing, and uncovering is nothing," as He does with circumcision. This difference need not disrupt a local fellowship, although it can, and sometimes does. Since Paul's instruction pertains to what an individual woman should do, some women might practice one thing and some another, but it doesn't have to affect our work as a whole in a local congregation. This doesn't mean it shouldn't be studied, taught on, etc. It just means wearing the covering should not be a collective work of the church.

The question of whether or not Christians ought to participate in carnal warfare is another personal matter that does not affect our collective action. God surely doesn't put the question of killing for the government in the realm of expediency. Very sincere and studious Christians take various positions on this question, yet whether or not a Christian participates in wars is not part of the work of a local congregation. Such issues shouldn't affect our local fellowship, though they might. Unfortunately, some might insist that their position become the collective position of the local church. In this case anyone who conscientiously cannot participate in these wars can no longer function as a part of that fellowship without violating his conscience.

Sometimes churches get involved in personal matters about whether it's right or wrong for individual Christians to pay taxes. This question may not affect you or me, but it affects some very fine Christians. Again, if a Christian studies the issue for himself and decides he cannot conscientiously pay taxes in certain situations, we don't have to be (nor do we have the right to be) the "sheriff" of every aspect of his life and insist he agree with us. Our difference doesn't have to affect our work together in a local church.

These comments do not imply these questions are not important. They are. Nor do we mean these issues shouldn't be studied, even collectively. We do mean that when the studying is over, our local fellowship doesn't demand we all agree on matters that do not affect our collective action.

Issues Potentially Involving Collective Action in Which We're Not Involved

In addition, we may differ on matters that *could* affect our collective action, but unless someone is insistent on our practicing them, they *need not* affect our collective action. Nearly every congregation contains individuals who believe we could do various things collectively that others conscientiously want no part of. Likewise, these same Christians who object to the others' beliefs, themselves believe they can collectively do things the others would blanche at. But in both instances, since neither one insists on making those things a part of the work of the local church, they can still be in fellowship.

We Don't Have to Agree with Everything That Is Preached

Those interested in the non-denominational way of Christ probably appreciate that our purpose in studying the Bible collectively and teaching it to others is not for handing down positions that have been taught before or to pass along "the party line" on various doctrinal questions. Since we have no alignment larger than a local church, our purpose is not to state what the brotherhood teaches on certain issues. We should simply strive to see what Jesus Christ taught in His word, make sure we obey it to the utmost of our ability, encourage others to do the same, and leave the denominational thinking and acting to others. If we have something we call "Bible Study," let's don't make it "Creed Rehearsal;" let's study the Bible to find out what the truth is for ourselves.

If, in the process of airing out an issue to determine the truth, some off-the-wall ideas are set forth, so be it. This happens many times in the search for truth. We can help pay someone's salary to come teach something we believe is wrong, if it's done in a setting where he and the rest of us are involved together in a search for truth. Of course, paying someone to come teach a false doctrine when he isn't searching for truth, and refuses to have an open forum where his doctrine can be questioned or answered, is repugnant to the very concept of the restoration of the New Testament way of the Lord. Indeed, it might well involve us in his evil works!

When We Cannot Be in Fellowship

After all these exceptions to one hundred percent agreement that still enable us to be in fellowship in a local church, one might wonder when we might not be in fellowship with one another. Such a time can come. When one Christian believes he *must* do a certain thing in order to maintain his allegiance to Christ, and another Christian believes he *must not* do the same thing to maintain his allegiance to Christ (i.e., he can't do it "of faith"), then those two brethren cannot be in fellowship in the matter. If it is going to be made a work of the local church, (i.e., it affects their collective worship, or involves work done through the treasury of the local church) then they can't serve Christ *in the same local church*. They simply cannot do so, and both live by faith.

Even then, Christians who can give those they differ with credit for being sincere and wanting to do right, should be able to break their fellowship without committing a lot of sin, in hope that one day they might be in fellowship once again. This type of behavior doesn't occur naturally too often, but it is scriptural. The next section of this chapter and Chapter 6, "Dealing with

Doctrinal Differences," have more to say on this subject. Also, see the author's book *Christians, Churches, and Controversy: Navigating Doctrinal and Personal Clashes*.

Principles to Guide Us in Making Decisions as a Local Church

A Church May Be Acceptable to God Without Elders

While it is not our purpose to fully discuss the organization of the local church and the qualifications and work of elders, the Old and New Testaments both clearly teach God has used a group of men known as "elders" to lead His people since the time He brought the Jews out of Egypt under Moses. In the New Testament, elders are the central figures of the organization of God's churches (Ac. 14.23; 20.17; Phil. 1.1; I Tim. 3.1ff, and Tit. 1.6ff).

Under the direction and guidance of the Holy Spirit, the elders are to guide, guard, and lead God's people from a state of spiritual childhood to the state of full-grown manhood in Christ Jesus. Their responsibility will not cease until they give account of every member under their care to the Master Himself, Heb. 13.17.

While it ought to be a temporary situation, a church may be acceptable to God without elders. To discover how a local church ought to work without them, we will examine principles from the Bible that will also be very helpful to those of us in churches with elders. These principles basically govern how Christians work together in nearly every collective circumstance, whether or not elders are superintending the flock.

First, notice that some congregations in the New Testament evidently did not have elders, yet they functioned in ways that pleased God. In Ac. 14.23, Luke said:

> And when they had appointed for them elders in every church, and had prayed with fasting, they commended them to the Lord, on whom they had believed.

This passage pertains to churches operating temporarily without elders. These churches were established near the beginning of Paul's first missionary journey, and had waited between six months and four years before Paul and Barnabas came back through their region. During this period of time these local congregations of Christians functioned without elders.

In Tit. 1.5, Paul commanded Titus to ordain elders in every city. This included churches on the island of Crete that Paul established when Paul was there, and left Titus behind to ordain elders. Thus, these churches existed temporarily without elders.

These examples are in contrast to churches in the New Testament that clearly had elders. God's intent is for all congregations to eventually to have elders, but in the New Testament some churches did not. Neither do some today.

Church Action with No Evidence of Elders

Quite an array of passages in the New Testament describe collective local church action with no evidence of elders. In Ac. 13.1-4, we read of the church in Antioch sent out Paul and Barnabas and yet they did this work without any evidence exists of elders in that congregation. This did not prevent that church from functioning in the realm of evangelism.

In Ac. 14.27, when Paul and Barnabas returned to Antioch, they assembled the whole church and rehearsed all that had been accomplished. No one would deny this church was a great evangelistic church, yet we have no proof they had elders at this time.

Likewise, a church with no elders can function in the realm of benevolence. If Ac. 11.27-30 is an example of a local church operating collectively in benevolence, it would be a church without evidence of elders doing so. The churches in Corinth and Galatia engaged in benevolence, as we read in I Cor. 16.1-3, and there is no evidence they had elders. In spite of the fact Paul wrote two letters to Corinth, and one to the churches of Galatia, and Paul never addressed himself to elders, nor referred to them. Yet he dealt with many problems in those churches.

In addition, a church may function in the realm of discipline without elders. In Mt. 18.15-18, Jesus instructs Christians how to deal with personal offenses, saying if a brother sins against you, won't hear you when you exhort him privately, and won't hear you nor your witnesses when you bring them into the process, then "tell it to the church." Jesus doesn't say, "If there are elders, take it to the church." Then Jesus says, "if he will not hear the church." Thus, the church, upon hearing the testimony of the witnesses, is to do some exhorting. Churches without elders can well be involved in disciplinary matters.

Churches without elders can also work in the realm of edification. In I Cor. 14.4-5 Paul speaks of edification using miraculous gifts, but aside from the miraculous element, notice that a church with no elders was involved in edification. Likewise, the Corinthian church in I Cor. 11.18ff carried out public worship, as Paul resolves some of their problems concerning the public observance of the Lord's Supper.

All of these examples show that when a local church does not have elders, it must still do many things that a fully organized congregation would do under the oversight of elders. Feeding the flock must still be done. In Eph. 4.12-16, Paul names other individuals, in addition to elders, who can carry out that work. "Watching in behalf of souls" must still be done when no elders exist, and in Gal. 6.1, Paul says "the spiritual" ought to do it.

A Church May Select Servants to Act for It

A church can select agents or servants to act for it, whether or not it has elders. These individuals are vested with authority from a local church. They do not act on their own authority, but with the church's authority. In I Cor. 16.3, Paul instructed the Corinthian church (as he had already instructed other churches) to select messengers to take their benevolent contribution to the needy saints in Jerusalem. These individuals were not going on a personal trip since they had authority from this local church to do a specific job. In II Cor. 8.19, 23 Paul referred to these same messengers again, and said they were "appointed by the churches." A local church can appoint agents to act for the church in any work that is lawful for the church to do.

The Jerusalem church functioned in this way. In Ac. 6.1-6, the apostles instructed the church to select seven men to take care of a benevolent work for the congregation. Many people wonder if these men were permanent deacons. Whether or not they were permanent deacons, they acted as servants of that local church.

The church selected them; they operated with the authority of the church. They did not work independently or individually, but they served as agents of the Jerusalem church.

In Rom. 16.1, Paul spoke of Phoebe, a lady who was a servant of the church in Cenchrea. Evidently, the church had selected her to do some job as an agent of that local church. We don't know what the assignment was, but obviously it was something lawful for a church and a woman to do. Local churches may do the same thing today. A local church might select a lady upon the basis of her qualifications to help in assessing the benevolent needs of other ladies, because women observe things men never notice nor inquire about. A lady who is qualified as an exhorter can very effectively be used in disciplinary situations with women, etc. Women perform as agents of the church when they teach Bible classes. Such work is not at their individual prerogative, since they teach with the authority of the church.

Principles to Guide Decisionmaking as a Church

This section is very important whether or not a particular local church has elders. These principles apply in any event, and are essential to understanding what makes up a local congregation of Christians. We've already seen a local church is not a group of people who agree on everything in the Bible, but they at least must agree on what actions they engage in collectively. Neither is a local church just a bunch of people who happen to live in the same area; it is much more than that.

The New Testament never suggests "one man, one vote." Instead, the Bible shows how different Christians are to submit to others in matters of judgment. The following principles embody the very essence of what is required for a local church to function as God wants it to. For further information on how Christians and churches make controversial decisions, see the author's book*Christians, Churches, and Controversy: Navigating Doctrinal and Personal Clashes,* particularly Chapter 3, "How Churches Make Controversial Decisions."

Younger Christians Submit to Older Christians

In I Pet. 5.5, after giving specific instruction to elders in a local church, Peter says:

> Likewise, ye younger, be subject unto the elder.

Since the term "elder" in the original text of this verse is plural, Peter instructs Christians younger in years and experience to be subject to Christians older in years and experience. Peter is not implying older Christians can order younger Christians around, but he is speaking of an attitude younger Christians ought to have. To be in subjection means to have an attitude of submission, a willingness to accommodate themselves to the guidance of older Christians, wherever possible. The writer of Heb. 5.13-14 gives a valid reason why they should:

> For every one that partaketh of milk is without experience of the word of righteousness; for he is a babe. But solid food is for fullgrown men, even those who by reason of use have their senses exercised to discern good and evil.

Peter commands younger, more immature Christians to subject themselves to older, more mature ones. They subject themselves because of their respect for the judgment the older Christians developed through many years of service to Christ.

For example, young Christians inexperienced in restorative or punitive discipline often want to drag discipline situations out. If they refuse to listen to the more knowledgeable older Christians, discipline problems can plague a church for years without being resolved.

All Christians Submit to Special Workers

In I Cor. 16.15-16, Paul says:

> Now I beseech you, brethren (ye know the house of Stephanas, that it is the firstfruits of Achaia, and that they have set themselves to minister unto the saints), that ye

> also be in subjection unto such, and to every one that helpeth in the work and laboreth.

These individuals in the Corinthian church had "set themselves" to serve other Christians. What their specific work was, we don't know. Paul instructed others in the Corinthian church to be subject to such. Paul does not mean we ought to let those individuals take the oversight of the local church as elders, but when someone tries to carry out a responsibility, whether as an agent of the church or as an individual, we ought to try to accommodate ourselves to him, rather than going out of our way to inconvenience or restrain him. We need to adapt to him and help him do that job, or at least stay out of his way.

For example, many times elders or a teaching committee makes major decisions regarding the teaching program of the church without consulting the men or women teachers. Often these men and women have dedicated years of their lives perfecting their teaching skills and have insights those outside the classroom lack. Because those in authority fail to seek the advice of the workers, they sometimes make decisions that hinder and discourage the teachers unnecessarily. Or they listen to the complaints of people who are not involved in the work of the church and make major decisions that hamper the workers, all because they fail to respect the experience and zeal of the laborers.

Women Submit to Leading Men

In I Tim. 2.12, Paul says:

> But I permit not a woman to teach, nor to have dominion over a man, but to be in quietness.

Since some women sometimes resent "subjection," I have purposely put this point near the end of the passages dealing with subjection to illustrate that "subjection" is not peculiar to women's responsibilities. All of us who are younger ought to submit to those who are older. All of us ought to submit to a Christian who has set himself to do a special work to serve Christ. As the next point shows, all of us are to submit to one another.

"Subjection" never means "let someone steamroll over you," "your opinion doesn't matter," or "you're a second class person," but the word does mean "arrange yourselves under." Women have just one more area of subjection than men have. If women have a problem in that area, they're probably going to have lots of problems in other areas that speak of subjection. For a fuller discussion of the role of women and men in a local church, see Chapter 4, "Women and Men in a Local Church" in the author's book *Christians, Churches, and Controversy: Navigating Doctrinal and Personal Clashes.*

All Submit to One Another

In Eph. 5.21, Paul says:

> ...subjecting yourselves one to another in the fear of Christ.

I Pet. 5.5 tells us the same thing:

> Yea, all of you gird yourselves with humility, to serve one another: for God resisteth the proud, but giveth grace to the humble.

These are words of paramount importance to our seeing how God's people can work together in a local church. In matters of judgment, we ought to do all we can to accommodate ourselves to those we're striving to work with.

Consider Weak Brethren

In Romans 14.1, Paul says:

> But him that is weak in faith receive ye, yet not for decision of scruples.

As a congregation makes decisions about it's collective work, the more mature Christians can often see that some things are more appropriate than a young Christian can. In these cases, they ought not ram it down his throat, or jam him into a situation that involves him in something he cannot conscientiously do. We are to consider weaker brethren in matters of opinion and expediency.

Follow After the Things That Make for Peace

In the context of expediency (matters in which God gives us a choice) Paul says in Rom. 14.19:

> So then let us follow after things which make for peace, and things whereby we may edify one another.

None of the six principles discussed above sound like Christians should be contentious about matters in the realm of opinion. These principles do not describe the behavior of someone politicking to get his way in a meeting of the church. Nor do they sound like someone trying to steamroll a pet project through the church. They are talking about Christians who have an attitude of humility toward each other, who listen to the opinions of others and give them careful consideration. Obeying these principles brings peace to a congregation.

Definition of a Local Church

We've commented earlier that a local church is not a group of Christians who agree on everything the Bible teaches, but they must agree on what they do together. From the study of the principles of how Christians ought to work together, we are now ready to complete the definition of a local church. *A local church is a group of Christians who agree on what they do collectively, and they share an attitude of subjection and humility toward one another in matters of opinion and expediency. In other words, they agree on what they do collectively, and they agree to treat each other properly in the matters they do not agree on, while they strive to arrive at agreement even in matters of judgment.*

According to this definition, which we believe to be in harmony with the Bible's teaching, the strength of a congregation doesn't come from the size of the church, but rather from the size of the work they can do collectively. Brethren who work together for many years, solve their problems together, and develop confidence in the spirituality of each other, will naturally enjoy a much larger area of common activity than a congregation composed of Christians who do not know each other very well, do not do much together, and fail to solve their problems together.

Chapter 6

Dealing with Doctrinal Differences

As previous chapters have shown, Christians in a local congregation do not have to agree on everything in the Bible in order to be in fellowship with each other. Practically speaking, they never will, try as though they might. This chapter discusses how brethren should conduct themselves when their doctrinal differences come to the fore. In I Tim. 3.14-15, Paul instructs Timothy:

> These things write I unto thee, hoping to come unto thee shortly; but if I tarry long, that thou mayest know how men ought to *behave* themselves in the house of God, which is the church of the living God, the pillar and ground of the truth.

This chapter deals with *how Christians ought to behave themselves in God's family in view of doctrinal differences.* We will not contemplate matters of sin, nor consider doctrinal differences with non-Christians, though many of the principles would also apply.

Indeed, doctrinal differences do occur, and many times our record has not been good at conducting ourselves properly in the midst of differences. Brethren divide from each other over doctrinal points, many times without serious study taking place before the division. Preachers, teachers, elders, and other teachers are sometimes abused over matters of private study and belief that they may not even have taught. Preachers and other Christians appreciate the need to stand for the truth and contend for the faith, for the Scriptures plainly teach such. *However, sometimes preachers and other Christians mistake contentiousness (which is clearly condemned) for contending for the faith.* This chapter explores the differences between the two, and proposes scriptural procedures for dealing with brethren we differ with.

For the first part of this chapter, we deal with a number of *seemingly unrelated* topics, that by the conclusion of the chapter will be seen as *clearly related.* These principles are also fundamental to our goal of knowing how to conduct ourselves in the house of God.

We Naturally Expect Lions and Lambs to Have Problems

Just realizing that we can expect differences is helpful in achieving scriptural methods of dealing with brethren in the midst of them. Brethren having doctrinal differences is not an unusual, weird, or unique circumstance. Once we understand that differences are common, the next step is to learn how to conduct ourselves properly in the midst of them.

In Isa. 2.1-4, Isaiah prophesied concerning the Messiah's kingdom, that Christians now comprise:

> Now it will come about that in the last days, The mountain of the house of the Lord will be established as the chief of the mountains, and will be raised above the hills; and all the nations will stream to it. And many peoples will come and say, Come, let us go up to the mountain of the Lord, to the house of the God of Jacob; that He may teach us concerning His ways, And that we may walk in His paths, for the law will go forth from Zion, and the word of the Lord from Jerusalem. And He will judge between the nations, and will render decisions for many peoples; and they will hammer their swords into plowshares, and their spears into pruning hooks. Nation will not lift up sword against nation, and never again will they learn war.

This passage shows that in contrast to the Old Testament kingdom of Israel that was national in scope, the Messiah's kingdom was prophesied to be, and is, an international or multinational kingdom. People from all nations are in it.

Similarly, in Isa. 19.23-25, Isaiah prophesied concerning the Messiah's kingdom:

> In that day there will be a highway from Egypt to Assyria, and the Assyrians will come into Egypt and the Egyptians into Assyria, and the Egyptians will worship with the Assyrians. In that day Israel will be the third party with Egypt and Assyria, a blessing in the midst of the earth, whom the Lord of hosts has blessed, saying, Blessed is Egypt My people, and Assyria the work of My hands, and Israel My inheritance.

These words were never true during the days of the physical nation of Israel. One can easily imagine how these words sounded to the physical Israelites in Isaiah's day. The very idea of Jews, Egyptians, and Assyrians, who were normally enemies, functioning together in the Messiah's kingdom, would have been altogether incomprehensible. Isaiah's proposition was that people of widely different backgrounds would be thrown together to serve God together under the rule of the Messiah.

Isaiah 11.6-10, perhaps the most familiar of messianic passages in Isaiah, showed how these people would get along with each other:

> And the wolf will dwell with the lamb, and the leopard will lie down with the kid, and the calf and the young lion and the fatling together; and a little boy will lead them. Also the cow and the bear will graze; their young will lie down together; and the lion will eat straw like the ox. And the nursing child will play by the hole of the cobra, and the weaned child will put his hand on the viper's den. They will not hurt or destroy in all My holy mountain, for the earth will be full of the knowledge of the Lord as the waters cover the sea. Then it will come about in that day that the nations will resort to the root

of Jesse, who will stand as a signal for the peoples; and His resting place will be glorious.

Premillennialists (those who do not believe Christ is presently ruling, but will return to earth before a literal thousand-year reign) view these verses as unfulfilled. They view them as prophecies that will be fulfilled when the Messiah sets up His kingdom on the earth. However, even if premillennialism were true, with our widely different backgrounds, the qualities we would need *in the future* to get along are the same ones we need *now*. The apostle Paul quotes verse 10 in Rom. 15.12 as fulfilled. In the midst of discussing relations between Jewish and Gentile Christians, he cites this very prophecy to show "the nations" in the day of the Messiah (1) would not hurt nor destroy (2) in all God's holy mountain, (3) because of the knowledge of Jehovah. Thus, Isaiah spoke of things fulfilled in the body of Christ, and he assuredly did not speak of literal wolves and lambs lying down together as a result of hearing the gospel of Christ!

Basically, Isaiah foretold that the Messiah's kingdom, i.e., the body of Christ, would be composed of people of widely different backgrounds, people who historically had not gotten along together. Consequently, *when people with widely different doctrinal positions come into the kingdom as a result of their obedience to the gospel, they must learn from the "knowledge of Jehovah" not to "hurt nor destroy" in all of God's holy mountain* (the kingdom of God in which Christians are now citizens, Heb. 12.22). This chapter teaches us how.

I encountered a good illustration of a lion and lamb lying down together in the kingdom of God when I preached in a small town in Idaho. Early in the week I met a young Christian who had a very violent past, and had participated in the racial riots in the Watts area of Los Angeles in the Nineteen Seventies. He described the weapons he and others in his motorcycle gang had used to assault the law enforcement officers in that area.

Later in the week when a number of the men of the congregation gathered in a private home for a bachelor's party, I asked that young Christian to relate some of the tales that he had told me earlier in the week. As he did so, one of the men sitting on the same couch with him was noticeably disturbed, so I stopped the storyteller, to ascertain what the problem was. He mentioned although he was then a law-enforcement officer in Northern Idaho, he had been a deputy sheriff in the Watts area at about the same time the other fellow had been there. These two men discussed the details of when they had been in the Watts riots, and soon found out they may well have been on opposing sides in some of the same conflicts. However, as a result of the knowledge of Jehovah, these men who were once natural enemies, nearly to the point of taking each other's lives, had obeyed the gospel of Christ and were now serving Christ together in the same local congregation.

On another occasion, I met two Christians who started a congregation in New Jersey. One, a Cajun-sounding man from east Texas who was an executive with a large petroleum company; the other, a biology teacher at Rutgers University, was an environmental activist in the Sierra Club. These were two men who, without the knowledge of Jehovah, would have had little in common, yet they served Christ together in that community.

This concept of Christians with widely different backgrounds having to "lie down together" in the kingdom of Christ, is also contemplated in many New Testament passages. In Gal. 3.26-29, Paul says:

> For ye are all sons of God, through faith, in Christ Jesus. For as many of you as were baptized into Christ did put on Christ. There can be neither Jew nor Greek, there can be neither bond nor free, there can be no male and female; for ye all are one man in Christ Jesus. And if ye are Christ's, then are ye Abraham's seed, heirs according to promise.

Paul shows that groups such as Jews and Greeks, servants and masters, and men and women, enjoy a relationship in Christ that historically they were not accustomed to. The failure of the Galatian Christians to realize this goal caused Paul to exhort them in Gal. 5.15:

> But if ye bite and devour one another, take heed that ye be not consumed one of another.

Biting and devouring was customary for wolves and lambs, but not for citizens in the Messiah's kingdom, who were not to hurt nor destroy in all God's holy mountain. Likewise, in I Cor. 3.3, Paul said to his carnally-minded brethren:

> ...for ye are yet carnal: for whereas there is among you jealousy and strife, are ye not carnal, and do ye not walk after the manner of men?

These young Christians were involved in worldly strife because they still conducted themselves toward brethren they differed with according to a worldly philosophy. They still thought in terms of wolves, lions, lambs, and kids, rather than in terms of citizens united in the Messiah's kingdom, as a result of the knowledge of Jehovah.

So how do we deal with brethren we differ with? What is our record? There are over three hundred prophecies about *the Messiah* (where He would be born, when, the fact He would be born of a virgin, He would perform miracles, teach in parables, be rejected by physical Israel, be crucified, be raised from the dead, etc.). Most realize that if Jesus did not fulfill every one of them, he was an impostor, and not the Christ of God. Similarly, there are many prophecies made about *the Messiah's people* (Christians), and specifically ones concerning how they are to treat each other in the body of Christ. Do we also realize that if we don't measure up to those prophecies, that is just how far we are from being the Messiah's prophesied people? Can it be that we are impostors?

Much of this material was developed several years ago when a small college-town church with a lot of doctrinal differences contacted me. Since I had a part in the beginning of the congregation a dozen years before, and although I knew only one family there when they contacted me, they thought I might be able to help. This congregation was somewhat unusual in that it was composed of young college students and instructors who nearly all had become Christians somewhere else. They had left home and were now thrust together with brethren with quite different backgrounds. They sent me a tape recording of a meeting of the men of the congregation to present their problems to me. The tape began by their going around the room and identifying themselves so I might recognize their voices as they spoke during the meeting.

Next, those men listed sixteen major doctrinal topics that agitated them. Then they gave the startling admission that although they didn't believe any of those doctrinal issues was their real problem, they didn't know what their real problem was. They requested I listen to them talk about all their differences to see if I could determine what their real problem was.

As I listened to their comments, and grasped the spectrum of differences, my first reaction was that there was no way Christians with so many different backgrounds, philosophies, and opinions could work together. I took the cassette out of the player and put it away, thinking the situation was hopeless. Several days later, I listened to it again, and this time I was impressed by two things: (1) the candor of these Christians, who clearly were trying to determine how they might work together, and (2) the obvious respect they had for each other in the midst of their many differences. I suggested to those brethren I put some material on fellowship together, and present it to them to see if it could help them work together in spite of the fact they lacked complete doctrinal agreement.

Later, as I drove across the state to meet with them, I thought this was an unusual situation, because most congregations are fairly stable doctrinally without a variety of backgrounds being thrust together at the same time in the same place. However, the more I thought about these passages from Isaiah, the more I was forced to the conclusion that these situations are to be expected.

The New Testament doesn't present a picture of stagnant congregations where everyone comes from the same direction, but rather groups of Christians where many are converted out of quite a variety of religious backgrounds, and having to learn how to deal with one another while they grow doctrinally. As a matter of fact, as long as Christians teach those in the world, this problem will exist, and never go away. It was never supposed to! Rather, God wants Christians to learn how to conduct themselves in these circumstances. Certainly, it helps to solve these problems if we first realize they are not unusual when a church grows as it should.

Solving Problems Together Builds Bonds Between Brethren

An individual Christian is a highly complex person, consisting of at least a body, spirit, mind, and personality as did Jesus in Lk. 2.52, where it is said He grew in wisdom, stature, and in favor with God and man. As a result, even a person who lives alone will have personal problems. If two such complex persons marry, marriage problems naturally occur. When children are added to the family, each with their individual bodies, minds, spirits, and personalities, family problems are inevitable. Likewise, as many diverse people are joined together in a local church, problems are bound to manifest themselves.

This chapter examines some things Christians can do from the teaching of Christ and that will (1) prevent many problems from arising in local congregations, and (2) solve some problems that may already exist. *Above all, local church problems do not have to be tolerated.* God tells us how to avoid and solve problems between Christians. When we don't solve them, but merely endure them, it shows either a *lack of knowledge* of or a *lack of faith* in God's teaching.

Ignorance of God's Word Causes and Magnifies Problems

God says His people are destroyed by ignorance. Ignorance of God's word causes many church problems. Many secondary causes of problems exist between Christians, some of which are discussed in this chapter. However, many of these secondary problems generally go back to a more fundamental factor, ignorance of God's word.

Historically, ignorance has always been the paramount cause of the disobedience of God's people. In Hos. 4.6, God spoke of the underlying cause of Jewish problems seven hundred years before Christ when He said:

> My people are destroyed for a lack of knowledge.

Likewise, when the Apostle Peter preached the second gospel sermon recorded in Ac. 3.17, he explained to the Jews why they crucified the very Messiah they looked for:

> And now, brethren, I know that in ignorance ye did it, as did also your rulers.

The gospels show that Jesus was put to death because of pride, envy, and love of money. Peter, however, got to the heart of the matter when he proclaimed Jesus was crucified in ignorance. The Jews were simply so ignorant of God's word they crucified His Anointed.

So it is today. Most doctrinal problems local churches get involved in go back to a dismal ignorance of God's word. Many personal problems between Christians stem from the same root cause. Christians worldwide starve for competent teachers of God's word, who can teach them the way of the Lord more perfectly. Therefore, since widespread ignorance of God's word is basic to church problems, a well-rounded knowledge of the word of God helps us avoid many church problems, as well as enables us to extricate ourselves and others from difficulties.

Solving Problems Together Builds Confidence and Bonds Between Brethren

Often a congregation contains able Christians with quite a reservoir of Bible teaching available to them, and yet the members may not work well together. Collectively, the congregation may do so little the people in their community don't even know they're there. Little personal evangelism is done, and Satan may well have that church exactly where he wants it, with its doing perhaps twenty percent of what it could.

Usually, a major reason those Christians cannot do more together is because of a lack of respect for and confidence in each other. They may be friendly and associate together on a social basis, and yet they still may not have developed confidence in one another on a large enough scale where they can work together.

Because of a lack of confidence and respect in one another, when doctrinal or personal problems arise, as they inevitably will, it is easy to "write off" the others as not being valuable compatriots anyway. Thus, efforts at collective church discipline are not effective. The person losing fellowship doesn't consider it to be too bad a penalty because after all, fellowship with the congregation wasn't all that grand to begin with!

Confidence in brethren does not occur naturally, and it doesn't come about by accident. Neither does that confidence develop by mere social contact, no matter how extensive it might be. Many in a congregation might get together socially very frequently. However, when problems involving doctrine or personal sin arise, some of them won't have sufficient confidence in each other to work together to solve the problems, even though they are veritable reservoirs of the teaching of God.

We can learn what produces confidence among Christians from the dealings of the Apostle Paul with Christians in Corinth in whom he had no confidence at first. In I Cor. 3.1, he declared he couldn't even talk to them like spiritually-minded people because they were still so carnally minded. He had to treat them like babies. Throughout the letter he rebuked them for their lack of understanding of preacher-church relations (Chapters 1-4). He demanded they quit being proud of an impenitent fornicator in the church and deliver him to his owner, Satan, so he might be ashamed and repent, and thereby be saved (Chapter 5).

He blistered them for taking their disputes before pagan judges (Chapter 6). He chided them for not conducting themselves properly in realms of expediency (Chapters 7-10), i.e., of not having the judgment to conduct themselves properly toward weak Christians. In Chapters 12-14 Paul made it clear they were sadly mistaken concerning a variety of aspects of miraculous spiritual gifts. In Chapter 15, he endeavored to correct serious misconceptions concerning the general resurrection at the end of time.

Imagine a similar church in our day! If a church of our acquaintance had members who were seriously mixed up and divided on a variety of matters, we wouldn't have any confidence in that group of Christians. Yet when Paul wrote his second letter several months later to the same church, his tone was entirely different. For example, in II Cor. 7.16, Paul told them:

> I rejoice that in everything I am of good courage concerning you.

Remember, in the first letter he did not speak of good courage about them. He confided elsewhere in the second letter that as he wrote the first one he cried because he was afraid his harshness might cause them to renounce their association with him. He had anything but good courage concerning them in the first letter. But Paul delighted in the good report his companion, who delivered the letters to them, brought back to him, so much so, that he began boasting about them in II Cor. 8.22:

> And we have sent with them our brother, whom we have many times proved earnest in many things, but now much more earnest, by reason of the great confidence which he hath in you.

Thus, Paul and his traveling companion both felt tremendous confidence in a church where just shortly before, they had none whatever. What produced this change?

Before answering that question, notice some additional events where Paul expressed great confidence in individuals and churches. For example, in Philemon 21, Paul mentioned his confidence in his friend Philemon:

> Having confidence in thine obedience I write unto thee, knowing that thou wilt do even beyond what I say.

Likewise in Phil. 1.14, Paul spoke of the confidence the Roman Christians had in him in the midst of a major trial directed against Christians in that city:

> ...and that most of the brethren in the Lord, being confident through my bonds, are more abundantly bold to speak the word of God without fear.

In all these instances, Paul had been through trying situations and weighty problems with certain brethren. When Paul and these brethren worked together according to God's word, even solving tremendous problems, they established bonds of confidence. Brethren merely associating together socially for years will not build bonds of confidence nearly like they were working in spiritual situations together according to God's word. *Solving problems together by applying the teaching of Christ builds not only faith in Christ, but also confidence in faithful brethren as well.* Then when new problems between those brethren arise, bonds of confidence will prevent them from writing each other off so quickly. In addition, church discipline will have a real chance to bring about repentance when needed, because loss of fellowship will cost brethren a great deal.

I remember a serious conflict between two Christians. It started when a mature Christian woman hired a babe in Christ to do some remodeling work in her home. She overheard him tell a lie in a phone conversation to one of his suppliers, and when he hung up, she confronted him about it. No one ever dealt with him so forthrightly, and being somewhat perturbed, he denied he had lied, thereby lying again.

The more he tried to extricate himself, the deeper in he dug himself. He simply never had anyone refuse to be shaken off like this lady. Since he had now sinned against her by lying to her, she dealt with him according to Jesus' direction concerning personal offenses as prescribed in Mt. 18.15-18.

When he wouldn't hear her private exhortations, she got two witnesses, of whom I reluctantly was one, to hear her continued efforts to get him to renounce his untruths. I well remember going to their meetings with an upset stomach, wishing to be anywhere else. I thought all along these two Christians would soon have nothing to do with each other again.

How wrong I was! When the young Christian finally realized this lady was not his enemy, but trying to get him to repudiate his past pattern of casual attitude toward the truth, and that she was not going to be put off, he finally repented of his lying. I'm glad to say those two Christians became the best of friends, and several years later, when the young man became a gospel preacher and needed some financial support, guess who was the first one to come forward to aid him financially? That's right, the woman who he had thought was out to destroy him in the beginning of his service of Christ. To this day, they have tremendous confidence in one another, and their solving a serious spiritual problem according to God's word was the foundation of that confidence.

Many other Christians of my personal acquaintance have developed confidence in each other this same way. Are you in a group of Christians who do not work confidently together? Do you have a problem with anyone that could be solved scripturally? If so, approach him with this attitude: since someone could probably have a lot more fun doing something else than being a Christian in that specific congregation, why not give him credit for wanting to do what is right? Then approach him with the idea of your working together with him on some spiritual project. It may well be the very thing your troubled congregation needs to start developing confidence among brethren.

This ought to be easy to do, especially in troubled congregations. Where brethren have been plagued with problems, and many sensible people have already left because of the seriousness of them, it ought to be easy to give the ones who have remained credit for wanting to serve Christ and do what is right. They may not do right, they may not even know what is right, but if they stick it out in an unpleasant situation, it's not for the fun of it. They must want to do what is right. Give them credit for that at least and striving to solve problems with them according to God's word will become much easier.

Is the Restoration Over?

A major thing that gets in the way of brethren solving doctrinal problems is their attitude toward the restoration of the way of Christ. To those who have been for some time involved in a "restoration movement," we simply ask, "Is the restoration over?" In other words, are we involved in going back to the Bible and seeing for ourselves what Christians did in the New Testament, or do we merely hand down what some early restorers determined to be the truth?

Stated another way, "Do we restore the New Testament way of righteousness or a restoration movement?" There is quite a difference! As a matter of fact, the two philosophies are thousands of miles apart. We shouldn't object to the Roman Catholic practice of setting forth the infallibility of one man, the pope, if we somehow believe in the infallibility of a group of men, a group of preachers, a previous generation of preachers, a brotherhood paper, etc. It is no worse to believe in the infallibility of one man than it is to believe in the infallibility of a group of men.

Another interesting question along this same line might be, "When did someone first speak of the restoration as something completed in the past?" Many do so now, but those involved in restoration movements didn't always. The restorers before Alexander Campbell definitely did not. Campbell himself absolutely did not. He viewed himself as right in the middle of restoring the New Testament way. I doubt any of us, had we lived in the time of Campbell, would have thought the restoration was over. Those in churches of Christ need to know that Campbell taught many things they would not endorse. For example, Campbell believed the sabbath rest was *commanded* in the Garden of Eden. This sounds fine to sabbatarians, but the Bible doesn't so teach. Campbell believed all his life the body of Christ is composed of congregations rather than individual Christians, a thoroughgoing denominational view. Campbell didn't know baptism is for the remission of sins when he was baptized. We certainly wouldn't view one who agreed with Campbell today as having arrived at the pristine way of Christ. The practice of offering an "invitation" to obey the gospel was unheard of in Campbell's early work, something most seem to think is absolutely mandatory today. Thus, had we lived in Campbell's time with our present understanding of the Scriptures, we would not have thought those brethren "had arrived."

If one believes the restoration is over, i.e., that someone somewhere at some time arrived at all the truth so all that remains for us to do is to hand it down to future generations, several questions naturally arise. First, "Who finished the restoration?" "When was it finished?" "In what city was it completed?" If it has been completed, someone must have done it somewhere at sometime.

All these questions are designed to help us realize that to view the restoration as completed in past time misses the whole concept of restoration. Even if someone had arrived at all the truth, either in the past century or in the current century, each one of us still has the same personal responsibility to study for ourselves and determine the truth of God for ourselves.

However, the restoration is not a movement of congregations, as Campbell conceived it. Instead, it should be the restoration of a person's personal fellowship with God, not organizational. Since we still should be involved in a renewal that is a continuing process, then we need to appreciate the following distinction.

Bible Study vs. Creed Rehearsal

Once we regard the restoration process as ongoing, then the distinction between "Bible Study" and "Creed Rehearsal" becomes clear. Once, when I had just begun work with one congregation, I noticed when questions that were a little off the beaten path arose during Bible classes everyone dove for cover. It was as though they thought they would be "fragged." One fellow seemed to get especially nervous when the discussion went longer than he deemed necessary. I knew from the background of the questions and the ones who asked them that the questions concerned real issues in those persons' lives. They were sincere questions that needed immediate application, but this fellow attempted to curtail all discussion so we could go to the next verses.

After noticing this for several weeks, I approached this Christian, and I asked him what the sign outside the building said was to take place at 9:45. He said he didn't understand. I said, "Does it say we have Bible Study or Creed Rehearsal?"

He thought about it a moment, and said, "I see your point, I guess we are here to study the Bible, aren't we?" It's important for us to see that if we are involved in a continuing process of determining the truth for ourselves, with lions and lambs from a variety of backgrounds involved in the search, we're bound to have some off-the-wall views and concepts expressed. To have it otherwise would not be normal.

Thus, we need to appreciate the necessity of Bible study instead of creed rehearsal, and realize we're all involved in a continual search for truth. We must learn not to be so defensive when ideas other than our own are expressed. At such times, we ought to be able to give each other credit for wanting to know the truth, then help each other find it, and behave ourselves toward each other while we strive to find it. The purpose of this chapter is to help us learn to behave ourselves toward brethren when we have doctrinal differences. In Chapter 5 we established the concept that a local congregation is a group of Christians who agree on what they do collectively and who agree to behave themselves on the matters they're not agreed on. Now we seek to see what "behaving ourselves" means in the case of doctrinal differences.

Unless We Learn Some Lessons, We're Doomed to Undergo Splits

It is of the utmost importance that we learn how to conduct ourselves in the midst of doctrinal differences, because unless we do, congregations are doomed to undergo a succession of splits. In the restoration movement in the United States, many splits occurred in fellowship between Christians in the same congregations as well as splits between coalitions of congregations (which coalitions should never have existed anyway, being denominational in nature). Churches of Christ split over the missionary society concept in the 1850s, and over instrumental music in worship sometime later. Earlier in the twentieth century, they split over benevolence, sponsoring churches, Bible classes, and the container used in the Lord's Supper, etc. Generally, these splits took place without a lot of study and understanding of the other side's arguments, but with much tension, labeling of each other, misrepresentation, and hard feelings. At the present time, some churches contemplate a similar split over various questions pertaining to divorce and remarriage. Others seem willing to draw the line on whether or not the fruit of the vine used in the Lord's Supper may be fortified with Vitamin C. In most of these splits, the breaks in fellowship take place between brethren who are not at all familiar with both sides of the issue. The break comes before a lot of studying has been done by most of those involved.

Unless we learn to solve the real underlying problem of how we ought to conduct ourselves toward brethren we differ with, we will continue to have comparable breaks in fellowship. We may always say it's over a different doctrinal issue, but we fail to deal with the real issue.

Not only are we doomed to a succession of splits, but the overall situation will also continue to get worse, because as one older, wiser preacher suggested, "In every split, the conservatives always get the cranks." In a controversy over an innovation, the conservatives get the ones who are honestly scripturally opposed to the innovation. These are not the cranks we speak of. The ones opposing the innovation also get the people who are opposed to doing anything they've never done before (i.e., Tuesday night Bible classes instead of Wednesday night), along with those who are opposed to doing anything at all. These latter two categories are indeed cranks. This being true, as the succession of splits goes on without the real problem (our mistreating each other) ever being addressed, the concentration of cranks will only increase, and lead to even more splits!

Question Showing the Extent of Doctrinal Differences

In the congregation where I was invited to present this material originally, to emphasize the overwhelming nature of their differences, one Christian asked this question during a question and answer period:

> The following illustrates the magnitude of some of the differences we have:
>
> One brother teaches Ac. 2:38 promises us the literal indwelling of the Holy Spirit and another teaches that the gift is not the literal indwelling, but salvation.

> One brother affirms that in Ac. 19.1-7 those baptized into John's baptism were baptized in Christ's name to receive the Holy Spirit (literally) and not the forgiveness of sins, because they had already received forgiveness under John's baptism, while another brother affirms that those people were baptized for forgiveness of sins and did not receive a literal indwelling of the Holy Spirit.
>
> One brother teaches that the phrases in Rom. 8.9-11 "if Christ be in you," "in the spirit," "if the spirit of God dwell in you," and "if a man have not the spirit of Christ" are all descriptions of the literal indwelling of the Holy Spirit, while another brother publicly affirms that this doctrine is wrong because he believes that the ideas and power of God's word is what dwells in us.
>
> One brother teaches that the Holy Spirit and Jesus Christ are literally one and the Holy Spirit is Jesus Christ ministering on earth in spirit form, while another brother teaches that the Holy Spirit and Christ are separate divine beings.
>
> One brother teaches that what was promised to Abraham was the Holy Spirit, but the other brother teaches the promise to Abraham was salvation through Christ.
>
> Can fellowship exist between these two brothers?

As I read this brother's question, I originally thought, "There's no way these two brethren can be in fellowship." Surely the fellow who wrote the question thought it was hopeless, and perhaps you do as well. After thinking about the matter for a moment, though, I answered the question this way: "Yes, it is possible for these two brethren to be in fellowship, but it will not be by accident." I meant they can enjoy fellowship in many cases. For instance, suppose one of these Christians is a new convert, while the other one has been a Christian for many years. It is entirely possible for a new convert to have all kinds of mistaken ideas about the Godhead, the indwelling of the Holy Spirit, etc.

When I obeyed the gospel and became a Christian, I was not even aware of most of these questions, much less their answers. I had not even heard of the proposition that God promised Abraham the Holy Spirit when I read this question. Can a mature Christian associate with me while I study to find the truth of the proposition? We can be if we agree to behave ourselves toward each other while the study goes on. Even then, it wouldn't have to affect our collective action if we differ on the nature of the promise made to Abraham. If one view wasn't pushed to the exclusion of all others, I could probably enjoy fellowship with both of these brethren.

We're Not Saved by Perfect Doctrinal Correctness

It will surely help us conduct ourselves properly toward brethren we differ with if we appreciate the fact none of us is in fellowship with God because we're completely doctrinally correct. Remember, *we're talking about differences only between brethren, i.e., between Christians*, who are in Christ, and have been baptized into Him upon the basis of their faith in Christ.

A recent debate proposition between two Christians clearly draws this issue: "Resolved: Absolute doctrinal conformity is necessary for scriptural fellowship." As previous chapters show, since *fellowship with God is based upon perfect faith, not flawless knowledge or performance*, the requirement of absolute doctrinal conformity cannot be right. Before reviewing the reasons why, observe that this contention does not work, practically. The man who signed to affirm the proposition didn't have absolute doctrinal conformity with God when he became a Christian, and thence he didn't have scriptural fellowship with God if his proposition is right. To be truthful, he still doesn't have absolute doctrinal conformity with God, and thus, according to his own proposition, he still doesn't have scriptural fellowship with God.

Likewise, if absolute doctrinal conformity is required to have scriptural fellowship between two Christians, there are not two Christians in the entire world who have absolute doctrinal conformity. The concept of perfect doctrinal precision makes fellowship with God or with any other Christian practically impossible.

We understand that perfect doctrinal conformity is not essential for mature Christians to be in fellowship with new converts. Everybody seems able to see it in that case. We understand the new converts in Acts 2 did not have absolute doctrinal conformity, either with God or with each other. Even though the Apostle Peter preached Gentiles would come into the kingdom on the same basis as Jews, he didn't believe it. Thus, Peter didn't even have perfect doctrinal correctness. In Acts 10, God performed miracles to convince Peter to practice what he had preached years before.

Many times we show extreme patience with those we teach the gospel. After they obey the gospel, we are still fairly patient with their off-the-wall ideas, at least until they've been Christians, let's say, for three to six months. But by then, woe be unto them if they are doctrinally incorrect!

We should be able to see it within ourselves if we are mature Christians. Who among us is perfectly doctrinally correct? Are you? Are you really? If you are, how long have you been? How long has it been since you've had to change on some doctrinal issue? If you believe complete doctrinal correctness is required for fellowship with God or with other Christians, were you in fellowship with God just before you changed doctrinally the last time?

Chapter 4 reviewed Paul's statement in Romans 4 that we will be saved like Abraham and David were. Abraham and David were two powerful choices for Paul to use because one lived under the Law of Moses and the other one did not. Therefore, the Law of Moses was not the means by which they were justified. Secondly, one was justified being circumcised, yet the other was justified before he was circumcised. Thus, circumcision had nothing to do with their justification. Imagine the force the justification of Abraham and David had on the Jews of Paul's day, who believed they were justified because they had the Law of Moses and had been circumcised!

Also, neither Abraham nor David were justified because they were perfectly doctrinally correct. Did Abraham have doctrinal perfection? When God promised all nations would be blessed through his seed, Abraham first thought Eliezer, a member of his household but not a descendent, would be his heir. This was not doctrinally correct. If I taught this today, you would know I was wrong, just as wrong as Abraham was when he believed it. Yet Abraham's position concerning Eliezer was not a lack of faith, but rather a lack of understanding. It appeared logical to him, based upon what God had told him up to then.

When God told Abraham that Eliezer was not the heir, but one coming from his own loins would be his heir, Abraham immediately stopped thinking of Eliezer as his heir. But he then mistakenly thought Ishmael (who came from his loins, but by Hagar, rather than Sarah) would be his heir. If anyone today taught Ishmael was the heir of whom God spoke, we would all know the doctrine was wrong, as it was wrong in Ishmael's day. Again, this was not a lack of faith on Abraham's part, because Ishmael fit what God had told Abraham at that time. It was a lack of understanding.

Finally, when Abraham understood Isaac was the heir, he was still doctrinally mistaken when he went to offer Isaac as a sacrifice. He believed after he killed Isaac, God would raise him from the dead. If I taught this today, I would certainly be mistaken, but it was not a lack of faith on Abraham's part, was it? To the contrary, it was a lack of understanding. Absolute doctrinal conformity must not be required for scriptural fellowship with God, for Abraham did not have such conformity, yet he was justified.

In spite of the clear example of Abraham, some of us continue to think we cannot be doctrinally mistaken and still be in fellowship with God. To illustrate, a lady once heard me preach a series of lessons on Matthew 24, presenting a view different from that held by preachers she had been exposed to. After the lessons she said: "Sam, I've read your teaching on Matthew 24 for many years, and I've enjoyed even more listening to you in person, and I think what you teach on the passage is the truth. But I have a question: If what you preach is the truth, then what about all the other preachers who have stood in the same pulpit and preached another view?"

I replied I didn't understand what she meant. She then asked, "Will these other preachers be lost if what you teach on Matthew 24 is the truth, and what they've taught is not true?"

I replied, "No, they won't be lost because they taught something wrong on Matthew 24, nor will I be saved because I may have taught the truth on it." None of us will be saved because we've got the truth on Matthew 24. Abraham wasn't saved because he had the truth on Matthew 24. We'll be saved because we have Abraham's kind of faith, faith you can walk in the steps of.

What About I Cor. 1.10 and II John 9?

Some may well ask, "What about passages like I Cor.1.10 and II John 9? Are you saying doctrinal correctness is not important?" Assuredly, doctrinal correctness is important, and these passages teach it is. However, I Cor. 1.10 and II John 9 do not teach we're saved by complete doctrinal correctness. A few moments' reflection will help us see no one really believes these passages teach this.

Before we notice the passage in detail, recall an aforementioned announcement of a religious debate between two brethren, both of whom believe doctrinal correctness is important. The proposition they debated illustrates the issue we are confronted with at present: "Resolved: Absolute doctrinal conformity is necessary for scriptural fellowship." (Sentry Magazine, *XIII*, No. 4, Floyd Chappelear, editor, pp. 7-11, June 1987.) Although the man who affirmed this proposition had several pages to prove his proposition, he used only two inches, and merely quoted I Cor. 1.10 and II John 9.

Before discussing these two passages individually, let's make some general observations concerning the significance of this proposition. First, if absolute doctrinal conformity is required for scriptural fellowship, then it would be required for both fellowship with God, and with other Christians. Thus, unless one had absolute doctrinal conformity with God, he could not be in association with God, and unless he had absolute doctrinal conformity with another Christian, he couldn't work with another Christian.

Second, in Mt. 28.19-20 Jesus told the apostles, "Go ye therefore, and make disciples of all the nations, baptizing them into the name of the Father and of the Son and of the Holy Spirit: *teaching them to observe all things whatsoever I commanded you*: and lo, I am with you always, even unto the end of the world."

Notice that Christ said to teach those who have been baptized. This should raise a question: "If people are already in fellowship with God because they have absolute doctrinal conformity, then what more could they be taught?" Why have Bible classes to teach those we have baptized, if one must have absolute doctrinal conformity in order to be in fellowship with God?

Third, Eph. 4.11-14 lists Christ's gifts to the church, "for the *perfecting* of the saints...till we all come in the *unity of the faith*...that we henceforth be *no more children, tossed to and fro* with every wind of doctrine." If absolute doctrinal conformity is required to be in fellowship with God, why do we need teachers, elders, evangelists, etc., to teach the way of the Lord more perfectly? We can't get more perfect than absolute doctrinal conformity, can we? We had to arrive at the unity of the faith before we could even get into fellowship with God, and we stopped being tossed to and fro at the same time. Why have Bible study in local churches, or why teach the Bible to Christians, if they already have absolute doctrinal conformity?

Certainly, we should all strive for absolute doctrinal conformity, and this author is so striving. But this is a far cry from a demand for doctrinal conformity in order for us to be in fellowship with God or other Christians.

I Corinthians 1.10

With these general observations in mind, let's now turn our attention to I Cor. 1.10, where Paul said:

> Now I beseech you, brethren, through the name of our Lord Jesus Christ, that ye all speak the same thing, and that there be no divisions among you; but that ye be

perfected together in the same mind and in the same judgment.

In the context, the apostle Paul addressed the Corinthians' practice of calling themselves after the name of the preacher who baptized them, and Paul condemns their division. But even then, he did not say the Corinthians were already out of fellowship with God. In verse 9, he mentioned, "God is faithful, through whom ye were called into the fellowship of His Son Jesus Christ our Lord," as though they were still in fellowship with God. If they weren't, they had no business withdrawing from an impenitent fornicator as Paul commanded them in Chapter 5. However, they risked losing fellowship if they continued in the error.

Additionally, throughout the book of I Corinthians, Paul mentions their differences with one another over eating meat offered to idols (Chapters 8 and 10), yet he did not tell them to withdraw fellowship over these differences. As a matter of fact, regarding the same problem in Rom. 14.1-2, he said the strong ought to receive the weak, not withdraw or fragment from them. Again, with respect to the weak, who bound more closely in the realm of expediency than God Himself, Paul called them in I Cor. 8.5-13 "brethren...for whose sake Christ died." Obviously, these weak Christians did not have absolute doctrinal conformity, yet Paul called them "brethren" and did not urge a break in fellowship between them and their more knowledgeable brethren. Rather, he encouraged the strong to bear the infirmities of the weak, even though they were doctrinally imperfect.

From our previous study on what we can differ on and still share fellowship with other Christians, we could say scripturally "being perfected in the same mind and in the same judgment" in I Cor. 1.10 does not require us to agree on matters in the realm of expediency. We may *differ* on matters that are not in the realm of expediency but that don't affect our collective action. We may *differ* on matters that would affect our collective action if we were to engage in them. We may *differ* with some things that are preached, as long as the forum is open in the search for truth. This doesn't mean we can be satisfied with doctrinal differences, nor that we shouldn't study the issues and resolve the differences. But all doctrinal differences don't have to be resolved in order for us to be in fellowship, either with God, or with other Christians.

II John 9-11

In this passage, John says:

> Whosoever goeth onward, and abideth not in the teaching of Christ, hath not God: he that abideth in the teaching, the same hath both the Father and the Son. If any one cometh unto you, and bringeth not this teaching, receive him not into your house and give him no greeting: for he that giveth him greeting partaketh in his evil works.

The "teaching of Christ" John speaks of is "the teaching from Christ," not the teaching about Christ. See Appendix 4 for a brief discussion of this issue. Given that, does this passage teach "whosoever *goeth onward* [transgresseth—KJV] past the teaching from Christ doesn't have God," or that "whosoever *differs* with Christ doesn't have God?" If you think the passage teaches whosoever differs with Christ hath not God, did it mean that the day you obeyed the gospel? If this is what the passage teaches, and you differed with Christ on anything the day you were baptized, then you still didn't have God! In fact, unless you are confident you don't differ with anything Christ teaches now, you still do not have God.

The word translated "goeth onward" in this passage does not mean "differ." It implies a *disregard* for the authority of the teaching of Christ, not ignorance, nor misunderstanding, nor difference. Those who have studied John's Epistles seriously have learned John wrote to combat a sect of false teachers known as Gnostics, and nearly every verse of these three letters contains some teaching that was anathema to the Gnostics. Among other false teachings, the Gnostics taught you didn't have to pay any attention to the teaching of Christ; you didn't have to be constrained by those teachings. John affirmed anyone who had a careless disregard for the teaching that came from Christ didn't have God. While the Gnostics had a disregard for Christ's teaching—many who misunderstand or are ignorant of Christ's teaching do not have such a disregard.

In addition, in verse 10, John said, "If anyone cometh unto you and bringeth not this teaching, receive him not into your house and give him no greeting, for he that giveth him greeting partaketh in his evil works. What is "this teaching" John spoke of? Is it the teaching of Matthew 24? Revelation 20? Any aspect of divorce and remarriage we might differ about? No, "this teaching" is the teaching John had just stated: *you have to abide in the teaching of Christ to be share fellowship with God.*

Next, did John teach that if a Christian has a doctrinal difference with another person (either a Christian or not) then he can't even invite the person into his house to study the issue? Many won't, but is this what John says? No, he affirms that one (like the Gnostic false teachers) who had no compunction about going beyond the teaching of Christ should not be given support, lest we be a partaker in his evil works. Support to the false teacher who *disregards the authority of the scriptures* is the subject.

Doctrine is important. It's so important if one is like a Gnostic and thinks it's not, he is not in fellowship with God. Something else that is important, though, is the Bible's teaching about how Christians treat each other while they seek to find the true doctrine. In Mt. 23.23, Jesus condemned the Pharisees for stressing doctrinal correctness to the extreme they forgot about justice, mercy, and faith. We who strive for doctrinal correctness may labor under a similar condemnation if we neglect justice, mercy, and faith while aspiring to attain complete doctrinal correctness.

What Can We Differ on and Still Be in Fellowship?

As shown in Chapter 5, "Fellowship with Other Christians," we may differ on matters of expediency where God gives us choices and the options are scriptural. In this realm, He leaves it to our best judgment how to conduct ourselves most expeditiously, and still not disrupt fellowship in a local church.

Also, we can differ on matters that are not in the realm of expediency, but that do not affect our collective action. In that chapter, we gave the example of whether or not a Christian can participate in carnal warfare. One may say, "Even though this doesn't affect our collective action, one of two Christians who differ on the war question is wrong." Yes, one of them is wrong, perhaps both are wrong. However, the one who is right on the war question is undoubtedly wrong on something else, and thus, he won't be in fellowship with God because he's right on every doctrinal issue. As a matter of fact, neither of these two Christians has ever been right on everything, any more than Abraham was.

Likewise, we might differ on questions that would affect our collective action, but we do not practice them. Along this line, we might deal with the question, "Must we agree with everything preached?" We shouldn't expect to if we're involved in a search for truth. We can help pay someone's salary to come preach something we differ with if we can view it as part of the truth-seeking process, in an open forum. Truth can stand the light, it has nothing to fear in open investigation, Jn. 3.21. God commands us to put everything proposed for our belief to the test, I Thes. 5.21. When the people he has the controversy with will no longer speak out in the open, they take the same tactic the rebellious Jews took with Jesus, Jn. 7.25-26. *Without an open forum, the search for truth is over, and so is the restoration of the New Testament religion of Jesus, insofar as that local church is concerned.*

A quotation from David Lipscomb, a restorer of the late 19th and early 20th centuries applies:

> When differences exist, the discussion of these differences is the only hope of union. The suppression of discussion is the direct and open road to division. Whoever opposes the free discussion of differences among brethren, in that favors speedy division. Differences existing will manifest themselves. If they are discussed freely, there is hope of reconciliation and harmony. Suppress the discussion, and unless the strong hand of arbitrary and despotic power holds by the terror of physical force, disruption and division must follow. When persons having a community of interest differ, so long as those who differ show a kindly interest in the others,

> listen to the remonstrances, treat with considerate kindness their feelings, wishes, and reasonings, they remain one. The moment the one party says: "We wish to hear no more your reasonings; we intend no longer to regard your feelings or wishes; we intend to go our own way, regardless of your course or purposes," those people become two distinct people. Division or an unmanly and unchristian submission to what we believe to be wrong is the only alternative.(David Lipscomb, *Gospel Advocate* [Nashville, TN: Gospel Advocate Publishing Company, 1906], p. 552.)

Lipscomb's advice for dealing with brethren we differ with is what we have lost in large part. The Christians in Lipscomb's day didn't have perfect doctrinal correctness, but they propagated the right standard (which the Gnostics in II John 9 did not do): the teaching of Christ rather than denominational creeds. Those with the attitudes Lipscomb describes conducted themselves properly toward each other while they studied to learn truth. They still respected each other; it was not uncommon for preachers who differed with each other to stay in each other's homes when preaching away from home so they could study together. We see these attitudes of open investigation all too rarely anymore.

An admirable modern plea like Lipscomb's recently came in a letter from a brother studying a controversial topic with a group of others. While the topic of their study is not pertinent to our present subject (it so happens I disagree with the brother on the topic), the plea for good behavior on the part of all involved is. Concerning their previous study session, he wrote:

> I want to thank you all for the time you have set aside to help me with a very important topic...Unfortunately, I was disappointed in our last meeting. I had serious questions in my mind which hinder me from taking your stand. But rather than deal with my questions seriously, as though you were helping me to learn truth; you dealt with them defensively, adversarily, as though you were *"batting them aside."* There are at least three serious problems with this approach: 1) it withholds your knowl-

edge from me (so I can't change my thinking); 2) it keeps you from looking closely at something which might change your thinking (cf. Acts 17:11); and 3) it left [my companion—SGD] in a quandary. He doesn't agree with me, but saw you unable or unwilling to deal seriously with my questions...

I know you want me to commit myself and expose a "position." This, I believe, is pre-mature. Now is the time for patience and study. The fact is, I don't know what the answer is (though I do have a prevailing line of thought—which I will pursue until proven false, or true).

I need you to help me see through the questions I've raised. I haven't raised them to "convert" you; but to show you where I see serious flaws that hinder me from embracing your stand. Continue patiently with me to overcome these "stumbling-blocks" by dealing studiously with my questions.

I am not a teacher of this subject, but a student. If I present my concerns and questions and leanings, it is in order to glean input and understanding; not to persuade. I feel that you have misunderstood this. There were a few adversarial statements Monday night which indicated that you would rather cast me and my questions aside than to take the time and energy necessary to seriously deal with them. Indeed, someone said, *"We've given you four hours and you still haven't said anything to change our minds."* Brothers, I wasn't trying to change your minds. I was trying to get you to change mine! I was showing you where my hang-ups were, not to unseat you, but so you could show me the answer.

So far you haven't done that for me. If what you have is truth, I both need it and want it. And, if my questions keep me from embracing truth, I need to lay them aside. But integrity will not allow me to lay aside nagging questions just because others, who know more accu-

> rately, say I should. Gentlemen, your duty, if you love me and deem me an honorable man, is to do for me what Priscilla and Aquila did for Apollos. Show me the answers. If you respond: *"we already have shown you;"* please, be patient with me. Obviously I didn't understand your answers. My questions still nag.
>
> I want to know the truth. I want to lay the nagging questions to rest. I want to be at peace within. I want to tell people only what God wants them to do. But, I don't want it to be superficial assertions. I want to have the confidence of a fellow worker in the cause of Christ who can ask the nagging questions (which may fly in the face of *"orthodoxy"*) without being reproached. Let there be serious concern, study and communication on such questions. I want to be in fellowship with brothers who won't cast me aside the first time I dig into God's word and ask questions which might indicate further study is necessary. I covet the freedom to study, to air ideas, and to come to a deeper knowledge of truth—and to do so without fear.
>
> Please deal gently, kindly and patiently with me—and with all who are eager for truth.

Again, the topic of their study is not material here. As a matter of fact, whether any of the people involved are Christians is not even material. If I can't behave myself toward a Jehovah's Witness who wrote me a letter like this while we study together, I've got character problems at least as serious as his doctrinal ones!

Of course, some doctrinal differences will finally lead to a break in fellowship. After intensive study of an issue that affects the collective action in a local church, when one Christian thinks he must do a certain thing out of his allegiance to Christ, and another Christian believes he must not do the thing, then their fellowship must cease. Even then, these two Christians do not have to be mean to each other. They can strive to keep the lines of communication open, hoping some day they may be able to work together once again. And they should both realize that even though they are not able to work with each other, they may both be in fellowship with God. Their fellowship does not depend upon complete doctrinal correctness, but perfect faith.

The restorers in the American restoration movement knew how to differ with each other. They discussed, debated, and discovered truths that previous generations had missed. If we've lost those qualities, then the restoration is, indeed, over for us.

Principles for Solving Problems

In this section, we discuss a number of tips for Christians to use in solving their doctrinal differences. To help us appreciate their validity, a comparison of how we *should* handle them with how *they're customarily handled* follows.

Need to Give Others Time to Study

In Rom.14.1, Paul instructed more mature Christians how to conduct themselves toward weak Christians, i.e, those less knowledgeable:

> But him that is weak in faith receive ye, yet not for decision of scruples.

While Paul speaks of things in the realm of expediency, this passage contains instruction applicable much more broadly than just that realm. In this context, the weak brother is always the fellow who makes a law where God did not, and who binds where God did not. He is always more conservative than God Himself, and never thinks the controversy is in the realm of expediency. The Christian who thought it was wrong to eat meat offered to an idol didn't think the controversy belonged in the realm of expediency. The fellow who thought it was wrong to esteem one day above another didn't think the controversy was in the realm of expediency, etc.

However, Paul's instruction for dealing with one who made a law where God didn't, and who didn't think it was in the realm of expediency, was not to withdraw, nor to fragment from him, but rather to receive him. Paul said he should be received, but not for the purpose of arguing with him about it all the time. These truths imply Christians should give others time for study to occur. The fact the weak brother is more restrictive than God doesn't mean he's lost, i.e., he's out of fellowship with God, or he ought not to work with us.

I remember a Christian woman I met when I first began preaching. Her brother was a preacher who had come to hold a new (for him) position concerning the woman's covering Paul speaks of in I Corinthians 11. While she visited him (they lived in different parts of the United States), he brought his new convictions to her. He told her he could be in fellowship with her because she had not studied the issue. He wanted to study it with her. Then if she differed, he would have to withdraw fellowship from her. She asked me, "Can he do that?" I replied, "He certainly couldn't withdraw from me, for I'm not in fellowship with people like that." Paul would give more time before drawing the line of fellowship.

I also recall two very fine Christians in a congregation that was trying to select elders. These two had a doctrinal difference that caused the lady to object to the man serving as an elder. Strangely, the woman had agreed with the man until recently, when she changed her position. Now she demanded he make the same change. It had taken her several years to come to her new conclusion. After quite a long discussion concluding with the man leaving her home, he made some comment that let her think perhaps he was coming around. She said, "Come back in, and I'll fix you a sandwich. If you don't agree after the sandwich, I'll still have to object to you."

These were both very fine people, but in Romans 14 Paul gives us more time than it takes to eat a sandwich before we have to come to a parting of the ways. I'm glad God has given me time to come around on His teaching, and on some of the more difficult passages and doctrines, I hope He continues to give me time. If God has allowed me more time than it takes to eat a sandwich, shouldn't I be able to allow God to give time to others?

Credit Others for Loving the Lord as Much as You

One thing that will help us behave ourselves toward brethren we differ with is to give them credit for loving the Lord at least as much as we do. This should be easy to do, since they do not serve the Lord for the fun of it, and could have more fun doing something else. They should be given credit for loving the Lord as long as possible.

Allow You Might Be Wrong

We have been wrong before, and we will be again. For many years, when studying controversial matters with brethren or non-Christians, I usually mention in the beginning that while I think I'm right on the matters we will discuss, I have to allow to myself I might be wrong, as I have been many times before. I then ask if they can allow the same thing of themselves. Most people do not allow they may be wrong. In studying with Jehovah's Witnesses, for example, the common answer is, "Why, no, we can't be wrong; we're God's organization." One can have this attitude and be as wrong as can be, whether he is a Jehovah's Witness, or a Christian. Solomon writes (Prov. 12.15), "Every way of a fool is right in his own eyes." Perhaps most important, truth isn't what's propagated by "God's organization." As we've seen, the universal church doesn't teach anything through an organization. Truth is taught in God's word (Jn. 17.17), and depends on no organization or person for its validity.

Be Open-Minded

In I Thes. 5.21-22, Paul instructs Christians:

> Prove all things; hold fast that which is good; abstain from every form of evil.

The word translated "prove" means to put something to the test, to see if it be genuine. Thus, God gives Christians the responsibility to put everything that is proposed for their belief to the test of His word. This is a solemn God-given responsibility that cannot be delegated to a favorite preacher, one's parents, an organization, or anyone else. A child of light (Eph. 5.8-11) simply must examine everything for himself. What he finds to pass the test of God's word he must hold to; what fails, he must reject.

Notice that Paul does not say that we should reject or ignore everything new to us. He says, test it. If we are unwilling to do so, we are willfully blinding ourselves to truth that may be new to us. Many times we demand an open mind on the part of those we teach. Yet if we are unwilling to practice what we require of others, there's a word that applies to us—hypocrite. Jesus condemned the religious conservatives of His day as two-faced in Mt. 23.4, saying, "Yea, they bind heavy burdens and grievous to be borne, and lay them on men's shoulders; but they themselves will not move them with their finger."

Too Much Talk, Not Enough Talk

Another major cause of church problems, including those involving doctrinal difficulties, is too much talk, not enough talk. You might say, "How can too much talk, not enough talk, be just one cause?" It's simple: too much talk to the wrong people and not enough talk to the right people. In human relationships, this is a major cause of problems. It causes personnel problems at work, marriage problems, problems in business, or church problems. When problems need to be dealt with, we almost always do too much talking to the wrong people, and hardly ever do enough talking to the right people.

In Mt. 18.15-18, Jesus gives a procedure for wisely dealing with personal offenses. If I am convinced a fellow Christian has sinned against me, I may tell a third and perhaps a fourth party about it rather than the person Jesus specified. Later, if I find out the offense was really just a misunderstanding (as personal offenses many times turn out to be), it will be a lot harder to straighten out all the talk and hard feelings than if I had just gone to the person who caused me the problem. In that case, by talking to the right person and not to any wrong ones, I won't have damaged his reputation with the others. While Jesus spoke of personal offenses, rather than doctrinal differences, it seems much of the wisdom contained in His instruction applies to this case as well. It simply works much better to do it the way Jesus says! The more times you try His way, the more confidence you'll have Jesus knew what He talked about. Again, solving problems according to the teaching of Christ builds confidence in Christ and in your brethren.

In Jn. 7.51, Nicodemus rightly said to the Jews who plotted to do away with Jesus:

> Doth our law judge a man, except it first hear from himself and know what he doeth?

Even the Jews who killed Christ waited a while in order to hear some more from Him. In Mt. 22.46, Matthew says:

> And no one was able to answer him a word, neither durst any man from that day forth ask him any more questions.

When the Jews quit talking with Jesus, the time had come to watch out! So it is today, as David Lipscomb said earlier. Also, notice that the following passages warning of the tremendous power of the tongue for harm in these cases:

> Psalm. 34.13: "Keep your tongue from evil, and your lips from speaking deceit."

> Psalm 52.2: "Your tongue devises destruction, like a sharp razor, O worker of deceit."

> Prov. 18.21: "Death and life are in the power of the tongue..."

> Rom. 3.13: "Their throat is an open sepulchre; with their tongues they have used deceit; the poison of asps is under their lips; whose mouth is full of cursing and bitterness."

Thus, misuse of the tongue plays a great role in causing problems. It greatly hinders their solution, as well.

Don't Answer Before Hearing the Other Side

In Prov. 18.13, 17, Solomon said:

> He who gives an answer before he hears, it is folly and shame to him...The first to plead his case seems just, until another comes and examines him.

Thus, a person who has a difference with a brother, and makes up his mind about the issue without studying the other side, may not only reject the truth his brother may have, but he also does a very foolish and shameful thing. Hearing the other person's side before jumping to conclusions is a good way to avoid being embarrassed. Moreover, *answering before we hear is no substitute for study.*

Don't Misrepresent the Other Side

Another thing that is not a substitute for study with a brother is misrepresenting him or his position. Misrepresentation has always been a dishonorable way of dealing with someone you differ with. A few moments reflection will remind us that misrepresentation of our own views is not an effective way of reaching us with a certain teaching. Is it?

When someone accuses us of believing Sunday is the Christian sabbath, when we don't believe it, will they make much headway with us? If one conscientiously doesn't believe in *certain methods* of providing care for orphans, it will not be effective to represent him as opposing taking care of orphans. When Christians strive to live by the teaching of the New Testament and not by the Mosaic Law, it will not do to accuse them of not believing in the Old Testament. When people who strive to be just New Testament Christians and reject denominational allegiance, doctrine, organization, etc., it will not be effective to accuse them of thinking they're the best denomination. If people believe in the necessity of water baptism in order to be in Christ, accusing them of believing in "water salvation" will not be an effective way of reaching them.

If a few moments' reflection convinces us the technique of misrepresentation doesn't work with us, surely we can see it will not work if we use it on those we differ with. *Misrepresenting the other side is not a substitute for study*, either.

Don't Hasten to Label

Hastening to label someone in the midst of a difference has always been a dishonorable way of dealing with controversy. In Lk. 7.33-34, when John the Baptist came neither eating nor drinking, the Jews said he had a demon. When Jesus came both eating and drinking, they said He was a glutton and a winebibber. You just can't win with those who would rather label than study. It's easier to label someone than it is to learn his position and deal with it from the scriptures. It's so much easier and faster to call someone by a prejudicial name than study. This may be why so many do so much of it. However, *hastening to label is no substitute for study.*

Don't Impugn Motives

We now want to discuss a major cause of church problems, actually a sin so common in mankind it affects every conceivable human relationship. Since it is a common fault, it may surprise some to find out that "judgment of others' unknown motives" is wrong. Once we realize what this sin is, we will easily recognize it in the workplace, in our family, with our neighbors, and even with the stranger on the street.

In I Cor. 2.11-13, in the greatest text on the subject of the inspiration of the New Testament, Paul says:

> For who among men knoweth the things of a man, save the spirit of the man, which is in him? even so the things of God none knoweth, save the Spirit of God. But we received, not the spirit of the world, but the spirit which is from God; that we might know the things that were freely given to us of God. Which things also we speak, not in words which man's wisdom teacheth, but which

> the Spirit teacheth: combining spiritual things with spiritual words.

This passage teaches at least four great truths: (1) Man has a conscious spirit, a spirit that "knows" his things. This is not our breath, as Jehovah's Witnesses, Seventh-Day Adventists or other materialists might affirm, for our breath knows nothing. (2) We don't know the things, the thoughts, intents, wishes, desires, likes, or dislikes of a person, unless he reveals them to us. (3) We don't know what God's things are, His likes and dislikes, unless He tells us. (4) The very words of the Bible are inspired by God. The Apostle Paul specifically denies the apostles spoke and wrote their own words, but the Holy Spirit guided their very words.

Most people probably don't have problems with the fact man has a conscious spirit. The majority will understand we don't know God's likes and dislikes unless He reveals them to us. Our readers probably believe in the verbal inspiration of the scriptures. However, many probably will fail to appreciate the devastating sin we commit when we judge or impugn another's unknown motives. Paul affirms we no more know what another human being thinks unless he reveals his thoughts to us than we know what God thinks unless He reveals His thoughts to us.

Think how prone we are to condemn the motives of those whom we differ with. Think how apt we are to judge the motives of those whom we have doctrinal differences with. Think how liable we are to impugn the motives of individuals who teach false doctrine. Think how inclined we are to malign brethren whom we differ with. We are quick to do this in our marriages, business dealings, families, dealings with people we strive to teach the gospel, and in local churches.

How easy it is to think that someone who criticizes us is out to get us. How naive it is to think our wives don't care about our wishes when they do something that displeases us. How simple it is to come to the conclusion that a person I have a doctrinal difference with simply doesn't love the Lord, or doesn't care what the truth is.

The truth is, some individuals don't care what the Bible says on a subject. You may know of cases, as I do, where a preacher has said, "I know that's what the Bible says, but I've got so much invested in my denominational pension plan I can't afford to start preaching that now." However, this doesn't give us the right to assume his followers have the same callous attitude toward serving God that he has. We don't have the right to assume all those who make his same arguments are so motivated. Paul affirms we don't know the things of a man unless his spirit tells us. Believe it!

In Ac. 1.24, the disciples wanted to know God's will concerning a replacement apostle for Judas, who had fallen away. When they addressed God in prayer, they said:

> Thou, Lord, who knowest the hearts of all men, show of these two the one whom thou hast chosen...

Mark it well: God is the only one who knows the hearts of all men. When we are involved in a doctrinal discussion, how easy it is for brethren to accuse others of not believing in the grace of God, of trying to get around what the Bible teaches, or of having a lack of faith in God.

Several reasons show why judging motives is extremely serious. First, judging others' unknown motives is a sin. We take upon ourselves a prerogative that belongs only to God, and hence we're guilty of blasphemy. These are strong words: examine them carefully and see if they are true. In Rom. 1.28-32, Paul recounts the sinfulness of the Gentiles in these words:

> And even as they refused to have God in their knowledge, God gave them up unto a reprobate mind, to do those things which are not fitting; being filled with all unrighteousness, wickedness, covetousness, maliciousness; full of envy, murder, strife, deceit, malignity, whisperers, backbiters, hateful to God, insolent, haughty, boastful, inventors of evil things, disobedient to parents, without understanding, covenant breakers, without natural affection, unmerciful: who knowing the ordinance of God, that they that practice such things are worthy of death, not only do the same, but also consent with them that practice them.

We often use this handy passage to condemn several horrible sins we want unalterably to oppose: whisperers, homosexuals (vv 26-27), covenant-breakers, etc. However, notice the word "malignity." This is same the sin we speak of: impugning the unknown motives of another. Paul said those who practice it are worthy of death!

Second, impugning motives is extremely harmful to us because it both determines and undermines the way we approach every person we have differences with. Now, how many relationships in your life involve people you have differences with? Isn't it every personal relationship you have? We can differ with our child's teacher, the clerk at the store, our next-door neighbor, our spouse, our children, or any other person whom we come in contact with.

If we do something that undermines the way we deal with every human being we come in contact with, then we'll have serious problems with a lot of people. If we're quick to decide those who differ with us on some doctrinal point are "not interested in the truth," or "trying to get around what the Bible says," then we certainly will not make much of an effort to teach them further, will we? So we easily repudiate people who differ with us doctrinally. We mourn, "No one is interested in the truth anymore." We quickly brand some as "liberals," others as "anti's;" and thus, we're done with them. In reality, we probably didn't even get started!

Practically speaking, more people are interested in the truth than we might think. The man we have a doctrinal difference with may be more interested in the truth than we are. We may just defend ourselves by judging his motives. After all, it's a whole lot easier to impugn somebody's motives and dispatch him, than it is to diligently study God's word so we can deal with his argument, isn't it?

Judging motives is one of the reasons why many churches are constantly plagued by problems from within. Churches may split every decade or so, ostensibly over some "doctrinal issue," when in reality, they may fail to engage in much mutual study of the issues involved. Likely, the persons involved don't know very much about how to deal with brethren they differed with. They may decide quickly that those they differed with were not interested in the truth. Then they may settle the issue by refusing to waste their time studying with people who couldn't care less what the Bible says. No doubt, they save themselves a lot of work, but they surely do not save themselves a lot of problems.

We need to recognize churches are doomed to a succession of splits until they teach and work on the real problem. The real problem is the absolute impropriety of passing on the motives of individuals when we simply do not have the ability to know their motives unless they reveal them to us. A person who is constantly in discord with other people needs to examine himself and see if he's guilty of impugning their motives. The next time we are involved in a religious discussion where someone impugns motives, let's realize we're dealing with only the second man on earth with the ability to do that. The first man was Jesus Christ. Finally, *maligning a brother is no substitute for study.*

Admonitions Concerning Misuse of the Tongue

As the last several suggestions concern the tongue, so a number of passages warn of the unrighteous use of the tongue. James 3 contains some familiar and provocative teaching about misuse of the tongue. For example, in Jas. 3.6, James says:

> And the tongue is a fire: the world of iniquity among our members is the tongue, which defileth the whole body, and setteth on fire the wheel of nature, and is set on fire by hell.

When I first lived in the northwestern part of the United States with its great forests, I learned that a very small, improperly controlled cigarette can easily cause a forest fire costing millions of dollars and perhaps even loss of life. James affirms the tongue similarly can cause great damage in the lives of men and women.

During the Senate Watergate hearings that led to President Nixon's resignation, I recall listening one afternoon while the Senate committee questioned one of the President's underlings, a man by the name of Alexander Butterfield. Unknown to the Senate committee, this man was responsible for the maintenance and operation of a secret tape recording system the President used in the White House.

While Mr. Butterfield answered another question, he casually mentioned "the tapes." When the Senate Committee heard those words, they became excited and of course closely quizzed Butterfield about the tapes.

You probably know the rest of the story. Both the House and Senate Committees subpoenaed those tapes. The President denied Congress access to the tapes, and the case went to the United States Supreme Court, that ruled President Nixon had to turn the tapes over to Congress. Within days, he became the first President to resign under fire.

What brought down the President of the United States? Russian premiers had threatened and tried for years to bring Nixon down. They had sought to destroy him economically. They had contemplated annihilating him with their missiles on several occasions. But the slip of one man's tongue led to his downfall. James says the tongue is a comparable fire, that has also brought down many Christians and congregations.

In James 3.2, we read:

> For in many things we all stumble. If any stumbleth not in word, the same is a perfect man, able to bridle the whole body also.

James affirms if a man can control his tongue, he can control his whole body. Think of it! The hardest sins to overcome are not sexual sins or alcoholism, but sins having to do with controlling the tongue. If a man can control his tongue, he can control himself in the sexual realm. Those who say they are homosexuals and cannot help it are mistaken. Some sins are harder to overcome than homosexuality, and they have to do with the tongue.

Now you might say, "Well, I just don't know if I can believe that!" or "That's hard to accept!" If so, your problem is not with me, but with what James says, by the inspiration of God.

In Jas. 3.7-8, he says:

> For every kind of beasts and birds, of creeping things and things in the sea, is tamed, and hath been tamed by

> mankind: but the tongue can no man tame; it is a restless evil, it is full of deadly poison.

We've all marveled at trained animals: elephants, dolphins, horses, lions, whales, etc. James explains that the man who can control his tongue ought to arouse our awe! In Jas. 1.26, he says:

> If any man thinketh himself to be religious, while he bridleth not his tongue but deceiveth his heart, this man's religion is vain.

"Vain" means "empty, worthless, of no value whatsoever." These are strong words, like those of Jesus in Mt. 15.6-9 when He affirmed that the Jews who set aside God's teaching with their own traditions made their worship of God "vain." James says we do the same thing when we do not bridle our tongues. James goes further, though, and says this man "deceives his heart." He may think he's in fellowship with God, but actually he's the furthest thing from pleasing his God.

Indeed, misuse of the tongue is a great cause of problems in local churches. In addition, the following passages reflect the responsibility of the listener when others misuse their tongues. In Prov. 20.19, we read:

> He who goes about as a slanderer reveals secrets. Therefore do no associate with a gossip.

Likewise, in Prov. 26.20:

> For lack of wood the fire goes out, and where there is no whisperer, contention dies down.

We Shouldn't Credit Others with the Foolish Statements of Those Who Hold Their Position

Preachers (and others) often try to put someone who differs with them in some camp so they can assume he believes everything the other person does. This gives them "pat" answers to what they "think" he believes. It sounds terrible to say that someone else agrees with Jack the Ripper or the Boston Strangler, but again, it's no substitute for study with the person.

Remember What "Sanity" Must Include

A disconcerting fact that breaks out in the press from time to time is that modern mental health experts cannot agree on what constitutes sanity or insanity. Apparently, drawing the line is a fine task to the workers in this field. However, Dr. Karl Menninger, a recognized expert on mental health who probably knows more about the subject than any man alive, has given the following definition of mental health:

> Mental health is the adjustment of human beings to the world and to each other with a maximum of effectiveness and happiness. Not just efficiency or contentment or the grace of obeying the rules of the game cheerfully. It is all of these together. It is the ability to maintain an even temper, an alert intelligence, socially considerate behavior and a happy disposition. This, I think, is a healthy mind. (Dr. Karl Menninger, cited by Ann Landers, *Seattle Post-Intelligencer*, October 24, 1986.)

Notice the term "socially considerate behavior." Menninger argues that a basic quality a person needs to be considered mentally healthy is the ability to put himself in another's shoes and understand his point of view. Isn't this exactly what Jesus requires of us in Lk. 6.31? There He said:

> As ye would that men would do unto you, do ye also unto them.

When we have a difference with a brother, how do we like to be treated? We like for him to be socially considerate of us. We like to be given credit for loving the Lord. We like for the person we study with to be open-minded. We want him not to answer before he hears our line of thinking. We want him not to misrepresent us, hasten to label us, or impugn our motives. Surely these desires are common to all of us. The next question then is, are we willing to treat a brother the same way we would like to be treated? If we're not, not only do we disobey one of the most basic teachings of Christ, but we don't even display one of the basic ingredients necessary to sanity!

Maintain the Independence of Local Congregations

Assuredly, when a congregation of Christians faces a doctrinal difficulty that has the potential of affecting their work together, *no earthly headquarters of the church or body of Christ exists that can solve the problem for them*. Nor is there a spokesman to say, "Here's what the body of Christ believes and teaches" on this or any other subject.

Many times someone asks, "I know what the Presbyterian church teaches on such-and-such, and the Adventist church, but what does the church of Christ teach?" But, as we have seen in the Bible's concept of the universal church, the universal church doesn't collectively teach anything! *No one on earth has the right to say what the universal church teaches!* Generally this question is asked from a denominational point of view, i.e., "What does a distinct coalition of congregations (Presbyterian or Adventist) teach?"

If someone actually wonders what a coalition of churches of Christ teach on a specific subject, I reply, "I don't care!" The extent of my concern is what does God teach in the Bible, and what do we teach collectively in the local church I am in fellowship with. The truth on the specific doctrinal question this congregation obeys is not what some man or group of men or churches (whether it's the Jehovah's Witnesses or nondenominational Christians) hands down, but it is ascertained by its own independent study.

In addition, *a local church confronted with a doctrinal difficulty needs to solve its doctrinal difference for itself, not for a brotherhood, congregationhood, religious paper, religious college, preacher, or coalition of preachers*. Its concept of fellowship with other Christians ought not to be larger than that local congregation. If a congregation will spend less resources and energy on what entities outside the local church think (other than Christ, of course) and devote its resources and energy to dealing with those within, it will fare much better. It won't squander limited resources on activities, interests, crises, and concerns the Lord never contemplated in His word.

Not only should a congregation not try to solve doctrinal problems for others congregations, but it should not let anyone outside the congregation settle their differences for them! No one has the right to try to impress the teaching of a religious paper, college, preacher, collection of preachers, or another church upon a congregation with a doctrinal question.

These last two points may be hard to do in practice, but with effort, they can and should be done. I recall once among churches of Christ, where it is customary to assemble twice on Sunday, one congregation's elders decided to eliminate Sunday night services. Many Christians in other congregations looked askance at their decision, not realizing what the other congregation did was *none of their business*.

Likewise, other congregations might do many things that are simply none of our business, unless we think of the body of Christ as a coalition of churches, a denominational view. Christians, including preachers, squander tremendous energy in this realm, and then wonder why their own efforts are so fruitless.

In addition, the congregation we work with may do many things in the realms of discipline, worship, and leadership that are not the business of any other congregation. Concern about our congregational affairs by other Christians in other congregations should make us recoil at such violations of congregational independence.

To sum up thus far, when a congregation has a doctrinal question, it should settle the question for itself. This is not to say a congregation can't ask for teaching or procedural advice from other Christians, but it is a long way from the church bowing to outside pressure. If we say we believe in the independence of local congregations, let's practice it. If we say we see the danger in denominational coalitions of congregations and allegiances, let's leave them alone.

To illustrate, what a local church believes, teaches, and practices concerning partaking of the Lord's Supper had better not be based upon the positions of prominent preachers, papers, or colleges, but on the basis of its own independent study and deliberation. What a local church believes, teaches, and practices on sponsoring church or benevolence issues had better not be based upon the positions of well known preachers, papers, or colleges, but on the basis of its own independent study and deliberation. Similarly, what a local church believes, teaches, and practices on various issues concerning marriage, divorce, and remarriage had better not be based upon the positions of preeminent preachers, papers, or colleges, but on the basis of its own independent study and deliberation.

Know the Difference Between Contending and Being Contentious

A concrete example illustrates how the previous procedures apply to solving doctrinal problems between brethren that have the potential of affecting their collective action. I once became aware of a congregation that had just arranged for a preacher to come work with them. I had been familiar with this congregation from its inception, and knew them to be interested in the truth wherever it might lead. However, the congregation was composed of Christians who in the vast majority had not been raised as children of God, i.e., they had not been "raised in the church," either universal or local. Thus, while they had quite a practice and reputation of being willing to seriously examine anything proposed for their belief or practice, they had very few human traditions to fall back on.

Within several months after the preacher's arrival, he became convinced that the congregation was involved in collective error, whereupon he preached a sermon or two "lowering the boom" on the congregation. When a significant number jerked back from his approach, he became disgusted with them and left. The whole episode took only two weeks, without the issue he thought so important being extensively taught or deliberated on. This failure to calmly study the issue with the congregation before writing them off is the calamity, regardless of what the doctrinal issue was, or whether or not the preacher had the truth on it. For the purposes of this illustration I could freely admit he was right! Likewise, I have no reason to doubt his sincerity, courage, or even that he did the best he knew how to do.

Incidents like this happen so frequently on so many different issues that the location or specific doctrine is immaterial. So is the fact that a preacher was involved: other Christians do the same.

The congregation was willing to study the issues he had raised, but he gave them no time for study before the eruption took place. They said, "We believe a preacher (and other Christians) must contend for the faith, but we also believe preachers (and other Christians) can be contentious as they propagate what they believe to be the truth. But we're not sure how we can tell the difference between contending for truth and just being contentious." This chapter grew out of wrestling with that distinction, and the following shows the difference.

Let's suppose that I as a preacher begin working with a congregation that practices something I no longer believe is scriptural. What the issue is or whether my position is right or wrong is immaterial to how the issue should be handled. If I no longer believe the practice can be substantiated by the Bible (and I could be wrong), and it affects our collective action, then it is a doctrinal difference that falls into the scope of this chapter.

We have two ways to approach the problem: First, after studying with them in Bible classes and sermons to let them get to know me, I would pick an opportune time to bring the matter to the attention of the congregation. It would not be the first thing I "tackled" after our working relationship had begun. When I finally did bring it to their attention, I would suggest we study the matter in a completely open forum, with plenty of time for all to consider and deliberate on the matter.

All would be urged to refrain from misrepresenting those who differed with them and impugning their motives. If we could all conduct ourselves in this way, either they would teach me, or I would teach them. More likely, we would teach each other, and perhaps we would collectively come to an entirely different conclusion from what any of us now have, as a result of our deliberate study together.

Another approach, much more popular it seems, would be for me to conduct myself in the following manner. Soon after commencing work with this congregation, I could think that specific doctrinal difference is the first problem I've got to work. If we think we're saved by perfect doctrinal correctness, we would have to come to the conclusion if the congregation differs with God on this single point, those Christians will be lost.

Further, we could think you shouldn't have any problems between "lions and lambs," assume the restoration movement is over, and have creed rehearsals instead of Bible studies. If anyone differs with us, we can become defensive. We can think we've got to agree on everything or we can't be in fellowship.

We can misrepresent those who differ with us, impugn their motives, and try to impress brotherhood, paper, or college positions. We might insist our position is what we've always believed, and imply the weakness of anyone who says study is needed. We can fail to learn the others' arguments, blast them, suppress the study, and press for an immediate answer with no time for study.

Surely we can see that if we conduct ourselves in this way, we won't work together very long, regardless of what the issue is, or what the truth of the matter is. We'll part company, and the doctrinal question will not have received the attention it deserved. *It's the difference between contending for the faith as God commands and dividing churches through the contentiousness of men.*

What God Always Has Required

In conclusion, all through His dealings with His people, God always has deplored the person who mistreated others while maintaining doctrinal strictness and rigorous obedience. For example, in Isa. 1.11-17, we read:

> What are your multiplied sacrifices to Me? says the Lord. I have had enough of burnt offerings of rams, and the fat of fed cattle, and I take no pleasure in the blood of bulls, lamb, or goats. When you come to appear before Me,

> who requires of you this trampling of My courts? Bring your worthless offerings no longer. Incense is an abomination to Me. New moon and sabbath, the calling of assemblies—I cannot endure iniquity and the solemn assembly. I hate your new moon festivals and your appointed feasts. They have become a burden to Me. I am weary of bearing them. So when you spread out your hands in prayer, I will hide My eyes from you, yes, even though you multiply prayers, I will not listen. Your hands are covered with blood. Wash yourselves, make yourselves clean; remove the evil of your deeds from My sight. Cease to do evil, learn to do good; seek justice, reprove the ruthless; defend the orphan, plead for the widow.

Although the sacrifices, feasts, offerings, prayers, etc. were all commanded in the Law of Moses, the way Jews treated one another was also just as important. This is not to discount the importance of true doctrine, but true doctrine will not let us diminish the importance of how God's people treat each other, either.

In Jer. 9.23-24, we read:

> Thus says the Lord, Let not a wise man boast of his wisdom, and let not the mighty man boast of his might, let not a rich man boast of his riches; but let him who boasts boast of this, that he understands and knows Me, that I am the Lord who exercises lovingkindness, justice, and righteousness on earth; for I delight in these things, declares the Lord.

To know God is, and always has been, to pay attention to lovingkindness, justice, and righteousness. When the Israelites placed emphasis on structured, ritualistic laws, and neglected their responsibilities to treat each other justly and compassionately, they were doomed. This was their problem with Jesus. We exhibit the same shortcoming, when we place emphasis on the Lord's Supper, attendance, and prayer to the neglect of dealing justly, mercifully, and faithfully with our brethren.

In Ps. 135.15-18, we have the following condemnation of idolatry:

> The idols of the nations are but silver and gold, the work of man's hands. They have mouths, but they do not speak; they have eyes, but they do not see; they have ears, but they do not hear; nor is there any breath at all in their mouths. Those who make them will be like them, yes, everyone who trusts in them.

This is one of several statements in the Old Testament that teaches one great consequence of idolatry—those who worship idols become like them. Thus, the idolaters in Corinth made for themselves gods of harlotry; the Corinthians were harlots themselves. The same principle applies to us—we'll become like the object of our worship, even if it's the true God, as Jesus said in Lk. 6.40:

> ...but every one when he is perfected shall be as his teacher.

As we grow in our confidence in God, and appreciate He gives us time to study, He doesn't save us because we are perfectly doctrinally correct, He doesn't hasten to write us off, impugn our motives, etc. Then we will be able to do the same with brethren we differ with. If we don't, then we make the same mistake as the Jews of old.

As we come into the New Testament, in Mt. 7.12, Jesus said:

> All things therefore whatsoever ye would that men should do unto you, even so do ye also unto them: for this is the law and the prophets.

Yet the Jews of Jesus' day missed the very emphasis of the law and the prophets, thinking they could be careful about doctrinal matters while mistreating their brethren. For example, in Mt. 9.10-13, the Pharisees, who were experts at mistreating those they differed with, grumbled at Jesus' dealings with tax collectors and sinners:

> And it came to pass, as he sat at meat in the house, behold, many publicans and sinners came and sat down with Jesus and his disciples. And when the Pharisees saw it, they said unto his disciples, Why eateth your Teacher with the publicans and sinners? But when he heard it, he said, They that are whole have no need of a physician, but they that are sick. *but go ye and learn what this meaneth, I desire mercy, and not sacrifice:* for I came not to call the righteous, but sinners.

Didn't Jesus depreciate the Jews' emphasis on strict obedience while at the same time treating their own brethren unmercifully?

In Mk. 12.28-34, we read of a scribe who apparently knew this lesson:

> And one of the scribes came, and heard them questioning together, and knowing that he had answered them well, asked him, What commandment is the first of all? Jesus answered, The first is, Hear, O Israel; The Lord our God, the Lord is one: and thou shalt love the Lord thy God with all thy heart, and with all thy soul, and with all thy mind, and with all thy strength. The second is this, Thou shalt love thy neighbor as thyself. There is none other commandment greater than these. And the scribe said unto him, Of a truth, Teacher, thou hast well said that he is one; and there is none other but he: and to love him with all the heart, and with the understanding, *and with all the strength, and to love his neighbor as himself, is much more than all whole burnt-offerings and sacrifices.* And when Jesus saw that he answered discreetly, he said unto him, Thou art not far from the kingdom of God. And no man after that durst ask him any question.

We close this section by noticing Eph. 4.29-5.2:

> Let no corrupt speech proceed out of your mouth, but such as is good for edifying as the need may be, that it may give grace to them that hear...Let all bitterness, and wrath, and anger, and clamor, and railing, be put away

> from you, with all malice: and be ye kind one to another, tenderhearted, forgiving each other, even as God also in Christ forgave you.

For a fuller discussion of what God always has required, see Chapter 1, "Formality vs. Humanity: When God Despises Scriptural Worship," in the author's book *Christians, Churches, and Controversy: Navigating Doctrinal and Personal Clashes.*

Chapter 7

Applications

In this chapter we apply what we've learned about the nature of the Lord's church to a number of doctrinal questions. As suggested in the Introduction to this volume, our basic conclusions will drastically affect many important topics related to the New Testament way of Christ. We now want to address ourselves to a variety of topics, and see how a non-denominational view of the Lord's church helps resolve an assortment of significant doctrinal issues.

How Our Language Should Change

In Chapter 1, we remarked that our use of words is important because words are vehicles of ideas. In I Tim. 6.3, Paul urged Timothy to hold fast to "sound [healthy—SGD] words, even the words of our Lord Jesus Christ." Healthy language depicts healthy concepts concerning the nature of the church of our Lord.

Recently a news report told of a small Roman Catholic group that had confiscated a church building over some difference with the hierarchy of that denomination (collective of congregations). A high-ranking Catholic spokesman told the news services, "That building doesn't belong to the people, but to the church." Since a church is a group of people, this language is not healthy. It depicts a concept of the people of God that contradicts Scripture. We need to take care we do not show by our language that we have that same concept.

"Do You Think You're the Only Ones Who Will Be Saved?"

The question, "Well, do you think you are the only ones who will be saved?" is often hurled at many who are interested in being just Christians, without loyalty to a denominational creed or organization. Those who ask this question need to understand that those interested in the nondenominational religion of Jesus do not avoid denominationalism because they consider themselves better than people in denominations. It's because they think *serving God as Christ revealed is better than any human design can be.*

Consider this question in light of the two uses of the word "church" in reference to the people of God in the New Testament. First, take the church universal. When someone asks, "Do you think you are the only ones who will be saved?", if they speak of the universal church, *we all* understand that only those in the universal church will be saved, and certainly no one else. The universal church, by definition, is the collection of all those in fellowship with God. It is the saved. Of course, *everyone* in the religious realm, whether he's in a denomination, a cult, a non-denominational church, or whatever, understands just one universal church exists, and it consists of all the saved. But the universal church is not the viewpoint that the question is asked from, for *all* agree that the universal church is all the saved, and one must be in that church to enjoy fellowship with God.

On the other hand, the New Testament uses the term "church" in a local sense. If the question, "Do you believe you're the only ones who will be saved?" is asked in that sense, then *no one* believes that only those in one local church will be saved.

Thus, if we use the term church the only two ways it's used of the people of God in the New Testament, the question becomes meaningless. However, the question is usually asked in a third, non-scriptural sense, the denominational sense: "Do you think only your denomination will be saved?" Of course, if we are determined to be just Christians, serving Christ in strictly a non-denominational capacity, in name, organization, or concept, we can see the question doesn't even include "just Christians." The question is asked in the only sense those with only a denominational concept know how to ask it. Perhaps all they've ever known is a universal church composed of local churches, yet it's a sense that is never used in the New Testament. This will help us turn a prejudicial question into a teaching opportunity. To answer the question correctly, we would say, *"Only those in Christ, and who live by perfect faith in Him, will be saved."*

"I'm a Methodist, What Are You?"—"Church of Christ"

Occasionally a persons says, "I'm a Methodist, what are you?" To which you might reply, "Church of Christ." If you've said this, it's not true. No, you're not. You're not church of Christ. You're not one church of Christ. You're not a church of Christ. You're not the church of Christ. You may be a Christian, but if you speak this way, your speech well may betray a denominational concept of the body of Christ.

Why not say, "I'm a Christian"? Your questioner may ask, "What kind?" But if he does, make a teaching opportunity of the situation and say, "The kind you read about in the Bible." In other words, don't perpetuate the denominational misconception!

"What Does the Church of Christ Teach?"

Once in awhile, someone asks, "The Lutheran Church teaches such-and-such; what does the church of Christ teach?" The universal church doesn't teach anything collectively. Since the time of the apostles, it has had no spokesman to tell what the universal church teaches. On the other hand, no one really cares what the position of a local church is on a specific point. Most often, this question comes from a person who thinks of the body of Christ as a coalition of churches, just like the denomination he may belong to. Again, don't perpetuate the denominational concept.

"Church of Christ" as an Adjective

Just about every time the term church of Christ is used as an adjective, it's used in a denominational sense. If one is said to be a "church of Christ preacher," no one really believes he preaches as an agent of the universal church, for the universal church has no spokesman. No one seems to care if he speaks only for a local church. Most likely, the thought is that he preaches for a coalition of congregations, a thoroughgoing denominational concept.

Years ago, in an announcement concerning a debate between a preacher in a Sabbatarian denomination and myself, it was said he represented the Seventh-day Church of God, and I represented the Church of Christ. Although neither of us represented the universal church, he represented a denominational coalition of congregations. Sad to say, the language of the announcement said I did, too! Even worse, the concept in my mind was denominational as well, as I didn't consider myself as representing just a local congregation of Christians.

The same thing could be said of "church of Christ" songbooks, colleges, etc. Those aren't imagined as belonging to just a local church, and no one believes they belong to the universal church, including both living and dead saints. They are generally thought of as belonging to a coalition of congregations.

These remarks are not given merely to be picky. We need to appreciate the fact that a great number of people are looking for just simple nondenominational service of God. They may not realize that many others try to be just Christians without the denominational teachings, organization, allegiance, creeds, etc. Let's not hide a nondenominational approach from them with denominational concepts and language. As the maiden told Peter as he stood warming his hands by the fire, "The way you talk gives you away" (Mt. 26.73).

"Unfaithful to the Church," "Quitting the Church," Etc.

While one may not be dependable as far as a local group of Christians is concerned, unfaithfulness to the church isn't nearly as critical as unfaithfulness to the Lord. Likewise, quitting the local company of Christians may be serious; however, quitting the Lord is what is usually referred to in this way. Similarly, we say a person "left the church" when, more seriously, he may have abandoned his allegiance to the Lord. We urge a person to "come back to the church," when he really needs to come back to the Lord, and live a life of allegiance to Him.

We have sometimes said, "The church is the most important thing in the world." The church is composed of people. Surely we do not consider ourselves to be more significant than the Lord. He, and our glorification of Him through our faithful obedience is more important than people.

When one sins, we sometimes say he's brought reproach upon the church, and perhaps he has. However, isn't the reproach he's brought upon his Lord much more significant?

Sometimes in our resistance to human institutions that men devise to do various works in service to God, we say we should resist them "so the church will get the glory." If the church is God's people, do we really want them to get the glory? The whole concept of our service of God is based upon the fact that God should be glorified, not men (Eph. 3.21). Surely, we can see that such language betrays a great interest in "churchianity," not the way of righteousness.

How to Teach People in the World

Chapter 9 shows in detail how to teach the gospel to those outside of Christ. In this section, we will merely show some shortcomings of ways traditionally used to teach the gospel.

Many times, our attempts to teach the gospel revolve around the idea, *How to Find the Right Church.* We cannot use the word *church* as God does in the Bible and continue to use such an approach. If by *the right church* we mean the universal church, as we saw in Chapter 2, the universal church cannot be found. It has no address, phone number, area code, or zip code. It has no earthly headquarters or collective work. A person cannot do anything to *find* the universal church.

If by *the right church* we mean a local church, then not just one *right one* exists. Many local churches pleased God in the New Testament, and the same is true now. *The local church we are joined to does not match the universal church as far as its founder, date of beginning, city of beginning, and terms of admission are concerned.*

Rather than suggesting to someone that he needs to find the right church, using the term in the universal sense, and then showing him a local church, or even more confusing, a mixture of characteristics of local churches and the universal church, why not approach him with the concept of fellowship? In other words, why not teach the person what he needs to do (1) to be in fellowship with God, and then (2) to be in fellowship with other Christians? This approach will do a better job of converting the individual to Christ instead of to an organization. And it will also help him understand more fully his responsibilities in a local church.

Church Discipline

Suppose congregation A, trying to follow the teaching of Christ and His apostles, withdraws fellowship from one of its members, either for impenitent sin, such as the fornication of I Corinthians 5, or for being "disorderly," as per II Thessalonians 3. If this individual approaches congregation B, seeking to "join himself to it," what should congregation B do? Is the action of the first binding on the second and "on all other faithful churches in the area"?

Our concept of the universal church will affect the way we answer this question. In the denominational view (that many churches make up a denomination), the disciplinary action of one of the congregations is generally binding upon all.

Some members of the body of Christ view the universal church as a collection of "faithful congregations." They also would think that the disciplinary action of one of those churches would be binding upon all. So if a congregation withdraws from a person, all the other congregations would treat the individual as if they had withdrawn from him themselves.

However, if we understand the body of Christ is composed of individual Christians rather than churches, then we will understand that congregation A does not control the fellowship of congregation B; only congregation B can do that. It is entirely congregation B's affair as to what they do with this prospective member. Just the fact he has been withdrawn from by another church is not binding on them. They must investigate the situation as best they can, probably asking for information from congregation A, and then make their own decision whether they will accept the person into their fellowship.

As a result of their investigation, they might come to the conclusion that someone like Diotrophes in the book of III John had actually kicked this Christian out without just cause. In that case, they would be honored to have him in their fellowship. They might even have him serve as an elder!

On the other hand, their investigation might show that this "disfellowshipped" person was like the impenitent fornicator in I Corinthians 5, and they should refuse to accept him into their fellowship. It's not as easy as just finding out whether the individual has been withdrawn from by "another faithful congregation." It wasn't in the New Testament, and it's not now.

Sometimes congregation B can't obtain enough facts from congregation A to make a just decision. If in this case congregation B decides to accept the individual into their midst, that is congregation B's business. We still ought to believe in the autonomy of the local church. If congregation B makes a mistake, and they will from time to time, wish them well, or at least realize the two congregations do not share fellowship with each other.

The question is sometimes asked, "When a church withdraws from someone, should they notify other congregations of their action?" The overriding principle should be for any congregation involved to act in the best interest of the person withdrawn from, rather than in the interest of an alignment of congregations. If congregation A wants to notify other churches to enable them to act in the best interest of the sinner, they might do so, understanding that their withdrawal is not binding upon other churches. Congregations that receive such information should use it justly, realizing what another church does should not necessarily affect their fellowship. Each congregation in the New Testament controlled its own fellowship, and each should do so now.

Another question along this line is, "What is the effect when you withdraw fellowship from someone who the congregation has no contact with?" For example, at one time this individual was a member of the congregation, then he drifted off and does not attend or work. What effect does it have to withdraw fellowship from someone who has no further contact with the congregation?

Withdrawing fellowship, or at least formally recognizing fellowship no longer exists, would have two good effects. The first would benefit the drifter. If an individual drifts off and gets involved in sin, then *for his protection*, we need to recognize and announce that he is no longer in fellowship with us. If he drifted out, he might have the concept he can drift right back in. If no disciplinary action is taken, and five or six years go by, he may have the mistaken concept that he can drift right back in. Then no real working relationship with its bonds of confidence will exist with the congregation. Thus, for his best interest and protection, both he and the congregation need to have early formal communication.

Second, whether or not it turns out for his best interest, some communication needs to take place in the best interest of the congregation. For example, somebody may drift off and lose contact with the congregation and rob a bank. We might read in the paper, "So-and-so of the such-and-such church robs local bank." This has actually happened.

In addition, many people check into hospitals and put down their affiliation with a local church they have never attended, or perhaps only visited one or two times. For the protection of the congregation and the individual Christian, the members need a clear understanding of exactly who is in the local church.

Sometimes the concept of fellowship has been so loose that some people "on the rolls" haven't attended or worked with the congregation for years. If they cannot be located or persuaded to establish a real working relationship with the local group, why not recognize them for what they are—visitors! If someone wonders what the authority is for this practice, Paul's command to "put away falsehood and speak the truth in love" in Eph. 4.25 suffices. It is a falsehood to call them members when they're not, and it is the truth to call them what they are or have been—visitors. While we appreciate visitors, we owe them no collective responsibility in discipline, nor do we expect them to contribute to our collective work since they have not "joined" themselves to us. Chapter 8, "Dealing with the Uncommitted," discusses these matters in detail.

Church Cooperation—Sponsoring Churches

We now want to apply our understanding of the relationship between the universal church and local churches to the sponsoring-church concept of cooperation between congregations. Churches in the New Testament cooperated in evangelism (II Cor. 11.8, where several churches supported Paul, and Phil. 4.15-16, where one church supported Paul) and in benevolence (I Cor. 16.1-3, where several churches sent benevolence to needy saints in Jerusalem). In all the examples of church cooperation in the New Testament, there never was any organization larger than a local church. There never was collective action of churches, i.e., common action of churches with common oversight and pooling of resources.

However, among churches of Christ (congregations of Christians historically striving to have no denominational allegiance, doctrines, organization, etc), in the 1950s the sponsoring-church form of cooperation became popular. This arrangement entails many churches sending money to one sponsoring church, whose elders then oversaw the entire project.

Some objected this was activating the church universal. From our study of the nature of the church, we can see the universal church is active, it's just not collective action! Collective action of congregations is the very essence of denominationalism. It fits the classic definition of denominationalism, and no surprise, as many people in local congregations thought of themselves in denominational terms at the time. Concerning their Herald of Truth (a network radio program, then later a television broadcast) cooperative effort, the elders of the Fifth and Highland Church of Christ in Abilene, Texas, (the sponsoring church) issued a statement that said:

> We believe the new "Herald of Truth" series will be the most fruitful effort of our great brotherhood. (*The Willis-Inman Debate* [Louisville, KY: Truth Magazine, 1968], p. 75.)

These elders and the participating churches thought of a coalition of churches functioning collectively, which is denominational action. Indeed, it was essentially denominational action. William Banowsky, a prominent preacher among churches of Christ, wrote about the development of the sponsoring church concept at Abilene Christian College (as it was then called), and explained how the Abilene Christian College Lectureship participants arrived at the concept:

> The lecturers came to desire a missionary procedure which would more effectively involve the hundreds of small congregations. But they also sought a program whose scope would be more far-reaching than even the best, but isolated efforts of any one large congregation. They could not resist the temptation to shop about and contrast their plight with the obvious strong points in denominational machinery. Thus, they sought for some practical, scriptural means of *brotherhood-wide co-ordination* without creating an agency for brotherhood-wide control [emphasis mine—SGD]. (William S. Banowsky, *The Mirror of a Movement* [Dallas, TX: Christian Publishing Co., 1965], p. 313.)

They wanted denominational machinery, and they got it! One other statement concerning the sponsoring church concept is from G. C. Brewer, a highly respected preacher among churches of Christ:

> When the "Herald of Truth" broadcast of Abilene, Texas was proposed, I told the brethren who were soliciting help for the venture that it would put the Lord's people before the world as a denomination, and, this program would be the "church of Christ Hour" just as distinctly as we have the "Catholic Hour" or the "Lutheran Hour." The brethren said they would avoid this by calling it the "Herald of Truth." This they have done but they have not avoided the error that I feared. (G. C. Brewer, *Autobiography of G. C. Brewer* [Murfreesboro, TN: DeHoff Publications, 1957], p. 139.)

Brewer was right. The thing that made the sponsoring church concept denominational was not the name, but rather the collective congregational action. Those brethren thought of the Lord's church in denominational terms. Many of those who opposed their concept also thought in denominational terms too, and some of us still do, as the problem did not end there.

When an alignment of congregations wanted to support the sponsoring-church concept, then an alignment of congregations developed in the minds of many to resist the first one. *If alignments of congregations with common oversight was denominational in nature, collective opposition by congregations is denominational action itself. As a matter of fact, if common oversight was supplied practically by preachers, papers, or colleges who thought in terms of an alignment of congregations, then those opposed to the sponsoring church concept were involved in the very thing they opposed, that is, denominational action.*

Rather than being involved in any alignment of congregations of whatever sort, I want to be just a Christian. I want to be in fellowship with Christ and other Christians (both alive and dead) in the universal church, and I want to be in fellowship with other Christians in a local church that I've "joined." This is now the extent of my fellowship. I have no association or fellowship with an alignment of congregations that are involved in sponsoring churches, nor with an alignment of congregations that are opposed to the concept. I no longer belong to a "camp." After all, which camp were the Ephesian Christians in? The Philippian church? The seven churches of Asia? If they could be just Christians without allegiance to a coalition of other congregations, so can we! The sponsoring church concept, both pro and con, is discussed further in Appendices 6 and 7.

Does the Universal Church Have Collective Work?

The question is asked, "Are you sure the universal church doesn't have a work? What about when some of us from different congregations teach our friends together outside the work of a local congregation, or encourage weak and discouraged Christians? Isn't that work taking place in the universal church?"

Of course, the universal church works. When Christians from the same local church or different local churches work together, certainly they function together in the universal church. However, the universal church does no *collective* work, that is, where resources are pooled with common action and oversight. Collective oversight and pooling of resources are missing in the work of the universal church.

As stated in Chapter 1, just because you have one or more elements of a collective acting, that does not imply the collective acts. When one or two cows act, the herd does not act. When two or three quail act in concert, the covey does not act. When ten or twelve soldiers do something together, the troop does not act, unless the overseer of the troop has authorized the action.

The neighborhood I live in is a unit, it is a recognizable located entity. The people are , yet my neighborhood is not a working unit. It takes no action as a unit. It might, but it does not.

Similarly, when two Christians, Tom and Dick, together do something in their service of Christ, two Christians function in the universal church. But they are not the universal church functioning collectively. No collective oversight couples the two, nor is there collective pooling of resources. Appendix 6, "Are There Examples of Denominational Action in the New Testament?" deals with several arguments that allege that denominational action can be found in the New Testament.

Attitudes Toward Brethren with Whom We Differ

Our non-denominational views of the body of Christ can affect our attitudes toward brethren we have doctrinal differences with. First, consider the case of doctrinal differences with brethren in the same local church where we are members. As we pointed out in our discussion of the relationship of the universal church to the local church, Tom, Dick, and Harry don't have to agree on everything to enjoy fellowship with each other in a local congregation. In fact, in no instance will they agree on everything in the teaching of Christ. Even if they were to do so, when a new Christian comes along, he won't agree with them on everything in the teaching of Christ. What is required for their fellowship in the local church is agreement on what *they do collectively.*

When differences on a doctrinal point arise, once it is determined doctrinal differences do not affect their collective action, they can maintain the proper attitudes toward each other while they study the issue and endeavor to come to an agreement on it. Again, the only thing that will require their fellowship to be broken is a doctrinal difference where one or more come to the conclusion that God *requires them* to do something others believe *they cannot* do and still please Christ.

Next, consider our attitudes toward brethren we differ with who are members in other local churches. The only way doctrinal differences could affect us would be in the universal church, where they might prevent our working together outside a local church. As far as the local churches are concerned, the congregations are not in fellowship with each other anyway. Regardless of how the doctrinal issue is resolved, it won't affect congregational fellowship anyway. This does not mean we don't study the issue, for we should. This doesn't mean the doctrinal issue is not important, for it well may be. It does mean our congregational fellowship will not be affected, because our fellowship in the body of Christ is not between congregations.

If, however, we view the body of Christ as composed of congregations, doctrinal differences will affect our congregational fellowship, and alignments of congregations will surely result. Our opposition to this view of the body of Christ is not just that it leads to alignments of churches, but rather that it is not in the teaching of Christ. The energy expended in maintaining these alignments of churches is squandered in areas where the Lord never intended His people to be involved. Wasting energy detracts from our scriptural efforts in which the Lord does intend our energy to be expended.

Extend this application one more step and consider an effect on the practice of debating. I have participated in several debates of religious topics, and may do so again. I believe debates can be quite an effective way of teaching. However, not viewing the body of Christ as an alignment of "faithful churches" has affected my view of the criterion of success.

Historically, many have viewed a successful debate as one where one local church "goes over to the other side" and begins practicing what the opposing church believes. The two congregations may then be thought to be in fellowship. However, if in truth congregations are not in fellowship, whether they agree or differ on the doctrine in debate, intercongregational fellowship will not be the criterion of success.

Suppose a sponsoring church calls me saying, "Sam, we hear you are opposed to the sponsoring church concept. Would you come and present a lesson on what you think is wrong with it?" I tell them I will. They then ask, "Would you mind if we ask you some questions when you get through?" I say no. They ask, "Would you mind if we had someone respond to your answers?" No, that's their privilege. "Would you mind debating it where we have equal time?" they ask. Again the answer would be no. When we had the debate, as I went home, the criterion of success would not be whether the congregation had changed to my position so I could now enjoy fellowship with the congregation, for I will not be in fellowship whether or not they agree. If, as a result of the debate, we agree on the issue, the two congregations will not be in fellowship (remember, collective action of congregations is denominational), but as individuals we'll gain fellowship in the universal church. Thus, the debate will have been a success if the participants conducted themselves properly, if the truth was taught effectively, and if fellowship in the universal church was increased. My goal is not to share fellowship with the congregation. My goal, after being in fellowship with God, is to be in fellowship with the congregation to which I am joined, and then with as many Christians in the universal church as possible.

Are Members of Other Congregations Our Brethren?

In Chapter 3 we said our fellowship with all Christians is in the universal church. That is why we are in fellowship with members of other local churches, and not because of a fellowship of congregations. I am asked the above question, "Are Christians in other churches brethren?"

Yes, they are our brethren. Bible writers speak of them in this manner, and so should we. Chapter 3 merely points out that we enjoy fellowship with those brethren in the universal church and not congregationally. If Christians in other congregations are in fellowship with Christ, and I also am, we have obeyed the same gospel, and we have the same Father. We are brethren.

Is It Correct to Speak of "Erring Brethren"?

We have stated several times that non-denominational fellowship is not between congregations. We have also noticed that congregations who do agree on collective matters are no more in fellowship with each other than they are with congregations that do not. Thus, I am asked, "What about brethren in congregations that are involved in work we think is unscriptural? Is it correct to speak of 'erring brethren'?"

Of course erring brethren exist. They did in the New Testament, and they do now. I may not be able to conscientiously participate with brethren in a local church because they err in their action. They may do it ignorantly, uncaringly, or rebelliously, but they do things I can't do with them.

I can share fellowship with other individuals who may believe those collective actions are scriptural, where it doesn't affect our action. If it is not part of our collective action, then I'm not a participant in their sin. I may differ with them about a lot of things, but I can participate with them because our differences aren't part of our collective action. In other words, they do not insist on doing what I cannot do.

Other erring brethren may have the right *actions*, as I view them conscientiously. They do not do anything as far as our collective action is concerned that I cannot go along with. They may do all the right *things*, but err in their *attitudes*. They may be like the Pharisees, doing the right things for the wrong reasons; thus, they are erring brethren. They may have the poorest attitude possible. Should I be in fellowship with them? No. Do those kinds of erring brethren exist? Assuredly.

In summary, I can be a partner with Christians whose actions I can conscientiously and collectively be involved in, and whose apparent attitude is one of faith in Christ. So our fellowship with brethren, like our fellowship with God, ought to be based, to the best of our knowledge, upon the actions and attitudes of brethren.

Along this same line, some ask, "What should be a person's attitude toward Christians who have joined a group that teaches and practices denominational methods of cooperating? If you associate in the same manner as you do with Christians who do not practice these things, do you encourage them to continue what they practice?"

We could broaden this question to include brethren who have joined any local church we could not conscientiously join, whether or not they are involved in denominational machinery. If a Christian of my acquaintance works with a congregation that I conscientiously could not, first, I do not write him off as being unfaithful to God; he may love the Lord more than I do.

Second, I do not automatically view him as in rebellion to God. He is still a brother; if I can, I go, express my concern, and offer to study the matter with him. I encourage him to be sure he has no doubts about what he supports. I remind him that we may participate in other peoples' sin and not even know it just by financially supporting it. I ascertain that he grasps that if we doubt the scripturality of something, we sin to do it even if it's right, for "whatsoever is not of faith is sin" (Rom. 14.23).

I do not give him unreserved support. I try not to give him any inadvertent support. If I have to pull back from him and cannot treat him like everything is all right, I should let him know I regret it, and would like to again be able to support him.

How About Brethren in Congregations Involved in Collective Action We Do Not Believe Is Scriptural?

This question concerns our relationship to brethren who are involved in collective practices we could not sanction. Are they brethren? Assuredly. If they have obeyed the gospel of Christ from a pure heart, they are Christians; they are children of God. Whether they continue to live by faith, I do not know. Whether they practice things that I could not do by faith in Christ, I do know. Whether they are in fellowship with Christ, I do not know.

As we've said before, whether or not they are in agreement with us in doctrine or practice, we do not enjoy fellowship with them on a congregational basis; this concept is strictly denominational. If we are in fellowship with them, it will be in the universal church, not in an alignment of local churches.

How Public Should Confession of Sin Be?

The question of how public confession of sin should be definitely relates to our view of the body of Christ. To answer it, first recall what confession is. "Confession" literally means, "to speak the same thing." When the police extract a confession from a suspect, it means they charge him with a certain crime. If he confesses to the crime, he "says the same thing" the police say, he admits to the charge.

When one confesses sin, he says the same thing God says about the sin, i.e., he acknowledges the sin. If he repents of the sin, he repudiates it.

The purpose of confession is integral to our study of fellowship. The purpose of confession is not to humiliate, but to restore fellowship. When one confesses his sins *to God*, he acknowledges them *to God* for the purpose of restoring his fellowship *with God*. If one confesses his sins to other *people*, it ought to be to restore his fellowship with *them*. Confession communicates to people with whom your fellowship has been broken that you have changed your mind and want to work with them in the way you once did.

Understanding what confession accomplishes makes it easy to determine how widely sin should be confessed. It should be confessed as widely as it affects our fellowship.

If you and I are on a hike and I sin, but only you and God know of the sin, then the only fellowship that sin affects is my fellowship with you and God. If I am impenitent about the sin, you will have to pull back from me. You can't treat me as if everything is all right, and God won't either.

If you and I work in the same local church, and you testify about my private sin to the church, on the basis of the testimony of only one witness, the church will not be able to make a just decision. Both in the Old and New Testaments, God has always required the testimony of two or more witnesses before punishment could be executed (Dt. 17.6, Mt. 18.16, II Cor. 13.1, I Tim. 5.19). Thus, on the basis of only one witness my fellowship with them will not be affected. When I publicly deny my private sin, then I become guilty of another sin, that of lying to the whole church. Now if I want to make things right, I will have to go to the whole church to do so.

On the other hand, if I commit some open sin, i.e., that is known by all the church, then other individuals are involved. It affects my fellowship with all of them. To restore our fellowship, I not only need to confess my sin to God, but also to my brethren.

A confession needs to be made that will enable all I am in local fellowship with to know I have repudiated my sin, to share fellowship with me. How must the communication be made? Some say, "Public confession in the assembly." Certainly, that would make the necessary communication, but so would calling each of the others, or writing each of them a letter, or discussing it with each one privately. Generally, it is easier just to stand up in the public assembly and communicate to all my brethren at once.

When the impenitent fornicator of I Corinthians 5 finally repented, and made his repentance known to the Corinthian church, exactly how did he do it? Did he walk down the aisle at the conclusion of the service? No one knows. We do know his confession was somehow made as widely as it had affected his fellowship, so fellowship could be restored.

Legalities on Discipline

In Chapter 5, "Fellowship With Other Christians," we discussed the communication that needs to take place between an individual Christian and a congregation of Christians he contemplates joining. It is helpful for the Christian to communicate to the church his beliefs and practices concerning collective action. It is also necessary for the congregation to communicate to those who contemplate joining it the work they are involved in, their goals, and how they presently go about achieving those collective goals.

An example of one way to achieve this is given in Appendix 5, "An Introduction to a Local Church." A main point of this introduction is that a local congregation is not a group of Christians who agree on everything in the Bible, but they are agreed on what they do collectively. They also agree to behave themselves toward each other according to Biblical principles in matters they differ on.

The introduction might include (as we have suggested) a description of the congregation:

> This church is an independent local congregation of Christians, i.e., believers who have been baptized into Jesus Christ for the remission of their sins, and who are committed to living by faith in Christ.

In light of recent legal cases involving churches withdrawing fellowship from impenitent members, this communication (and agreement to it by prospective members) might protect a congregation from lawsuits. If one who joins himself to a local church agrees to live by faith in Christ, then it will be easy to show "living by faith in Christ" has a scriptural connection to certain sins along with preventive, restorative, and even punitive discipline regarding impenitent sin. Thus, when one is guilty of impenitent sin, he has already agreed he is subject to disciplinary action when he joined the congregation. This in no way resolves the difficulty that arises when individuals, who claim no longer to be members of a local congregation, are subject to punitive discipline, but it will help in the cases where the person is still a member of a local church.

Is There an Exclusive Proper Name for a Local Church?

Believers in Christ who strive to be just Christians have long been concerned about scriptural names, both for themselves as individual Christians and for the local church. Some have gone so far as to affirm an exclusive proper name for the body of Christ, some saying it must be "church of God" or "church of Christ." The integrity of those brethren we have no reason to call in question, but our study of the nature of the church will have some effects on the way we deal with this question as well.

If we consider the two ways the word "church" is used in the New Testament, we could use "The Church of Christ" or "The Church of God" to talk about the universal church. It is not likely we would call a local church these names, since *many* churches of Christ (Rom. 16.16) and churches of God (I Cor. 1.2) exist. In speaking of a local church, we could say "a Church of Christ" or "a church of God," and use the term as it was used in the New Testament.

Local churches that are insistent on one of these names use neither the definite article "the" or the indefinite article "a," but merely "Church of Christ" or "Church of God." This may reflect that they think of neither the universal church nor a local one, but possibly of some alignment of local churches. The absence of an article is interesting, to say the least. Occasionally, a sign in front of the building of a non-denominational group says, "Christians meet here."

As the maiden told Peter in Mt. 26.73, "The way you talk gives you away" on this subject. Listen to the following words that use a scriptural name (church of Christ) in definitely an unscriptural, denominational sense:

> My childhood was of the strict and straight Church of Christ variety. As a teenager, I was the moral and doctrinal example of Church of Christ orthodoxy. I memorized all the scriptures that are important to the Church of Christ. I mesmerized myself with the Church of Christ doctrines and vigorously defended the Lord's church! I was proud of my religion. I was conscientious and zealous. I chose to go to a Church of Christ college because of my affection for the Church of Christ doctrines. (Wayne Willis, "The Plight of the Church of Christ Liberal," *Mission*, June 1973, pp. 9, 10.)

Reflection on this person's use of "church of Christ" reveals he doesn't use it of the universal church, that scripturally has no college, no collectively set forth doctrines, etc. Nor does he speak of a local church. Rather, he uses the term in a denominational sense, in other words, the doctrines and colleges of a collective of congregations. Thus, we hear of "church of Christ preachers," "church of Christ songbooks," etc. *All similar uses of the term neither speak of the universal church that belongs to Christ nor of a local church, but of an alignment of local churches acting collectively, i.e., a denomination.* This is not to say these folks consider themselves a denomination, nor that they are; but they certainly use the term denominationally.

One church put "The Acts 2:38 Church of Christ" on their building, while another wrote the following:

> The Church of the New Jerusalem—The One John Saw Coming Right Down Out of Heaven. (Talmadge F. McNabb, "The Church with the Right Name," *Sentinel of Truth,* IV, 4, October 1968, cited by Monroe Hawley, *Redigging the Wells* [Abilene, TX: Quality Publications, 1976], p. 135.)

All of which leads us to ask, "Is there an exclusive proper name for the Lord's church?" Were the terms "church of Christ" and "church of God," used in the New Testament, used in the sense of an exclusive proper name, or were they used to show ownership and relationship?

The fact that the Bible uses several different terms shows none of them is exclusive. The term "churches of Christ" is used in the New Testament to speak of people who belong to Christ, who are in Christ in specific locales. So with the term "church of God," whether used universally or locally, the term comprises people who belong to God, not the text of the sign on their building, nor a proper name.

Note these examples: There is "the dog of Sam," "the car of Sam," "the wife of Sam," expressions that are grammatically equivalent to "the church of Christ." Are they exclusive proper names? Not at all. The proper name of "the dog of Sam" may be Fido; the proper name of "the car of Sam" is Honda. The proper name of "the wife of Sam" is Patsy! Dog, car, and wife of Sam are not proper names; they show relationship or ownership. So with the terms in the New Testament.

Some who disagree with this argue, "If we don't call it 'church of Christ,' the traveling brethren won't know who we are!" Is this an argument *for* its use, or *against* its use? By the use of a standardized name, do we seek an affiliation larger than a local church after all? Whether we do or not, the expression can well work against the exclusive use of even Biblical terminology. Many understand the exclusive use of "church of Christ," to align one with congregations we are not in fellowship with, nor would we conscientiously be if we could.

For example, many non-Christians confuse the term with various Pentecostal or "Holiness" churches of Christ, the Church of Christ, Scientist, the Church of Jesus Christ of Latter-day Saints, and the United Church of Christ, which is a denomination that largely denies the verbal inspiration of the Bible, the deity of Christ, the resurrection of Christ from the dead, etc. From these observations, we can see we may not want visitors to know who we are just from our name, if they confuse us with groups that are denominational!

While we appreciate the zeal of those who want to call Bible things by Bible names, the popular terms are not used exclusively, and we should not insist on them. As one writer observed, *"The main problem in speaking about the church is not confusing the church with a building. A far more serious problem is confusing the church with a denomination!"*

Who Can Baptize?

The question arises sometimes as we study with someone who has been baptized into some denomination, "When we teach them to be just Christians, do they need to be re-baptized?" The answer is pertinent to all who would be just Christians without any denominational affiliation, since nearly everyone in the religious world practices *something* they call baptism. Of course, some denominations do not practice baptism at all, rather sprinkling or pouring.

This is the way I approach the question: we have seen in our study that baptism puts us into the universal church. Most of the time, people who have been baptized into a denomination fail to realize the importance of baptism. Though they were baptized, they were not baptized in the name of Christ, that is, by the authority of Christ. They don't have the same knowledge of the purpose of baptism as people in the New Testament had. For example, the penitent believers in Ac. 2.38 recognized that *baptism was for the remission of sins*. Likewise, Jesus taught in Mk. 16.16 that *salvation was obtained through baptism*. Paul taught the Corinthians that baptism put a person into the body of Christ, I Cor. 12.13. Paul knew that *baptism washed away sins*, Ac. 22.16. Peter understood that *baptism saved man*, I Pet. 3.21. The Corinthians understood that *baptism in Christ's name was necessary to be called "Christian,"* I Cor. 1.13. Paul understood *it is at baptism that one enters the new life*, Rom. 6.3-4, and that *baptism is what makes men free from sin* through faith in Christ, Rom. 6.17, Col. 2.12-13. Most people who study the subject of baptism come to the conclusion they didn't understand any of these things about baptism when they were baptized in a denomination. Upon gaining this knowledge they want to be baptized, not to get into any denomination, but to obey Christ and enjoy fellowship with Him.

However, this is not always the case. I remember one gentleman who had listened to me on the radio for several years. As a result of hearing me teach on the subject of baptism, he concluded, "I'm not a Christian; I have never been baptized. This is what I need to do for the remission of my sins."

This man lived across the street from a denominational church. Unaware of the distinction between the way of Christ and man's denominations, he went across the street and asked the preacher to baptize him, not intending to become a member of the preacher's denomination. The preacher agreed to baptize him, but told him their baptistry was being repaired. He asked him to come back in two weeks. The man said, "What do you mean, come back in two weeks? What if I die in the meantime?"

The preacher told him, "Nothing, because baptism has nothing to do with salvation anyway." They argued about baptism for a while, the preacher getting nowhere with this man. Finally, the man allowed the preacher to put him off for two weeks.

Two weeks later, he went back to the preacher. They argued about the significance of baptism some more before the preacher baptized him. Neither of them believed what the other one thought about the subject of baptism.

This man understood the same gospel and obeyed the same gospel all Christians have obeyed. The unusual thing about his case was that he did not agree with the doctrine of the person who baptized him. Normally one agrees with the doctrine of the person who baptizes him. This man believed the truth, and obeyed the truth. He acted by the kind of faith Romans 4 describes, and he obeyed the same gospel those in Romans 6 obeyed.

Who can baptize? Surely, a denominational preacher can baptize. *The Bible doesn't place the emphasis on the faith or the doctrinal correctness of the one who does the baptizing; the Bible places the emphasis on the faith of the one who is baptized.* If we try to guarantee the faith of the person who does the baptizing, then ultimately we will have to trace the validity of everyone's baptism back to the days of the apostles.

The major concern is did the man have saving faith in Christ? He did if his faith led him to obey the gospel, and he therefore is in the universal church. Of course, his responsibility to the Lord was not over, it had just begun. He needed to learn what to look for in a local church, and find a group of Christians he could conscientiously work and worship with, which, I'm glad to report, this man did.

Are There Saved in Denominations?

It is possible some individuals in denominations have heard the gospel of Christ and have obeyed it (with the assistance of someone in a denomination) from the heart fervently, though this is rare. It is rare because most denominations do not tell a believer in Jesus Christ what to do for the remission of his sins so he can enjoy fellowship with God. For example, Baptists teach that a person is saved prior to baptism. Methodists, Lutherans, and Catholics insist that baptism is for little babies who can't believe. If, as has happened, an individual encounters the pure gospel, desires to obey it, and without knowing where all the denominations came from and what they are up to, he enters a denominational building to be baptized, he is a Christian. He is not a Christian because he obeyed denominational doctrine, but because he obeyed the gospel, even though he was just baptized by a denominational preacher.

The previous question related the example of a person who heard how to become just a Christian, wanted to obey the gospel, but he permitted a denominational preacher to delay his obedience. When he was finally baptized by that same preacher, neither one of them believed what the other believed about baptism. This individual obeyed his Lord in baptism and became a Christian.

Suppose though that one joins the denomination. Now he has a problem. Now he participates in denominational practices. He is involved in things outside of his faith in Christ, but ignorantly, and in so doing, he assuredly sins. This is not a problem peculiar to new converts. Older Christians have to contend with the same problem even if they have been Christians for thirty years. As we pointed out in Chapter 4, "Fellowship with God," we're not saved by our sinless obedience, nor by our perfect doctrinal understanding, but by our perfect faith in Christ.

As this man continues to study (after all, he is a disciple, a student), he will learn he cannot participate in the propagation of denominational doctrines and practices that are not in harmony with the doctrine of Christ, and so he will repudiate them entirely. He then will begin to worship with Christians who had no denominational allegiance or attachment whatever.

If our Lord had returned for judgment the day after this man was baptized, the man would have been judged on the basis of whether he was in Christ, and whether he served God with all his heart, soul, and mind. Since Christ did not return that day, what should this man have done? Exactly what he did: question everything that was proposed for his belief (I Thes. 5.21, I Jn. 4.1, Eph. 5.8-10), and serve the Lord with all his heart, soul, and mind. He should resolve that since he had not yet learned all truth, he should examine every facet of his religious practice to see whether he did it by faith in Christ or in men. As a matter of fact, this individual needed to "prove all things" exactly like any new convert who has no attachment to a denominational organization. We all need to live every day by perfect faith in Christ so we can be saved.

Assembling While Traveling

I'm often asked, "Are Christians who are traveling obligated to worship with another congregation they're not in fellowship with?" When I'm traveling I seek a congregation I may assemble with on the first day of the week. I do it to partake of the Lord's Supper, to edify them, and to be edified myself. However, the issue is not what I do, or what I like to do; but the issue is whether the Bible teaches I am *obligated* to assemble with them.

From the study thus far, we understand we're not in fellowship with any congregation we're not *joined* to. We see this in our practice, in that we are not bound to contribute to the work of that congregation, though we could if we so desired. Likewise, we're not bound to participate in their weekly Bible classes, though we could if we wanted to. We're not bound to that congregation in any way. Since we haven't agreed to be in subjection to them in matters of expediency and judgment, we don't have the fellowship with them that we enjoy in the congregation we regularly work with.

In the same sense, my present opinion is that we're not bound to assemble with this congregation and partake of the Lord's Supper with people we're simply not in fellowship with. Again,

I do, and will continue to. The question is whether or not I'm obligated by Christ to do so.

Some will blanch at the suggestion that they are not bound to attend congregations they're not in fellowship with, since in the minds of many, attendance means faithfulness. "Is so-and-so faithful? Sure, he's here every time the doors are open!" To many people, not attending is a sign of unfaithfulness. A significant number of Christians put more energy and resources into worshipping with a congregation they're not joined to than they put into working with the one they are in!

We should be faithful, both to Christ in the universal church and to the brethren we're bound to work with in the local church. How about faithfulness to Christians in a congregation we're not joined to? Some might say faithfulness to Christ demands our faithfulness to other congregations as well. But, how? Why? Does the New Testament even contemplate our relationship to a congregation we're not joined to? I presently believe not.

The only passage that talks about assembling with another congregation is Ac. 20.7, where Paul met with the disciples in Troas on the first day of the week as he passed through on his way to Jerusalem. He did not join that congregation as he did in Jerusalem and Antioch. Yet the apostle had a special relationship with the Troas church (and all others) that no man has today. As an apostle, he functioned as an agent of Christ in the universal church. Thus, in I Corinthians 5, Paul could *command* the church at Corinth to withdraw from an impenitent fornicator. For preachers today to exercise authority in a congregation they aren't joined to is an entirely inappropriate exercise of authority belonging to apostles. In II Cor. 9.28, Paul mentioned his anxiety for all the churches. While modern preachers might have an interest in the welfare of Christians in many local churches, they do not have the responsibility that Paul had in the affairs of local congregations. Obviously, Paul's relationship to Troas isn't parallel to our visiting a local congregation while we're traveling.

When Do Private Sins Become the Church's Concern?

Someone has asked, "In view of your remarks concerning the existence of erring brethren and confession of sins, at what point does the private sin of a member of a local church become 'sin in the camp;' and thus, affect others' fellowship with God even though they do not jointly participate in the sin?"

This is a practical question, and one that is well-related to our subject. The reference to "sin in the camp" comes from Joshua 7, which describes the defeat of Israel at Ai immediately after their great victory at Jericho. Israel was defeated because of "sin in the camp," the sin of the idolater Achan, who was inadvertently harbored by the nation of Israel.

The private sins of a member should become the concern of the church only when they can legitimately be made the church's concern. A time comes when the private sins of a member should not be a concern of the church collectively.

For example, in Mt. 18.15-18, when Jesus gave instructions concerning the handling of personal offenses, He said:

> And if thy brother sin against thee, go, show him his fault between thee and him alone: if he hear thee, thou hast gained thy brother. But if he hear thee not, take with thee one or two more, that at the mouth of two witnesses or three every word may be established. And if he refuse to hear them, tell it unto the church: and if he refuse to hear the church also, let him be unto thee as the Gentile and the publican.

This passage shows there can be a time when private sins are not the legitimate concern of the congregation. It would be wrong for the church to become involved in a matter of personal offense before the one sinned against had tried individually to resolve the matter, first alone, then with witnesses. If in a case where the one sinned against then brought the matter to the church, the church refused to obey Jesus' instructions, then the matter, indeed, would be "sin in the camp." In addition, if a member knew of such irresponsibility on the part of that local church, and he could not aid in its resolution, he would have to disassociate himself from the church rather than participate in their collective sin. This would be "partaking in others' sins" by consenting with their sins, and by improper association.

Conclusion

As stated in the "Introduction" to this volume, our concept of fellowship with God and with other Christians will affect drastically our views on many issues. This chapter has presented brief discussions of a wide spectrum of applications of the basic concepts of fellowship. In the time to come, we are confident that many other applications will manifest themselves.

Chapter 8

Dealing with the Uncommitted

This chapter is not designed to be a complete treatment of the subject of "church discipline." A complete study would discuss the collective action of a local church to *train* its members to live faithfully to Christ and to avoid sinning. It would also consider the *restoration* to faithfulness of those who sin, and proper *punitive action* when they refuse restoration. Instead, this chapter summarizes the Bible's teaching on the subject and then notices how the Bible's concept of the local church and its relationship to the universal church affects some of the "stickier" questions on discipline. It especially deals with Christians who are on the roll, but are uncommitted to working with other members in a local church.

Generally, these more difficult questions concerning church discipline involving uncommitted Christian are a weak area in local churches. Many congregations are ignorant of the Bible's teaching on the subject. Others have been taught what to do, but do not even try to obey. Those who try to solve discipline problems should be commended, because it's certainly not an effort they're involved in for fun. They could have a lot more fun doing something else!

Among churches who know what God says on the subject and strive mightily to obey Him, many are not satisfied. They fear that they are not consistent, fair, or sensitive enough. Hopefully, this chapter will help local churches be more consistent, fair, and sensitive to the needs of Christians who either do not participate wholeheartedly in the work of the local church or who are involved in sin.

A Brief Review of the Bible's Teaching on Church Discipline

Briefly, the Bible teaches about three kinds of discipline or training of Christians in a local church. First, and most important, is *preventive discipline*. Many of the efforts by Christians in local churches are devoted to preventing one another from sinning. Our assembling together to consider and provoke one another unto love and good works (Heb. 10.24-25) and our collective and individual teaching efforts from God's word are conducted for this purpose. The confidence we develop in each other and in God as we strive to serve Him according to His will helps us live faithfully to Christ. *Probably ninety-five percent of a local church's efforts in discipline ought to be in the preventive realm.*

However, times come when preventive efforts are not altogether effective, and members occasionally sin. Then *restorative efforts* are necessary. In Mt. 18.15 Jesus speaks of an individual's restorative efforts with a brother who has sinned against that individual. If the individual's efforts are not sufficiently persuasive, then the church is to get involved in restorative discipline. In Gal. 6.1, Paul instructs the "spiritual" Christians to restore Christians who have sinned. *Thus, approximately four percent of a church's disciplinary efforts ought to be in the restorative realm.*

Finally, when all else has failed, *punitive discipline* seeks to make an *impenitent sinner* ashamed so he will repent. Then his fellowship with God and his brethren can be restored. Paul spoke of this type of discipline concerning the impenitent fornicator in I Corinthians 5 and the impenitent non-workers in II Thes. 3.6. This form of discipline is enacted for the destruction of one's fleshly desires (I Cor. 5.5, Gal. 5.24), for the salvation of his spirit (I Cor. 5.5), that he may be ashamed (II Thes. 3.14), and to cleanse the church of sin (I Cor. 5.7-8). *Perhaps one percent of a church's disciplinary efforts ought to be in the punitive realm.*

In these cases, the discipline that consists of viewing the sinner as a Gentile and publican, that is, one who does not enjoy fellowship with God (Mt. 18.16-17), and turning him over to his master, Satan (I Cor. 5.5). Other Christians are to have no company with him (I Cor. 5.9), and they are to withdraw themselves from him (II Thes. 3.6).

God has blessed His people with all three of these methods of training to keep them as His partners. God gives every Christian the *privilege* of being taught, restored, and withdrawn from before he is recognized as belonging to Satan and no longer enjoys fellowship with God or with a local congregation. In II Cor. 2.9, Paul says a local church's efforts in this realm are the true test of faithfulness to Christ. Any church can teach people what to do to become Christians, how to worship God collectively and individually, have elders, partake of the Lord's Supper appropriately, etc. However, when a church has the faith and courage to obey God in the disciplinary realm, then one can know that church is faithful in all things.

Subjection Cannot Be Forced

In the concluding pages of Chapter 5, "Fellowship with Other Christians," we saw that a local congregation is not a local chapter of a parent organization nor simply one congregation of a coalition of similar congregations. Rather, a local church is a group of Christians who agree on what they do collectively and who are in subjection to one another. This subjection is actually the "glue" that holds them together in spite of many (though not all) doctrinal differences. If the members of a local congregation don't have this subjection to one another, they're not only disobedient to God, but they simply don't enjoy the relationship with each other that God desires.

By its very nature, subjection cannot be forced. Though this may come as a surprise to many husbands, in the marriage relationship, God never told husbands to put their wives in subjection. In Eph. 5.22, He instructed the wives to put *themselves* in subjection unto their own husbands. Since subjection must be voluntary on the part of the wife, the husband should conduct himself toward her so that she confidently wants to submit to him.

Likewise, in the servant-master relationship, Christ didn't instruct Christian masters to put their servants in subjection.

Rather, in Eph. 6.5, He told the servants to be in subjection to their masters.

This seems to be the point of Paul's controversial statement concerning the woman's covering in I Cor. 11.16:

> But if any man seemeth to be contentious, we have no such custom, neither the churches of God.

After all that Paul said about the covering to be worn by Christian women to show subjection in certain circumstances, did Paul say it really wasn't important after all and that the women he was associated with had no custom of wearing a covering? Paul, after teaching the purpose of the covering in those circumstances, said that if anyone wanted to be contentious about a matter of subjection, this custom would be useless. *Paul simply couldn't badger people into subjection. They had to enter into it voluntarily for it to mean anything.* The only apparent exception to this pattern is parents who God instructs to "have their children in subjection" (I Tim. 3.4).

One does not "arrange himself under" others if they must coerce cooperation from him. Along this same line, it was prophesied in Ps. 110.3 that the Messiah's people would offer themselves willingly in the day of His power. Christ does not contemplate His people coercing, badgering, or pestering uncommitted Christians into performing their spiritual service.

God Hates Obedience Motivated by Wrong Attitudes

Many elders, preachers, and dedicated workers have engaged in nearly forcing other Christians to work with them, either by "giving them a job so they'll be faithful," or by continually badgering or pestering them to "be faithful." Thus, it might be good to notice what God thinks of service rendered to Him that is not motivated by voluntary allegiance.

For example, Isa. 1.10-14 contains the following scathing denunciation of Israel, so wicked at this time that God refers to her as Sodom and Gomorrah:

> Hear the word of the Lord, you rulers of Sodom; give ear to the instruction of our God, you people of Gomorrah. What are your multiplied sacrifices to Me? Says the Lord. I have had enough of burnt offerings of rams, and the fat of fed cattle. And I take no pleasure in the blood of bulls, lambs, or goats. When you come to appear before Me, who requires of you this trampling of My courts? Bring your worthless offerings no longer. Their incense is an abomination to Me. New moon and sabbath, the calling of assemblies—I cannot endure iniquity and the solemn assembly. I hate your new moon festivals and your appointed feasts, they have become a burden to Me. I am weary of hearing them.

The Jews offered scriptural sacrifices that were stipulated in the Law of Moses. However, when they failed to offer them with the proper spirit, God spurned the people. Likewise, in Mal. 1.10, during the restoration of the Jews after the Babylonian captivity, they again offered sacrifices to God with improper attitudes:

> Oh that there were one among you who would shut the gates, that you might not uselessly kindle fire on My altar! I am not pleased with you, says the Lord of hosts, nor will I accept an offering from you.

God wished for someone to put a stop to the Jews' worthless sacrifices by closing the gates to the temple! He was weary with their sacrifices, and He would not accept them.

Notice a similar passage in Amos 5.21-22:

> I hate, I reject your festivals, nor do I delight in your solemn assemblies. Even though you offer up to Me burnt offerings and your grain offerings, I will not accept them; and I will not even look at the peace offering of your fatlings.

With these statements of God's aversion toward sacrifices offered with improper motives ringing in our ears, let's contemplate the following questions: Have we badgered people to do something God hates? Have we pestered uncommitted brethren to render service to God He would rather someone would stop? Unquestionably, it's proper to teach and encourage fellow Christians their spiritual responsibilities. It's also possible psychologically to force Christians, who demonstrate no more commitment to do right than a *kamikaze* pilot on his seventh mission. Doesn't God hate coerced obedience?

Can you think of an example when Jesus constrained obedience? Unquestionably, Jesus displayed tremendous patience and compassion in teaching God's will, and in encouraging men to obey it. However, Jesus never begged anyone to do right. He taught them their responsibility, and then He let them accept responsibility for carrying it out. In the case of Judas, Jesus frequently exhorted His betrayer to do right, but He didn't beg Judas not to sin. To the contrary, He said, "What thou doest, do quickly." In other words, Jesus put the ball in Judas' court, and demanded that he play it!

Likewise, in Rev. 22.10-11, Jesus concluded the Revelation by saying:

> And he saith unto me, Seal not up the words of the prophecy of this book: for the time is at hand. He that is unrighteous, let him do unrighteousness still, and he that is filthy, let him be made filthy still: and he that is righteous, let him do righteousness still: and he that is holy, let him be made holy still.

After the story has been told, and every effort to show Christians why they ought to remain faithful even if it costs them their lives (Rev. 2.10), Jesus still leaves Christians the choice of being either unrighteous and filthy, or righteous and holy. Even the Master Himself didn't badger or pester Christians to be faithful to Him.

Thus, we read in Ps. 110.3 (a Messianic psalm) where Jehovah tells the Messiah how true Christians today will act:

> Thy people will volunteer freely in the day of Thy power;

It has always been so. The only service acceptable to God has been that voluntarily offered. God has never accepted service that was coerced and not based upon true allegiance to Him.

Like God and Jesus, we ought not to coerce uncommitted brethren into working with us in a local church. God gives us the responsibility to teach them our mutual accountability toward God and each other in a local church, then let them make their choice. They don't have to work with other Christians. Jesus didn't make them, and we shouldn't either. Let's not squander our energy on the uncommitted so that we become too weary to teach those outside of Christ. As someone said, "Jesus did more with *eleven committed* fishermen in Acts 2 than he did with *five thousand non-committed* fisheaters in John 6." This is good to remember, for Jesus never accomplished anything with people who were not committed to doing right. In Christ, the quality of service and servants is more important than is the quantity.

My experience is that uncommitted Christians generally respond to being told they will not be badgered and pestered into serving Christ with their brethren any longer. If you are determined to continue squandering lots of exhortation, visits, calls, letters, etc., over a number of years, why not see if you can find an example of Christ engaging in such fruitless efforts. You will not find an example like that.

For What Sins Should Fellowship Be Withdrawn?

The first sticky question we wish to address on the subject of church discipline is, "for what sins should a local church withdraw fellowship?" Some argue that we should withdraw only for sins that are specifically named in the Bible. For example, we use I Corinthians 5 as authority for withdrawing from a fornicator and the other sins listed there (covetous, extortioners, idolaters, drunkards, and revilers). Likewise, we use II Thes. 3.6 to withdraw from the disorderly who will not work.

If punitive discipline is limited to these specific sins, a local church could not withdraw from a liar, because lying is not a sin listed in either of these passages. Likewise, a murderer could not be withdrawn from, for the same reason. Likewise, this reasoning exempts a lying murderer.

To carry this argument a little further, if we could use these two passages to withdraw from only the sinners specified, then we could only use I Corinthians 5 to withdraw from one who committed fornication with his father's wife. What about one who committed fornication with his father or with another man's wife? If we can only use II Thes. 3.6 to withdraw from one who acts disorderly and will not work, it would apply only to those who would not work because of false concepts concerning the return of Christ. Those were the disorderly in Thessalonica. Where would we go for specific authority to withdraw from one who is just a sluggard?

These questions and similar cases ought to convince us to take a different look at the point of withdrawal of fellowship. *The man in I Corinthians 5 was not withdrawn from merely because he was a fornicator.* Thousands of Christians have been fornicators and they weren't withdrawn from, nor should they have been. They repented of their fornication! Neither were the idle in II Thessalonians 3 withdrawn from simply because they would not work. *The real reason both of these types were excluded from their collective fellowships was not the specific sins they were guilty of, but because of their impenitent attitudes.* In the case of the fornicator at Corinth, once he repented and repudiated his fornication, he was accepted back into their fellowship (II Corinthians 2).

Any sinful Christian who refuses to repent (when taught and admonished) should be withdrawn from. He demonstrates he has the same attitude of impenitence as these specific cases in the New Testament. The person who will not spurn his sin rends the bonds that hold Christians together in a local congregation. Remember, a local church is Christians who have banded together to work for Christ as they live by faith in Him, and who strive to conduct themselves properly toward one another. One who determines not to repudiate his sin goes back on his promise to live by faith in Christ. As such, he cannot practically share fellowship with the other Christians in the group. Even if they will not exclude him for his impenitence, he is not in fellowship with them. The withdrawal serves to notify him that regretfully they can no longer have the relationship with him that they once enjoyed because of his breaking faith with Christ and them. Hopefully, he will feel ashamed and repudiate his sin.

The Difference Between Withdrawing Fellowship and Recognizing It Does Not Exist

We now address the question of "withdrawing from the withdrawn," i.e., the case of a Christian simply drifting off and ceasing to work or even assemble with other Christians. Hopefully, the working relationship between Christians in the congregation would prevent long delays in attending to these cases. The fact is, even well-meaning churches often allow them to occur. Sometimes after several years have elapsed, a church determines that something needs to be done and attempts to formally "withdraw fellowship" from the person who "forsakes the assembly." Some noble Christians question: "Do we have the authority to withdraw from a person who has already withdrawn himself from the local church?" Others insist that he should be withdrawn from and that the very words "withdraw" or "disfellowship" should be in a letter notifying him of the church's action.

The importance of a Christian assembling with others is covered later, but for now consider another approach to this situation. After ascertaining that the person doesn't even want to be considered a member of the congregation any longer, why not simply notify him that he is no longer recognized as a part of the congregation, for the benefit of both him and the congregation? For his benefit lest he consider his relationship to the local church so meaningless that he can just quit it without notice. Should he later desire to establish a working relationship again, he won't assume that he is still part of the group. For the benefit of the congregation, so that should he commit blatant public sin and bring reproach upon the name of Christ, he won't be identified with the congregation.

Some will certainly object, "Where is the authority in the scriptures for merely recognizing that fellowship no longer exists rather than withdrawing fellowship?" The simple answer is: the authority comes from the command to speak or write the truth on a sheet of paper (Eph. 4.25: "putting away falsehood, speak the truth each man with his neighbor"). In other words, if it is *true* that he is no longer a co-worker, it is all right to *say* that!

The result is the same whether the person who drifted away is withdrawn from or he is simply recognized as no longer working with this group of Christians. The purpose of either action is to obtain consistent treatment of this one by Christians who meet him in public. This way, some won't treat him like he's a faithful Christian, while others shun him completely. Whether or not a church uses the word "disfellowship" in the letter, its desire should be to admonish him to greater faithfulness, and not treat him as though he pleases God.

Five Common Cases of Discipline

Many Christians have submitted questions regarding five common cases of discipline. Any Christian experienced in dealing with disciplinary matters will immediately recognize these cases as ones he has also agonized over before, as have Christians everywhere. Notice first, that the five cases are defined, and then some general observations are made about all of them as a whole. Finally, they are analyzed individually in light of the Bible's concept of a local congregation.

Case Number One: A Weak Uncommitted Christian

What action should the church take in regard to a weak uncommitted Christian who comes only occasionally? Let's assume (1) he does not take part in any church work, (2) he is not rebellious, but is apathetic about spiritual matters, and (3) he does not take any classes.

Case Number Two: A Weak Committed Brother Who Sins

What action should the church take in regard to a weak committed brother who sins, but is willing to work on his problem?

Case Number Three: A Christian Who Quits Attending

What action should the church take in regard to one who quits coming? Let's also assume that when questioned regarding his intentions, he states that he does not wish to be a member any longer.

Case Number Four: A Christian Who Attends Only Sunday Mornings

Should the church take any action on a person who comes only on Sunday morning and is not active in any church work? He does not take any classes or participate in other spiritual work.

Case Number Five: A Christian Who Is Withdrawn From

What association can we have individually with a person who has been withdrawn from? What association can we have with a person who is recognized as no longer being a member of this congregation, and who does not attend another faithful church?

Use of the Word "Weak"

Before discussing these cases, notice how Christians customarily use the word "weak" in these five cases, and then compare that with how the Bible uses the word "weak." We ordinarily use the word "weak" in talking about discipline, and have commonly heard it said, "We don't want to be too harsh on weak Christians; we're supposed to support the weak." While these comments are correct, perhaps we should look at this word "weak" a little closer.

Our translations render three words "weak." First, the word *adunatos* is used for example in Rom. 15.1, "support the weak." Thayer, in his *Greek-English Lexicon of New Testament Words* defines this word as "1. without strength, impotent, 2. impossible." This is a combination of two Greek words, one that means "no" and the other that means "power," hence "no power" or "impossible." This word is used in Ac. 14.8 of the man impotent in his feet. Paul used this same word in Rom. 8.3 when he mentioned what the Law of Moses *could not* do. This same Greek word is used in Heb. 10.4 to speak of what it is *not possible* for the blood of bulls and goats to do. Obviously, from these examples, as well as all occurrences of this word in the Bible, the word translated "weak" in Rom. 15.1 ("support the weak") does not speak of those who *will not*, but those who *cannot*. In other words, "weak" refers to the unable, not the unwilling! A congregation with an invalid in its midst, for example, has one who is *weak*. *Those who are not willing to participate are not weak, they are simply uncommitted.*

The second word translated "weak" is *asthenseo*, used for example in Ac. 20.35 where Paul instructed the Ephesian elders to "support the weak." Thayer defines this word as "to be weak, feeble; universally to be without strength, powerless." To grasp how this word is used, look at Mt. 10.8 where Jesus told the apostles to heal the *sick*, Jn. 5.3 where the word was used of *impotent* folk, and I Cor. 12.22 where Paul spoke of the members of our body that are more *feeble*. This word is used in Rom. 5.6 when Paul said we would be *without strength* had not God sent Christ into the world. Like the previous word, this word refers to the powerless, those who *cannot*, not those who *will not*. It describes the unable, not the unwilling.

The other word translated "weak" in the New Testament (*asthenees*) is closely related to the second. Thayer defines it as "weak, infirm, feeble, unable to achieve anything great...destitute of power among men." To illustrate its meaning, see I Cor. 2.3 ("I was with you in *weakness*"), I Cor. 15.43 (our dead physical body will be "sown in weakness"), Rom. 8.26 that speaks of our *infirmities* in prayer, and Gal. 4.13 that refers to Paul's *infirmity* in the flesh. Again, this word means those who are *powerless* to do a certain thing, not those who *will not* do it?

Certainly, Christians ought to support the *weak* or those who cannot serve in some capacity. However, none of these passages encourage Christians to support those who *will not* serve—the uncommitted.

Extreme Seriousness of Unreliable Attendance

These cases of unreliable attendance at various collective activities of the local church, necessitate that we discuss the importance of Christians assembling together. I frankly admit that although I have done significant teaching on the subject, I'm afraid I haven't appreciated the extreme seriousness of unreliable attendance at those assemblies.

First, reliable attendance is not a sufficient gauge of faithfulness to Christ. Many times we hear the question asked, "Is So-and-So faithful?" to which the reply is often given, "Why sure, he's here every time the doors are open." But is there necessarily any concept of faithfulness to God in this yardstick? Some Christians attend even though they do not want to, perhaps because someone pestered or badgered them into it. Their attendance may be an example of service rendered involuntarily or with improper attitudes so God hates it. Others may attend regularly, but their hearts are corrupt and faithless beyond belief.

Even though reliable attendance at Christian assemblies is not a sufficient gauge of faithfulness, it is an indicator. The lack of reliable attendance by an able Christian is a positive indicator that the Christian is probably not carrying his part of the load in the congregation. It indicates his lack of faithfulness to his brethren whom he has banded together with to work. If he doesn't participate in the assemblies, he likely doesn't participate financially in the work of the congregation. Likewise, he probably doesn't contribute his other abilities and resources to the work of the congregation. Thus, his lack of attendance indicates other, more serious problems.

In Mt. 25.23, in the parable of the talents, Jesus affirms the principle that those who are faithful in small things are faithful in important things; those who are unfaithful in small things will also be unfaithful in important things. In Lk. 16.11 Jesus says, "If therefore ye have not been faithful in the unrighteous mammon, who will commit to your trust the true riches?" Consequently, if a person isn't reliable in the small things, what makes us think he'll be reliable in the big things?

Jesus argues from the less to the greater. Paul makes the same argument concerning elders in I Tim. 3.5: "But if a man knoweth not how to rule his own house, how shall he take care of the church of God?" Paul implies that if a man is not able to rule his own house well, we should not think he would be able to handle the house of God. This principle is universally believed. If a man cannot handle the job of being the superintendent of a small school district, why would we think he could supervise a much larger one? If a man cannot capably coach a high school team, why would anyone think he could lead a college team?

This principle applies in the present case. If a person participates unreliably in the assemblies of the local church, a little thing, he probably won't be reliable in the big things either. For example, he probably will fail to remember the Lord's death as He taught (I Cor. 11.23-25). He will neglect to imitate the apostles (I Cor. 11.1 cf. 11.23). He will probably flag in his responsibility to teach and admonish others (Col. 3.16). He will overlook considering others (Heb. 10.24). He will neglect provoking unto love and good works (Heb. 10.24). He is not in subjection to his brethren (I Pet. 5.5, Eph. 5.21). He declines to grow (I Pet. 2.2). He fails to walk as he has attained (Phil. 3.16). While attendance is a little thing, these common areas of failure are big things. They are, indeed, serious matters!

What Does It Mean to Forsake Our Assembling Together?

Many times when discussing Heb. 10.24-25, the question arises as to what constitutes "not forsaking our own assembling together." The question is generally stated thusly: "How many times must one be absent in order for it to be forsaking?", as though it might be three times in a row or a dozen times per year. Thayer's lexicon defines "forsaking" in terms that are not related to a number of times or a frequency of being absent, but more in terms of an attitude: "to abandon, desert, to leave in straits, leave helpless." The word is used throughout the New Testament not to show the *frequency* of a certain action, but the *attitude behind* the action.

For example, when Jesus asked the Father in Mt. 27.46: "My God, My God why hast Thou forsaken Me?", even though God turned His back on Jesus *only one time*, Jesus was still forsaken. This was not something that would happen three times in a row or a dozen times a year. Jesus was left in the lurch because of the Father's attitude toward the sins of the world that Jesus had taken upon Himself as He was sacrificed as the Lamb of God.

Likewise, in Heb. 13.5, God promises us: "I will never forsake thee." Does this mean He might abandon us twice, but not three times; or perhaps ten times, but not a dozen? Of course not! The point is, God will never leave us in the lurch, not even once. The concept in Heb. 10.24-25 was that some Christians did not appreciate the value of their assembling together. They thought they didn't need the mutual provocation unto love and good works that God ordained take place therein. In the context of Hebrews, the Christians didn't quit assembling because they were tired or just living busy lives. They took a lax attitude toward assembling with their brethren *because of the fear of religious persecution*! The Hebrew writer's emphasis is that even in those circumstances, they took much too casual an attitude. They were not to leave in the lurch brethren they had bound themselves to work with, even to protect their own physical well-being. With these points in mind, let's go back and analyze the five common cases of dealing with uncommitted brethren:

Case Number One: A Weak Uncommitted Christian

What action should the church take in regard to a weak uncommitted Christian who comes only occasionally? Let's assume (1) he does not take part in any church work, (2) he is not rebellious, but is apathetic about spiritual matters, and (3) he does not take any classes.

After discussing the term "weak" as it's used in the scriptures, this question uses the term inconsistently with the scriptural usage. Obviously, the question uses weak in the sense of being uncommitted. Thus, if we're dealing with one who is uncommitted to working with his brethren, we recommend the following course of action:

> (1) Teach the Christian the need to submit to other Christians: that he is bound to work with a group of Christians and to be in subjection to them in realms of opinion (Eph. 5.21, I Pet. 5.5).

(2) Try to help him ascertain any problems that might keep him from being in subjection to this group of Christians.

(3) Urge him to become committed, while realizing subjection cannot be forced upon him. He doesn't have to be in subjection with this group of Christians.

(4) If he refuses to become committed to working with the group, recognize that scriptural fellowship does not exist. Until he commits himself to working with the other Christians, he is simply a "visitor."

(5) Make sure he knows visitors are appreciated, but they are not obligated to contribute either financially or of other resources. Neither is the congregation responsible to him in the matter of collective discipline.

Case Number Two: A Weak Committed Brother Who Sins

What action should the church take in regard to a committed brother who sins but is willing to work on his problem?

Evidently this person is overtaken in a trespass while he's committed to working with a group of Christians, and he also struggles to overcome his sin. In this case, passages like Gal. 6.1, "Brethren, even if a man be overtaken in any trespass, ye who are spiritual, restore such a one in a spirit of gentleness: looking to thyself, lest thou also be tempted," certainly apply.

Case Number Three: A Christian Who Quits Attending

What action should the church take in regard to one who quits coming? Let's also assume that when questioned regarding his intentions, he states he does not wish to be a member any longer.

Obviously, this person is not committed to working with the congregation; he doesn't demonstrate an attitude of subjection. If, after trying to ascertain if some legitimate problem exists that might be solved, he still doesn't wish to be a part of the congregation, acknowledge that he doesn't have to be. Urge him to work with some group of Christians somewhere, wish him well, and let him go.

Case Number Four: A Christian Who Attends Only Sunday Mornings

Should the church take any action toward a person who comes only on Sunday morning and is not active in any church work? He does not take any classes or participate in other spiritual work.

The answer to this question depends on the extent of the congregation's collective endeavor. If coming on Sunday morning is the extent of their activity, then this fellow is as active as any of them and he should probably be commended. If on the other hand, he joined the congregation and bound himself to participate in its collective work, but he is no longer committed to working with them, he no longer has the critical attitude of subjection. He should be urged to develop that attitude if possible. If he can't muster it, the congregation should realize that he's a visitor as per the first case.

Case Number Five: A Christian Who Is Withdrawn From

What association can we have individually with a person who has been withdrawn from? What association can we have with a person who no longer is recognized as a member in this congregation, and who does not attend another faithful church?

This case actually contains two questions. First, if the person has been withdrawn from by this congregation, we should treat him as an alien sinner, only more detached, I Cor. 5.9-13, Mt. 18.17. We should avoid all social contact along with any action that might inadvertently support him in his evil deeds and give him the impression that we thought he still shares fellowship with God. When the opportunity arises, we should admonish him as a brother, II Thes. 3.11-15. Hopefully, our lack of fellowship will cause him to reflect on his impenitence, be ashamed, repudiate his sin, and be restored to fellowship with God and with his brethren.

Second, if the person is no longer recognized as a member but has not been withdrawn from, i.e., "a newly recognized visitor," for example, we should simply treat him as we would other visitors: encourage him to investigate the work of the congregation to make sure he can conscientiously participate without involving himself in something he considers unscriptural. Encourage him to commit himself to working with the other Christians in the congregation if he can conscientiously do so. If he cannot, encourage him to realize that God expects him to work with other Christians in a kindred group, if possible. However, in discipline the congregation has no collective responsibility toward this Christian.

Procedures in Discipline

The Bible teaches that qualified people should be involved in the collective disciplinary efforts of a local congregation. Naturally, if a local church has elders, those elders will take the lead in conducting these efforts, but even then, the Christians they use to help in their efforts should fit the following Biblical description.

Who Should Be Involved in Restorative Discipline?

As far as *individual efforts* are concerned, any Christian can do what he believes to be scriptural concerning discipline, but *collectively*, we should use the efforts of the following people:

(1) *The spiritual*, Gal. 6.1, are commanded to restore Christians who trespass. Thayer says the spiritual person is filled with and governed by the teaching of God, i.e., a Christian mature in knowledge and experience.

(2) Only *Christians whose personal lives are in order* should be used to help restore other Christians, Mt. 7.5, "...cast out first the beam out of thine own eye; and then shalt thou *see clearly* to cast out the mote out of thy brother's eye." If Christians are blinded by their personal sin, they cannot see clearly to help others.

(3) *Bible students* should be used, II Tim. 3.16-17, who can give teaching, reproof, correction, and training in righteousness, rather than advice based upon worldly wisdom.

(4) *Men working toward becoming elders*, Tit. 1.9-11, should be used to further develop their disciplinary skills. It also provides the congregation an occasion to develop confidence in their abilities.

(5) *Men working toward becoming deacons* also should be used, because of qualifications they are developing, I Tim. 3.13.

(6) *Wise persons*, should be used, I Cor. 6.5-6, "What, cannot there be found among you one wise man who shall be able to decide between his brethren...?" Their insights will aid others in avoiding and overcoming spiritual problems.

(7) *Experienced Christians* have developed talents valuable in this realm, Heb. 5.14, "But solid food is for fullgrown men, even those who by reason of use have their senses exercised to discern good and evil."

(8) *Those full of the Spirit and wisdom* were used by early congregations as problem solvers, Ac. 6.1-6.

(9) *Qualified older women*, Tit. 2.3-4, are especially helpful in training the young women. "Train" means "to make one, restore one to his senses; duty; to admonish, to exhort earnestly" (Thayer).

In the absence of elders, a committee of men and women who have the above qualifications can see that discipline is carried out fairly. Prov. 24.6 tells us: "In a multitude of counselors there is wisdom." In the presence of elders, they would be well-advised to use the above-described individuals to assist them in their disciplinary efforts.

In the absence of responsible people taking care of disciplinary matters, people who are babes in Christ and without Bible knowledge or experience often hamper effective disciplinary efforts. Some want to visit sinners twenty times before taking any kind of action. Others think the church is too harsh no matter what it does. Some who volunteer aren't qualified, and others doubt the effectiveness of their exhortations. Others don't follow through until just before they're scheduled to report the results of their efforts, and then report that they couldn't get in touch with the person. As a result, a church often becomes bogged down in disciplinary efforts to the point of perhaps even a three to seven year backlog.

However, such a congregation may have plenty of qualified people to discipline members in the preliminary stages when the person's heart might still be receptive and before matters need to be brought before the whole church. Then these workers can serve as competent witnesses if the problem requires being brought to the attention of the whole church.

Elders should use qualified people to aid them with disciplinary matters to help prevent their becoming worn out as Moses was when he tried to do everything himself as the leader of Israel (Exodus 18.13-23).

Who Should Not Be Involved in Restorative Discipline?

Just as the Bible describes certain people who are qualified to exercise discipline, it excludes others from that work. When unqualified people are used and allowed to make decisions regarding discipline, a congregation loses its ability to deal with sinners in a just, compassionate, and consistent fashion.

(1) *Immature older Christians and new converts*, Heb. 5.12-14, should not be used by the congregation. However, these could express their concern and exhort on an individual basis.

(2) *The wicked* have no right to take God's word in their mouths for the purpose of teaching or reproving others. In Ps. 50.16, God expresses His indignation when sinners quote His Law: "But to the wicked God says, What right have you to tell of My statutes, and to take My covenant in your mouth?"

(3) *Christians who are unlearned, or who are not disciples* (students), may wrest the scriptures to their own destruction and the harm of those they want to help, II Pet. 3.17.

(4) *Members who are involved in sin in their own lives* do not have the ability to justly point out the faults of others, Mt. 7.5. For example, God does not even hear the prayers of men who mistreat their wives (I Pet. 3.7), yet many of these men are used to serve the Lord's Supper, offer public prayers, and exhort known sinners.

When Should Collective Discipline Begin?

Churches shouldn't delay the onset of their restorative efforts until the righteous are disgusted and the sinner leaves of his own accord. The following principles should be used in determining when such efforts should begin:

(1) When it's apparent that an able Christian is not involved in collective activity.

(2) Eccl. 8.11, "Because the sentence against an evil deed is not executed quickly, therefore the hearts of the sons of men among them are given fully to do evil," suggests that discipline must be executed speedily. This will avoid encouraging sinners, Isa. 26.10, because when the wicked are shown favor, they do not learn righteousness. It also avoids discouraging the good, Mt. 24.12, since when lawlessness increases the love of most people grows cold. This is a frequent cause of burnout among preachers and many others when congregations fail to properly exercise corrective discipline.

In the absence of elders, this group of qualified people might meet once or twice a month to ascertain discipline needs quickly and to prevent action from being delayed.

When Should Discipline Matters Be Brought to the Local Church's Attention?

As we've noticed earlier in this study, some sins are not the concern of the church, while others are. This section deals with when disciplinary matters rightly deserve the church's recognition:

(1) Personal offenses should be brought to the attention of the church after two or three witnesses verify the problem as unsolved, Mt. 18.15-17.

(2) In the case of sins that are *not* personal offenses, the church should be made aware after two or three witnesses verify the problem. However, this is not because of Mt. 18.15-18, that deals with personal offenses! The Bible has always demanded a plurality of witnesses to establish a matter. In Jn. 5.31ff, Jesus recognized a need for witnesses regarding His life and referred the Jews back to the Law of Moses. In II Cor. 13.1, Paul affirmed

that every fact is to be confirmed by the testimony of two or three witnesses. In I Tim. 5.19, Paul instructed Timothy to have two or three witnesses to receive an accusation against an elder. In Heb. 10.28, Paul reminds us of the Mosaic Law's requirement for witnesses before someone was punished by death.

SUGGESTION: After the above-mentioned group or the elders verifies that restoration is not possible through their efforts, then the matter should be brought to the whole church. The members of this group can serve as competent witnesses in substantiating matters regarding the sinner.

What Should the Church Do When a Discipline Matter Is Brought to Its Attention?

(1) Determine if repentance has taken place, Mt. 18.21-35.

(2) If it has not, then fellowship should be withdrawn, as per case number five above.

(3) If it has, he should be forgiven, comforted, and our love should be reaffirmed, II Cor. 2.4-11.

Chapter 9

Teaching Others

This chapter presents a concise method of teaching our fellowman the gospel of Christ. It is designed to teach a person the gospel in one sitting, and baptize him into Christ the same evening. Although less time-consuming than filmstrips and multi-session approaches, it is logically organized to effectively and sufficiently teach a person so he can obey the gospel. It follows the approach suggested in earlier chapters: it teaches one how to be in fellowship with God in the universal church, and then teaches him how to find a group of Christians he can be in fellowship with in a local congregation.

The approach consists of three charts that depict a simple three point outline:

Chart One: Allegiance to God

Chart Two: Fellowship with God

Chart Three: Fellowship with Other Christians

I use this method in my personal evangelism, and it has proved very effective. Sitting at the kitchen tables of those I'm studying with, I usually draw the three charts on blank pieces of paper. However, if you aren't sufficiently familiar with the material, you can teach it from a pre-printed leaflet with equal results.

Some have adapted this material to videocassettes, audiocassettes, and public lectures as well. This approach enables one to provide Bible answers to any religious issue the Bible deals with in an orderly, logical manner.

All those involved in the study should read every passage for themselves. This can be done by them taking turns reading aloud from their own Bibles, which involves everyone in the study.

When studying with someone who is not familiar with the location of the books of the Bible, help the student find the books in his own Bible. *It is important that every person read every verse for himself, so that his confidence will be in God through His word rather than in the teacher.*

The teacher introduces each passage by developing the context briefly. He describes who is speaking and to whom the words are addressed. He also encourages each one involved to feel free to inquire about any passage discussed. After all, this is the student's personal study, and he is entitled to ask questions.

The study begins at a point that is ordinarily satisfactory. If the student believes in the existence of God, and has even a mediocre respect for the inspiration of the Bible, this method will result in his learning the simple gospel of Christ with no appeal to denominational creeds, allegiance, or loyalty. The vast majority of the time, a student who finishes the first chart will obey the gospel and become just a Christian. Even though you are confident your student believes in the existence of God, you should still begin at the same point, to impress upon him that you will deal with religious matters consistent only with divine authority. If your student doesn't believe in the existence of God and the inspiration of the Bible, you'll generally know it prior to the time of the study, so that you will be able to prepare even for that eventuality.

If you are unaccustomed to teaching others the gospel, you will probably want to begin teaching this approach just as it appears here. As you gain experience and confidence in your teaching ability, and in the truth of the gospel, you may want to modify this technique to fit your personality, and the personality of the ones you teach.

Regardless of what subject brings about the study session, always began at the same foundation point: the Bible is the final authority in God's dealings with man. I point out to the student that we all realize religion and politics are the most controversial topics in our society today, and that most people try to avoid controversy.

One way to avoid the unpleasantness of controversy in religious discussions is to appeal to a common source of authority, that is, the Bible. I illustrate this by saying that if we were to get into an argument about how long the kitchen table is, or how warm the room is, a number of ways exist to settle these questions. We could agree that since I'm the oldest, or the youngest, or the most handsome, or the ugliest person in the group, we could take my word in the matter. At least we would all be agreed. However, if we were to accept common standards of authority, like a ruler and a thermometer, we could settle all these differences, and we would all be correct!

People can see that the same thing is true in determining God's will in religious matters, and most will tacitly agree that the Bible should be our standard of authority. The purpose of the first chart is to demonstrate this truth in detail. I normally tell the person that I'm confident we won't have any major differences on the first chart. Everybody understands Christians ought to follow the teaching of Christ, just as Buddhists ought to follow the teaching of Buddha.

Chart One: Allegiance to God

As you can see from Figure 12, our allegiance should be to God. I usually say, "Now let's just begin where the Bible begins, that is, the Bible says, 'In the beginning, God...' Now you do believe God exists, don't you?" The vast majority of folks you study with believe in the existence of God, and if they don't, you'll know it and will be prepared to show evidence for the existence of God. Although many unanswerable arguments are available to show that an eternal spiritual being exists who is responsible for the physical creation, the presentation of that evidence is not within the scope of this brief study.

I then discuss how all authority stems from God because God has authority over everything. Even an atheist will admit that "if God exists, He has all authority." God has all authority because He created everything, and everything belongs to Him. Just like I have authority over my things (my car, my Bible), then since

ALLEGIANCE TO GOD

GOD HAS INHERENT AUTHORITY

GOD DELEGATED ALL AUTHORITY TO JESUS

Mt. 28.18; Jn. 12.49

JESUS DELEGATED AUTHORITY TO HIS APOSTLES

Jn. 20.21; Jn. 13.20

THE HOLY SPIRIT GUIDED THE APOSTLES

Jn. 14.26; I Cor. 2.10-13

THE APOSTLES WROTE THE BIBLE

Eph. 3.3-4

WE CANNOT ADD TO, TAKE FROM, OR CHANGE THE BIBLE

II Jn. 9; Rev. 22.18-19; Gal. 1.8

IN THE BIBLE, GOD HAS TOLD US EVERYTHING HE IS GOING TO TELL US

Jude 3:

"the faith" - Gal. 1.11, 23
"once for all" - Heb. 9.26-27
"delivered"

II Pet. 1.3

"all things pertaining to life and godliness"

Figure 12

everything belongs to God, He has inherent authority over everything simply because of who He is.

Jesus Has Delegated Authority: Mt. 28.18; Jn. 12.49

We then want to show that God delegated authority to Jesus. We begin by reading together in Mt. 28.18, where Jesus said to His apostles shortly after His resurrection and just before His ascension into heaven:

> All authority hath been given unto me in heaven and on earth.

It is normally obvious to the student who delegated authority to Jesus, but I always ask them who delegated it. The person usually readily sees that God the Father delegated authority to Jesus. This helps the student realize from the very beginning that even Jesus had divine authority from God for everything He said and did. I emphasize that since Jesus had all authority both in heaven and on earth, He does not lack any authority whatsoever.

The next passage used to demonstrate the fact that Jesus had delegated authority from God is Jn. 12.49, where Jesus spoke to His apostles the night before He died:

> For I spake not from myself: but the Father that sent me, he hath given me a commandment, what I should say, and what I should speak.

Again, Jesus respected divine authority in all His activity. He didn't just do and teach what He wanted, but He always acted with authority from the Father. If Jesus had such respect for divine authority, can we be so presumptuous as to have less?

The Apostles Had Delegated Authority: Jn. 20.21; Jn. 13.20

Jesus then delegated authority to His apostles, those He sent out with His gospel. In Jn. 20.21, shortly after His resurrection, Jesus told the eleven apostles, with Judas absent from the group:

> Peace be unto you: as the Father hath sent me, even so send I you.

Likewise, in Jn. 13.20 Jesus said to the apostles the night before He died:

> Verily, verily, I say unto you, he that receiveth whomsoever I send receiveth me; and he that receiveth me receiveth him that sent me.

This verse is a little complicated to some on first glance, and I let them recognize that. I then point out that to receive the apostles was to accept their teaching and obey it. He then can see that to receive the apostles' teaching was to receive Christ, and to receive Christ was to receive God. Conversely, if one rejects the teaching of the apostles, he rejects Christ, and hence God Himself.

Christ's Apostles Wrote the Bible: Eph. 3.3-5

With the divine authority delegated to them by Christ, the apostles wrote the New Testament. Paul claims this in Eph. 3.3-4:

> ...how that by revelation was made known unto me the mystery; as I wrote before in few words, whereby when ye read, ye can perceive my understanding in the mystery of Christ; which in other generations was not made known unto the sons of men, as it hath now been revealed unto his holy apostles and prophets in the Spirit.

The mystery Paul speaks about is nothing but the gospel of Christ (Rom. 16.25-26). The gospel was called a mystery simply because it was not revealed in the Old Testament period of time, as Paul affirms in verse 5.

Having established this, notice with the student that Paul declares when one reads the gospel, he can perceive Paul's understanding of the gospel. Often this is remarkable to the average person because he probably believes one must be a preacher or have attended a seminary to understand the Bible.

Paul says the gospel was written for the common man, and can be so understood. (Eph. 5.17 even commands us to understand it!)

However, the main point from this passage is that the gospel was made known unto Paul and the other apostles by revelation. It was revealed to the apostles from God Himself.

The Holy Spirit Guided the Apostles: Jn. 14.26; I Cor. 2.10-13

Most people realize neither God nor Jesus would make a mistake in the Bible, but sometimes they reasonably wonder if the apostles could make mistakes. Jesus covered this possibility by having the Holy Spirit guide the apostles so their teaching would be infallible. In Jn. 14.26, Jesus told His apostles the night before He was put to death, that the Holy Spirit would guide their teaching:

> But the Comforter, even the Holy Spirit, whom the Father will send in my name, he shall teach you all things, and bring to your remembrance all that I said unto you.

All too often these verses are applied to others than the apostles, that only the apostles were included in this promise. Only the apostles were given a remembrance of all that Jesus had told them, which would include statements Jesus made that are not even recorded in the Bible. If someone claims that this promise was given to him, it is a simple claim to test: just see if he has a remembrance of everything Jesus told the apostles that *is recorded in the Bible*!

The next passage, I Cor. 2.10-13, explains in what detail the Holy Spirit guided the apostles. In the most extensive passage in the Bible on its inspiration, Paul says:

> But unto us God revealed them through the Spirit: for the Spirit searcheth all things, yea, the deep things of God. For who among men knoweth the things of a man, save the spirit of the man, which is in him? Even so the things of God none knoweth, save the Spirit of God. But we received, not the spirit of the world, but the spirit which

> is from God; that we might know the things that were freely given to us of God. Which things also we speak, not in words which man's wisdom teacheth, but which the Spirit teacheth: combining spiritual things with spiritual words.

In this passage, Paul states at least four great truths:

1. *Man has a conscious spirit that knows his things*, i.e., his desires, his likes, his dislikes, his goals, etc. (This truth is convenient for those who don't believe man has a conscious spirit.)

2. *We don't know a man's likes and dislikes unless he tells us*. (This is easy to demonstrate to the student: just ask your student, "Do I like eggplant or black walnut ice cream?" He has no way of knowing unless you tell him, thus demonstrating the truth of Paul's statement. We simply don't know the things of a man unless his spirit tells us.

3. *We don't know God's things, i.e., His likes, dislikes, or His will unless He tells us*. This truth shows that just because we like something, it doesn't mean God likes it. We simply don't know what God likes unless He tells us, for we don't even know the desires of a man unless he tells us. If we presume to know what God likes without His telling us, we do not act by confidence or faith in God, but confidence in our own wisdom. This is why we must have divine authority for what we do to serve God.

4. *These verses also reveal the Bible doctrine of inspiration*, i.e., verbal inspiration. The apostle Paul specifically denies that the apostles wrote the Bible according to their own wisdom. They wrote according to the teaching of the Holy Spirit, even down to the very words they used. Thus, when we read the Bible, we have access to the precise words authorized by God through Christ and the Holy Spirit.

Cannot Add to the Bible: Rev. 22.18; II Jn. 9

Since God placed the very words He wanted in the Bible, He doesn't want us to add to the Bible. In Rev. 22.18, John says:

> I testify unto every man that heareth the words of the prophecy of this book, If any man shall add unto them,

> God shall add unto him the plagues which are written in this book:

In this context, his prohibition against adding to God's word includes only the book of Revelation. However, it illustrates a principle God has always desired man to honor. For example, in Dt. 4.2 and Prov. 30.6, God taught the same thing in the beginning and the middle of the Bible. The same principle is spelled out in II Jn. 9-11, where John says:

> Whosoever goeth onward and abideth not in the teaching of Christ, hath not God: he that abideth in the teaching, the same hath both the Father and the Son. If any one cometh unto you, and bringeth not this teaching, receive him not into your house, and give him no greeting: for he that giveth him greeting partaketh in his evil works.

This passage teaches several important truths: (1) If one is not content to stay within the truth that came from Christ, i.e., the Bible, he does not have God. That is, he does not please God, he is not in fellowship with God, and God does not dwell in this individual. (2) We shouldn't support teachers who do not affirm that one must abide in the teaching of Christ to be in fellowship with God.

I customarily illustrate this by saying, "So far tonight, we've used Bible teaching for everything we've said. Suppose after a while I put down something without a substantiating Bible passage, and when you ask me for a Bible verse, I reply, 'The Bible doesn't say that, that's just the way it is.' What should you tell me to do?" The person invariably says that he'll tell me to leave. That's good!

(3) This passage also declares that when we act outside the divine authority of the teaching of Christ, our works are evil. Of course, they are evil because they're not works of faith, but works that we've presumed please God.

Cannot Subtract from the Bible: Rev. 22.19

Similarly, in Rev. 22.19, we are forbidden to subtract from God's word:

> ...and if any man shall take away from the words of the book of this prophecy, God shall take away his part from the tree of life, and out of the holy city, which are written in this book.

Cannot Change the Bible: Gal. 1.8

In Gal. 1.8, Paul affirms:

> But though we, or an angel from heaven, should preach unto you any gospel other than that which we preached unto you, let him be anathema.

This verse contains two remarkable statements: (1) If one of the apostles arose from the dead and taught something not in the Bible, he should be anathema, that is, accursed, set apart for destruction. (2) Even if an angel came to earth and taught us something not in the Bible, he ought to be set apart for destruction, too. (To Mormons, this should mean that even if Joseph Smith saw an angel on the hillside in New York, he should have told the angel to get lost!)

These are impressive truths. The Bible is as authoritative as if God Himself spoke out of heaven. It is divine truth.

In the Bible, God Has Told Us Everything He Will Tell Us: Jude 3; II Pet. 1.3

God makes it clear that He doesn't want us to tamper with His word. The reason is because in the Bible, God has told us everything He will tell us in this life. In Jude 3, Jude says:

> Beloved, while I was giving all diligence to write unto you of our common salvation, I was constrained to write unto you exhorting you to contend earnestly for the faith which was once for all delivered unto the saints.

"The faith" Jude speaks of is nothing but the gospel. See Gal. 1.11 where Paul says he preached "the gospel," and Gal. 1.23, where he says he preached "the faith." "The gospel" is called "the faith" because it contains a system of salvation by faith, and because it produces faith (Rom. 10.17).

Thus, Jude professes that the gospel was delivered once for all. We have shown the student how the gospel was delivered, i.e., from God, through Christ, through the Holy Spirit, through the apostles, to us on earth. The term "once for all" means *once so that it needs no repetition.* For example, in Heb. 9.27-28, Paul declares with this same term that Christ was *once* offered, and man dies *once.* We die exactly as many times as Christ died, once for all. This verse contends the gospel was delivered exactly that many times, once for all.

For the last verse on the first chart, Peter says in II Pet. 1.3:

> ...seeing that his divine power hath granted unto us all things that pertains unto life and godliness, through the knowledge of him that called us by his own glory and virtue...

Peter maintains the Bible doesn't claim to teach us everything on every subject, but it does claim to teach us *everything we need to know* on every subject, that is, to please God. Thus, we cannot read the best recipe for our favorite dish in the Bible, nor can we read the best brand of automobile to buy. We can be ignorant of those matters and still please God. Everything we need to have true life and please God is revealed in the Bible! This is precisely why God does not want us to tamper with the Bible.

This completes the first chart. If a person is determined to obey God according to His revealed will without addition and subtraction, he will complete the study and become a Christian. Also, any issue that comes up in the study must be settled by the Bible, or some truth on this first chart must be violated.

TIP ON DENOMINATIONAL CREEDS: Before I leave this chart, I normally show the student how denominational creeds are standards of allegiance that do not fit the pattern we've just noticed. I normally illustrate how one must hold to the creeds of the Lutheran church to be in fellowship with that denomination.

Using a copy of *Our Church and Others*, published by the Evangelical Lutheran denomination itself, we read together:

> The Evangelical Lutheran Church is the total of all who unreservedly accept all canonical books of the Old and New Testament as God's revealed Word and who confess agreement with the teaching again brought to light through Luther's reformation and presented concisely in writing to Emperor and Empire at Augsburg in 1530 and repeated and expanded in the other so-called Lutheran symbols. (Lewis W. Spitz, Ph.D., *Our Church and Others* [Saint Louis, MO: Concordia Publishing House, 1969], p. 23.)

On the next page, we read the following:

> The Lutheran Church is a Bible church. She receives the Word of God, the Holy Scriptures of the Old and the New Testament, as the only source and standard of doctrine, the sole authority in matters of faith and life. (*Ibid.*, p. 24.)

Yet just across the page, we have:

> If someone asks a Lutheran: "What does the Lutheran Church teach?" or: "What do you as a Lutheran believe?" he can direct the inquirer to the Lutheran confessions...The Lutheran confessions may also be regarded as a standard around which Lutherans rally in their common defense of the doctrines of the Scriptures against error, or they may be regarded as a flag to which the teachers of the church pledge loyalty. Every member of the Lutheran Church is expected to subscribe not only to the Bible but also to the confessions as a correct presentation of Biblical doctrines. (*Ibid.*, pp. 25-26.)

Of course, these quotations establish how one becomes an Evangelical Lutheran: he must have allegiance for Jesus according to His teaching in the Bible, as well as loyalty for the creed of that denomination. Most people have no idea where denominations come from, believing perhaps that they result from different interpretations of difficult passages in the Bible. This quotation, which I let the student read for himself, demonstrates that the problem is one of divided allegiance, not difficult interpretation.

Just like allegiance to the Bible and the Lutheran creeds produces a Lutheran, so the Bible plus the *Methodist Discipline* produces not a Lutheran, but a Methodist. Likewise, using the Bible with the Seventh-Day Adventist Manual produces a Seventh-Day Adventist. The standard of allegiance in the Roman Catholic Church is the Bible along with the traditions of the church. This concept, although very simple, is likely to open the eyes of your student. You may use any creed books you have to accomplish this same effect.

Chart Two: Fellowship with God

Once we settle on the Bible as our only standard of authority, I then present the second chart (Figure 13), that is concerned with teaching the person how to get into fellowship with God. I begin before the creation.

God Planned to Save Us in Christ: Eph. 1.3-4

In Eph. 1.3-4, Paul says:

> Blessed be the God and Father of our Lord Jesus Christ, who hath blessed us with every spiritual blessing in the heavenly places in Christ: even as he chose us in him before the foundation of the world.

I tell the student these verses in the early part of Ephesians 1 are very meaty. While we might like to examine many things at length, we want to observe that before the foundation of the world, before God ever created Adam and Eve, He planned for the salvation of man, and his plan involved Jesus Christ. Rather

FELLOWSHIP WITH GOD

Eph. 1.3-4: Before Creation, God Planned to Save Us in Christ
Ac. 20.28: When Christ Shed Blood, He Purchaed the Church
Eph. 3.10: God Also Planned That Church
(a group of people in fellowship with Him)
Eph. 1.22, 23; 4.4: How Many Churches Did Christ Purchase?

SALVATION BY PERFECT FAITH

Rom. 1: All Gentiles Have Sinned
Rom. 2: All Jews Have Sinned
Rom. 3.23: All Have Sinned
Rom. 3.21: God's Plan to Save Us in Christ
Rom. 4.1-3: Example of Abraham
Rom. 4.6: Example of David
Rom. 4.12, 22-25: Us Too (Jas. 2.24)
Rom. 6.3-6, 17-18: Here's How

WHO SHOULD BE BAPTIZED?

Mk. 16.16: Believers
Col. 2.13: Faith in Working of God
Ac. 2.38: Penitent Believers
Rom. 6.5: Old Man in Sin

WHAT IS BAPTISM?

Jn. 3.23: Much Water
Ac. 8.38: Going Down into Water
Roim. 6.3-4, Col. 2.12: Burial

WHY BE BAPTIZED?

Rom. 6.4: Newness of Life
Col. 2.13: Alive, Forgiven
Ac. 2.38: Remission of Sins
Mk. 16.16: To Be Saved
Ac. 22.16: Sins Washed Away
I Cor. 1.13: To Be Called a Christian
Rom. 6.1-2, 6.17-18, 22-23: Manner of Life

All Based On Confidence in Christ!

Do You Want Newness of Life in Christ?

Figure 13

than using Christ as an auxiliary effort in His dealings with man, God always planned to save man in Christ.

When Christ Shed His Blood, He Purchased the Church: Ac. 20.28

We next notice Ac. 20.28, where Paul, speaking to the elders from the church at Ephesus, says:

> Take heed unto yourselves, and to all the flock, in which the Holy Spirit hath made you bishops, to feed the church of the Lord which he purchased with his own blood.

When Christ came, He died and shed His blood, and with His blood He purchased "the church," that is, people who were redeemed with Christ's blood. Those redeemed people were also in the eternal plan of God. In Eph. 3.10-11, Paul, speaking of the universal church, says:

> ...God created all things to the intent that now unto the principalities and the powers in the heavenly places might be made known through the church the manifold wisdom of God, according to the eternal purpose which he purposed in Christ Jesus our Lord...

God's eternal plan to save men in Christ and Christ purchasing the church with His blood were not two isolated events, for the church was also in God's eternal plan. As a matter of fact, these verses state two great truths: (1) God's plan for the church was from all eternity before the creation just like His plan for salvation in Christ, and (2) the church was to show the manifold wisdom of God.

The fact God designed the church to show His eternal wisdom needs to be impressed upon the student, as well as upon us all. The church Christ purchased ought to show God's wisdom, not man's. When men seek to change something about the church that was designed to show God's wisdom, in effect, they place their own wisdom over God's infinite eternal wisdom.

How Many Churches Did Christ Purchase? Eph. 1.22-23, 4.4

To show that just one relationship exists in which men may be redeemed by Christ's blood, notice Eph. 1.22-23 where Paul says:

> ...and he put all things in subjection under his feet, and gave him to be head over all things to the church, which is his body, the fulness of him that filleth all in all.

Accordingly, Paul speaks of God putting all things under Christ, which is the same thing Jesus said in the first verse we used in this study ("All authority hath been given unto me [Jesus—SGD] in heaven and on earth" Mt. 28.18). Paul adds that Christ is the head of the church, that is, the body of Christ. In Eph. 4.4, Paul also says concerning Christ's body:

> There is one body...

Thus, just one universal church, the Body of Christ, exists. It consists of all those redeemed by Christ's blood, and who are in fellowship with God through Christ's redemption.

These passages in Ephesians are tremendously instructive. Since the relationship between Christ and His church are like that of the head and body, we learn that just as one head exists, so is there just one body. Likewise, just as in the human body, the head controls the body in its entirety, so it is with Christ. Everything His church does ought to be controlled by Christ through His word. This is the same lesson we learned on the first chart: God's people must have divine authority for all they do to act by faith in Christ.

How to Be in Fellowship with God

This approach is based upon briefly summarizing the first six chapters of Romans:

Rom. 1: All Gentiles Have Sinned

Romans 1 shows all Gentiles (non-Jews) have sinned, and stand condemned before God.

Rom. 2: All Jews Have Sinned

Romans 2 shows all Jews have sinned, and stand condemned before God.

Rom. 3: All Have Sinned

Romans 3 shows that both all Jews and all Gentiles have sinned, and therefore all men stand condemned before God. As Paul summarizes in Rom. 3.23:

> ...for all have sinned, and fall short of the glory of God.

Rom. 3.21-22: God Saves Us Without Flawless Obedience

As Paul says in Rom. 3.21-22:

> But now apart from the law a righteousness of God hath been manifest, being witnessed by the law and the prophets; even the righteousness of God through faith in Jesus Christ unto all them that believe; for there is no distinction;

Thus, God planned a way to make men who have sinned righteous, a way that is based upon faith in Christ.

Rom. 4.1-3, 6: Abraham and David

Romans 4 illustrates the salvation by faith of two men, Abraham and David. Neither of these men was saved by a perfect understanding of God's will or by perfect obedience of God. They were both justified upon the basis of their faith in God.

Rom. 4.11-12, 22-25: Us Too (Jas. 2.14-24)

In Rom. 4.11-12, Paul states that we can be saved the same way Abraham was:

> ...and he received the sign of circumcision, a seal of the righteousness of the faith which he had while he was in uncircumcision: that he might be the father of all them that believe, though they be in uncircumcision, that righteousness might be reckoned unto them: and the father of circumcision to them who not only are of the circumcision, but who also *walk in the steps of that faith* of our father Abraham which he had in uncircumcision.

So Abraham is the father of those who share his kind of faith. This faith is not mere mental assent, but obedient faith, *faith that one can walk in the steps of* as Abraham did. James speaks of this faith in Jas. 2.18-24 when he says:

> Yea, a man will say, Thou hast faith, and I have works: show me thy faith apart from they works, and I by my works will show thee my faith. Thou believest that God is one; thou doest well: the demons also believe, and shudder. But wilt thou know, O vain man, that faith apart from works is barren? Was not Abraham our father justified by works, in that he offered up Isaac his son upon the altar? Thou seest that faith wrought with his works, and by works was faith made perfect.

James asserts the same thing Paul does, that Abraham's faith was perfect faith, faith that wrought with his works. These were not works of merit, but works of faith in God. Paul affirms we will be justified on the basis of the same kind of faith.

TIP ON JAMES 2.24: Before leaving this passage, another quotation from a denominational creed book generally helps the student to see denominational divisions are not produced by varied interpretations of difficult scriptures. For example, the

Discipline of the Methodist Church, the creed of the Methodist denomination states:

> We are accounted righteous before God only for the merit of our Lord and Saviour Jesus Christ, by faith, and not of our own works or deservings. Wherefore, that we are justified by faith only is a most wholesome doctrine, and very full of comfort. (Emory Stevens Bucke, editor, *Discipline of the Methodist Church* [Nashville, TN: The Methodist Publishing House, 1960], p. 32.)

After making sure the student understands this direct contradiction of Bible teaching, I hold out both the Bible and the *Methodist Discipline* to him and ask which book he wants. He invariably takes the Bible.

Rom. 6.3-6, 17-18: Here's How

Romans 6.3-6 shows how early Christians exercised Abraham's kind of faith:

> Or are ye ignorant that all we who were baptized into Christ Jesus were baptized into his death? We were buried therefore with him through baptism into death, that like as Christ was raised from the dead through the glory of the Father, so we also might walk in newness of life. For if we have become united with him in the likeness of his death, we shall be also in the likeness of his resurrection; knowing this, that our old man was crucified with him, that the body of sin might be done away, that so we should no longer be in bondage to sin.

In verses 17-18 of the same chapter, Paul explains further:

> But thanks be to God, that, whereas ye were servants of sin, ye became obedient from the heart to that form of teaching whereunto ye were delivered: and being made free from sin, ye became servants of righteousness.

Paul shows in both these passages that early Christians exercised saving faith when they, as penitent sinners, obeyed their Lord in baptism, and thus entered newness of life: fellowship with God. This is in accord with the proclamation of the gospel the first time it was preached in Acts 2. When the apostle Peter convinced the Jews they had actually killed the very Messiah they were looking for, we read in Ac. 2.37-38:

> Now when they heard this, they were pricked in their heart, and said unto Peter and the rest of the apostles, Brethren, what shall we do? And Peter said unto them, Repent ye, and be baptized every one of you in the name of Jesus Christ unto the remission of your sins: and ye shall receive the gift of the Holy Spirit.

These individuals were baptized for the remission of their sins, not because baptism was a work of merit, but because it exercised Abraham's kind of faith. In connection with this command, in Ac. 2.41, we read:

> They then that received his word were baptized:

Recall earlier in our study that Jesus said (in Jn. 12.49):

> Verily, verily, I say unto you, He that receiveth whomsoever I send receiveth me: and he that receiveth me receiveth him that sent me.

Those who received the teaching of the apostle Peter were baptized, and it was the same as receiving Jesus on that occasion. People who receive Jesus now do the same thing: they receive His word and are baptized for the remission of their sins.

TIP ON BAPTISM: Since many people have undergone something called "baptism," I try to find out what action was taken, when it was taken, and why it was taken long before I teach the person what the Bible says concerning baptism. If the person mentions he was baptized, I say, "Oh, when?" He may then tell me that he was sprinkled when he was christened as a baby or he was baptized after he thought he was saved. Whatever action and reason he gives me, I just remember it to help him compare what he did with what the Bible says concerning baptism. I do it before I teach him because most of us have a tendency to judge what we did perhaps years ago on the basis of what we now know. After he's learned the truth on baptism, I want him to judge his motive for what he did before on the basis of what he knew then, not on what I've just taught him.

ANOTHER TIP ON BAPTISM: Depending on the religious background and receptiveness of the student to the teaching of these passages on baptism, I may write or display the following simple outline. It basically shows the who, what, and why of baptism.

WHO IS TO BE BAPTIZED?

Mk. 16.16: Believers (not infants, or mentally incompetent people)
Col. 2.12-13: Those with faith in the working of God (again, those who can understand the gospel and resolve to obey Christ out of allegiance to Him)
Ac. 2.38: Penitent believers
Rom. 6.5-6: The old man (not the new man, not Christians)

HOW TO BE BAPTIZED:

Jn. 3.23: Baptism requires much water (sprinkling and pouring don't)
Ac. 8.38: Going down into water is required
Rom. 6.3-4: Baptism is a burial (like Christ was buried)
Col. 2.12: Baptism is a burial

WHY BE BAPTIZED?

Rom. 6.4: For newness of life
Col. 2.13: To be made alive, forgiven
Ac. 2.38: For remission of sins
Mk. 16.16: To be saved
Ac. 22.16: For sins to be washed away
I Cor. 1.13: To be called a "Christian"

I then compare this teaching with one or two denominational creeds to demonstrate that the controversy about baptism is not a problem of interpretation. It is a problem of allegiance!

In *The Truth that Leads to Everlasting Life*, Jehovah's Witnesses make the following statement concerning baptism:

> What, then does Christian baptism signify? It is not a washing away of one's sins. (*The Truth that Leads to Eternal Life* [New York: Watch Tower Bible & Tract Society of New York, Inc., 1968], p. 183.)

Likewise, our Baptist friends deny the Bible's teaching concerning the necessity of baptism. Notice carefully the following words from *The Standard Manual for Baptist Churches* by Edward T. Hiscox, D.D.:

> Baptism is not essential to salvation, for our churches utterly repudiate the dogma of "baptismal regeneration"; but it is essential to obedience since Christ has commanded it. (Edward T. Hiscox, D.D., *The Standard Manual for Baptist Churches* [Philadelphia, PA: American Baptist Publication Society, 1890], p. 21.)

On the next page we read:

> It is most likely that in the Apostolic age when there was but "one Lord, one faith, and one baptism," and no differing denominations existed, the baptism of a convert by that very act, constituted him a member of the church, and at once endowed him with all the rights and privileges of full membership. In that sense, "baptism was the door into the church." Now, it is different... (*Ibid.*, p. 22.)

Again, I give the student the choice of these books or the Bible. I've never had anyone take a creed book over what the Bible says on the subject. For a fuller discussion of arguments against the necessity of baptism to be a Christian, see Appendix 3, "Arguments Against Baptism Answered."

Rom. 6.1-2, 16-18, 22: Manner of Life

Completing our study of Romans 1-6, we then note the manner of life one lives after he becomes a Christian, again based on his faith in Christ. In Rom. 6.1-2, Paul said:

> What shall we say then? Shall we continue in sin, that grace may abound? God forbid. We who died to sin, how shall we any longer live therein?

In Rom. 6.16-18, Paul continues along this same line:

> Know ye not, that to whom ye present yourselves as servants unto obedience, his servants ye are whom ye obey; whether of sin unto death, or of obedience unto righteousness. But thanks be to God, that, whereas ye were servants of sin, ye became obedient from the heart to that form of teaching whereunto ye were delivered: and being made free from sin, ye became servants of righteousness.

Finally, in Rom. 6.22, Paul says:

> But now being made free from sin and become servants to God, ye have your fruit unto sanctification, and the end eternal life.

All Based on Confidence in Christ

Through perfect faith in Christ one can enjoy fellowship with God, and be in the universal church or the body of Christ. We've taught the student concerning the manner of life he is expected to live, and it's all based on confidence in Christ.

Do You Want Newness of Life in Christ?

Now is the time to ask the student if he wants newness of life in Christ, or fellowship with God. He can have it by exercising Abraham's kind of faith, obedient faith. I normally ask the student if he understands how people in the New Testament came into fellowship with God through Christ. If he says, "Yes," I ask, "Well, would you like to confess your faith in Christ and your determination to live according to His will to the best of your ability, and be baptized into Him to be in fellowship with God?"

Then I stop talking. In the course of the class, I have done most of the talking, but now it's the student's turn. Usually a student will answer affirmatively. If he has faith that Jesus is who He claimed to be, the divine Son of God, and if he has repented, that is, determined to live by faith in Christ to the best of his ability, and confesses that he has that kind of faith, he should be baptized into newness of life. This will put him into the universal church, the collection of all who are in fellowship with God through the blood of Christ.

Sometimes a student will not say anything for a while, and it will seem like an eternity to you, but let him alone. He's working some important issues in his mind, and he needs time to think. The student may even put his head between his legs.

If the student finally says something that is not "Yes," respond forthrightly to the reason he gives you. For example, if he says, "I'm not sure," I remind him that he read every one of these verses for himself. I ask him if he were baptized and the next day saw in the morning paper a picture of me with a bottle of whiskey in one hand and a blond in the other, standing in front of a bank that I had just robbed, would that prove his baptism was wrong? He will see his understanding and obedience doesn't depend on me, and will say so. I ask him again if he would like to be baptized into Christ for newness of life, and then be quiet.

If the student is a young person or married, and he wants to talk to his parents or spouse before obeying the gospel, I don't hinder them. However, I remind him of Jesus' statement in Mt. 10.37:

> He that loveth father or mother more than me is not worthy of me; and he that loveth son or daughter more than me is not worthy of me.

If the person understands what it means to obey the gospel, and just says, "No, I don't want newness of life," or "No, I don't want to live that manner of life." When I'm convinced of that, I tell him, "Fine, I've done the best I can." I urge him to remember what he's learned in our study, for he's probably learned a great deal. In the future he will have a lot of teaching to fall back on that he did not have before. I encourage him to contact me if he changes his mind and decides to obey his Lord. I counsel him to be sure in such a case to place his confidence in Christ, not a man, nor an organization. However, the vast majority of individuals, who complete the first chart, will obey the gospel by the time they have completed the second.

Chart Three: Fellowship with Other Christians

After the person has been baptized into Christ, he needs to be taught about establishing fellowship in a local congregation of Christians. This is the purpose of Chart Three (Figure 14).

God Desires It: Heb. 10.24-25

From the beginning of the New Testament church God has desired for His people to associate and work together in local churches. This is easily established by noticing local congregations whom most of the letters in the New Testament were written to, i.e., the letters to the church at Corinth, the churches of Galatia, the church at Rome, the churches at Ephesus, Philippi, Colossae, and the seven churches of Asia in Revelation.

God certainly could have made man so he didn't need the mutual provocation unto love and good works that is available to him in a local congregation. But the fact is, God did not so make man. In Heb. 10.24-25, the writer says:

> ...and let us consider one another to provoke unto love and good works; not forsaking our own assembling together, as the custom of some is, but exhorting one another; and so much the more, as ye see the day drawing nigh.

This passage was written shortly before the destruction of Jerusalem in AD 70. At this time, some Christians of a Hebrew

FELLOWSHIP WITH OTHER CHRISTIANS

God Desires Such: Heb. 10.24-25, Existence of Local Churches
Even Apostle Paul: Ac. 9.16, 13.1, 28.11 cf. Phil. 1.14
Word of Caution: I Tim. 5.21-22; Eph. 5.8-11
Supporting Error: Phil. 4.15-16, 1.5-7; III Jn. 8; II Jn. 9-11

WHAT TO LOOK FOR IN A LOCAL CHURCH

NOT: Entertainment or Mere Convenience, Large Crowds, Certain Ages
BUT: Scriptural Collective Action

Name: Ac. 11.26 - "Christian"

Organization

Elders: Ac. 14.23, 20.28 (Qualifications: I Tim. 3.1-7)
Deacons: Phil. 1.1 (Qualifications: I Tim. 3.8ff)

Worship

Prayer: I Tim. 2.8
Lord's Supper: Ac. 20.7
Singing: Eph. 5.19
Preaching: Ac. 20.7
Giving: I Cor. 16.2; II Cor. 9.6, 7

Submit in Matters of Opinion

All to Elders: Heb. 13.17
Younger to Older: I Pet. 5.5; Heb. 5.13-14
All to Laborers: I Cor. 16.15-16
Women to Leading Men: I Tim. 2.11-12
All to One Another: Eph. 5.21; I Pet. 5.5

Concern for One Another: Rom. 12.5-8

Teaches Christians: Ac. 2.42

SUCH A CHURCH SHOULD BE "JOINED" - Ac. 9.26

Figure 14

background, because of persecution by Jews (Heb. 10.32-39), had the idea their assemblies were not worth the cost. But, this passage shows that even during times of persecution, God views assemblies of Christians as extremely important. They give Christians the opportunity to fix their minds on the needs of each other to provoke one another unto love and good works. God intends for Christians to do the same thing today.

Even the Apostle Paul: Ac. 9.26, 13.1, 28.15 cf. Phil. 1.14

I use Ac. 9.26 and Ac. 13.1 to show how Paul associated with local churches. Acts 28.11 depicts Paul being encouraged by brethren in Rome, while Phil. 1.14 describes his emboldening them to teach others. The example of Paul demonstrates that if a Christian of our time thinks he doesn't need the mutual consideration and provocation unto love and good works that early Christians did, he is making himself greater than the apostle Paul.

Word of Caution: I Tim. 5.22; Eph. 5.11

When one considers associating with a group of Christians, he needs to exercise caution, so that he will not get involved in the sins of others. Paul warns about this in I Tim. 5.22:

> Lay hands hastily on no man, neither be partaker of other men's sins: keep thyself pure.

Similarly, in Eph. 5.11 Paul instructs:

> ...and have no fellowship with the unfruitful works of darkness, but rather even reprove them...

Financially Supporting Error: Phil. 4.15-16, 1.5-7; III Jn. 5-8; II Jn. 9-11

One prominent way a Christian can partake in another's error is by financially supporting it. In Phil. 4.15-16, Paul teaches positively that when one supports a good spiritual work, he is a partner in that work, and God regards it so:

> And ye yourselves also know, ye Philippians, that in the beginning of the gospel, when I departed from Macedonia, no church had fellowship with me in the matter of giving and receiving but ye only; for even in Thessalonica ye sent once and again unto my need. Not that I seek for the gift; but I seek for the fruit that increaseth to your account.

In Phil. 1.5-7, Paul comments along this same line when he thanks them:

> ...fellowship in furtherance of the gospel from the first day until now...in the defence and confirmation of the gospel, ye all are partakers with me of grace.

By financially supporting the collective work of a local church, we may actually accomplish much more in the propagation of the gospel than we could accomplish as individuals. It is with this principle in mind that John says in III Jn. 5-8:

> Beloved, thou doest a faithful work in whatsoever thou doest toward them that are brethren and strangers withal; who bare witness to thy love before the church: whom thou wilt do well to set forward on their journey worthily of God, because that for the sake of the Name they went forth, taking nothing of the Gentiles. We therefore ought to welcome such, that we may be fellow-workers for the truth.

The negative side of this principle is if we support a collective work that is not scriptural, then we're not fellow-workers for the truth, but fellow-workers in that error. Thus, in II John 9-11, we have:

> Whosoever goeth onward and abideth not in the teaching of Christ, hath not God: he that abideth in the teaching, the same hath both the Father and the Son. If anyone cometh unto you, and bringeth not this teaching, receive

him not into your house, and give him no greeting: for he that giveth him greeting partaketh in his evil works.

John does not prohibit inviting a Christian you have a doctrinal difference with to your home to study the issue. This passage is in the context of supporting a false teacher, one who shows a disregard for the necessity of abiding in the teaching of Christ. If we support teaching not based upon the teaching of Christ, then we become a partaker (we're in fellowship) in that evil work.

What to Look for in a Local Church

Obviously, we need to teach a young Christian what to look for in a local congregation. But the Bible does not use the criteria that people so many times use. For example the Bible's criteria are not entertainment or mere convenience, large crowds, or certain age groups. On the other hand, a Christian needs to be concerned about getting involved in scriptural collective action. Note some examples of scriptural collective activity:

Name: Ac. 11.26—"Christian"

Local churches in the New Testament were called "churches of Christ" in Rom. 16.16, a "church of God" in I Cor. 1.2, or many times simply "the church," that is, the "bunch" of God's people in a specific location. These were not exclusive proper names as Chapter 6 demonstrated. Of course, denominational names like "St. Matthew's Lutheran," etc., would involve one in unscriptural collective action. On an individual basis, according to Ac. 11.26, in New Testament times disciples of Christ were called simply "Christians."

Organization

The organization of the local congregation is important. In contrast to complex denominational organizations so prevalent in the world today, the organization of the local church in the New Testament was extremely simple. It consisted of

Elders: Ac. 14.23, 20.28

In Ac. 14.23, while Paul and Barnabas were on their first missionary journey, they helped appoint a plurality of elders in each local church. In Ac. 20.28 Paul makes it clear that the elders' authority is limited to the local church where they served. I Pet. 5.1-2 teaches the same thing. It needs to be impressed upon a young Christian that he should not associate with a congregation involved in collective action larger than a local church, i.e., denominational action.

In Ac. 20.28 and I Pet. 5.1-3, the terms elders, bishops (overseers), and shepherds (pastors) are used interchangeably of the same group of men.

The elders are a very highly qualified group of older men whose qualifications are found in I Tim. 3.1-7 and Tit. 1.5-11. Briefly mention that they are mature Christians, married, with children, teachers, rule their families well, and with high qualifications of character.

Deacons: Phil. 1.1

In addition, local churches should have deacons who functioned under the oversight of the elders as specially designated servants. Of course, all Christians are servants, but these deacons are also highly qualified men. A brief summary of the qualifications of deacons in I Tim. 3.8ff is appropriate.

Saints: Phil. 1.1

Phil. 1.1 shows the simplicity of the organization of the local church in the New Testament:

> Paul and Timothy, servants of Christ Jesus, to all the saints in Christ Jesus that are at Philippi, with the bishops and deacons...

Bishops and deacons we've seen before. The only other individuals in the local church are saints. Since this term is tremendously abused in the religious realm, the student may think in terms of Roman Catholic saints, i.e., notable Christians who have been dead for a number of years, worked four miracles, and have been voted on by the College of Cardinals in Rome. However, Paul uses the term to denote plain ordinary Christians whose lives are sanctified or set apart for the service of God; hence they are saints.

TIP ON ORGANIZATION: After covering Phil. 1.1, and remarking on the simplicity of the organization of a New Testament church, I illustrate how simple the Bible's organization is compared to denominational organizations. Sometimes I draw a pyramid and assert that nearly all denominational organizations can be depicted using the same picture. For example, the Roman Catholic church has local congregations, dioceses, etc. on the lower level up to Metropolitans and Cardinals with the Pope at the top of the organization. Although the titles are different, Mormons have essentially the same organization with their Prophet, Apostles, Seventies, etc. So with Jehovah's Witnesses with their districts, regions, branches, and zones. So with mainline protestant denominations with their synods, conferences, etc. In contrast to these complicated forms of organization, Christians in New Testament times had no organization nor allegiance larger than a local church.

God's wisdom shows in this arrangement. While the leadership of a local church may be corrupted and carry the whole congregation away from the Lord, since New Testament churches were completely independent, corruption in one congregation wouldn't have to affect another church at all. Contrast this with denominations where the hierarchy makes decisions that the grassroots-level congregations are told to either "like it or lump it!"

ANOTHER TIP ON ORGANIZATION: I usually use the *Methodist Discipline* again just to show how complicated denominational organization can be, and none of it is in the Bible. My edition of this volume runs over seven hundred pages. I quickly leaf through the last 650 pages noticing the headings that read like: "The Quarterly Conference," "The Church Conference," "The Official Board," "Episcopacy," "The General Conference," "The Jurisdictional Conference," "The Central Conference," "Provisional Central Conferences," "The Annual Conference," "The District Conference," "The Judicial Conference," "Coordinating Council," "Interboard Commission," "Board of Missions," "Board of Education," "Board of Evangelism," "Board of Lay Activities," "Board of Christian Social Concerns," "Commission on Worship," "Commission on Chaplains," "Commission on Church Union," "Interagency Commissions," "Council of Secretaries," "Interdenominational Agencies," "General Board of Pensions," "Annual Conference Organizations," "Judicial Council," "Quadrennial Commissions," etc., etc. Not a verse of scripture is cited for any of it! Usually, with the simplicity of the New Testament church in his mind, the student is astounded. If I ask him which he wants, the denominational creed or the New Testament, invariably the student takes the scriptures.

This completes the teaching concerning the organization of the local church. Of course, any change man makes in the organization reflects on the wisdom of God Himself.

Worship

To describe the worship of the local church as it was in the New Testament, I cover the following topics with their associated passages:

Prayer: I Tim. 2.8

I've never had anyone object to prayer in the worship of a local congregation. Any number of passages will suffice for showing its necessity.

Lord's Supper: Ac. 20.7

Basically, in the New Testament local churches partook of the Lord's Supper weekly, on the first day of the week. The context of Acts 20 shows Paul didn't lay over in Troas to eat a common meal with those Christians, but to partake of the Lord's Supper with them.

Although the first day of the week is not the sabbath (Mt. 28.1; Lk. 23.56-24.1), I parallel the early Christian practice with that of the Jews under the Law of Moses. Although the Jews were told to "remember the sabbath," they understood in *each week* that had a seventh day, they were to refrain from working on the seventh day. God didn't tell them *which* week, and they understood *every* week.

We do the same thing now. If the banker tells us to make payments on our auto loan on the twentieth of the month, we don't wonder, "Which month?" We make payments every month that has a twentieth until the loan is paid off. The same concept implies weekly participation in the Lord's Supper.

Singing: Eph. 5.19

No one argues that New Testament Christians sang in their worship. However, most people are used to mechanical instruments of music in denominational worship. If a question arises concerning mechanical music, I merely tell them I'm not personally opposed to it, and would personally like it, providing we can do it out of our allegiance to Christ. If Christ taught it, I want it. If He didn't, we must leave it alone.

TIP ON INSTRUMENTAL MUSIC: The Old Testament contains many references to instrumental music, for the Jews were commanded in II Chron. 29.25 to have instrumental music in their collective worship in the tabernacle and temple service. The Levitical musicians had specific instruction from God for instrumental music. If the New Testament contains a similar passage as in the Old Testament, we should have instrumental music as well.

If someone says playing an instrument is a God-given talent and therefore should be introduced into Christian worship, I remind him of a friend who is an airline pilot. He flies with a God-given talent, but no one thinks we should make flying his Boeing 747 a part of our collective worship. Neither do we let a welder use his God-given talent in our collective worship.

It is helpful to trace the history of instrumental music in so-called Christian worship century by century. No one affirms that instrumental music was used by the apostles or Christians in the New Testament. Passing into secular history, instruments weren't used in the second, third, fourth, fifth, or sixth centuries.

The first mention of instrumental music in the worship of people called Christians occurred in the seventh century. Philip Schaff, celebrated religious historian, writes:

> The use of organs in churches is ascribed to Pope Vitalian (657-672). Constantine Copronymos sent an organ with other presents to King Pepin of France in 767. Charlemagne received one as a present from the Caliph Haroun al Rashid, and had it put up in the cathedral of Aix-la-Chapelle...The attitude of the churches toward the organ varies. It shared to some extent the fate of images except that it never was an object of worship...The Greek church disapproved the use of organs. The Latin church introduced it pretty generally, but not without the protest of eminent men, so that even in the Council of Trent a motion was made, though not carried, to prohibit the organ at least in the mass. (Philip Schaff, *History of the Christian Church, IV* [New York: Charles Scribner's Sons, 1887], p. 439.)

Secular history is silent as to the instrument's use through the thirteenth century, except that in 1250 AD, Thomas Aquinas objected to its use by Catholics, lest they "seem to Judaize," i.e., seem like the Jews:

> Our church does not use musical instruments as harps and psalteries, to praise God withal, that she may not seem to Judaize. (Joseph Bingham, *The Antiquities of the Christian Church, II* [London: Reeves & Turner, 1878], p. 483.)

In the *Catholic Encyclopedia* we find:

> For almost a thousand years the Gregorian chant, without any instrumental or harmonic addition was the only music used in connection with the liturgy. The organ, in its primitive and rude form, was the first, and for a long time, the sole, instrument used to accompany the chant. (*Catholic Encyclopedia, X* [New York: The Encyclope-

> dia Press, Inc., 1911], edited by Charles G. Herbermann, *et al*, p. 657.)

Long after Thomas Aquinas, Erasmus, a Catholic scholar who lived in the sixteenth century, said:

> We have brought into our churches certain operatic and theatrical music; such a confused, disorderly chattering of some words as I hardly think was ever in any of the Grecian or Roman theatres. The church rings with the noise of trumpets, pipes, and dulcimers; and human voices strive to bear their part with them. Men run to church as to a theatre, to have their ears tickled. And for this end organ makers are hired with great salaries, and a company of boys, who waste all their time learning these whining tones. (John L. Girardeau, *Instrumental Music in the Public Worship of the Church* [Richmond, VA: Whittet & Shepperson, Printers, 1888], p. 166.)

Although instrumental music in supposedly "Christian" worship originated within Roman Catholicism, thereby being the origin of the denominational use of it, it is astounding to notice the opposition the very founders of those denominations had to it. John Girardeau, Professor at Columbia Theological Seminary (Presbyterian) said:

> It has thus been proved, by an appeal to historical facts, that the church, although lapsing more and more into defection from the truth and into a corruption of apostolic practice, had no instrumental music for twelve hundred years; and that the Calvinistic Reformed Church ejected it from its services as an element of Popery, even the Church of England having come very nigh to its extrusion from her worship. The historical argument, therefore, combines with the Scriptural and the confessional to raise a solemn and powerful protest against its employment by the Presbyterian Church. It is heresy in the sphere of worship. (John L. Girardeau, *Instrumental*

Music in the Public Worship of the Church [Richmond, VA: Whittet & Shepperson, Printers, 1888], p. 179.)

James Pierce, Presbyterian scholar of the eighteenth century, said:

> I come now to say somewhat of the antiquity of musical instruments. But that these were not used in the Christian Church in the primitive times is attested by all the ancient writers with one consent. Hence, they figuratively explain all the places of the Old Testament which speak of musical instruments, as I might easily show by a thousand testimonies out of Clement of Alexandria, Basil, Ambrose, Jerome, Augustine, Chrysostom, and many others...From what has been said, it appears no musical instruments were used in the pure time of the church. (James Pierce, *A Vindication of the Dissenters*, cited by John L. Girardeau, *Instrumental Music in the Public Worship of the Church* [Richmond, VA: Whittet & Shepperson, Printers, 1888], pp. 157-158.)

John Calvin, a founder of Presbyterianism, wrote:

> Musical instruments in celebrating the praises of God would be no more suitable than the burning of incense, the lighting up of lamps, and the restoration of the other shadows of the law. The papists, therefore, have foolishly borrowed this, as well as many other things, from the Jews. Men who are fond of outward pomp may delight in that noise; but the simplicity which God recommends to us by the apostle is far more pleasing to Him. (John Calvin, *Commentary* on Ps. 33 and on I Sam. 18.1-9, cited by M. C. Kurfees, *Instrumental Music in the Worship* [Nashville, TN: Gospel Advocate Co., 1969], p. 191.)

David Benedict, the Baptist historian, said:

> In my earliest intercourse among this people, congregational singing generally prevailed among them...The Introduction of the Organ among the Baptists...This instrument, which from time immemorial has been associated with cathedral pomp and prelatical power, and has always been the peculiar favorite of the great national churches, at length found its way into Baptist sanctuaries, and the first one ever employed by the denomination in this country, and probably in any other, might have been standing in the singing gallery of the Old Baptist meeting house in Pawtucket, about forty years ago, when I then officiated as pastor (1840)...Staunch old Baptists in former times would as soon tolerated the Pope of Rome in their pulpits as an organ in their galleries, and yet the instrument has gradually found its way among them...How far this modern organ fever will extend among our people, and whether it will on the whole work a *de*-formation or *re*-formation in their singing service, time will more fully develop. (David Benedict, *Fifty Years Among the Baptists* [Glen Rose, TX: Newman & Collins, 1913], pp. 204-207.)

John Wesley, founder of Methodism, was quoted to say:

> I have no objection to instruments of music in our chapels, provided they are neither heard nor seen. (John Wesley, cited by Adam Clarke, *Commentary, IV* [Nashville, TN: Abingdon Press, n.d.], p. 686.)

Adam Clarke, famous Methodist commentator himself, said:

> I am an old man, and an old minister; and I here declare that I never knew them productive of any good in the worship of God; and have had reason to believe that they were productive of much evil. Music, *as a science*, I esteem and admire: but instruments of music in the house of God I abominate and abhor. This is the abuse of music; and here I register my protest against all such corruptions in the worship of the Author of Christianity. (Adam

> Clarke, *Commentary, IV* [Nashville, TN: Abingdon Press, n.d.], p. 686.)

In a discussion of the Presbyterian Confession of Faith, we find:

> Question 6. Is there any authority for instrumental music in the worship of God under the present dispensation? Answer. Not the least; only the singing of psalms and hymns and spiritual songs was appointed by the apostles; not a syllable is said in the New Testament in favor of instrumental music nor was it ever introduced into the Church until after the eighth century, after the Catholics had corrupted the simplicity of the gospel by their carnal inventions. It was not allowed in the Synagogues, the parish churches of the Jews; but was confined to the Temple service and was abolished with the rites of that dispensation. (*Questions on the Confession of Faith and Form of Government of the Presbyterian Church in the United States of America* [Philadelphia: Presbyterial Board of Publications, 1842], p. 55.)

Even during the nineteenth century, nearly every denomination in the United States continued to fight its introduction. One hundred and fifty years ago, we would not even have had a conversation about the subject, for no one except Catholics used it in "Christian worship." Now those who do not use it are viewed as peculiar. However, the teaching of Christ has not changed since New Testament times. Those content to abide in the teaching of Christ will refrain from it until they find it sanctioned therein.

Preaching: Ac. 20.7

The word translated "preaching" here means to give a reasoned discourse, in this context from the teaching of Christ. This is what Paul did on this occasion in Troas.

Giving: I Cor. 16.2; II Cor. 9.6, 7

These passages show Christians are to give bountifully, purposefully, and cheerfully into the treasury of their local congregation on the first day of the week (every week—NASV, NIV). I emphasize that the New Testament nowhere tells Christians to tithe, or to give ten percent of their capital gains. Israelites in the Old Testament were so commanded. Yet they didn't tithe their capital gains, but the produce of their flocks and agriculture. God commanded the Jews to bring the tithe to the Levitical priests so it could be stored in the storehouse in the temple (Mal. 3.10).

No one today does any of this. Preachers presume to bind tithing on people not under the Law of Moses. It's imposed on capital gains, not flocks, herds, and crops to feed the Levitical priests. No Levitical priests exist. No storehouse exists in the temple to put the tithe in.

Submit in Matters of Opinion

Here are a series of passages demonstrating how Christians must work together in a local church. These passages do not require that we agree on everything in the Bible to be in fellowship, but they do require that we agree on what we do collectively. At the same time, we are to behave ourselves toward each other in matters of opinion, expediency, and that which we're not agreed on.

All to Elders: Heb. 13.17

Younger to Older: I Pet. 5.5; Heb. 5.13-14

All to Laborers: I Cor. 16.15-16

All to One Another: I Pet. 5.5; Eph. 5.21

Women to Leading Men: I Tim. 2.11-12

Concerned for One Another: Rom. 12.5-8

Teaches Christians: Ac. 2.42

Such a Church Should Be Joined: Ac. 9.26

This is the time to encourage your student (who is presumably now a Christian) to find a group of saints without denominational allegiance, and in whose collective worship he can conscientiously participate. If he lives in your area and you can commend the group you work with, invite him to investigate and join it.

Conclusion

In closing this chapter, let me remind you this approach is merely a guide. As you use it, you will probably make your own improvements to it. Let me counsel you to know your material and get the major commitments as you go through it. Remember, you cannot make the material too simple.

Appendices

Appendix 1

The Harm of Denominationalism

The basic premise of this entire volume is based upon the desire to be just New Testament Christians, i.e., without any denominational ties or allegiance whatsoever. But some may not be impressed with the desirability of the nondenominational way of Christ, so this appendix considers the harm of denominationalism.

The Atheist's Unanswerable Argument Against the Way of Christ

Several years ago I debated a professor in one of our state universities who was the faculty sponsor of a group called The League For the Promotion of Militant Atheism. This group challenged religious groups to debate the evidences for the existence of God and the inspiration of the Bible. A local group of Christians selected me to respond to his challenge. In preparation for the debate I read several interviews with this professor. One contained an argument against the existence of God and the inspiration of the Bible that is unanswerable. As a matter of fact, it is the strongest argument atheists and skeptics can use. It has produced more atheists than all the militant atheists put together!

The Atheist's Argument

This professor based his argument upon religious division. He said:

> Common sense tells us that atheism is a much more rational stand in the face of the conflicting claims of the world's religions than fleeing to the Bible.
>
> The fact that there are so many religions shows, at best, that human beings have a weakness for irrational beliefs.

The Atheist Agrees with Jesus

This argument is unanswerable because this militant atheist agrees exactly with what Jesus said about the harm of religious division! This militant atheist preached exactly like Christ on this subject. As a matter of fact, he preached more like Christ on this subject than many preachers do.

In Jn. 17.20-21, on the night before He died, Jesus prayed for all the believers in Him who would come after Him. Thus, if you believe in Christ, this is Christ's prayer for you. Jesus began by praying in His own behalf, then in behalf of the apostles. Then He said:

> Neither for these only do I pray, but for them also that believe on me through their word; that they may all be one; even as thou, Father, art in me, and I in thee, that they also may be in us; that the world may believe that thou didst send me.

Paul, in I Cor. 1.10, 11, taught much the same thing when he told the Corinthian Christians:

> Now I beseech you, brethren, through the name of our Lord Jesus Christ, that ye all speak the same thing, and that there be no divisions among you; but that ye be perfected together in the same mind and in the same judgment.

Likewise, Paul prayed in Rom. 15.5, 6:

> that with one accord ye may with one mouth glorify the God and Father of our Lord Jesus Christ.

Then in Gal. 5.20, Paul said concerning religious division:

> Now the works of the flesh are manifest, which are these: fornication, uncleanness, lasciviousness, idolatry, sorcery, enmities, strife, jealousies, wraths, factions, divisions,...of which I forewarn you, even as I did forewarn you, that they that practice such things shall not inherit the kingdom of God.

With these passages fresh in our minds, we must ask ourselves some questions, "Do all believers in denominations speak the same thing? Are there any divisions that are works of the flesh? Do all denominational believers speak with one mouth?"

The answer to all these questions is a dismal, "No!" Over 760 separate religious denominations exist in the United States alone, all claiming allegiance to Christ. But they all teach different things that contradict the others. Yet they all claim to teach their distinctive doctrines right out of the Bible.

Greatest Enemy of True Religion Is Religion Itself

A person doesn't have to look very far to find examples of how modern denominations ignore Jesus' prayer for unity.

Newsweek Magazine

What do you imagine any intelligent person thinks about this notice in *Newsweek* magazine several years ago?

> The Good Shepherd Baptist Church in Denver, Colo., has refused to meet the payments on a small stucco building it contracted to buy from the Wisconsin Evangelical Lutheran Synod in 1965—precisely on the ground that the property already belongs to God. The Baptists say "the Holy Spirit revealed to them that once you buy a church property, it belongs to the Lord and nobody can sell it." The Lutherans say, "But the Holy

> Spirit did not speak to us in this way. The Baptists got it from a special revelation and there is no way to deal with that." (*"Divine Property?" Newsweek*, July 5, 1971, p. 51.)

What did the several million people who read this in *Newsweek* think of the concept that the Holy Spirit taught these two denominations two different and contradictory doctrines? What do you think?

Martin Luther

What happens when people realize that the great reformation leader Martin Luther wrote:

> I ask that men make no reference to my name, and call themselves not Lutherans, but Christians. What is Luther? My doctrine, I am sure, is not mine, nor have I been crucified for any one. St. Paul, in I Cor. iii, would not allow Christians to call themselves Pauline or Petrine, but Christian. How then should I, poor, foul carcase that I am, come to have men give to the children of Christ a name derived from my worthless name? No, no, my dear friends; let us abolish all party names, and call ourselves Christians after Him Whose doctrine we have. (Hugh Thomson Kerr, *A Compend of Luther's Theology* [Philadelphia: The Westminster Press, 1943], p. 135. Also cited by Lewis W. Spitz, Ph.D., *Our Church and Others* [Saint Louis, MO: Concordia Publishing House, 1969], pp. 23-24.)

yet people who call themselves Lutherans are in blatant disagreement with Luther himself, who on this point was in agreement with Christ?

John Wesley

Another great reformation leader, John Wesley, among whose followers are the Methodists, Wesleyans, etc., said:

> Would to God that all party names, and unscriptural phrases and forms which have divided the Christian world, were forgot and that the very name [Methodist—SGD] might never be mentioned more, but be buried in eternal oblivion. (John Wesley, *Universal Knowledge, A Dictionary and Encyclopedia of Arts, Science, History, Biography, Law, Literature, Religions, Nations, Races, Customs, and Institutions, Vol. 9,* Edward A. Pace, editor [New York: Universal Knowledge Foundation, 1927], p. 540.)

In violation of Wesley's plea, his followers still call themselves Methodists, Nazarenes, and Wesleyans.

Charles Spurgeon

What transpires when people hear Charles Spurgeon, one of the great Baptist preachers who ever lived, say:

> I look forward with pleasure to the day when there will not be a Baptist living! I hope that the Baptist name will soon perish, but let Christ's name last forever. (*Spurgeon Memorial Library, Vol. I,* n.d., p. 168.)

Instead of Spurgeon's desire coming true, we have at least twenty-six different Baptist denominations in this nation alone. Likewise, Calvinists today disagree with Calvin, and right on down the line.

Preachers Teach Contradictory Doctrines

Many people seem to have no problem with all the contradictory doctrines in the religious realm, and yet if a single preacher taught all those contradictory doctrines himself, all would realize he had serious mental problems. Imagine what happens when an intelligent person sees so-called Christians claiming that the Bible can be understood hundreds of different ways, and the amazing thing about it, each way is right if religious division is right!

In truth, denominationalism has produced more atheism than all the atheists, militant atheists, hypocrites, and false teachers put together. Jesus knew it, Paul knew it, most of the founders of these denominations knew it, and pleaded it wouldn't happen.

Fruits of Denominationalism

With respect to religious division, compare the teaching of Jesus Christ with the statements of many prominent atheists:

Jesus

> ...that they may all be one...that the world may believe. (Jn. 17.20-21)

Benedict Spinoza

This prominent Dutch Philosopher blamed theological creeds with all their contradictions as his rationale for becoming an atheist.

Voltaire

This famous French philosopher blamed the contradictions and abuses of Roman Catholicism for his atheism.

David Hume

This foremost Scottish philosopher blamed the creeds of Calvin and Presbyterianism for his unbelief.

Diderot

The eminent French encyclopedist blamed the creeds of orthodoxy for his atheism.

Robert Owen

Robert Owen was the greatest European atheist of the 19th century. He was a genius and a philanthropist, and concerning his background before debating Alexander Campbell on the evidences for the existence of God, historian Bill J. Humble says:

> At the time when Robert Owen came to debate Campbell in 1829, he was 58 years of age and already a world figure of renown, appealing to the popular imagination by his schemes for the betterment of humanity, and arousing the ire of united clergy by his denunciations of all religions. This international figure was born in New Montgomeryshire, North Wales, on May 14, 1771. At an early age the boy was enrolled in a day school where he evidenced a precocious mental development; for at seven he had mastered all the information which his instructor could impart and was himself teaching. The intellectual growth of the young man was so rapid that before attaining his tenth birthday, he had investigated a number of theological works and examined their contents so critically as to lead himself to doubt the fundamental nature of all religion. (Bill J. Humble, *Alexander Campbell and Controversy* [Rosemead, CA: Old Paths Book Club, 1952], p. 81.)

The Bible didn't produce this distinguished atheist. The contradictions in denominational creeds did!

Charles Darwin

Many do not realize that the renowned agnostic Charles Darwin at one time studied at a seminary to become a clergyman in the Church of England. How did Charles Darwin, a believer in Christ and a creationist, become an agnostic whose name is inevitably connected with the hypothesis of evolution? What swayed the man who has swayed so many? Why did Darwin, who prepared for the work of a clergyman, become the chief apostle of evolution?

His son, also his biographer, wrote:

> We had an earnest conversation about going into Holy Orders; and I remember his asking me, with reference to the question put by the Bishop in the ordination service, "Do you trust that you are inwardly moved by the Holy Spirit, etc." whether I could answer in the affirmative, and on my saying I could not, he said, "Neither can I, and therefore I cannot take Orders." (Francis Darwin, *Life and Letters of Charles Darwin, Vol. I* [New York: D. Appleton and Co., 1898], p. 147.)

Darwin didn't reject Christ, or the Bible. He rejected a doctrine that was not even in the Bible, something in the creed book of the Church of England! Darwin's works influenced the minds of Marx, Engels, Lenin, Stalin, and Hitler, and gave them the "ethical basis" for many of their horrible actions. Who would dare say religious division isn't really so bad?

Robert Ingersoll

The greatest American atheist of the last third of the nineteenth century claimed that theological creeds led to his religious downfall.

Charles Smith

Charles Smith, the first president of the American Association for the Advancement of Atheism, explained how he became an atheist:

> Let me tell you something of how I came to be an Atheist. I used to live in Maud, Oklahoma—was there before the town was built; and have lived in Shawnee. I was in this town some twenty years ago, working for the Farmer's Union. I joined the First Methodist church. A few years later, I went to a Methodist school, Epworth University, in Oklahoma City...The next session I went to the State University at Norman. I tried to continue to believe the

> Christian religion, but began to investigate its doctrines. One day when watching a football game with my pastor, I asked him if he believed the virgin birth story, and the Adam and Eve story. He said, "Why, of course not." I demanded: "Why do you not tell your congregation that?" He replied: "That would do a great deal of harm, and no good." (Charles Smith, *Oliphant-Smith Debate* [Nashville, TN: Gospel Advocate Company, 1952], pp. 23-24.)

In every case, these renowned atheists and skeptics became unbelievers, not because of the Bible and the teaching of Christ or His apostles, but because of their lack of ability to believe religious confusion came from God. People's allegiance to human creeds produced their unbelief.

This is why Jesus prayed that His followers would not be divided. This is the reason we ought to avoid man-made religion: names, doctrines, institutions, organizations, and practices that come from man, not God. This is why Jesus said, in Mt. 15.6-9:

> ...And ye have made void the word of God because of your tradition...This people honoreth me with their lips; but their heart is far from me. But in vain do they worship me, teaching as their doctrines the precepts of men.

Creeds Produce Denominationalism

Many times people think denominationalism is produced by an inability of mankind to agree on how the Bible ought to be interpreted. Rather, it is produced by allegiance to something other than God and Christ: allegiance to human creeds.

Webster's New World Dictionary, says concerning the term "creed":

> (...Latin, *credo*, lit., I believe...) 1. a brief statement of religious belief; confession of faith; 2. a specific statement of this kind accepted as authoritative by a church; 3. a statement of belief, principles, or opinions on any

> subject. (*Webster's New World Dictionary*, Second College Edition [New York: The World Publishing Company, 1970].)

It is important to realize a distinction between a personal creed and an organizational one. I have the right to state what I believe, and other men may state their beliefs as well. However, denominational creeds are not statements of personal belief, but statements of what someone says you must believe to be in fellowship with them. It follows from this that a denominational creed must be a condition of communion in a specific coalition of congregations. This concept did not exist among New Testament Christians.

Thus, *The Philadelphia Confession of Faith* (Presbyterian), *The Standard Manual for Baptist Churches, The Methodist Discipline*, etc. are not personal statements of belief, but authoritative (that is, based upon human authority) standards of fellowship other than the Bible. When one is involved in denominationalism, he is subject to human authority rather than divine authority.

For example, the *Discipline of the Free Methodist Church* prescribes allegiance to it as a condition of fellowship in that denomination:

> Let none be received into full connection unless they give evidence of a renewed heart, by living up to the requirements of the General Rules,...(6) Do you subscribe to our articles of religion, our General Rules, and our Discipline, and are you willing to be governed by the same? (*Discipline of the Free Methodist Church* [North Chili, NY: B. T. Roberts, Publisher, 1887], p. 24.)

Be assured, none of Christ's apostles or other early Christians, nor any Christians for eighteen hundred years after Christ subscribed to the requirements of the General Rules of the Free Methodist Church. They never heard of the rules, or the denomination! These simply did not exist in New Testament times.

Similarly, one must hold to the creeds of the Lutheran church to be in that denomination. In *Our Church and Others*, published by the Evangelical Lutheran denomination itself, we read:

The Evangelical Lutheran Church is the total of all who unreservedly accept all canonical books of the Old and New Testament as God's revealed Word and who confess agreement with the teaching again brought to light through Luther's reformation and presented concisely in writing to Emperor and Empire at Augsburg in 1530 and repeated and expanded in the other so-called Lutheran symbols (*Our Church and Others*, p. 23.)

If someone asks a Lutheran: "What does the Lutheran Church teach?" or: "What do you as a Lutheran believe?" he can direct the inquirer to the Lutheran confessions.

The Lutheran confessions may also be regarded as a standard around which Lutherans rally in their common defense of the doctrines of the Scriptures against error, or they may be regarded as a flag to which the teachers of the church pledge loyalty. Every member of the Lutheran Church is expected to subscribe not only to the Bible but also to the confessions as a correct presentation of Biblical doctrines...

Therefore pastors and professors are asked at the time of their ordination or installation: "Dost thou accept the three Ecumenical Creeds—the Apostles', the Nicene, and the Athanasian—as faithful testimonies to the truth of the Holy Scriptures, and dost thou reject all the errors which they condemn?" and: "Dost thou believe that the Unaltered Augsburg Confession is a true exposition of the Word of God and a correct exhibition of the doctrine of the Evangelical Lutheran Church; and that the Apology of the Augsburg Confession, the two Catechisms of Martin Luther, the Smalcald Articles, and the Formula of Concord as contained in the Book of Concord—are also in agreement with this one Scriptural faith?" *To both of these questions the candidate must answer, "I do."* The officiating minister then asks: "Dost thou solemnly promise that thou wilt perform the duties of thy office in accordance with these Confessions and that *all thy teach-*

> *ing* and thy administration of the Sacraments *shall be in conformity* with the Holy Scriptures and *with the aforementioned Confessions*?" (*Ibid*., pp. 25-26.)

In addition, one who holds to the Bible and *The Methodist Discipline* will become a Methodist, not a Baptist. To be a Baptist, one must hold to the *Baptist Manual* plus the Bible. However, you cannot follow that course and become a Mormon. Mormons are those who hold to both the Bible and the *Book of Mormon.*

One last illustration that shows denominationalism is not produced by difficulties of interpretation but by adherence to denominational creeds is found in the following statement from Edward T. Hiscox's *Standard Manual for Baptist Churches*:

> It is most likely that in the Apostolic age when there was but "One Lord, one faith, and one baptism," and no differing denominations existed, the baptism of a convert by that very act, constituted him a member of the church, and at once endowed him with all the rights and privileges of full membership. In that sense, "baptism was the door into the church." Now, it is different; and while the churches are desirous of receiving members, they are wary and cautious that they do not receive unworthy persons. The churches therefore have candidates come before them, make their statement, give their "experience," and then their reception is decided by a vote of the members. (Edward T. Hiscox, D.D., *The Standard Manual for Baptist Churches* [Philadelphia: American Baptist Publication Society, 1890], p. 22.)

It's an absolute impossibility to follow just the Bible and become involved in these denominations or any others. None of them existed in Bible times.

The Harm of Denominational Creeds

We've all been around denominational creeds all our lives. Are they as innocuous as many think?

Creeds Hinder Fellowship

One of the arguments for the existence of creeds is that they are necessary for unity. While they produce unity *within the denomination*, on a scale larger than the denomination, they produce exactly the opposite. *Creeds are walls that prevent the fellowship of believers in Christ* in different denominations, in the sense that fellowship is contemplated in the Bible.

Creeds Impeach the Wisdom of God

Will the Bible as God gave it produce the unity God desires? If it won't, we imply that men must write creeds because God didn't know what to say.

Creeds Impugn the Good Will of Christ

If Christ were wise enough to give us everything we needed (which He promised to do in Jn. 14.26, 16.13, and that the apostles affirmed he did, II Tim. 3.16; II Pet. 1.3; Jude 3), but He didn't, then if God's wisdom is not impeached, Christ's goodness must be. Did Christ deliberately reveal the Bible in such an ambiguous fashion that it remained for men to write creeds to make God's meaning understandable?

Creeds Harm Believers in Christ

Creeds not only harm the reputation of God, Christ, and the Holy Spirit, who brought the complete revelation into the world, but they cause inestimable harm to believers in Christ. Rather than obey Paul's command to test everything to see if it's genuine (I Thes. 5.21), and "prove what is well pleasing to the Lord" (Eph. 5.8-11), those who place their confidence in creeds are obliged to approach the Bible with an interpretation already placed upon it. Obeying the apostle's teaching requires Christians to examine the scriptures with no established opinion. Those who place their confidence in creeds are not so free to examine the scriptures for themselves. They are compelled to conduct their investigations in light of the creed. Thus, creeds are opposed to independent Bible study and those believers who would profit thereby. Human creeds simply did not exist in the time of Christ, his apostles, or early-day Christians.

The argument of the atheist from religious division is still unanswerable. When one understands it's great harm, he cannot entertain a benevolent attitude toward denominationalism and maintain his allegiance to Christ.

Appendix 2

Faith: The Least Understood Bible Subject

The subject of faith is one all atheists and all Christians are agreed upon: the Bible teaches the absolute necessity of faith. Even though an individual may not believe in the inspiration of the Bible, no one denies the absolute essentiality of faith in the religion of God.

Indeed, in Heb. 11.6, the writer says, "And without faith it is impossible to be well-pleasing unto God; for he that cometh to God must believe that he is, and that he is a rewarder of them that seek after him." In John 8.24, Jesus says: "I said therefore unto you, that ye shall die in your sins: for except ye believe that I am he, ye shall die in your sins."

In view of passages like these, no one could deny that the Bible teaches faith is a requisite to salvation. Faith is such a basic subject in the Bible that the Gospel is called "the faith" (Gal. 1.11, 23) because it produces faith, and contains a system of salvation by faith. In the Lord's church, everybody realizes faith is the most fundamental subject in all the Bible. Among those who are not Christians, and among those who don't even pretend to be religious, everyone knows about faith, and yet *faith is the least understood subject in all the word of God.*

While nearly everyone agrees on the necessity of faith in order to please God, utter confusion exists in the religious realm about what faith is, how it is obtained, and its relationship to salvation. Some believe faith is a blind, unquestioning attitude that leads a person to accept the most ridiculous things either without evidence, or in spite of all the evidence. Some say faith is an indescribable gift that is injected by God when the recipient neither expects it nor desires it. Others say faith is obtained only after hours, perhaps days and weeks, or even years of praying at a mourner's bench for God to bestow it. Nothing is more misunderstood in all the Bible than faith!

Many times Christians think faith is so basic that they don't need to study what the Bible says about it. Because of all the confusion on the subject in the religious world, it's obvious we all need to be thoroughly familiar with what the Bible says about faith for our own benefit, as well as for those we want to teach.

What Is Faith?

The Bible defines faith in Heb. 11.1 where the writer says, "Now faith is assurance of things hoped for, a conviction of things not seen." To begin with, faith is a conviction concerning things not seen.

Many irreligious individuals who do not value faith at all may be surprised to learn they indeed do have faith. Many people have faith that a city exists in Russia called Moscow, even though they have not seen it themselves. Many believe in electric and magnetic fields, even though no man has ever seen any kind of electromagnetic field. Nearly everyone now believes matter consists of molecules and atoms that are composed of even smaller elements, although no one has seen even one of these elements.

We even advocate these convictions about things we have not seen because of supporting testimony and authentic evidence. Even though we might not have seen Moscow personally, we have seen pictures and heard testimony about that great city from those who have seen it first hand. We have enough conviction about electromagnetic fields to treat them with respect when necessary because of the authentic evidence we've seen. Likewise, we believe in the atomic theory of matter, not because any of us has actually seen an atom, but because we have seen an overwhelming amount of evidence that matter consists of these components. So faith, a conviction concerning the unseen that is supported by authentic evidence, is something all of us have every day of our lives.

Faith Is Not Peculiar to Religion

Many times someone says, "Oh, I couldn't possibly be involved in anything having to do with faith!" Frequently, the more education an individual acquires, the less he may feel like involving himself in matters of faith. However, everyone of us, every day of our lives, is involved in faith, from the most militant atheist to the most faithful Christian.

All of us begin using faith at birth, when we start accepting the word of others concerning food, medicine, poison, etc. For example, we may have very strong convictions that certain foods are good for our body, not because we've actually been inside another body to see their effect on the human body, but because of authentic evidence that those foods are vital to good health.

Likewise, we all share a strong conviction that arsenic is a deadly poison although we may never have seen anyone die of arsenic poisoning. We have those convictions simply because authentic evidence has instilled them within us. From the time an atheist (who prides himself in not being involved in faith) is a little baby, he indeed possesses convictions concerning things not seen.

Not only are we all involved in faith every day of our lives, but faith pervades every realm of life. Banks extend credit based on faith. Without a strong conviction that their money will be returned, that conviction supplied by authentic evidence about previous transactions, a bank would be foolish to loan money.

When an atheist phones an order in to Sears, and they tell him to pick up the package at a certain time, the fact he will get into his car and drive to the store shows he has conviction his order will be there, In reality, he has not seen his order there; he simply acts upon a conviction concerning things not seen. In this case, his conviction might be produced by authentic evidence based upon Sears' past record, the testimony of a friend who works at Sears, or simply from reading the catalog.

These examples show we all use and act upon faith every day of our lives, whether we are atheists, Buddhists, or Christians. Faith is not peculiar to religion at all!

Faith Is an Act of the Mind

In Rom.10.9, Paul says, "Because if thou shalt confess with thy mouth Jesus as Lord, and shalt believe in thy heart that God raised him from the dead, thou shalt be saved." From this passage we see that man believes with his heart.

What Is the Bible "Heart"?

Webster's dictionary defines "heart" something like "the central blood pump situated in the thorax." Obviously, no one believes this muscle of the body produces faith.

In the Bible, "heart" depicts nothing more nor less than the mind of man. As a matter of fact, "heart" in the Bible cannot mean the literal physical heart, for in Hos. 7.11, Hosea says concerning apostate Israel, "Ephraim is become as a silly dove, without heart." Of course, a dove has a "central blood pump situated in the thorax," but the dove does not possess what the Bible refers to as the heart of man.

The following table shows the Biblical functions of the heart of man:

Commit Adultery: Mt. 5.28
Think: Mt. 9.4; Lk. 9.47; Ac. 8.22; Heb. 4.12
Understand: Mt. 13.15; Jn. 12.40
Reason: Mk. 2.6
Imagine: Lk. 1.5
Ponder: Lk. 2.19
Conceive: Ac. 5.4
Lust: Ro. 1.24
Desire: Ro. 10.1
Purpose: II Cor. 9.7
Love: Mk. 12.30; I Pet. 1.22
Obey From: Ro. 6.17

Obviously, the mind of man performs all of these functions, yet the Bible says they're the functions of man's heart. With this same mind or heart, man believes unto righteousness.

Not only is the mind of man the Bible heart, but the Bible also uses the heart and mind interchangeably. In both Heb. 8.10 and 10.16, the Hebrew writer quotes from Jer. 31.33 and uses the terms "heart" and "mind" in the place of each other to describe Christians:

> Heb. 8.10: I will put my laws into their mind, and on their heart also will I write them.
>
> Heb. 10.16: I will put my laws on their heart, and upon their mind also will I write them.

Men speaking by inspiration in the Bible recognized the heart of man was nothing more nor less than his mind. In addition, Paul in Rom. 12.1 says, "I beseech you therefore, brethren, by the mercies of God, to present your bodies a living sacrifice, holy, acceptable to God, which is your spiritual service." The word "spiritual" comes from the Greek word *logiken*, that our word "logical" comes from, and literally means, "belonging to the reason."

Thus, our faith and service of God is to be based upon a logical consideration of the evidence God has presented both for His existence and the inspiration of the Bible. In addition, Peter in I Pet. 3.15 says, "But sanctify in your hearts Christ as Lord: being ready always to give answer to every man that asketh you a reason concerning the hope that is in you, yet with meekness and fear." These passages show the faith God expects His people to have is a reasonable one; it can be answered for. Any faith that is not of this nature is simply not Biblical faith.

Many times we've all heard individuals talk about "heart faith" versus "head faith," but this distinction is unscriptural. Several years ago, the Stake President of the Mormon church in our community gave the following reason for not defending the claims of Joseph Smith to be a prophet of God (even though he was commanded to by Joseph Smith in the *Doctrine and Covenants*, 71.7.): "Mormon faith is not a product of the intellect." If he's right, that's exactly what's wrong with it! Bible faith is a product of the intellect!

How Does Faith Come?

The scriptures teach God does not bare the total responsibility for our having faith, but He also holds us responsible. In Jn. 5.24, Jesus says: "Verily, verily I say unto you: He that heareth my word, and believeth him that sent me, hath eternal life, and cometh not into judgment, but hath passed out of death into life." Obviously, Jesus teaches that if an individual does not believe on Him, he will suffer punishment. Jesus holds every man responsible for having faith.

Similarly, in Jn. 8.24, Jesus says, "Except ye believe that I am he, ye shall die in your sins." Again, the responsibility for belief rests squarely on the individual. In Jn. 6.28-29, some Jews asked Jesus, "What must we do, that we may work the works of God? Jesus answered and said unto them, This is the work of God, that ye believe on him whom he hath sent." All these passages show man is responsible for believing in Jesus Christ.

Further, in Heb. 11.6, the writer says, "For without faith it is impossible to be pleasing unto God, for he that cometh to God must believe that he is, and that he is a rewarder of them that diligently seek after him." In Mk. 16.16, Jesus says, "Go ye into all the world and preach the gospel to the whole creation. He that believeth and is baptized shall be saved; but he that disbelieveth shall be condemned." Certainly, in these two passages, God holds the individual responsible for believing.

Imagine, as some do, that faith is a gift God gives an alien sinner, and that the individual does nothing to obtain faith. If an individual dies and spends eternity separated from his God, whose fault would it be? If God must give an individual faith, and then punishes individuals when they don't have it, then it would be God's fault when the individual was punished as faithless! Yet not so, for the Bible plainly teaches faith is the responsibility of the individual. It nowhere teaches that God gives an alien sinner faith.

How then does faith come? In Rom.10.14-16, Paul says, "How then shall they call on him in whom they have not believed? and how shall they believe in him whom they have not heard? and how shall they hear without a preacher? So belief cometh of hearing, and hearing by the word of Christ." This passage gives man the responsibility to hear the evidence contained in the gospel, so that his faith comes from hearing God's word.

A parallel passage is found in Jn. 6.44-45, where Jesus says, "No man can come to me, except the Father that sent me draw him:" and then Jesus explains how the Father draws individuals to Him: "And they shall all be taught of God. Everyone that hath heard from the Father, and hath learned, cometh unto me."

Thus, God's role in our faith is to supply the authentic evidence, the gospel, which, when we hear and learn, produces faith in our heart or mind.

Likewise, Jn. 20.30-31 shows this is the very purpose of the gospel accounts of the life of Jesus: "Many other signs therefore did Jesus in the presence of the disciples, which are not written in this book: *But these are written, that ye may believe* that Jesus is the Christ, the Son of God; and that believing ye may have life in his name." In Jn. 17.20-21, the last night of his life, Jesus prayed to His Father on behalf of His apostles and Christians today. He said, "Neither for these only do I pray, but for them also that *believe on me through their* [the apostles'—SGD] *word.*"

Other examples of faith coming through hearing God's word are found in:

> Ac. 14.1: And it came to pass in Iconium that they entered together into the synagogue of the Jews, and *so spake* that a great multitude both of Jews and of Greeks *believed.*

> Ac. 17.11: Now these were more noble than those in Thessalonica, in that they *received the word* with all readiness of mind, examining the scriptures daily, whether these things were so. Many of them therefore *believed.*

> Ac. 15.7: Brethren, ye know that a good while ago God made choice among you, that by my mouth the Gentiles should *hear the word* of the gospel, *and believe.*

Ac. 18.8: And many of the Corinthians *hearing believed.*

God doesn't give *faith* to an alien sinner, but *the testimony to produce faith*. God holds us responsible for examining the evidence so that it will instill faith in our minds.

Mental Assent Alone Is Not Enough

As we conclude our brief study of Biblical teaching on faith, it is important to learn the faith that pleases God is more than just mental assent that Jesus is who He claimed to be. Soul-saving faith involves placing one's trust and confidence in Christ.

To illustrate this distinction, suppose you are advised to go to a physician you have never consulted before, and as you enter his office you notice his diplomas on the office wall. You read them and become convinced the man is actually what he claims to be, a medical doctor, and that he's not an impostor. At this point, you have mentally assented to the fact that he is a doctor, based upon the evidence you have seen.

Suppose, however, that while you have conviction that he is a doctor, upon examining you he diagnoses your medical problem and prescribes treatment. If you reject his diagnosis and prescribed treatment, because it doesn't agree with what you thought should be done, then while you have mental assent that the individual is a doctor, you have not placed your confidence and trust in him.

So it is with Christ. Many individuals have mental assent that Jesus is who He claimed to be, and yet they have not placed their complete trust and confidence in Him. Tragically, many believe they will be saved by faith only.

An individual can believe in Jesus Christ and still be a child of Satan. In spite of the fact many believe one is saved by faith only, Jn. 8.30-44 says, "As he spake these things many believed on him." Beginning in verse 31, "Jesus therefore said to those Jews that had believed him...," and then Jesus spoke further to those believers. Those who claim we are saved by faith alone would assume these whom John calls "believers" were children of God. However, speaking to these same individuals in verse 44,

Jesus told them, "Ye are of your father the devil, and the lusts of your father it is your will to do." John and Jesus tell us it's possible to be a believer in Jesus and still be a child of the devil. These individuals had mental assent, but they still obeyed the desires of Satan, rather than the will of Christ.

Similarly, in Jn. 12.42, John says concerning the Jews, "Nevertheless even of the rulers many believed on him; but because of the Pharisees they did not confess it, lest they should be put out of the synagogue; for they loved the glory that is of men more than the glory that is of God." These believers were still children of Satan because they did not obey the will of Christ, who said, "Every one therefore who shall confess me before men, him will I also confess before my Father who is in heaven. But whosoever shall deny me before men, him will I also deny before my Father who is in heaven." (Mt. 10.32-33)

In Jas. 2.19, James tells us, "Thou believest that God is one; thou doest well; the demons also believe, and shudder. But wilt thou know, O vain man, that faith apart from works is barren?" And then in verse 24, James says, "Ye see that by works a man is justified, and not by faith only." Certainly, James does not speak of meritorious works, i.e., works that would deny the grace or unmerited favor of God, but rather acts of obedience that demonstrate we have placed our full trust and confidence in Christ. The demons had mental assent, and in Mk. 1.24-25, a demon was one of the first to confess Jesus as the Messiah. Yet demons will obviously not be saved by faith only because they have not placed their confidence in Christ by obeying His will.

Likewise, many today have mental assent that Jesus is the Christ, but they have failed to place their full confidence in Him by obeying His will without addition or subtraction. In the New Testament, those who believed Jesus was the Son of God, who determined to live according to Christ's will (or repented), and who confessed their faith in Christ were then told to be baptized in the name of Jesus Christ for the remission of sins (Ac. 2.38). Those who have more than just mental assent in Christ, and have placed their confidence and trust in Christ, obey Him today in just the same way, realizing that mental assent alone is not enough.

Conclusion

Thus, in this brief study on faith, perhaps the least understood subject in the Bible, we see that faith is not something to be ashamed of, nor is it an unquestioning blind faith. Soul-saving faith is based on facts supported by authentic evidence; it can be defended, and answered for, and is demonstrated in our complete reliance on Jesus by obeying His revealed will.

Appendix 3

Arguments Against Baptism Answered

In Chapter 4, "Fellowship with God," the relevance of baptism to fellowship was seen. Since baptism has been controversial at various times in religious history, this appendix is included to examine various arguments that have been used to depreciate its importance.

The New Testament's Teaching on Baptism

On the first Pentecost following the resurrection of Christ, the apostle Peter preached the first gospel sermon in fact. In Ac. 2.37-41, Luke recorded the reaction of Peter's audience on that occasion:

> Now when they heard this, they were pricked in their heart, and said unto Peter and the rest of the apostles, Brethren, what shall we do? And Peter said unto them, Repent ye, and be baptized every one of you in the name of Jesus Christ unto the remission of your sins; and ye shall receive the gift of the Holy Spirit. For to you is the promisc, and to your children, and to all that are afar off, even as many as the Lord our God shall call unto him. And with many other words he testified, and exhorted them, saying, Save yourselves from this crooked generation. They then that received his word were baptized: and

> there were added unto them in that day about three thousand souls.

Not only at the occasion of the first preaching of the gospel do we find an important statement made concerning baptism, i.e., it was for the remission of sins, but in many other New Testament passages, clear statements are also made about its importance. For example, in Ac. 22.16, Ananias told Saul:

> And now why tarriest thou? Arise, and be baptized, and wash away thy sins, calling on his name.

In Rom. 6.3-4, Paul teaches us baptism puts us into Christ and into His death:

> Or are ye ignorant that all we who were baptized into Christ Jesus were baptized into his death? We were buried therefore with him through baptism into death: that like as Christ was raised from the dead through the glory of the Father, so we also might walk in newness of life.

In I Cor. 12.13, Paul affirms baptism puts us into the body of Christ (which is the church, Eph. 1.23, Col. 1.18):

> For in one Spirit were we all baptized into one body, whether Jews or Greeks, whether bond or free; and were all made to drink of one Spirit.

In Gal. 3.26-27, Paul teaches again that baptism puts us into Christ and makes us children of God by faith:

> For ye are all sons of God, through faith, in Christ Jesus. For as many of you as were baptized into Christ did put on Christ.

In I Pet. 3.21, the apostle Peter affirms that like as Noah and his household were saved by means of water, we are too:

> ...which also after a true likeness doth now save you, even baptism, not the putting away of the filth of the flesh, but the interrogation of a good conscience toward God, through the resurrection of Jesus Christ.

These are the basic passages containing the New Testament's teaching concerning baptism. Sad to say, they are not universally accepted, even among those professing to be Christians.

Many Today Do Not Accept This Teaching

Although the first time the gospel was preached, "they that received his word were baptized," many today do not receive these words. For example, our Jehovah's Witness friends, in their official publications, say concerning baptism:

> Baptism Does Not Wash Away One's Sins. (*Make Sure of All Things* [Brooklyn: Watch Tower Bible & Tract Society, Revised in 1957], p. 40.)

> What, then does Christian baptism signify? It is not a washing away of one's sins. (*The Truth that Leads to Everlasting Life* [Brooklyn: Watch Tower Bible & Tract Society, 1968], p. 183.)

Likewise, our Baptist friends deny the Bible's teaching concerning the necessity of baptism. *The Standard Manual for Baptist Churches* by Edward T. Hiscox, D.D. shows the position of many of them:

> Baptism is not essential to salvation, for our churches utterly repudiate the dogma of "baptismal regeneration"; but it is essential to obedience since Christ has commanded it. (Edward T. Hiscox, D.D., *The Standard Manual for Baptist Churches* [Philadelphia: American Baptist Publication Society, 1890], p. 21.)

> It is most likely that in the Apostolic age when there was but "one Lord, one faith, and one baptism," and no differing denominations existed, the baptism of a convert by that very act, constituted him a member of the church, and at once endowed him with all the rights and privileges of full membership. In that sense, "baptism was the door into the church." Now, it is different. (*Ibid*., p. 22.)

These quotations could be multiplied from other denominational publications. But rather than look at them all, this appendix primarily examines the reasons why many in the religious world today do not accept the plain teaching of the Bible on this obviously important subject.

Jesus Wasn't Baptized for the Remission of Sins and We Are to Follow His Example

We can agree with much within this argument. For example, we are to follow the example of Christ, I Jn. 2.6; I Cor. 11.1. We can also agree that Jesus was not baptized for the remission of His sins, for indeed He had no sin, Heb. 4.15. However, the very fact He had no sin itself might indicate something different between His baptism and ours.

Why was Jesus baptized anyway? Do those who make this argument against baptism follow it consistently, and submit to baptism for the same reason Jesus did? In Jn. 1.29-34, John the Baptist tells us why Jesus was baptized:

> On the morrow he seeth Jesus coming unto him, and saith, Behold, the Lamb of God, that taketh away the sin of the world! This is he of whom I said, After me cometh a man who is become before me: for he was before me. And I knew him not; but that he should be made manifest to Israel, for this cause came I baptizing in water. And John bare witness, saying, I have beheld the Spirit descending as a dove out of heaven; and it abode upon him. And I knew him not: but he that sent me to baptize in water, he said unto me, Upon whomsoever thou shalt see

> the Spirit descending, and abiding upon him, the same is he that baptizeth in the Holy Spirit. And I have seen, and have borne witness that this is the son of God.

Indeed, the reason Jesus was baptized by John was not for the remission of His sins, but to indicate to John the Baptist that Jesus was the Messiah who was promised in the Old Testament! John the Baptist had been told by God that one day while he baptized people, the Spirit would descend on one of them in the form of a dove. When this happened, John would know he had baptized the Messiah.

Now, who do you know who ought to be baptized for the same reason Jesus was? Who has been baptized for the same reason Jesus was? Obviously, none of us today follow the example of Jesus in being baptized so God can show we are the Messiah!

The Blood of Christ Remits Our Sins, Not Baptism

Without exception, everyone who reads these words, and who believes the Bible accepts the fact the blood of Christ was shed for the remission of our sins. Before we discuss the relation of baptism to the remission of sins, let's ask ourselves why Bible believers universally agree Jesus' blood was shed for the remission of our sins? Wasn't it because the Lord Himself said in Mt. 26.28, "for this is my blood of the covenant, which is poured out for many unto remission of sins"? Certainly, we can all accept this plain statement from the lips of our Lord Himself.

Why then can we not accept the words of his apostle Peter, when in Ac. 2.38, Peter used identically the same language in the Greek and in the English concerning baptism: "And Peter said unto them, Repent ye, and be baptized every one of you in the name of Jesus Christ unto the remission of your sins"?

If we can't believe Peter in Ac. 2.38 when he says baptism is for the remission of sins, why would we believe Jesus when He uses the same words to say His blood was shed for the remission of sins? If on the other hand, we believe Jesus when He said His blood was shed for the remission of sins, why shouldn't we as well believe Peter when he used the same words to say baptism was for the remission of sins?

If someone should argue that "for" or "unto" means "because of" in Ac. 2.38, i.e., we are to be baptized because our sins have already been remitted, why would not the identical same language mean that Jesus shed his blood because our sins had already been remitted, and therefore the blood of Christ has nothing to do with the remission of sins? Surely, we can see whatever purpose Jesus accomplished by shedding His blood, the same purpose is accomplished by the baptism of a penitent believer in the name of Jesus Christ.

It is interesting to note that it is by no means unusual to meet denominational preachers who have had a smattering of exposure to the Greek language who insist the word translated "for" or "unto" means "because of" in Ac. 2.38. However, when pressed for a New Testament translation that so translates the word, they universally meet with failure. Denominational scholars generally will not sacrifice their scholarship in favor of their denominational doctrine.

Charles B. Williams, at one time Dean of Southwestern Baptist Theological Seminary, Fort Worth, Texas, said in his translation, *The Charles B. Williams Translation*:

> Peter said to them, You must repent—and, as an expression of it, let everyone of you be baptized in the name of Jesus Christ—that you may have your sins forgiven; and then you will receive the gift of the Holy Spirit... (Charles B. Williams, *The New Testament in the Language of the People* [Chicago: Moody Press, 1966].)

J. R. Mantey, Department of New Testament Interpretation, Northern Baptist Theological Seminary, Chicago, Illinois, said, in a quotation on the back cover of Williams' translation:

> ...It is the best translation of the New Testament in the English language.

Likewise, G. R. Beasley-Murray, Principal of Spurgeon's College in London, later Senior Professor at Southern Baptist

Seminary in Louisville, Kentucky, wrote a modern classic, *Baptism in the New Testament*. He gives chapters which thoroughly discuss baptism in the gospels, in Acts, in Paul's writings, and in other apostolic writings. In his Introduction, Beasley-Murray says:

> This book is intended to offer a Baptist contribution to the discussions on baptism that are taking place throughout the Christian world. But the indefinite article should be observed; the impression must not be given that my interpretations are characteristic of Baptist thought generally. At most it can be claimed that they represent a trend gaining momentum among Baptists in Europe. I have striven to interpret the evidence of the New Testament as a Christian scholar, rather than as a member of a particular Christian Confession. (G. R. Beasley-Murray, *Baptism in the New Testament* [Grand Rapids: Wm. B. Eerdmans Publishing Co., 1962], pp. v-vi.)

From his chapter on baptism in Acts, Beasley-Murray says:

> Consequently, baptism is regarded in Acts as the occasion and means of receiving the blessings conferred by the Lord of the Kingdom. Admittedly, this way of reading the evidence is not characteristic of our thinking, but the intention of the author is tolerably clear. (*Ibid*., p. 102.)

> Whatever the relationship between baptism and the gift of the Spirit elsewhere in Acts, there appears to be no doubt as to the intention of Acts 2.38; the penitent believer baptized in the name of Jesus Christ may expect to receive at once the Holy Spirit, even as he is assured of the immediate forgiveness of his sins. (*Ibid*., p. 108.)

From his chapter on baptism in the apostolic writings, concerning Rom. 6.3-4, Bealsey-Murray says:

> We that are Baptists have largely ignored this aspect of Pauline teaching; even when we have heard it we have hesitated to accept, partly no doubt because of the one-sided emphasis it has often received but partly also because we have not known how to deal with it. But misapplication of truth must never be permitted to make us insensitive to it. (*Ibid.*, pp. 142-143.)

Some concluding statements are:

> In light of the foregoing exposition of the New Testament representations of baptism, the idea that baptism is a purely symbolic rite must be pronounced not alone unsatisfactory but out of harmony with the New Testament itself. Admittedly, such a judgment runs counter to the popular tradition of the Denomination to which the writer belongs...The extent and nature of the grace which the New Testament writers declare to be present in baptism is astonishing for any who come to the study freshly with an open mind...the "grace" available to man in baptism is said by the New Testament writers to include the following elements: forgiveness of sin, Acts 2.38 and cleansing from sins, Acts 22.16, II Cor. 6.11; union with Christ, Gal. 3.27, and particularly union with Him in his death and resurrection, Rom. 6.3ff, Col. 2.11f, with all that implies of release from sin's power, as well as guilt, and the sharing of the risen life of the Redeemer, Rom. 6.1-11; participation in Christ's sonship, Gal. 3.26f; consecration to God, I Cor. 6.11, hence membership in the Church, the Body of Christ, I Cor. 12.13, Gal. 3.27-29; possession of the Spirit, Acts 2.38, I Cor. 6.11, 12.13, and therefore the new life in the Spirit, i.e., regeneration, Tit. 3.5, Jn. 3.5; grace to live according to the will of God, Rom. 6.1ff, Col. 3.1ff; deliverance from the evil powers that rule this world, Col. 1.13; the inheritance of the Kingdom of God, Jn. 3.5, and the pledge of the resurrection of the body, Eph. 1.3f, 4.30. (*Ibid.*, pp. 263-264.)

Beasley-Murray states his conclusions in a chapter entitled "Baptismal Reform and Church Relationships":

> First, there ought to be a greater endeavour to make baptism integral to *the Gospel*. It is taken as axiomatic amongst us [Baptists—SGD] that the proclamation of the Gospel consists of making the redemptive acts of God in Christ known and calling for faith in Christ as the due response; baptism is then a proper subject for exposition in the enquirers' class, along with instruction as to the nature of the Church, of worship, of Christian obligation in the Church and to the world etc. Peter's response, however, to the cry of his conscience stricken hearers on the Day of Pentecost was not "Repent and believe", but "Repent and *be baptized*"! (Acts 2.38). Naturally faith was presumed in repentance, but Peter's answer told the Jews how to become Christians: faith and repentance are to be expressed in baptism, and *so* they are to come to the Lord. Baptism is here a part of the proclamation of Christ. In an Apostolic sermon it comes as its logical conclusion. An effort ought to be made to restore this note in our [Baptist—SGD] preaching. (*Ibid*., p. 393.)

Thus, we believe the blood of Jesus was shed for the remission of sins, because the Bible says it. Likewise we believe baptism is for the remission of sins, because the same Bible says it in identically the same words.

Baptism Is a Work, and We're Not Saved by Works

Baptism is a work, or a thing done, and we're not saved by works of a distinct kind, that is, works of merit. We ought to be impressed with what many people in the religious world have been exposed to in the way of false teaching concerning the subject of baptism, and why they're leery about believing that baptism has anything to do with man's salvation.

Our Roman Catholic friends believe baptism is a work of merit, i.e., the act itself merits salvation whether any faith exists behind the act or not. For example, the following quotations, from several official Catholic publications, show that baptism in many cases is not an act of faith at all:

> Valid reception does not require faith...Therefore, an unbeliever who so desires may be validly baptized even tho he have no faith. (Jone-Adelman, *Moral Theology*, p. 320, cited by O. C. Lambert, *Catholicism Against Itself, Vol. II* [Winfield, AL: O. C. Lambert, Publisher, 1966], pp. 218-222.)

Likewise, Catholic sources teach one need not even be conscious when he is baptized:

> Baptize any person found unconscious and in a dying condition. (Ayrinhac, *Legislation on the Sacraments*, p. 32, cited by O. C. Lambert, *Ibid.*)

On baptizing infants, Catholics teach:

> Many priests find this the least spiritualizing of all their works in the Church. The fact that the recipient of the sacrament is unconscious of what is being done, and often in consequences behaves in a manner not befitting the occasion, undoubtedly detracts from the solemnity of the rite. (Ward, *The Priestly Vocation*, p. 89, cited by O. C. Lambert, *Ibid.*)

Two of the most amazing statements showing Catholics don't view baptism as an act of faith, but a mere meritorious work, are the following:

> A miscarried fetus or embryo, no matter how small, must always be baptized--absolutely if certainly alive, conditionally if doubtfully alive. (Gerald H. Fitz Gibbons, *Spiritual First Aid Procedures*, p. 3, cited by O. C. Lambert, *Ibid.*)

> The general rule is, of course, that a child should not be baptized until fully born. But if there is a danger that the child will die of suffocation, or from some other cause before complete delivery, it should be baptized on the first available members. (Rumble, *Quizzes on Hospital Ethics*, p. 56, cited by O. C. Lambert, *Ibid.*)

These statements regarding baptism as a meritorious work not contingent under any circumstances on the faith of the subject are as repulsive to us as to the one who argues that since baptism is a work, it has nothing to do with our salvation. However, just because Roman Catholicism goes to one extreme concerning baptism, we shouldn't go to another extreme where we don't teach the truth about baptism either. The argument that works have nothing to do with salvation is just as false as the idea that meritorious works do.

For example, the statement that works have nothing to do with salvation is not just an argument against baptism, but also an argument against repentance, for it is a "thing done." Likewise, confession is a work—not a meritorious one, but certainly "unto salvation" (Rom. 10.9-10). Similarly, faith itself is a work, for Jn. 6.28-29 says: "They said therefore unto him, What must we do, that we may work the works of God? Jesus answered and said unto them, This is the work of God, that ye believe on him whom he hath sent." Thus, if works have nothing to do with our salvation, then faith itself would have nothing to do with the salvation of man!

The truth of the matter is, *God* works in baptism: Paul says in Col. 2.12, "having been buried with him in baptism, wherein also ye were raised with him through faith in the working of God, who raised him from the dead." In the next verse Paul tells about the work God does when we are baptized with this faith: "And you, being dead through your trespasses and the uncircumcision of your flesh, you, I say, did he make alive together with him, having forgiven us all our trespasses." When we have "faith in the working of God," rather than thinking baptism has nothing to do with our salvation or perhaps even being unconscious to the act, and are baptized, God forgives us our sins, and raises us up with Christ to walk in newness of life.

Paul Said Christ Didn't Send Him to Baptize, Therefore Baptism Must Not Be Essential to Our Salvation

People who take this position use I Cor. 1.11-17 to substantiate their view:

> For it hath been signified unto me concerning you, my brethren, by them that are of the household of Chloe, that there are contentions among you. Now this I mean, that each one of you saith, I am of Paul; and I of Apollos; and I of Cephas; and I of Christ. Is Christ divided? was Paul crucified for you? or were ye baptized into the name of Paul? I thank God that I baptized none of you, lest any man should say that ye were baptized into my name. And I baptized also the household of Stephanas: besides, I know not whether I baptized any other. For Christ sent me not to baptize; but to preach the gospel:

Rather than showing Paul didn't think baptism was very important, this passage clearly demonstrates the essentiality of baptism. First, notice the context of these words. Corinth, a church that was wracked with nearly every conceivable problem, also had a problem with its attitude toward preachers.

In this very passage, Paul mentioned he learned that they were divided over the preacher who baptized them. In this context, Paul said he was glad he hadn't baptized any more of them than he had, *not because he didn't think baptism was important, but lest any man should say that he was baptized into Paul's name.* Indeed, Paul baptized a few of them while there. *Many were baptized* by other men, as Luke's account of Paul's work in Corinth in Ac. 18.8 shows: "And Crispus, the ruler of the synagogue, believed in the Lord with all his house; and many of the Corinthians hearing believed, and were baptized." So *many* were baptized, yet because of the specific problem in Corinth, Paul was glad that he hadn't personally baptized more of them, lest an even greater number would be calling themselves after him.

Concerning the structure of Paul's language in I Cor. 1.17, "For Christ sent me *not* to baptize *but* to preach the gospel," this is an excellent example of an *ellipsis*, a figure of speech where certain words that are not directly expressed are understood. Other scriptural examples illustrate how these words are to be interpreted. For instance, in I Pet. 3.3, Peter says, "Whose adorning let it *not* be the outward adorning of braiding the hair, and of wearing jewels of gold, or putting on apparel: *but* let it be the hidden man of the heart, in the incorruptible apparel of a meek and quiet spirit." In this passage, which is similar in construction to I Cor. 1.17, Peter doesn't forbid putting on apparel—certainly women are to adorn themselves with clothing, but he places the emphasis upon the woman's inward adorning, the adorning of their spirit!

Similarly, in Jn. 6.27, Jesus uses this construction when he says "Work not for the food which perisheth, *but* for the food which abideth unto eternal life." Obviously, Jesus doesn't prohibit working for physical food (Paul in II Thes. 3.10 says: "If any will not work, neither let him eat.") but He shows where we should place the *emphasis*, i.e., spiritual food should take precedence over physical food.

Likewise, when Paul said Christ sent him not to baptize, but to preach, he didn't depreciate baptism, but merely showed where Paul should place the *emphasis*, i.e., upon preaching the word of God. When the apostles delivered the gospel, it was definitely more important that they preach, because at that time, not just anybody could teach the word of God, but they could baptize! Thus, the apostles rightly emphasized their preaching over actually baptizing the believers themselves.

In addition, Luke in Ac. 18.8 said Crispus *believed*, whereas Paul said Crispus *was baptized* in his account in I Cor. 1.14. This merely shows that "belief" in the Bible included baptism. Crispus was a believer because he placed his confidence in Christ enough to obey Him—he believed in Christ enough to be baptized for the remission of his sins! Those who argue about Jesus' teaching on baptism ought to have the same faith Crispus had!

In this passage Paul also teaches two things must happen before one may call himself after another person. He said for one to call himself after Paul, (1) Paul would have to be crucified for the person, and (2) the person would have to be baptized in the name of Paul. The fact neither of these was true should prohibit the Corinthians from calling themselves after Paul. Consider carefully what Paul's argument means positively: *for one to be called after Christ, two things must happen:* (1) Christ would have to die for the person, and (2) the person would have to be baptized in the name of Christ! Thus, the very passage so many people use to show that baptism is not essential proves true belief includes baptism (as it did in the case of Crispus) and for one to be called a "Christian," he must be baptized in the name of Christ!

What About the Thief on the Cross? He Wasn't Baptized, Yet Jesus Said He Would Be with Him in Paradise

The case of the thief on the cross has to be the most frequently offered objection to the necessity of penitent believers being baptized in our time. People argue, "The thief on the cross wasn't baptized, and yet Jesus said he would be with Him in paradise." This argument deserves an honest and forthright reply.

First, *how do you know the thief on the cross wasn't baptized? What makes you think he wasn't?* Remember how John the Baptist preached and baptized in this region, and the gospels tell how he met with stupendous success (Mt. 3.1, 2, 5, 6; Lk. 3.7, 12):

> And in those days cometh John the Baptist, preaching in the wilderness of Judea, saying, Repent ye: for the kingdom of heaven is at hand...Then went out unto him *Jerusalem, and all Judea, and all the* region round about the Jordan: and they were baptized of him in the river Jordan...

> He said therefore to the *multitudes* that went out to be baptized of him...and there came also *publicans* to be baptized.

Suppose someone could make statements like this about the community where you live, i.e., *all the city* had gone out to be baptized, that *all the region around* your city had, that *multitudes* had, and *even the federal employees* had! Would you be dogmatic that a certain individual in your community had not been baptized?

Of course, no man knows for sure whether or not the thief on the cross was baptized by John's baptism. However, the success of John's preaching shows that those who assume the thief was not baptized have no basis to make this assumption.

Whether or not the thief on the cross was baptized by John, he was not baptized in the name of Jesus Christ! *No one in the whole world had been commanded to be baptized in the name of Jesus Christ* at the time Jesus was crucified. The thief on the cross was never commanded to be baptized in the name of Jesus Christ! Not until fifty days later, when the gospel was first preached in fact on the first Pentecost following the resurrection of Christ, were believers told: "Repent ye, and be baptized every one of you in the name of Jesus Christ unto the remission of your sins." So the thief on the cross couldn't have been baptized in the name of Jesus Christ—*he wasn't commanded to!* Have you been commanded to?

Suppose that someone refuses to pay his income tax, and when confronted by a federal judge, argues he doesn't have to pay income tax on the grounds that Abraham Lincoln didn't pay income tax. That judge will inform him the laws have changed somewhat since the times of Lincoln and now demand it.

Similarly, one might argue that he doesn't have to put money in parking meters on the grounds his great grandfather didn't. He, too, will be informed the laws have changed since great-granddad's day. We are to obey the laws we live under, not the laws someone else lived under.

Likewise, the thief on the cross lived under the Law of Moses. He was not under the covenant you and I are subject to, for Christ's covenant didn't go into effect until He died (Heb. 9.16-17). The thief never heard the words Christ directs to believers today: "Repent ye, and be baptized everyone of you in the name of Jesus Christ unto the remission of your sins; and ye shall receive the gift of the Holy Spirit."

Conclusion

When all of men's arguments fall, the Bible's teaching on this subject is still the same: Ac. 2.38 still teaches baptism is for the remission of sins; Ac. 22.16 still teaches baptism washes away sins. Mk. 16.16 still teaches "he that believeth and is baptized shall be saved." I Cor. 12.13 still teaches baptism puts us into the body of Christ. Gal. 3.27 still teaches baptism puts us into Christ. Rom. 6.3-4 still teaches baptism puts us into the death of Christ. Col. 2.12-13 still teaches that through baptism we obtain the newness of life. I Pet. 3.21 still teaches that baptism saves us.

The first time the gospel was preached, "They then that received his word were baptized," (Ac. 2.41). Men today who receive the gospel do the same thing. Friend, if you believe in Jesus Christ, and have repented, i.e., determined that you will live according to His teaching, won't you confess His name before men and be baptized for the reasons *He* said while you have opportunity?

For a discussion of other denominational errors, see the author's *Denominational Doctrines: Explained, Examined, Exposed.*

Appendix 4

II John 9 and the Teaching of Christ

The affirmation that we are not in fellowship with God on the basis of our complete doctrinal perfection may alarm some who wonder about passages like II John 9 where John says:

> Whosoever goeth onward and abideth not in the teaching of Christ, hath not God...

This is a legitimate question that deserves a careful answer. II John 9-11 has received a great deal of attention in recent years concerning matters of fellowship. Some conclude from the passage that doctrinal differences other than the teaching about the nature of Christ shouldn't divide Christians.

Carl W. Ketcherside's Position

Carl Ketcherside, an influential preacher in the restoration movement in America, makes the expression "teaching of Christ" in this passage mean "teaching about Christ," rather than "teaching from Christ," the New Testament. For example, in *The Twisted Scriptures*, he says, concerning II John 9:

> This is one of the "twisted scriptures." It has become the handle for every factional tool used to pry apart the living stones in the temple of God. It is the murderous knife employed to dismember the body of the Lord. It was written by the apostle of love to protect the flock of God

> from prowling wolves who sought to seduce them through denial of the fundamental fact that Jesus has come in the flesh. It is now used to convert the sheep into snarling dogs, snapping at each other over every stray scrap of doctrine. It has substituted the law of the pack for the love of the flock."(Carl Ketcherside, *The Twisted Scriptures* [Swengal, PA: Reiner Publications, reprint edition, 1965], page 81.)

On page 87 of the same book, Ketcherside says:

> The doctrine of Christ, in this case, does not consist of the things Jesus taught, but of the thing taught about Jesus.

What shall we say to these things? Is the doctrine of Christ the same doctrine Jesus taught, or is it, as Ketcherside says, the doctrine taught about Jesus?

Background of Gnosticism

Ketcherside argues correctly when he says that the doctrine of Christ ought to be interpreted in the context of John's writing to combat the Gnostic false teachers. The Gnostics taught a first century heresy concerning the nature of God (He had both a good and evil side, a physical and a spiritual side), Christ (Jesus was not the Christ, but He had the Christ), man (also has a dual nature, the physical side that is responsible for sin and the spiritual side that cannot be guilty of sin), and sin itself.

A significant class of Gnostics taught that it really didn't matter how you lived, since your spirit was saved anyway, rather than your body that was guilty of sin. While this volume does not thoroughly investigate Gnosticism, once one is aware of the Gnostic heresy in the latter part of the first century, he will then realize that nearly every verse in John's Epistles is a very pointed statement against Gnosticism.

Many who study John's letters are not aware of this background, and so when Ketcherside says these verses need to be interpreted in light of that background, he is altogether correct. However, he goes too far when he says that because of the background of Gnosticism, the expression doctrine of Christ means the teaching about Christ.

What Is the Doctrine of Christ?

John fought against much more of the Gnostics' teaching than just their false concept of the nature of Christ. As mentioned above, they also held false positions concerning the nature of God, the nature of man, the nature of sin, etc. As a matter of fact, one important theme of John's argument against Gnosticism was the manner of life Christians were to lead.

For example, in I Jn. 1.7, John says:

> But if we walk in the light, as he is in the light, we have fellowship one with another, and the blood of Jesus his Son cleanseth us from all sin.

John directs this slam against the Gnostic teaching that the manner of life of a Christian is not germane to fellowship with God. John specifically states that one's fellowship with God is contingent upon him walking in the light, that is, his pattern of life causes him to walk in the truth of God. He is not an habitual sinner, as the Gnostics were. In I Jn. 2.6, John says:

> ...he that saith he abideth in him ought himself also to walk even as he walked.

Again, this directly contradicts the Gnostic teaching that you can abide in God and still live anyway you want to.

In I Jn. 2.15, John says:

> Love not the world, neither the things that are in the world. If any man love the world, the love of the Father is not in him.

This opposes the Gnostic teaching that you could love the world and still share fellowship with the Father. Not so, John affirms.

In I Jn. 3.6-8, we have:

> Whosoever abideth in him sinneth not: whosoever sinneth hath not seen him, neither knoweth him. My little children, let no man lead you astray; he that doeth righteousness is righteous, even as he is righteous: he that doeth sin is of the devil; for the devil sinneth from the beginning.

With the understanding of Gnosticism, John pointedly sets aside the Gnostic teaching that Christians could sin all they wanted to. Yet Gnostics claimed to have a superior knowledge of God. In II Jn. 4, John counters another Gnostic heresy:

> I rejoice greatly that I have found certain of thy children walking in truth, even as we received commandment from the Father.

The "walking in truth" that John speaks about is not just the truth of the nature of Christ, although that was a problem with Gnosticism. It also refers to the pattern of life of those who fell into the Gnostic doctrine. See verse 6 of this same chapter:

> And this is love, that we should walk after his commandments. This is the commandment, even as ye heard from the beginning, that ye should walk in it.

John clearly is not just concerned about the Gnostic teaching concerning the nature of Christ, but also their beliefs about their manner of life.

John includes similar teaching in his third epistle (verse 4) when he says:

> For I rejoiced greatly, when brethren came and bare witness unto thy truth, even as thou walkest in truth.

> Greater joy have I none than this, to hear of my children walking in the truth.

Walking in truth that John is so concerned about, is not just the truth concerning the deity of Christ, but rather the behavior of these Christians who have fallen prey to the Gnostic influence.

These passages show that when we become familiar with Gnosticism to help us understand John's Epistles, we do well. However, if we limit the extent of the Gnostic heresy to teaching concerning the nature of Christ, we violate the context that the letters manifest. "The truth" in John's Epistles is not just the truth concerning the nature of Christ.

Yet another approach shows the weakness of this position, seeing just how the "teaching" or "doctrine" of a person or persons is used elsewhere in the New Testament. At least twenty-one other times in the New Testament, we have the "doctrine" of a person or persons. Apparently it never means the doctrine *about* the person, as Ketcherside asserts above, but rather always the doctrine or teaching *from* the person.

For example, Mt. 16.12 speaks of the "doctrine of the Pharisees." However, Jesus warns of the teaching *from* the Pharisees, not the teaching *about* them.

In Ac. 2.42, when the early Christians continued in the "apostles' doctrine," they were not concerned about the teaching *about* the apostles; they were seeking the teaching *from* the apostles.

In Ac. 13.12, some were astonished at the doctrine of the Lord. Yet they were not astonished at the teaching *about* Christ, but rather the teaching that came *from* Christ.

In Rev. 2.14, Jesus speaks of the "doctrine of Balaam." This was not the teaching *about* Balaam, but the teaching that came *from* Balaam.

In Rev. 2.15, Jesus speaks of the doctrine of the Nicolaitans. This was not the doctrine *about* the Nicolaitans, but the teaching *from* the Nicolaitans.

In Col. 2.22, Paul speaks of the philosophies and the doctrines of men. This doesn't refer to doctrines *about* men, but doctrines that come *from* men, man-made philosophies.

In I Tim. 4.1, Paul warns of the doctrines of devils, and then he names some of those doctrines. They are not doctrines *about* devils, but *from* devils, such as eating of meats, forbidding to marry, etc.

In II Tim. 3.10, we have the "doctrine of Paul." However, this passage does not concern the doctrine *about* Paul, but the teaching that came *from* him.

These examples could be multiplied, but apparently every time in the New Testament that the teaching or doctrine of a person is referred to, it never speaks of the doctrine *about* the person, but always the doctrine *from* him. Thus, when we come to the "doctrine of Christ" in II John 9, we would be highly suspicious if in all the New Testament, this expression meant anything other than the teaching from Christ, not the teaching about Christ.

John says that anyone who transgresses the doctrine of Christ, who without regard goes beyond it, who like the Gnostics didn't stay in the commandments or teaching of Christ, does not have God. He is not in fellowship with God, regardless of how loudly he might proclaim that he is.

The Positive View

If this is the teaching of II John 9, as we believe it is, then it is also positively stated elsewhere in the New Testament. In I Jn. 3.24, John says:

> And he that keepeth his commandments abideth in him, and he in him.

This teaches the same thing positively that II John 9 teaches negatively. II John 9 affirms that one is not in fellowship with God if he's not content to dwell in Christ's teaching, while this verse teaches that if one keeps His commandments, he abides or dwells in (or is in fellowship with) Christ.

In addition, in Jn. 14.23, Jesus states the truth of II John 9 in a positive manner:

> Jesus answered and said unto him, If a man love me, he will keep my word: and my Father will love him, and we will come unto him, and make our abode with him.

Jesus affirms that one condition of fellowship with the Father and the Son is keeping the word of God. II John 9 affirms that if we're not content to do so, we do not have God, i.e., we're not in fellowship with Him.

While Ketcherside's contention that the "teaching of Christ" is the teaching about the nature of Christ falls far short of the mark, John still does not profess that one must be perfectly doctrinally correct to be in fellowship with God. In striking out against the Gnostics' teaching that one could willfully disregard the teaching from Christ. John does not declare that one must perfectly understand and obey Christ to be in fellowship with Him, but continuing to study and grow and use the Bible for our standard of authority. Let's leave the teaching in its context.

After preaching this material in a meeting once in the Kansas City area, one especially studious fellow gave me some reaction to my material on II John 9, and asked me a particularly interesting question. I had taught much the same as I've written here, that II John 9 was written to combat Gnostics, who taught that Christians didn't have to be restrained by the teaching from Christ. I concluded that the "whosoever" that "goeth onward" was not the fellow who misunderstood or disagreed with the teaching of Christ, but the fellow (like the Gnostics) who just barged beyond its boundaries.

The fellow said he was giving serious consideration to that view, but he was afraid of how far I might take it. He asked, "If I come to you holding my New Testament in my hand, and tell you that we've got to be governed by this, and you say the same thing; and yet I believe that we must use instrumental music, can you use II John 9 to draw a line of fellowship with me?" My answer was no, but that we had other passages which would limit our fellowship in such cases, such as Eph. 5.11 ("have no fellowship with the unfruitful works of darkness") and I Tim. 5.22 ("neither be a partaker in other men's sins"). It seems simple to me now, but we don't have to use II John 9 to draw every line of fellowship that has to be drawn, do we? Yet it seems that's what many of us have been doing, and applying the passage to situations not contemplated by John. In the accompanying chart, I've sought to show how these three passages are related.

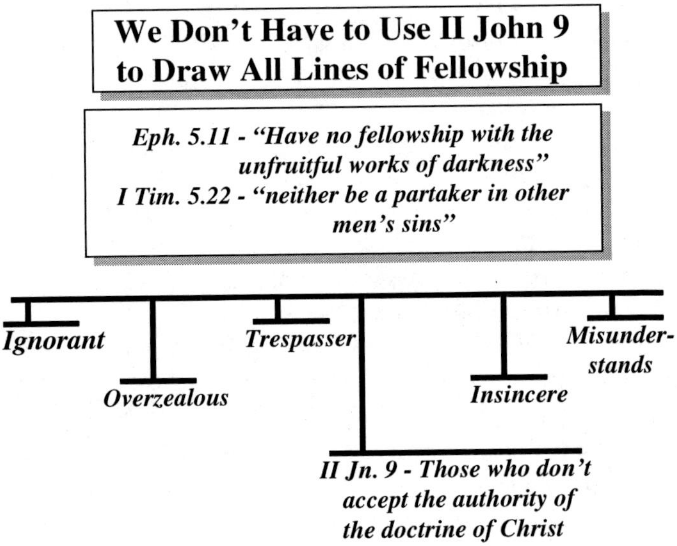

Figure 12

Appendix 5

An Introduction to a Local Church

Several times in the course of this volume, the suggestion has been made that a local congregation of Christians would do well to prepare a document that would forthrightly inform visiting Christians what the congregation does collectively. The purpose of this appendix is to give an example of this kind of document.

This document enables newcomers to see if they can conscientiously join themselves to a specific local church. An understanding of the work of the congregation helps contribute to the unity of the congregation, and serves to keep away those who don't want to be involved in similar unified efforts. A mutual commitment to work together would also serve as the basis of restorative discipline efforts when members no longer participate in the collective activity of the congregation or no longer seek to live by faith in Christ.

As mentioned earlier, this document is not a creed, a statement of belief of the congregation. Nor does it state what must be believed by prospective members in order to establish fellowship. It reveals the activities of the congregation. It assumes that one is in Christ (by baptism as a penitent believer), that he has a resolve to live by faith in Christ, and a commitment to work with other Christians in the collective activity of a congregation.

The statement that follows is intended only as a suggestive sample, and is not designed to be a standard for any congregation of Christians. The collective work of each congregation depends greatly upon the resources of its members. Whether or not a congregation has elders also influences how the collective activity of the congregation is arrived at. The exact makeup of each congregation determines as well the specific areas of action they can conscientiously participate in with each other.

Getting Acquainted with the ____________Church

An Introduction to the Church Meeting at

________________________.

This church is an independent local congregation of Christians, i.e., believers who have been baptized into Jesus Christ for the remission of sins and who are committed to live by faith in Christ. We are joined together to serve God and to encourage each other to become more faithful to Christ. We seek no affiliation larger than this local congregation. When we have the opportunity to cooperate with other congregations of the Lord's people, these cooperative efforts are always done in a way as to protect the independence of this local church.

We all earnestly desire to come to a full understanding of the teaching of Christ. While we work together toward this goal, we agree to be in subjection to one another in matters of opinion and to not be contentious about matters that we may differ on. Our joint action is based on those things that we all agree the Bible teaches a local church is authorized to do. At the present time we collectively participate in the following areas:

Evangelism

We actively support the teaching of the gospel of Christ in this local area, and when we are able, support teaching efforts in other areas. We also strive to develop each individual's abilities to teach the gospel.

Edification

We are earnestly committed to learning the word of God and teaching it to our children. Willing, qualified teachers are supported by the congregation is this effort. We have developed study plans covering all levels of spiritual maturity. These are available for inspection. Specifically, the following classes are offered:

ADULT CHRISTIANS: We have an overall goal of teaching the entire Bible every four years. This plan is subject to change when special studies of Biblical subjects are deemed necessary by the congregation.

JUNIOR AND SENIOR HIGH STUDENTS: The entire New Testament (except Revelation, due to lack of Old Testament background) is taught in the seventh through ninth grades, and then repeated in the tenth through twelfth grades. Again, this goal is subject to change when specific studies of Biblical subjects are deemed necessary by the congregation.

TODDLERS THROUGH SIXTH GRADE STUDENTS: Class material rich in audio-visual aids has been developed for all ages in this group. This plan of study provides parents and teachers with the lesson material and emphasizes the responsibility of the parents to provide the proper spiritual food for their children on a daily basis.

NEWLY CONVERTED CHRISTIANS: We strive to give newly converted Christians every opportunity possible to grow and mature as God expects them to. To assist these babes in Christ in their development, a member of the congregation teaches the new Christians several important lessons, while making himself available to answer any questions or help deal with any problems.

Public Worship

We assemble on the first day of the week to encourage each other unto love and good works, and to worship the God of heaven by praying, singing, partaking of the Lord's Supper, contributing into the church treasury, and publicly teaching His word. During these weekly assemblies, any physical or spiritual needs of the members of the congregation are made known, in order that we might serve our brethren and relieve them in any way possible.

Congregational Meetings

When this congregation has no elders, our collective action is determined in monthly meetings of the entire congregation. In order to efficiently accomplish the Lord's work, certain individuals are assigned specific responsibilities. These individuals then report to the congregation.

Benevolence

This church is willing and able to care for its own members and other needy Christians. However, we are also aware of the responsibility of the individual to care for the needs of his own family so as not to burden the church. We encourage Christians to support their own, while this church uses its resources to care for Christians with no family to relieve them. Individual Christians in this congregation have always been interested in the plight of their fellow man and will continue to care for those outside of Christ who need help with legitimate physical needs.

Discipline

To help prevent the necessity of restoring or disciplining members, the vast majority of our efforts are preventive measures. The teaching program, assemblies, and our working together are intended to help us remain committed to Christ and

His word, thereby living more faithfully to Him. Still, we recognize a person's right to make his own choices. If a member chooses to stop striving to live by faith or refuses to be in subjection to the congregation and rejects all efforts to be restored, this church will withdraw fellowship. This action applies moral force to the sinner so that repentance can take place and the church be cleansed.

If You Are Considering Joining Us

IF YOU ARE A CHRISTIAN, and you are considering joining the disciples here (Ac. 9.26), and can be committed to the work we are doing to the best of your ability, we invite you to join us. You can do so by making an announcement to that effect at the conclusion of one of our services or by making your desires known to one of the members, who will inform the congregation. Work sheets are available on different types of recurring jobs to help you see where you can work with us.

IF YOU HAVE BEEN WITHDRAWN FROM BY ANOTHER CONGREGATION, we do not recognize another congregation's actions as binding on us. However, it will be necessary for us to investigate your situation somewhat before we decide if we can work with you.

IF YOU ARE NOT A CHRISTIAN, we would very much like to study with you and present God's plan to you as revealed in the New Testament. Please contact one of the members and arrangements will be made for a class at a time convenient for you.

(NOTE: This Introduction is not conceived of by us, nor should it be by anyone else, as a creed, i.e., a doctrinal standard of belief for the Christians in this congregation. Rather, it is a statement of what we are presently doing, to inform those who may be interested in joining our collective activity.)

IF YOU HAVE ANY QUESTIONS OR COMMENTS you would like to discuss, please bring them to the attention of one of the members.

Appendix 6

Denominational Action in the New Testament?

Appendix 7 presents an examination of the sponsoring church concept. This appendix examines the major arguments for the concept. Two major lines of argument have come to light in recent years, one based upon Phil. 4.15-16 and II Cor. 11.8, the other on Ac. 11.27-30.

Though these arguments are prevalent among churches of Christ, they are not peculiar to them. For instance, I once debated the sabbath question with a leader in the Church of God—Seventh-day. During the debate, I met my respondent's son who was a preacher in the Seventh Day Church of God. Discussing the differences between the two denominational groups, I found that the two groups were divided over the very passages discussed in this appendix. The son argued for collective action of congregations using the same two arguments answered here. His father approached those arguments in essentially the same way I do herein. We ought to expect those defending denominational action to use these arguments, regardless of their denominational affiliation, and the answers to their arguments will work just as well, again regardless of the denominational affiliation.

Phil. 4.15-16 and II Cor. 11.8

These two passages read thusly:

Phil. 4.15-16: And ye yourselves also know, ye Philippians, that in the beginning of the gospel, when I departed from Macedonia, no church had fellowship with me in the matter of giving and receiving but ye only; for even in Thessalonica ye sent once and again unto my need.

II Cor. 11.8: I robbed other churches, taking wages of them that I might minister unto you.

The argument for the sponsoring church concept goes like this: (1) On his second missionary journey Paul received funds only from Philippi, Phil. 4.15-16. (2) Other churches contributed to his support (II Cor. 11.8). (3) Therefore, the other churches sent to Philippi, who, acting as a sponsoring church, received funds and sent them on to Paul while he was in Corinth.

This is an impressive argument at first glance. However, the context of Paul's two statements helps determine whether or not this argument is indeed valid. Thus, a brief chronology of Paul's second missionary journey as described in Ac. 16-18 follows:

1. Paul in Derbe-Lystra: Ac. 16.1
2. Paul in Phrygia-Galatia: Ac. 16.6
3. Paul in Troas: Ac. 16.8
4. Paul at Philippi: Ac. 16.12, the chief city of Macedonia
5. Paul at Thessalonica: Ac. 17.1, 2
    a. This was "in the beginning of the gospel," Phil. 4.15.
    b. This was "When I departed from Macedonia," Phil. 4.15.
    c. "For even in Thessalonica ye sent once and again unto my need," Phil. 4.16.
6. Paul at Berea: Ac. 17.10. When Paul left Berea, he left Macedonia.
7. Paul at Athens: Ac. 17.15. Now Paul is definitely out of Macedonia.
8. Paul at Corinth: Ac. 18.1. Here Paul dwelt eighteen months, verse 11: "I robbed other churches, taking wages of them to do you service," II Cor. 11.8.
9. Paul at Ephesus: Ac. 18.19
10. Paul at Antioch: Ac. 18.22, end of Second Journey

Examination of Phil. 4.15-16 in Light of Paul's Second Journey

First, Paul's statement in Phil. 4.15-16 makes it clear that *at a specific time* Paul received funds only from Philippi. In fact, Paul used three expressions to specify the precise time of their contribution to him: (1) "In the beginning of the gospel," (when Paul crossed the Aegean Sea from Troas to Philippi, he carried the gospel to European soil for the first time in his life); (2) "When I departed from Macedonia;" and (3) "For even in Thessalonica, ye sent once and again unto my need."

These statements limit the time when no other church sent funds to Paul. They do not apply to Paul's stay in Athens or during his 18-month stay in Corinth while he waited for his companions, or in Athens conversing with the Athenians in the synagogue, the marketplace, and on Mars Hill. Likewise, they do not apply while he spent time making tents with Aquila, and reasoned in the synagogue every sabbath (Ac. 17.16-18.4). *After all this* brethren (Silas and Timothy) came from Macedonia to supply his needs from *other churches* (II Cor. 11.8).

Lenski, in his commentary, makes this point in a similar fashion:

> When I departed from Macedonia: Note: the time when I left, before I got entirely away. For Thessalonica is located in Macedonia, and there the two gifts that were sent from Philippi reached Paul. That is why *kai* "even" is added, "even in Thessalonica," before I actually got farther away. (R. C. H. Lenski, *The Interpretation of St. Paul's First and Second Epistles to the Corinthians* [Minneapolis, MN: Augsburg Publishing House, 1937], p. 892.)

Likewise, the distinguished Greek grammarian A. T. Robertson says:

> Both once and twice they did it "even in Thessalonica" and so before Paul went to Corinth. (A. T. Robertson,

Word Pictures in the New Testament, IV [Nashville, TN: Broadman Press, 1931], p. 462.)

In addition, Paul's words in Phil. 4.15-16 do not describe the action of a sponsoring church: (1) Paul didn't say "sending and receiving" (as is done by a sponsoring church) but "giving and receiving." A big difference! If you give me one hundred dollars to send to someone, I don't give it. At a specific time, Philippi was the only church that gave. If other churches had contributed, Paul said they didn't give! Try telling the contributing churches who send to a sponsoring church that they don't give! Surely, Philippi sent, but what Philippi sent, Philippi gave.

The way Paul gives proper credit needs to be considered. In Phil. 4.15-16, Paul gave credit to a solitary church. In verse 15, he says that no church had fellowship with him but Philippi only. In verse 17, he said, "I seek for the fruit which aboundeth to your account." If Philippi served as a sponsoring church, no other church was credited for its contribution! Paul gives only Philippi any expression of appreciation for the action. If Philippi was a sponsoring church, only Philippi was in fellowship with Paul. All the contributing churches truly were robbed! Further, suppose a preacher in our time confessed he had only one sponsoring church at a specific time!

The sponsoring church concept argued from Phil. 4.15-16 and II Cor. 11.8 confuses several things with the facts of Paul's second journey: (1) It confuses the time difference between the two passages. Paul says, "When I departed from Macedonia," not "after I had left Macedonia, stayed awhile at Athens, and then had been settled for some time in Corinth." (2) It confuses the number of churches. Paul said Philippi only supported him, not other churches, as he departed from Macedonia. The sponsoring church concept involves other churches, not Philippi only, at Corinth.

Guy N. Woods, notable defender of the sponsoring church concept among churches of Christ, made the following statements concerning these passages before the sponsoring church concept gained widespread popularity:

> Here too, we see the simple manner in which the church at Philippi joined with Paul in the work of preaching the gospel. There was no "missionary society" in evidence, and none was needed: the brethren simply raised the money and sent it directly to Paul. This is the way it should be done today. No organization was needed to accomplish the work the Lord has authorized the church to do. When men become dissatisfied with God's arrangement and set up one of their own, they have already crossed the threshold of apostasy. Let's be satisfied with the Lord's manner of doing things. (Guy N. Woods, *Annual Lesson Commentary* [Nashville, TN: Gospel Advocate Publishing Company, 1946], p. 341.)

I agree with these comments. Philippi sent to Paul as he departed Macedonia, other churches sent to Paul while he was at Corinth. Examples like this show that one church can support a preacher, Phil. 4.15-16, or several can, II Cor. 11.8, but no sponsoring church exists in Paul's dealings on his second missionary journey.

Acts 11.27-30

The second passage used to try to demonstrate the sponsoring church concept in the New Testament is Ac. 11.27-30. The passage reads thusly:

> Now in these days there came down prophets from Jerusalem unto Antioch. And there stood up one of them named Agabus, and signified by the Spirit that there should be a great famine over all the world: which came to pass in the days of Claudius. And the disciples, every man according to his ability, determined to send relief unto the brethren that dwelt in Judea: which also they did, sending it to the elders by the hand of Barnabas and Saul.

To justify the sponsoring church concept, some people assume that when the collection was sent to Judea, it was sent to Jerusalem. As the "sponsoring church of Judea" Jerusalem received the funds, and then dispersed them to the surrounding churches.

Since in the New Testament local churches were autonomous or self-ruling, and each church had its own elders (Ac. 14.23; I Pet. 5.1-3; Ac. 20.17; Phil. 1.1; Tit. 1.5), the elders in Judea would surely be where the brethren in Judea were, that is, scattered throughout all Judea. After all, they were not the elders *of* Judea, i.e., sponsoring church elders. Instead they were the elders *in* Judea, and many different churches existed in Judea (Ac. 9.31; I Thes. 2.14, specifically Lydda, Ac. 9.32; and Joppa, Ac. 9.38).

However, the argument for the sponsoring church rests on more than just the assumption that the collection was sent to Jerusalem. The argument is made from Ac. 12.25 that when Paul and Barnabas finished this benevolent journey, they returned to Antioch from Jerusalem! Thus, we are told, those who oppose the sponsoring church concept assume Paul and Barnabas traveled throughout Judea, when Luke identifies only one city in Judea where they actually traveled to, Jerusalem.

What shall we say to these things? Again, the chronology of Paul's life answers these arguments, along with Paul's statement in Ac. 26.19-20. First, consider the benevolent journey in Ac. 11.27-30 in the overall picture of Paul's life. In Acts 9, Paul was in Jerusalem (vv1-2) obtaining permission to persecute Christians in Damascus. In verse 20, Paul was in Damascus after he saw Christ on the way there. Gal. 1.17 describes how Paul then went to Arabia, then back to Damascus. From Damascus, Paul went to Jerusalem for the first time as a Christian (Ac. 9.28; Gal. 1.18). This was when he sought "to join himself to the disciples which were at Jerusalem," (Ac. 9.26). Gal. 1.18 tells us that Paul was in Jerusalem only fifteen days on that visit. Then Paul went to Caesarea and on to Tarsus, as revealed in Ac. 9.30.

From Acts 11.26, we learn that Barnabas brought Paul to Antioch, and then they began their trip to Judea of our present concern (Ac. 11.27-30). Then in Ac. 12.25 Paul returned from Jerusalem to Antioch, as the proponents of the sponsoring church concept point out. Of course, later in Acts 13, Paul began his travels among the Gentiles.

Paul's statement to King Agrippa in Ac. 26.19-20, as he recounted how he became a Christian, and what he did thereafter sheds more light on his activities:

> Wherefore, O king Agrippa, I was not disobedient unto the heavenly vision: but declared both to them of Damascus first...

This refers to Ac. 9.20, after Paul first obeyed the gospel. Then Paul continued to Agrippa:

> ...and at Jerusalem,...

This was Paul's first visit to Jerusalem after becoming a Christian (Ac. 9.28, the 15-day trip). Then Paul continued his description of his travels:

> *...and throughout all the country of Judea*, and also to the Gentiles,...

Of course, Paul didn't go to the Gentiles until Acts 13, when he began the first of his three great missionary journeys. Now the question: When in Paul's life, after he went to Damascus and Jerusalem, and before he went to the Gentiles, did he go *throughout all the country of Judea*? Wasn't the only time he could have done it on the benevolent journey of Ac. 11.27-30? It has to be.

Thus, it is not an assumption to believe Paul and Barnabas traveled throughout the country of Judea with the benevolent collection from Antioch, ending up at Jerusalem, from which they returned to Antioch, Ac. 12.25. Jerusalem was not the sponsoring church some may have thought.

J. W. McGarvey, regarded as a brilliant scholar and commentator by those on both sides of the sponsoring church controversy wrote concerning these matters:

> The remark of Paul alluded to above, "I was still unknown by face to the churches in Judea" (Gal. 1.22), has

> reference to the interval in which he was 'in the regions of Syria and Cilicia" (21); and this was between his departure to Tarsus, and his being called thence to Antioch by Barnabas (9:30-11:25). Of course, his tour among the Judean churches with Barnabas, distributing the gift from Antioch, brought this ignorance of his person to a close. (J. W. McGarvey, *Biblical Criticism* [Cincinnati: Standard Publishing Company, 1910], pp. 377-379.)

Thus, those most familiar with the chronology of Paul's early travels are agreed that direct evidence exists for Paul's travels throughout Judea at the very time he was dealing with this benevolent work.

An Unbreakable Parallel with Baptism

Three questions concerning both baptism and church cooperation, (1) Who? (2) How? and (3) Why? show an unbreakable parallel between them. First, notice baptism:

Baptism

Who is to be baptized? Mk. 16.16 says believers are. Ac. 2.38 tells us penitent believers are. When we baptize penitent believers, we do something that we have plain Bible teaching for. If someone wants to baptize babies, the dead, or mentally incompetent people, we object. Not because we don't like babies, the dead, or the mentally incompetent, but because we don't have Bible teaching to baptize anyone except penitent believers.

How are penitent believers to be baptized? Rom. 6.3-4 and Col. 2.12 explain that baptism is a burial. When we bury penitent believers in baptism, we do something that we have plain Bible teaching for. If someone wants to sprinkle for baptism, we object, although we sprinkle our clothes, our lawns, etc. Sprinkling in itself is not immoral, but to sprinkle for baptism is to do what the Bible simply does not teach.

Why are penitent believers to be baptized? Ac. 2.38 indicates for the remission of sins. Ac. 22.16 says to wash away sins. When we baptize penitent believers for the remission of their sins, again, we do something that we have plain Bible teaching for. If someone wants to baptize a baby to give him a name, we object. Not because we dislike babies, nor because we believe they shouldn't have names, but simply because the Bible knows one, but not the other.

Church Cooperation

Who received funds in the New Testament when churches cooperated? II Cor. 8.13-14 says that the receiving churches were destitute. When one church sends benevolence to a destitute church, that church simply does what the Bible teaches. If a church wants to send funds to another church when the receiving church is not destitute, we object. Not only because it engages in denominational action, but because it also does something that no Bible authority exists for, just like baptizing babies.

How were those funds sent? Ac. 11.27-30, I Cor. 16.1-3, II Cor. 8-9, and Rom. 15.24-31 reveals that the funds were always sent directly. If someone wants to send those funds through a third congregation or agency, we object. Not only because it is denominational action, but because it also does something no Bible teaching supports, just like sprinkling for baptism.

Why were funds sent from one church to another in the New Testament? II Cor. 8.14 instructs us it was to equalize need. When one church sends funds to another church to equalize need, it does what the Bible says. When a church wants to send funds to another church for another reason, we object. Not only because it reeks of denominational action, but because it also does something the Bible does not teach, just like baptizing babies to give them a name.

Clearly, when we quit preaching the *who*, *how*, and *why* of cooperation, we will have to quit preaching the *who*, *how*, and *why* of baptism. This is also true of any other Bible subject!

I Believe in Church Cooperation

I am not opposed to church cooperation *per se*. Church cooperation was practiced in the New Testament, and was not denominational. That is, churches of the apostolic era did not participate in collective action of congregations. Thus, when the churches of Galatia, Corinth, and Rome each sent benevolent collections to the needy saints in Jerusalem (I Cor. 16; II Cor. 8-9; Rom. 15.25-31), they cooperated, yet not collectively or denominationally. Churches can and ought to do the same today.

When I began preaching, I participated in several "Ask Your Preacher" call-in radio programs. Three or four congregations each contracted with a radio station and purchased the time for certain days each week. Each congregation determined who preached, when they preached, what they preached, and how they preached on their days. This form of church cooperation was not collective action of congregations, nor denominational. It hardly compares to congregations that send funds to sponsoring churches when they have no say about who preaches, when, what, or how, etc.

In addition, their money was not spent to beg more money from other congregations, but rather it purchased radio time. Likewise, the elders of each participating congregation oversaw their own work and no one else's. Finally, none of the elders pleaded with other churches to let them continue their own work, as we will see in the sponsoring church concept. This method of church cooperation is in stark contrast to the sponsoring church or denominational concept.

So while Phil. 4.15-16; II Cor. 11.8, and Ac. 11.27-30 do not authorize denominational cooperation through a sponsoring church, they do permit churches to work together. In these efforts, however, each congregation must maintain control of its own work.

Appendix 7

The Sponsoring Church: An Example of Denominational Action

This chapter discusses a concept that has plagued churches of Christ since the late 1940s and has led to division and hard feelings. The realization of what constitutes denominational action (collective action of churches) will help us analyze the concept of the sponsoring church. We will examine specifically the Herald of Truth, a sponsoring church project supported by several thousand churches of Christ and overseen entirely by the elders of the Fifth and Hghland Church of Christ in Abilene, Texas. i

Many Think Problems Should Be Ignored

We are aware in the beginning that many believe that controversial issues among the Lord's people should not be talked about. As a result of this attitude, many have sought to sweep these problems under the rug. Yet in the New Testament, every letter, with the exception of the book of Philippians, concerned church problems.

After those letters were written, God spread and preserved them so that every atheist, infidel, Hindu, and denominational person could see that problems plagued the church in the New Testament. So not only in our age, but also in every age, the church of our Lord has had problems. Early Christians didn't shrug their problems aside saying, "We won't deal with them and maybe they will go away." One by one, they dealt with their problems face to face. They realized that sin was like a cancer, that if ignored, it only becomes worse. In this manner, they dealt with their problems and solved them by the forthright application of the word of God.

Likewise, in this appendix we seek to identify the problem clearly and then solve it by the proper application of the word of God. It is not written to hurl accusations or to impugn anyone's motives, but solely to study God's word relative to the problems that confront us.

Clearing Up a Misconception

We might notice by way of introduction that people like myself are often spoken of as being *against* certain things. The congregations that I preach among are often spoken of as being *against church cooperation*. But we are not and have not been opposed to church cooperation. Rather, we are in favor of church cooperation, and believe it should occur when necessary.

The prejudicial term "anti" is many times applied to us; that we are an *anti* church or I am an *anti* preacher. When asked, "What am I *anti*?" the answer many times comes back, "You are anti church cooperation." First, we want to drive the point home, we are not! I believe in church cooperation. The churches I have worked with believe in churches cooperating. We believe churches ought to cooperate in evangelism, exactly like churches did in the New Testament. We believe churches ought to cooperate in benevolence, exactly like they did in the New Testament. So we believe in church cooperation.

Now, if we believe in the form of church cooperation found in the Bible, is it fair to refer to us as anti-church cooperation? In Mt. 19.9 Jesus made it clear He was opposed to every kind of marriage except one. Does that make Jesus *anti-marriage*? In I Cor. 8.5-6, Paul said, "For though there be that are called gods, whether in heaven or on earth: as there are gods many, and lords many, yet to us there is one God, the Father, of whom are all things, and we unto him; and one Lord, Jesus Christ...." When he made it clear he was opposed to every god but one, was Paul *anti-God*? In Eph. 4.5, Paul affirmed one baptism existed. When he declared one and opposed all others, was he *anti-baptism*? Surely we can see that when God says one thing, and an individual stands for what God says, it is not fair to refer to him as *anti* the practice.

What the Issue Is Not

Many facets of the sponsoring church controversy can be eliminated immediately simply by clarifying what the issue is *not*. For example, the issue is *not* the integrity or sincerity of those who uphold such an arrangement. I am firmly convinced that those who support the Herald of Truth do so honestly, with just as great a desire to know and obey the truth as I do. We surely have no reason to think otherwise.

The issue is *not* whether any of us believe in church cooperation, for we do. The issue is *not* that we oppose preaching the gospel on radio or television, for we do not. The issue is a specific type of cooperation that is practiced in the Herald of Truth, that we cannot conscientiously participate in.

What the Issue Is

The central issue regarding the Herald of Truth specifically and all sponsoring church projects in general is that they are inconsistent with New Testament teaching concerning the non-denominational nature of the church. We have seen in the New Testament where elders had the oversight of local congregations. In Ac. 14.23, as Paul and Barnabas returned on their first missionary journey, they appointed elders in every church, because God intended for each congregation to have its own elders, i.e., God never intended elders to exercise the oversight of other congregations. Collective action of churches is classically denominational.

This is further brought out in Ac. 20. 28 where Paul told the elders from the church in Ephesus, "Take heed unto yourselves, and to all the flock, in which the Holy Spirit hath made you bishops." Again in I Pet. 5.1-2, Peter exhorted, "Tend the flock of God which is among you." In the New Testament, the elders of local congregations were the sole individuals who exercised the oversight of *what* work the congregation was to do, *when* the congregation would do it, *how* the congregation would do it, and *who* the congregation would use to do it.

In addition to these plain scriptural precepts, one can appreciate the wisdom of God in so ordaining His church. In the many denominations that have a pyramid of organization above the local congregations (Lutheran, Episcopal, Presbyterian, Nazaberene, Methodist, etc., etc.), if a high ecclesiastical official becomes corrupt, the entire denominational organization is in fellowship with his evil works. In the cults (Jehovah's Witnesses, Seventh-day Adventists, Mormons, etc.) that have the same type of organization, the same danger exists for a false teacher to carry away the entire denomination from the truth of God.

In the early 1970s, when the hierarchy of the Presbyterian church determined to give $10,000 to the communist Angela Davis' defense fund, the Presbyterian membership had no choice but to either go along with the hierarchical decision, or to leave the denomination entirely. These are the consequences of ecclesiastical domination and the denominational concept. It always makes one a partner with works that he has no control over. Thus, believers in denominations that ordain homosexuals as ministers, participate in works over which they have no control. Those in denominations with rank modernists at the helm, who deny the virgin birth of Christ, the inspiration of the Bible, and the resurrection of Jesus, are in fellowship with evil works over which they have no control. In the televangelism scandals of the late 1980s, many find themselves participating in evil works in which they have no say as those scandals are dealt with on a denominational scale rather than in a local congregation. However, when the Lord's will is followed His congregations will remain independent of each other, each ruled by its own eldership. Even if one entire eldership becomes corrupt, it need not effect any other congregation in the whole world.

This View of the Eldership Used to Be Held Generally Among Us

This has been the position of churches of Christ in the past. For example, David Lipscomb, viewed by many in churches of Christ as a defender of the faith for nearly fifty years as editor of *The Gospel Advocate* said:

> All meetings of churches or officers of churches to combine more power than a single church possesses are wrong...A Christian, one or more, may visit a church with or without an invitation and seek to stir them up to a more faithful discharge of their duties. But for one or more to direct what and how all the churches shall work, or to take charge of their men and money and use it, is to assume the authority God has given to each church. (*The Gospel Advocate*, 1890, p. 295.)

In 1931, brother F. B. Srygley wrote on those same pages the following words:

> These elders had no authority to take charge of the missionary money or any other money or means of any church except the one over which they were "overseer." Elders of one church should not try to get hold of money that has been contributed by others to direct for them in foreign fields or other places. (*The Gospel Advocate*, December 3, 1931.)

About that same time, W. E. Brightwell wrote in the pages of The *Gospel Advocate*:

> I submit this proposition: Any individual Christian, or group of individuals, smaller than a local congregation; or any group of individuals or churches larger than a local church; or any individual church itself that begins thinking in terms of what the whole brotherhood should do, and goes or sends somebody to the churches to see that

> they do it, and acts as an agent or agency through which the brotherhood does it, thereby constitutes itself full-grown, blown-in-the-bottle, fourteen-karat missionary society of the deepest dye! There is no way on earth to whitewash it. There is no city of refuge where he may hide from God's displeasure. To call it something else, or to leave it unnamed, is a mere technical dodge. It is not condemned because it is similar to a missionary society, but because it *violates the same fundamental principle the society violates*—namely, the initiative and autonomy of the local congregation. (*The Gospel Advocate*, December 20, 1934, p. 1223.)

Our approach in this chapter is that the Herald of Truth provides a form of cooperation not found in the New Testament; its form of cooperation violates what is found in the New Testament, i.e., *the Herald of Truth is a denominational work under a local eldership*. Naturally, to make this statement is not to prove it, thus we wish to set about proving it.

The Herald of Truth Is a Denominational Work, Not Local

Figure 13 shows each New Testament church with its own work overseen by its own elders. Figure 14 shows the sponsoring church organization with many churches turning the oversight of a part of their work over to the elders of the sponsoring church that, in turn, oversees the work that they all participate in. When the sponsoring church provides the collective oversight, it activates the denominational or collective action of churches.

In the case of the Herald of Truth in the 1970s, approximately 4500 churches around the United States sent funds to the Fifth and Highland Streets Church of Christ in Abilene, Texas, that in turn oversaw several brotherhood works. They included the production of the Herald of Truth radio and television broadcasts, the Heartbeat broadcast on the National Broadcast Company network of radio stations, and *Restoration*, a monthly magazine published in connection with the Herald of Truth.

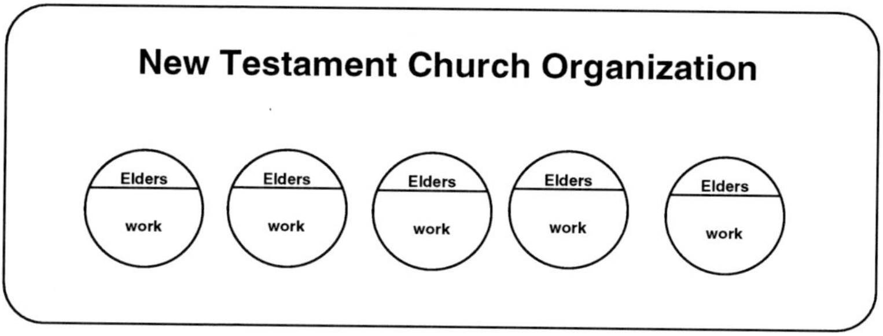

Figure 13

We can know for certain that the Herald of Truth is a collective work of churches (i.e., denominational work), because the participating churches say it is. The elders of the Skillman Avenue Church of Christ in Dallas, Texas (one of the congregations supporting the project) explain:

> Our elders decided to contribute to the program because they felt that it was a good work in which they desired to have a part. In making such a contribution, it is my belief that we at Skillman are discharging our own responsibility in doing *our own work* under the Great Commission.

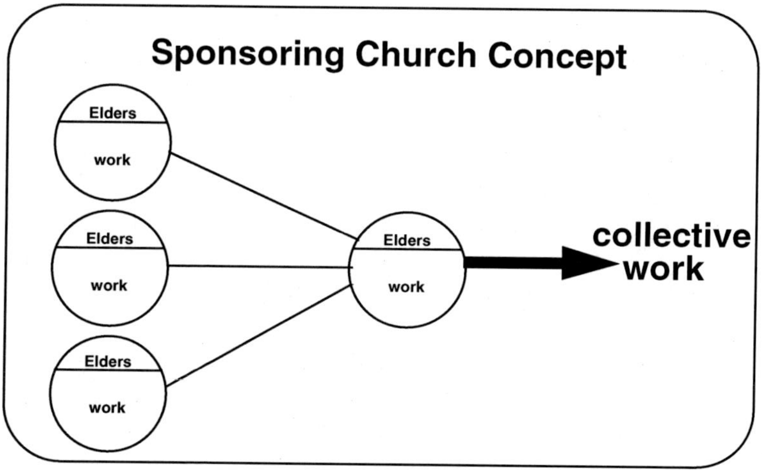

Figure 14

(Cited in *The Cogdill-Woods Debate* [Lufkin, TX: The Gospel Guardian Company, 1958], p. 199.)

The elders at the Broadway congregation in Lubbock, Texas (another supporting congregation) think it is:

> We contribute to the Herald of Truth radio program because we feel that this is a method of preaching the gospel of Christ in an effective manner to many people. When we contribute money to this radio program, we feel that this is a *part of our work*. (*Ibid.*)

So the contributing congregations, as well as the sponsoring congregation, understand that the Herald of Truth is not just a congregational effort. *It is the effort of an entire brotherhood.*

The Herald of Truth Is a Denominational Work Under a Local Eldership

Even though the Herald of Truth is admittedly a collective work of congregations, it has always been made clear that it was collectively under the oversight of the Fifth and Highland elders. In a statement entitled "That the Brethren May Know," published by the Highland elders and signed by all of them, they write:

> The Herald of Truth radio program is a work of the church of Christ at Fifth and Highland, Abilene, Texas. The elders of this congregation direct and oversee every phase of this work from preparation of sermons to mailing of printed copies of these sermons. The Highland elders have never delegated any authority to any person, but as a unit have directed this work. ("That the Brethren May Know," p. 2, cited in *The Cogdill-Woods Debate* [Lufkin, TX: The Gospel Guardian Company, 1957], p. 221.)

Thus, the Highland elders determine *what* is preached, *when* it's preached, *how* it's preached, and *who* preaches it. Yet it's a work of all the contributing congregations! This is the thing that is wrong: elders who oversee even part of the work of other congregations.

Readily, if the elders of one congregation could oversee *part* of the work of another congregation, no reason exists why they could not oversee *all* of it, and certainly some have carried the sponsoring church concept to its logical conclusion. From time to time we see local church bulletins which speak of the elders of one congregation "assuming the oversight" or "assuming the responsibility" of another congregation. These brethren have simply carried the sponsoring church organization to its next logical step. Their statements are scriptural and right if the Herald of Truth is scriptural and right.

The Sponsoring Church Destroys the Autonomy of Every Congregation Involved

Brethren in the past (David Lipscomb, F. B. Srygley, etc.) opposed similar arrangements in the past for the same reason we oppose them now: the sponsoring church arrangement produces an unscriptural dependency upon churches who cooperate in this way. Stated more precisely, *the Herald of Truth destroys completely the autonomy, equality, and independence of every congregation associated with it.*

A more dependent church in the world than Fifth and Highland in Abilene doesn't exist. This was demonstrated in 1973 when a major controversy erupted in churches of Christ concerning reports of compromised and false teaching in connection with the Herald of Truth. In order to deal with the criticism, a meeting of some two-hundred concerned Christians, consisting mostly of preachers and elders, including some from Fifth and Highland, took place in Memphis, Tennessee on September 10, 1973. A record of this meeting was published by the Getwell Church of Christ, 1511 Getwell Road, Memphis, TN, 38111, and contains some very revealing statements that demonstrate the unscriptural relationship existing among these churches.

For example, Art Haddox, a Highland elder, made the following statement to those present:

> We plead with you to allow us to continue to pray and work with this problem. (*Memphis Meeting with the Representatives of the Herald of Truth, September 10, 1973* [Memphis, TN: Getwell Church of Christ, 1973], p. 2.)

Can you imagine the elders, in the congregation where you worship, traveling hundreds of miles to plead with preachers and elders from many other congregations to let them continue a certain work in the congregation they oversee? Would it be proper, for example, for them to plead with Christians from other areas of the country to let them continue your disciplinary program, or perhaps your teaching program? Elders in congregations in the New Testament didn't plead with preachers and elders from other congregations in other cities and states to let them continue anything—they exercised the oversight of the flock that was among them!

Frank Cawyer, a former elder at Highland, who now opposes the abuses of the Herald of Truth, though not the sponsoring church concept itself, said:

> I'm not trying to kill the Herald of Truth, but it ought to be moved from Highland to a good sound eldership and carried on. (*Ibid*., p. 3.)

Again, considering the work of the congregation where you are a member, can a group of elders or preachers meet several hundred miles away from your congregation and make decisions concerning moving part of the work of your congregation? If they can, the congregation must be involved in something unscriptural, because in the New Testament, congregations were ruled only by the elders among them.

Garland Elkins, minister of the Getwell Church of Christ, Memphis, TN, and a strong supporter of the Herald of Truth (at least until 1973), said:

> Brother Baxter said earlier that today might determine whether or not the Herald of Truth program would live

> or die. But you know, brethren, really the survival of the church is involved in this, too. (*Ibid.*, p. 17.)

How about if the church were I labor has a meeting about the church were you are a member to determine whether part of your work lives or dies? Would that really be appropriate? Surely, we can see that the only way such meetings could take place, or that we could begin to think that the survival of the church depends upon the outcome of similar meetings is if the churches are involved in some unscriptural organization.

Lynn Anderson, who was at the time preaching at Highland, said:

> Maybe this ministry should be transferred to an eldership that feels more capable of coping with the unusual pressures that come. (*Ibid.*, p. 68.)

These statements demonstrate how the Herald of Truth destroys the autonomy of both the contributing churches, and Highland as well.

Opposition to the Sponsoring Church Concept Is Not New

With the advent of these issues that have faced the church of our Lord over the past decades, many brethren charge myself and those believing as I do on these questions with dividing the church with some new hobby, or splitting the church with a new doctrine. We here present what should effectively answer this charge, i.e., many statements made by well-known and highly regarded preachers of past years. These preachers, although many of them died long before I even began preaching, taught exactly the same thing that those who hold similar convictions and I preach and practice today. Yet the brotherhood highly regards them as faithful preachers of the gospel.

I believe the statements reproduced herein, *not* because I attach any importance to these men's' opinions, but because their teaching was consistent with what the Bible teaches on these matters. The only reason to quote these men is to show that we do not preach a new doctrine. If these men are not condemned as anti's and church-splitters, it is unfair and inconsistent to brand me so, for I do not oppose anything today they did not oppose then.

As you read these statements, see if you can determine who preaches a new doctrine: those who propagate and support institutional projects throughout the brotherhood today or those who oppose them as without authority from God's word.

> David Lipscomb: I have never published, or approved without publication, the assumption of elders of one church sending out a man to induce the members of other churches to direct their means from their own church treasury, and to take it from the direction of their own elders and place it under the elders of one church...All such concentration of power is destructive of the activity and true liberties of the church. It tends to exalt the elders of one church and degrade and dishonor those of the other. (*The Gospel Advocate*, December 3, 1931.)

> F. B. Srygley: The work of the elders stopped at the church in which they lived and labored. The elders had no authority to take charge of the missionary money or any other money or means of any church except the one over which they were overseers. Elders of one church should not try to get hold of the money that has been contributed by others to direct for them in foreign fields or other places. (*The Gospel Advocate*, December 31, 1931.)

> F. B. Srygley: The agent system of collecting funds from many churches, even if it is done under some eldership without authority, ties churches together and has a tendency to destroy the independence of the local church. The greatest objection to the whole scheme is that it is not in the New Testament. (*The Gospel Advocate*, November 1, 1934, cited in *The Willis-Inman Debate* [Louisville, KY: Truth Magazine, 1968], p. 49.)

H. Leo Boles: The churches acted in this work as individual and independent congregations. The missionary received help from the church that sent him out, from those in the field where he labored, and from other churches; but in all of this work there was no common fund for churches, no "central church" with a treasurer to receive the funds from the other churches, no general treasury to take care of the funds, no call from any church to other churches to help them do the work which fell in their province to do. (*The Gospel Advocate*, November 10, 1932, cited *Ibid.*)

Foy E. Wallace, Jr.: The missionary society usurps the functions of the church...On the same principle, if the elders of one congregation solicit the funds of other congregations for general distribution, then the elders of one congregation usurp the functions of the congregations whose funds they receive and disburse. It is the same in principle as if a society should do so. (*The Gospel Advocate*, May 14, 1931, p. 880.)

Foy E. Wallace, Jr.: For one church to help another church bear its own burdens, therefore, has scriptural precedent. But for one church to solicit funds from other churches, is quite a different question. Such procedure makes a sort of society out of the elders of a local church and for such there is no scriptural precedent or example. (*The Gospel Advocate*, May 14, 1931, p. 909.)

The Sponsoring Church Concept Is New

With these statements of well-respected gospel preachers of the past in mind, certainly we are forced to ask the question, "*Why has there been such a change in practice and preaching over the years?*"

nSeveral statements of a historical nature will help us understand the change. William S. Banowsky, past president of Pepperdine University and later President of the University of

Oklahoma, made the following statement concerning the thrust of the Abilee Christian College Lectureships that led directly to the formation of the sponsoring church concept underlying the Herald of Truth arrangement:

> The lecturers came to desire a missionary procedure which would more effectively involve the hundreds of small congregations. But they also sought a program whose scope would be more far-reaching than even the best, but isolated efforts of any one large congregation. They could not resist the temptation to shop about and contrast their plight with the obvious strong points in denominational machinery. Thus, they sought for some practical, scriptural means of *brotherhood-wide co-ordination* without creating an agency for brotherhood-wide control [emphasis mine—SGD]. (William S. Banowsky, *The Mirror of a Movement* [Dallas, TX: Christian Publishing Co., 1965], p. 313.)

The obvious question that arises just now is, "Why didn't they cast about in the Bible for this arrangement?" This statement sounds similar to one made by iram Christopher, an ex-supporter of the Missionary Society after he changed:

> The Missionary Society had its origin in a false pride and shame, and a desire to be like the denominations around us. With all our condemnation of denominationalism, we have not yet the independence of mind to discard their machinery. We are afraid that they will get ahead of us, and this fear leads us to adopt some of their machinery. (*American Christian Review, X*, No. 27, July 2, 1867.)

The matter of elders overseeing the work of another congregation is a matter of faith, not opinion. It's a matter of law, not expediency. It's a doctrine that will affect the destiny of those involved in it!

The Sponsoring Church Concept Is Older Than the Abilene Lectures

Students of the American restoration movement should recognize that the concept of the sponsoring church is much older than the Abilene Christian College Lectures of the thirties and forties. The TexasState Missionary Society was a comparable brotherhood project under a local eldership. Historian Earl West wrote:

> Beginning in 1867, it had been the practice of the churches to put the work each year under the elders of one Texas congregation. The work was under the Sherman Church perhaps more than any other one congregation. (Earl Irvin West, *Search for the Ancient Order, II* [Indianapolis, IN: Religious Book Service, 1950], p. 424.)

David Lipscomb wrote of this same situation:

> This very same course was pursued in Texas a number of years ago. The elders of the church at Dallas were made the supervisors of the work, received the money, employed the preacher, directed and counseled him. For a number of years they employed G. M. Wilmeth. He then dropped out of the work and the *Texas Missionary Society took the place*. Other experiments along the same course have been made. *All of them went into the society work*. (*The Gospel Advocate*, 1910, cited by Herbert E. Winkler, *Congregational Cooperation of the Churches of Christ*, 1961, p. 56.)

A similar project began in Tennessee in 1910 when the church at Henderson proposed to become the "sponsoring church" to oversee the work of an evangelist in west Tennessee. As many other congregations as would voluntarily do so were asked to cooperate by sending funds. Lipscomb commented about the arrangement:

> Now what was that but the organization of a society in the elders of this church? The church elders at Henderson constitute a board to collect and pay out the money and control the evangelist for the brethren of West Tennessee. (*The Gospel Advocate*, 1910, cited by Winkler, *Ibid.*, p. 56.)

As Lipscomb fought these projects he made this statement:

> All meetings of churches or officers of churches to combine more power than a single church possesses are wrong...A Christian, one or more, may visit a church with or without an invitation and seek to stir them up to a more faithful discharge of their duties. But for one or more to direct what and how all the churches shall work, or to take charge of their men and money and use it, is to assume the authority God has given to each church. (*The Gospel Advocate*, 1890, p. 295, cited by Winkler, *Ibid.*)

Obviously, the concept of one congregation's elders overseeing another congregation's work was fought for at least ninety years before the Herald of Truth came into existence!

The Herald of Truth's Teaching Compromised

Until 1973, most of the controversy surrounding the Herald of Truth focused on the unscriptural organizational arrangements. Even though some complaints existed concerning the quality of the program's teaching, in the main brethren opposed only the alliances of congregations that were not visible to the listening or viewing audience.

When the problems confronting Highland and the Herald of Truth surfaced in 1973, even among brethren who thought the sponsoring church concept was right, serious concerns arose over the compromised nature of the teaching. Actually, as far back as 1950 public statements were made concerning it. These concerns peaked during the 1973 crises which prompted the Memphis meeting. Garland Elkins, in the introduction to the *Memphis Meeting*, p. ii said:

> The brethren in the Memphis meeting made it unmistakably clear, that, aside from the doctrinal error under consideration, they and multitudes of others were disappointed by the largely non-distinctive type of preaching currently done on the program.

Batsell Barrett Baxter, featured speaker for many years on the program, acknowledged the same thing:

> From time to time in person and in letters to me directly and sometimes letters sent to me—forwarded to me by others, I have received criticism about "you are not preaching solidly or firmly enough," and frankly, I have some of that same feeling, like the elders under whom I work at the Hillsboro church in Nashville. (*Memphis Meeting*, p. 6.)

Brother Baxter then explained that he could not teach on baptism on the air like he wanted to:

> Now it just isn't easy to do that. We have a program, we submitted it to channel 5 in New York City awhile back. They had a vacant time; they had a religious program that they took off the air; they were looking for one; they viewed one of our films; they said "Its quality is excellent; we would accept it except for that part in it where you talk about baptism *and therefore we can't*."

Frank Cawyer, former elder at Highland, said concerning the Heartbeat program with speaker Landon Saunders:

> It's been compromised and as they published the other day, a little sixteen year old girl wrote brother Saunders and said, "Is your Heartbeat a religious program?" Brethren, when we are spending thousands, yea millions of dollars to broadcast and a sixteen year old girl will have

> to ask the question "Is this a religious program," there is something wrong. (*Memphis Meeting*, p. 12.)

These statements echo a concern of brother G. C. Brewer back in the 1950s:

> When the Herald of Truth broadcast of Abilene, Texas was proposed, I told the brethren who were soliciting help for the venture that it would put the Lord's people before the world as a denomination and this program would be the *Church of Christ Hour* just as distinctly as we have a *Catholic Hour* or a *Lutheran Hour*. The brethren said they would avoid this by calling it the Herald of Truth. This they have done, but they have not avoided the error I feared. In the announcer's "Churches of Christ Salute You" he just as definitely tells who or *what* denomination is *heralding this truth* as he could if he said, "The Methodist Churches greet you." This is as definitely a *commercial* for churches of Christ as any commercial is a plea for any sponsor. And, of course, then the listeners will expect the preacher to plead for and attempt to prove what the churches of Christ *teach* and *what they believe*—hence their creed. Thus the truth is hindered and the preacher is handicapped before he starts. This is not a condemnation of the Herald of Truth effort, nor is it even a criticism of the preaching itself, but *it is another illustration of the denominational use of scriptural terms and also of the denominational conception that the brethren today have of the church. It is lamentable*. [emphasis mine—SGD] (G. C. Brewer, *The Autobiography of G. C. Brewer* [Murfreesboro, TN: Dehoff Publications, 1957], p. 139.)

Worse Than Compromise, Just Plain False Teaching

Brother Juan Monroy, the Herald of Truth representative to Spain, has written many controversial statements in the monthly magazine *Restoration*, published in connection with the Herald of Truth. In the October 1971 issue, brother Monroy wrote and referred to one

> Doctor Jose M. Naredo Vidal, who performed an important task in the Ministry of Education during the government of General Batista in Cuba, *has been converted to the gospel of Christ and is a member, along with his family, of a Baptist church in Abilene, Texas*. (Juan Monroy, "Cuban Personality Converted to Christ," *Restoration*, October 1971, p. 25.)

Monroy continued:

> The group of Cuban men residing in Spain continues working with genuine interest to win other compatriots for Christ. From the 22nd to the 29th of August *they conducted a special campaign of evangelism in the temple of the Church of Jesus in Madrid. The pastors Rodolfo Loyola, Jose Gonzales, and Alfonso Guevara preached.*

In *Restoration*, April 1972, Monroy wrote under the title, "Let's Pray for Paul VI" (the Roman Catholic Pope at the time):

> If in these times there is on earth one human needy of celestial help, this one is *Paul VI, Pope of the Catholic Church, Apostolic and Roman,...This man must have the most grieved soul since that of the own Lord Jesus in the Garden of Gethsemane. No one knows how many nights Paul VI might have sweated drops of blood*. (*Restoration*, April 1972, n.p.)

In *Restoration*, May 1972, we read of the death of D. Ernesto Trenchard in Madrid:

> On the night of Wednesday, April 19, *the outstanding evangelic leader, Ernesto Trenchard died.* He was 70 years of age...Mr. Trenchard spent almost half a century

> working among the Evangelic churches of Spain...*This death happens when this edition of Restoration is in production. After this hurried note of urgency, in our next issue we will publish an explanation of the same, describing the personality of the servant who already rejoices in the abodes of his Lord.* (*Restoration*, May 1972, n.p.)

From the above three quotations, we glean the following false teachings:

1. One who has been converted to the gospel of Christ can still be a member, along with his family, of a Baptist church, in Abilene, Texas.

2. It is right to refer to preachers as pastors, even though the Bible refers only to elders as pastors. And it is all right for said "pastors" to conduct evangelistic campaigns for other than the church authorized in the New Testament in Madrid.

3. The Roman Catholic Church is apostolic, which it is not.

4. The worries of Pope Paul VI are comparable to the grief of our own Lord Jesus in the garden of Gethsemane.

5. Pope Paul VI, in his worry, may have sweated drops of blood, just like Jesus.

6. If Roman Catholics are not capable of helping Pope Paul VI in his work, then Christians should make it their duty to pray for the Pope in this regard and would thus be praying for a false teacher to succeed.

7. God will hear our prayers for Pope Paul VI, conserving the serenity in his heart, maintaining his mind clearly, and giving illumination to his spirit while he continues on as Pope. Likewise, Monroy assumes God will work with a false teacher.

8. One who died as a member of the Assemblies of Brothers after almost half a century of work among the evangelical churches of Spain, nevertheless, was a servant of the Lord and now rejoices in the abodes of his Lord. Thus, Monroy intimated that denominational preachers were servants of the Lord who would spend eternity with God.

Reaction of Former Supporters

Because of the current corruption and unscriptural practices within the Herald of Truth organization, it is easy to understand the reaction of men, who although they have defended the Herald of Truth in debate in the past, now are troubled about supporting it. For example, Thomas Warren said at the Memphis meeting:

> I would not today engage in a public debate in defense of this particular program. (*Memphis Meeting*, p. 11.)

Alan Highers, who also defended the sponsoring church concept in debate, wrote after the Memphis meeting:

> I have defended cooperative efforts such as the Herald of Truth in public debate, and I would still defend the principle of church cooperation; but I have no stomach for defending the Herald of Truth. We no longer support it or announce it, and I could not at this point conscientiously recommend it to any eldership for one penny of support.

W. L. Totty, who likewise debated in behalf of the Herald of Truth, wrote:

> Brother Guy N. Woods and I have defended the Herald of Truth in a number of debates. I would still do so, so far as the principle is concerned, if I were able; but I could no longer defend the program. (W. L. Totty, *Contending for the Faith, IV*, no. 6, August 1973, p. 6.)

We want to make it clear that *our objection is not just to the abuse of the sponsoring church arrangement*, for certainly an abuse of a thing doesn't mean the thing itself is unscriptural. It is just here that we can appreciate the unscripturalness of the arrangement the most because when the supporting churches became aware of the abuses in the teaching, *what could they do about it?* When elders of supporting congregations became aware of the problems, could they, even though they considered the Herald of Truth part of their own work, step in and make the necessary changes? Of course not, because the Highland elders have always taught, "The elders of this congregation direct and oversee every phrase of this work from preparation of sermons to mailing of printed copies of these sermons. The Highland elders have never delegated any authority to any person, but as a unit have directed this work."

Thus, the elders of supporting congregations cannot oversee the Herald of Truth, or change it, because they have no say about *what* is preached, *who* preaches it, or *how* or *when* it's preached. Just as Presbyterians could not change the decisions of their hierarchy in supporting the communist Angela Davis in her terrorist trial, they must put up or shut up. *Yet the elders of these supporting congregations admit the Herald of Truth is part of their work!*

We can also appreciate the fallacy of an argument made to justify these arrangements. Many times we are told, "Nobody forces these contributing churches and their elders to support the Herald of Truth, they do it voluntarily." That doesn't make the situation better at all! If someone voluntarily does something he has no authority for, it *increases* the enormity of his sin!

The Size of the Problem

In conclusion, compare the benefits claimed for the Herald of Truth with the cost in unity it has exacted from the brotherhood. Batsell Barrett Baxter, at the Memphis meeting estimated of the concrete results from the program currently:

> We're getting 235 letters on an average every day of the year—85,000 in a year. We believe, conservatively, that we are baptizing 200-300 every year. (*Memphis Meeting*, p. 7.)

Think seriously concerning these figures for a moment. The year brother Baxter made this estimate, the Herald of Truth budget amounted to four million dollars, that was contributed by approximately 4500 congregations. Three hundred conversions accomplished by 4500 congregations results in one conversion for each fifteen congregations per year, or one conversion for each congregation every fifteen years, at a cost of $13,333 per conversion! Has the division that resulted over the Herald of Truth done more harm than one conversion per congregation every fifteen years?

To put it another way, suppose that instead of the Herald of Truth, we had a preacher who was similarly "efficient." What if your congregation had a preacher who (1) was paid $13,333 per year (full salary the year these figures were first released), (2) was not under the rule of the elders who paid his salary, (3) spent fifteen percent of his money and time to beg more money, (4) split many churches over his work, (5) taught in a compromised fashion so that his own brethren rose up against him, (6) people who heard him wondered if he was religious, (7) left new converts in Baptist churches, (8) called denominational preachers pastors and commended their work in denominational campaigns, (9) called the Roman Catholic church "apostolic," (10) called denominational preachers servants of the Lord, who die and go be with the Lord, (11) had many of his previous defenders refuse to endorse him, (12) came from a college producing 300 comparable preachers per year, and (13) converts only one out of every 300 people who write him? Question: Would you fire this preacher to maintain unity among brethren?

Surely, no congregation would tolerate this preacher. Why can't we see the same with the behavior of the Herald of Truth? Many have, even among those who have supported the Herald of Truth in the past. The late Eldred Stevens, who defended the sponsoring church arrangement that made the Herald of Truth possible, lamented the beginning of the Herald of Truth:

> I wished there had never been a Herald of Truth. My reasons were threefold: First, the price paid in the dividing of the brotherhood was too high a price to pay. Second, the trend toward centralization of influence and control over churches has been fearfully fraught with severe dangers. The proof of that is quite clearly seen in the development of the Roman hierarchy, and later in the

> digression of the "Disciples." Third, as strange as it sounds, considerably more work is done when churches all move in their congregational capacities than when joint efforts are used. We saw this vividly demonstrated in our big downtown meetings of a few years ago. We were all starry-eyed until it dawned on us that if churches had not dismissed their services to cooperate in the meeting, considerably more people would have in services listened to the gospel preached. We were amazed at the number of baptisms...until we realized that the same money would have financed enough "ordinary" gospel meetings to yield probably two or three times as many baptisms. (*Contending for the Faith,* May 1979.)

Even though this appendix discusses a specific denominational trend in churches of Christ, it shows what happens when churches get involved in any denominational action. They lose control of their work. In addition, they lack the ability to correct their wrongs. When a denominational coalition becomes corrupt, it can affect thousands of churches. Not only is the non-denominational way of Christ scriptural, it is also the most practical way and produces more fruit. As each congregation maintains its autonomy, it controls its money and work. When abuses or sins occur, as they do, it possesses the power to deal with them. One congregation here and there may cease to wholeheartedly serve Christ, but its evil influence is confined to its own membership. Thus, God's wisdom and love for His people shines through in the non-denominational way He designed for His people to share fellowship with Him and with each other.

Appendix 8

Should Local Churches Exist? An Examination of the Teaching of Charles A. Holt

Charles A. Holt, a gospel preacher among churches of Christ for many years, has recently begun exercising considerable influence through his paper, *The Examiner.* This appendix is written out of concern for the basic premise of Holt's system of teaching, that there is no such thing in scripture as a local church. If this is true, there should be no such thing among us. If the idea of a local church is scriptural, then we should desire to associate with other Christians in such groups. Thus, the question is: Should Local Churches Exist?

While Holt's teaching frustrates many who briefly dismiss him as a crank and malign his character or motives, we propose to deal honorably with his teaching. In fact, concerning my general sentiments toward Holt's work, there is much with which I agree. For example, when Holt attacks denominational concepts that many Christians have of the body of Christ, he exhibits sensitivity we all ought to imitate. When he disparages high-handed treatment of people by some preachers, elders, and churches, he is imminently correct. When he decries much traditional activity in churches of Christ, handed down not from the apostles, but by a denominational system of churches, he does us all service. When he condemns confidence in an organization rather than in Christ, we are foolish not to heed his teaching. Further, although I do not know Holt well, I have extensive correspondence with him. Thus far, I have no reason to have any problem whatever with his character, motives, love for the Lord, or his intelligence and ability.

However, these positive sentiments do not prevent me from having serious problems with Holt's idea that local churches should not exist. Likewise, those serious problems don't prevent me from taking Holt's efforts seriously, nor do I think they should you. This is true of even Bible characters. I have problems with some of Abraham's behavior, but that doesn't keep me from taking him seriously. I can't understand some of the Apostle Peter's behavior, but that doesn't keep me from treating him earnestly. I have great problems with some of Solomon's behavior, but I still regard him seriously.

Likewise, crucial problems that we might have with much of Holt's teaching shouldn't prevent us from treating his work seriously either. Holt addresses some very legitimate grievances with churches of Christ. One's irritation at some of his methods and positions should not keep him from seeing that.

I recently heard a reliable report that Holt had roughly 16,000 readers on his mailing list. Since Holt frequently purges this list of people who do not request to remain on it, we may reason that these people are in part sensitive to the same issues Holt is. Should this estimate be even remotely accurate, Holt is probably exercising more influence among Christians than all the non-institutional gospel papers in America combined. This is perhaps more than six times the next largest circulation publication. This would be the equivalent of about 160 moderately-sized congregations of Christians. What other one person do you know who exercises such influence? Thus, we should take Holt's efforts seriously.

Holt's Position Concerning a Local Church

Gaylon Embrey (a regular writer in *The Examiner*) actually stated the foundation of Holt and *The Examiner's* position about a local church in the second issue of *The Examiner*. The fact that Holt republished this article in its entirety only two years later reflects its basis to his whole doctrine about the local church. Embrey reasons this way:

> Let us suppose that I, my wife, and my son John, you, your wife and your son John, along with two other couples have just been transferred to a strange town where the gospel has never been preached. We are all baptized believers, brothers and sisters in the family of God, members of the body of Christ. We are all Christians. We have all arrived in town. But according to the popular concept of what a Church is, the "Church of the Lord" has not arrived yet. For as yet no local "Church" has been "set up." Therefore at this time the community is thought still to be un-Churched. Alas, there is "no Church anywhere in town."

Later in this same article, Embrey says:

> What is it (make a list) that we as fellow disciples of Christ cannot do in the absence of one?
>
> Some kind of action must be taken that will make a "Church" among us where heretofore there has been no "Church."
>
> Suppose we have one more meeting, say on Wednesday night, and decide that Sunday is the day we will start "the Church" this coming Lord's Day. This means two things: there will be no Church in town till Sunday, but there will be one after that. Fine. But the question lingers. Come Sunday, how, oh how, are we going to pull off this feat? Sunday arrives and we all show up at the place where we have agreed to meet. There is no Church there, unless one has miraculously materialized since Wednesday night when we had our last planning session. So here we are, a group of disciples gathered together, but as yet no "Church" is present. We have a brief prayer together; but still there is no "Church" among us. We sing a few hymns together; but we don't have a "Church" yet. We have a Bible lesson; still no "Church"…

> We are told these days that the disciples in a community do not in and of themselves constitute the Lord's church.

Then Embrey asks:

> But, what do we have that we did not have before we started it? Before we started our Church all we had was a group of Christians, brothers and sisters in the family of God. Now that we have established a "Church" all we have is the same group of Christians. Of WHAT, then, does this mysterious "local Church" consist? It does not consist solely of the Christians; we had them before we started it. It does not consist of Church officers; we don't have any, scriptural or otherwise. It does not consist of a church building; we do not have one of these yet. This Church does not appear to consist of anything you can lay your hand or mind on. Frankly, I am at a loss. I fear that "the Church" we have started may be a figment of our imagination.
>
> Is it just possible, do you think, that we may have a few chinks in our "Church concept"? Frankly, I believe it is time for all Christians to look again at the *ecclesia* of the New Testament, and see it in a more scriptural and simple light. Hopefully the pages of this journal will encourage efforts in this direction. (Gaylon Embrey, "Starting A Church," *The Examiner, Vol. I*, No. 2, March, 1986, pp. 22-25, reprinted in *Vol. III*, No. 1, pp. 24ff.)

Similarly, Holt declares:

> Put this down as fact: In the beginning of the gospel of Jesus Christ as proclaimed by His apostles there was no such thing as a church, a religious institution. There was no "universal church" nor a "local church." There was no religious institution or organization. The early saints did not build, establish, join or hold membership in a church of any kind...Christians without a church? Yes,

> that is the way it was in the beginning. There is no church in the Scriptures. There should be no church today. (Charles A. Holt, "The Myth of the CHURCH of the Bible," *The Examiner, II*, No. 6, November, 1987, pp. 5, 6.)

Again, Holt writes:

> Hold to this simple truth: The saints, the redeemed people of God, constitute His *ekklesia*. There is one and only one *ekklesia* of Christ, just like there is only one body of Christ and one kingdom of Christ. (Charles A. Holt, "What Do We Do If There Is No Local Church Institution?" *The Examiner, III*, No. 3, May, 1988, p. 4.)

To this last statement we say, "Sorry, but it's just not true that there is one and only one *ekklesia* of Christ." Even if I wanted it to be true, or if we had a convention and we all agreed that it was true, it just isn't.

Reportedly seen on the wall of the Oriental Institute in Chicago is a classic statement which applies here:

> One of the greatest tragedies of life is the murder of a beautiful theory by a gang of brutal facts.

Here are some brutal facts that murder the foundation of Holt's beautiful theory. In Rom. 16.16, Paul said that "the *ekklesias* of Christ salute you," even though he never spoke of the bodies or kingdoms of Christ. In Rev. 1.4, John spoke of the "seven *ekklesias* of Asia," though he never spoke of the bodies or kingdoms of Asia. In Ac. 14.23, Luke said that Paul and Barnabas appointed for them "elders in every *ekklesia*," though he never mentioned every body or kingdom.

In Ac. 15.41, Luke said that Paul traveled through Syria and Cilicia, "strengthening the *ekklesias*," though Paul never strengthened bodies and kingdoms. In Ac. 16.5, Luke said "so the *ekklesias* were being strengthened," though he never said the bodies and kingdoms were strengthened. In Rom. 16.4, Paul spoke of "all the *ekklesias* of the Gentiles," though he never mentioned all the bodies or kingdoms of the Gentiles. In I Cor. 7.17, Paul said, "and thus I direct in all the *ekklesias*," though he never said he directed all the bodies and kingdoms. In I Cor. 11.16, Paul spoke of "the *ekklesias* of God," though he never spoke of the bodies or kingdoms of God. In I Cor. 14.33, Paul spoke of "all the *ekklesias* of the saints," though he never spoke of all the bodies or kingdoms of the saints. In I Cor. 14.34, Paul commanded: "Let the women keep silent in the *ekklesias*," though he never said for the women to keep silent in the bodies or kingdoms. In I Cor. 16.1, Paul said he "directed the *ekklesias* of Galatia," though he never directed the bodies or kingdoms of Galatia. In Cor. 16.19 Paul said "the *ekklesias* of Asia greet you." Can you find a passage where he said the bodies or kingdoms of Asia greeted anybody? In II Cor. 8.1, Paul spoke of "the *ekklesias* of Macedonia." Let Holt find where Paul spoke of the bodies or kingdoms of Macedonia. (For other uses of *ekklesia*s, please see: II Cor. 8.19, 23, 24, 11.8, 11.28, 12.13; Gal. 1.2, 1.22 (*ekklesias* of Judea); I Thes. 2.14, I Thes. 1.4; Rev. 1.4. 1.11. 1.20 (twice), 2.7, 11, 17, 2.23, 2.29, 3.6, 3.13, 22, 22.16.)

Thus, Holt's "simple truth," that "there is one and only one *ekklesia* of Christ," is not true in the least. He doesn't use *ekklesia* as either Paul, John, or Luke did in every one of these passages. His concept of *ekklesia* is not the same as that of Paul, John, or Luke. Other than that it may be alright—which means that it's not right at all!

What Is Missing?

In his original article, Embrey asks:

> What is it (make a list) that we as fellow disciples of Christ cannot do in the absence of one [a local church—SGD]?

We will use the Bible to make a list of the requirements for a local church to exist that fellow disciples acting independently do not have. We first notice that the term *ekklesia* (for which the word "church" is given in most of our translations) is a collective noun. Webster says a collective noun is:

> ...a noun which in the singular form denotes a collection of individuals (e.g., army, orchestra, crowd): it is treated as singular when the collection is thought of as a whole and as plural when the individual members are thought of as acting separately (*Webster's New 20th Century Dictionary*.)

To illustrate, when one says "The jury is out," he intends for his audience to picture the jury as a whole. If he says, "The jury went to their homes," he intends for the members of the jury to be pictured.

Both within and outside the Bible, collectives of people which act must have four things: (1) collective will, (2) collective action, (3) subjection to one another, and (4) recognition of collective entity. Collective will occurs when a group of people act according to joint will, not independently of each other. Collective action is the action the group takes, and is not the action of members of the group acting independently. Subjection to one another is the voluntary submission of one's own will to the collective will of the group. Paul spoke of such subjection of Christians one to another in Eph. 5.21, where he told the Christians in Ephesus:

> ...subjecting yourselves one to another in the fear of Christ.

Likewise, Peter, in I Pet. 5.5, said:

> Yea, all of you gird yourselves with humility, to serve one another: for God resisteth the proud, but giveth grace to the humble.

Though the idea of a collective noun is an elementary grammatical principle, it is easily seen in the pages of the New Testament, as the following points show:.

Ekklesias of Non-Christians Had Four Characteristics

For example, in Ac. 19.32, concerning the riotous mob of silversmiths seeking to kill Paul, Luke said, "the *ekklesia* was in confusion." In this *ekklesia*, we see collective will in verse 29, where they had one accord, to do something about Paul's preaching. They had collective action when they rushed into the theatre and seized Gaius and Aristarchus, Paul's companions in travel. They had recognition of group entity in verse 38, where Luke said the *ekklesia* was in confusion. Recall that Webster says a collective noun is treated as singular when the collection is thought of as a whole. This *ekklesia* was a group of silversmiths. Finally, these silversmiths were not acting independently of each other, they were in subjection to one another. Verse 29 again said they "rushed with one accord." These four things (collective will, collective action, recognition of collective entity, and subjection to one another) show that these silversmiths were not just several silversmiths who happened to be in the same place at the same time.

In Ac. 19.39, we find another *ekklesia* in this same context, the town assembly. The town clerk, hoping to avoid the Roman government's further restraining the people of Ephesus, said to the mob of silversmiths:

> But if ye seek anything about ot=her matters, it shall be settled in the regular assembly [*ekklesia*].

This *ekklesia* also demonstrates the four requirements for collective action. There was collective will contemplated, as the *ekklesia* would "settle" certain matters. Their collective action would be determined by how they "settled" those matters. There was recognition of group entity, the town council. These men were in subjection to one another, for they "regularly assembled." In other words, this *ekklesia* was not just several citizens who happened to meet coincidentally. It was a group of men with the above four characteristics.

In Ac. 7.38, Stephen mentioned the "*ekklesia* in the wilderness," the nation of Israel. This *ekklesia* also exhibits the same four characteristics necessary for collective action. The nation of Israel had collective will, the law of Moses. Their collective action was national action, the action of the entire nation. Recognition of group entity existed, it was the nation of Israel. There was subjection to one another. In Ex. 19.8, they had said, "All that the Lord has spoken we will do," binding themselves not to act independently, but in agreement with God's covenant. Again, these same four characteristics made this *ekklesia* of Israelites much more than just several Jews who happened to be in the wilderness of Sinai at the same time.

Local Groups of Christians in the New Testament Had These Same Four Characteristics

Local *Ekklesias* and Their Own Fellowship

In Ac. 9.26, we have the account of Paul's coming to Jerusalem three years after he became a Christian. Luke said:

> And when he was come to Jerusalem, he assayed to join himself to the disciples: and they were all afraid of him, not believing that he was a disciple.

Recognition of group entity existed among these disciples. If Embrey is right that the church is the Christians in a certain town, whether they know each other or not, then Paul was in the church in Jerusalem as soon as he got to town. They couldn't have kept him out! However, he wasn't in the Jerusalem *ekklesia*—they kept him out! We can see their collective will in that they didn't want him as a part of their group! Their collective action was that they rejected him. We can see that they were in subjection to one another, for they had a relationship to one another that they didn't want Paul to share.

Similarly in III Jn. 10, the contentious Diotrophes ejected Christians from that local *ekklesia*. John said:

> Therefore, if I come, I will bring to remembrance his works which he doeth, prating against us with wicked words; and not content therewith, neither doth he himself receive the brethren, and them that would he forbiddeth and casteth them out of the church [*ekklesia*].

Obviously, Diotrophes cast nobody out of the "general assembly and church [*ekklesia*] of the firstborn"—the universal church (Heb. 12.23), for only God can do that. Instead, Diotrophes rejected certain Christians from a local *ekklesia*. That Diotrophes could do so shows recognition of group entity. On the other hand, if Embrey is correct when he says that there is no difference between a local *ekklesia* and Christians who happen to be in a certain locale, Diotrophes could not have ejected anybody, unless he kicked them out of town! This local *ekklesia* had collective will, the will of the dictator Diotrophes. Diotrophes dictated their collective action, and their cooperation in obeying him shows subjection to one another. This local *ekklesia* was more than just some Christians who happened to live in the same town!

Local *Ekklesias* and Evangelism

Just like local *ekklesias* controlled their own fellowship, a local *ekklesia* could also act collectively in evangelism. In Ac. 13.1-3, we read:

> Now there were at Antioch, in the church [*ekklesia*] that was there, prophets and teachers, Barnabas, ...and Saul. And as they ministered to the Lord, and fasted, the Holy Spirit said, Separate me Barnabas and Saul for the work whereunto I have called them. Then, when they had fasted and prayed and laid their hands on them, they sent them away.

We can see recognition of group entity in Luke's statement "in the church that was there." The singular verb "was" shows, as Webster said, that the collection is "treated as singular when the collection is thought of as a whole." Their collective will was that of the Holy Spirit. Their collective action took place when they sent Paul and Barnabas away. Their subjection to one another is shown in that they were bound not to act independently, but according to the Holy Spirit. They had a relationship with each other in supporting Paul that just an unrelated number of Christians who happened to be in Antioch at the same time could not have.

Similar examples of a local *ekklesia* acting collectively in evangelism are seen in Ac. 15.3, in Antioch's sending Paul and Barnabas to Jerusalem, and II Cor. 11.8 where Paul "robbed other churches" taking wages of them to preach elsewhere.

Local *Ekklesias* and Doctrinal Unity

In the demonstration of doctrinal unity in Acts 15, Luke said in verse 22:

> Then it seemed good to the apostles and the elders, with the whole church [*ekklesia*], to choose men out of their company, and send them to Antioch with Paul and Barnabas, …

Again, we see the same four characteristics of collective action of a local *ekklesia*. Their recognition of group entity is shown by the whole church choosing men out of their company. Their collective will is shown when Luke said "It seemed good to the whole church." The collective action was the choosing of men to act as messengers. The relationship they shared with the apostles and elders shows their subjection to one another. Thus, the *ekklesia* in Jerusalem was more than just several Christians who happened to be in Jerusalem simultaneously.

Local *Ekklesias* and Discipline

In the example of collective action in dealing with impenitent sin found in I Corinthians 5 and II Corinthians 2, we can see these same four characteristics that made the Corinthian *ekklesia* more than just some Christians who happened to be in Corinth at the same time.

In I Cor. 5.9, Paul said, "I wrote unto you in my epistle to have no company with fornicators..." In verse 11, he says, "I wrote unto you not to keep company, if any man that is named a brother be a fornicator, ...with such a one no, not to eat." His use of the singular "you" in these verses shows recognition of group entity. Again, as Webster says, a collective noun (*ekklesia* this case) is treated as singular when the collection is thought of as a whole. Corinth's collective will was that enjoined by Paul, who changed their collective will by this very letter. II Cor. 2.9 mentions their collective action where Paul said the "punishment was inflicted by the many" and II Cor. 2.9, "that I might know the proof of you," where again, the singular "you" shows group action. Finally, their subjection to one another is seen in their relation with one another toward the impenitent fornicator as directed by Paul. They did not act independently toward him, as would an independent number of Christians who happened to be in Corinth at the same time.

Local *Ekklesias* and Benevolence

Collective action of the Corinthian *ekklesia* can be seen in I Cor. 16.2, where Paul said in regard to a collection for needy saints in Jerusalem:

> Upon the first day of the week let each one of you lay by him in store, as he may prosper, that no collections be made when I come.

Their recognition of group entity is seen in Paul's use of the singular "you." *Ekklesia* (according to Webster) is treated as singular when the collection is thought of as a whole. So does each church choosing its own messengers to carry their bounty to Jerusalem. Their collective will was expressed in the selection of the messengers for each church (I Cor. 16.3, II Cor. 8.23). Their collective action was the sending of their bounty to Jerusalem (I Cor. 16.3). The subjection to one another is shown by their acting together according to Paul's instruction. Thus, they had a relationship with one another with respect to the needy Jerusalem saints based on Paul's directions.

Local *Ekklesias* Selecting Servants

In Romans 16.1, Paul said:

> I commend unto you Phoebe our sister, who is a servant of the church [*ekklesia*] that is at Cenchrea, that ye receive her in the Lord, worthily of the saints, and that ye assist her in whatsoever matter she may have need of you...

Paul's use of the singular verb "is" shows the recognition of collective entity of the Christians in Cenchrea (Webster says a collective noun is treated as singular when the collection is thought of as a whole.) Their collective will is expressed in Paul's hope that they will be willing to use her as one of the group's servants. Their collective action is their use of her as a servant of the *ekklesia* in Rome. Their subjection to one another is seen in their working relationship, and Paul's hope they will include Phoebe in that relationship. The four ingredients of collective action are clearly shown.

Local *Ekklesias* and Public Assemblies

The *ekklesia* at Corinth also shows collective action in their public assemblies. In I Cor. 11.18, Paul mentioned their divisions:

> For first of all, when ye come together in the church, I hear that divisions exist among you; and I partly believe it.

This singular "you" shows Paul thought of the collection as a whole. In I Cor. 14.23-25, Paul said in regard to the use of spiritual gifts in the assembly:

> If therefore the whole church be assembled together...and so he will fall down on his face and worship God, declaring that God is among you indeed.

The term "whole church" and the singular "you" show Paul contemplated the *ekklesia* acting collectively. These verses show recognition of group entity, as does Paul's statement in I Cor. 11.17: "In giving you this charge..." Their collective will is shown in their willingness to come together. Their collective action is their coming together. Their subjection to one another is the result of Paul's rebuke of them. They didn't have it at first, when they weren't waiting for one another (I Cor. 11.21). Later, if they followed Paul's instruction, they were in subjection to one another, and waited for one another (I Cor. 11.33).

Summary Thus Far

In this section we have seen collective action of *ekklesias* in 1) control of local fellowship, 2) evangelism, 3) doctrinal unity, 4) discipline, 5) benevolence, 6) selecting servants, and 7) in their public assemblies. In each case, collective entity, will, action, and subjection made each of these *ekklesias* more than just Christians who happened to be in the same locale.

Sometimes Holt Agrees

> Saints may congregate or gather when, where and with other disciples as they please to "provoke one another unto love and good works" (Heb. 10.24); but this does not make them a church or an institution such as the White Rock C of C [Church of Christ—SGD] in Dallas ...It takes more than getting a number of Christians together to constitute a church. (Charles A. Holt, "What Do We Do If There Is No Local Church Institution?" *The Examiner, III*, No. 3, May, 1988, p. 3.)

I agree with this statement. Just Christians do not make a church. It takes more than getting some Christians together to constitute a church. It takes collective entity, collective will, collective action, and subjection to one another to have a collective of people, or an *ekklesia.*

Sometimes Holt Disagrees

> There is no such thing as "collective responsibilities," as some of our preacher/clergy now try to "con" us into believing. If there are collective or corporate responsibilities, then there would of necessity have to be collective or institution accountability. (Charles A. Holt, "What Do We Do If There Is No Local Church Institution?" *The Examiner, III*, No. 3, May, 1988, p. 5.)

Holt here argues merely from consequence. Collective responsibility is called "subjection to one another" in the New Testament (Eph. 5.21, I Pet. 5.5), and Holt's disdain for collective accountability doesn't negate it.

Brief Review of Embrey

In this section we wish to briefly review Gaylon Embrey's scenario of how Christians who happen to be in the same community cannot start a local *ekklesia*, because, whether they even know one another or not, they are already the Lord's *ekklesia* in that community.

Confuses Individual Christians, a Local Church, and the Universal Church

Again, Embrey says, with my comments:

> Let us suppose that I, my wife, and my son John, you, your wife and your son John, along with two other couples have just been transferred to a strange town where the gospel has never been preached. We are all baptized believers [individual Christians—SGD], brothers and sisters in the family of God, members of the body of Christ. We are all Christians. We have all arrived in

> town. But according to the popular concept of what a Church is, the "Church of the Lord" [universal church—SGD] has not arrived yet. For as yet no local "Church" has been "set up." Therefore at this time the community is thought still to be un-Churched. Alas, there is "no Church [either universal or local—SGD] anywhere in town."

Embrey starts out speaking of individual Christians, then speaks of them as the universal church, then speaks of a local church. Anyone who so mixes those concepts in one paragraph can prove just about anything. An individual Christian is not a church, any more than one quail is a covey, or one lion is a pride. He is not a collective of persons. Mixing the universal church indiscriminately with a local church is inexcusable. For the differences between these two *ekklesias*, please see Chapter 2.

Embrey then asks :

> What is it (make a list) that we as fellow *disciples* of Christ cannot do in the absence of one? [i.e., a local *ekklesia*—SGD]

We've already given our list, and shown each one of the items on it directly from scripture, and shortly we'll see them in Embrey's own words:

Collective Entity
Collective Will
Collective Action
Subjection to One Another

Embrey then says:

> Some kind of action must be taken that will make a "Church" among us where heretofore there has been no "Church."

I agree. There has to be

Collective Entity
Collective Will
Collective Action
Subjection to One Another

To see these same four characteristics in Embrey's own example, consider the following paragraph:

> Suppose we have one more meeting, say on Wednesday night, and decide [collective will—SGD] that Sunday is the day we will start "the Church" this coming Lord's Day. [Here is recognition of the group entity and subjection to one another—SGD] This means two things: there will be no Church in town till Sunday, but there will be one after that. Fine. But the question lingers. Come Sunday, how, oh how, are we going to pull off this feat? Sunday arrives and we all show up [collective action—SGD] at the place where we have agreed to meet. There is no Church there, unless one has miraculously materialized since Wednesday night when we had our last planning session. So here we are, a group [Embrey recognizes the group entity—SGD] of disciples gathered together, but as yet no "Church" [I disagree, SGD] is present. We have a brief prayer [collective action—SGD] together; but still there is no "Church" among us. We sing a few hymns together; but we don't have a "Church" yet. We have a Bible lesson; still no "Church" ...

I disagree! There are four things that weren't there before: (1) Collective will—these Christians had collective will on Wednesday night: "We have one more meeting, say on Wednesday night, and decide that Sunday is the day." (2) Collective action—these Christians had collective action on Sunday: "We all show up at the place where we have agreed to meet...We have a brief prayer together...We sing a few hymns together...We have a Bible lesson." (3) Recognition of collective entity—Embrey even calls them a group. (4) Subjection to one another—they're no longer acting completely independently of each other, but now have a relationship with each other they didn't have before. These four characteristics were necessary to have an *ekklesia* of silversmiths, the *ekklesia* of the town council, the *ekklesia* with Moses in the wilderness, and *ekklesias* of Christians in the New Testament.

Embrey then says:

> We are told these days that the disciples in a community do not in and of themselves constitute the Lord's church.

I agree, and sometimes, so does Holt!

> Saints may congregate or gather when, where and with other disciples as they please to "provoke one another unto love and good works" (Heb. 10.24); but this does not make them a church or an institution such as the White Rock C of C in Dallas...It takes more than getting a number of Christians together to constitute a church. (Charles A. Holt, "What Do We Do If There Is No Local Church Institution?" *The Examiner, III*, No. 3, May, 1988, p. 3.)

Next, Embrey says:

> But, what do we have that we did not have before we started it? Before we started our Church all we had was a group of Christians, brothers and sisters in the family of God. Now that we have established a "Church" all we have is the same group of Christians. Of WHAT, then, does this mysterious "local Church" consist? It does not consist solely of the Christians; we had them before we started it. It does not consist of Church officers; we don't have any, scriptural or otherwise. It does not consist of a church building; we do not have one of these yet. This Church does not appear to consist of anything you can lay your hand or mind on. Frankly, I am at a loss. I fear that "the Church" we have started may be a figment of our imagination.

Again, I disagree. To have collective action, an *ekklesia*, the Bible doesn't require officers, or a building. But it does require four things that we have already laid our hands on: collective entity, collective will, collective action, and subjection to one another.

Finally, Embrey says:

> Is it just possible, do you think, that we may have a few chinks in our "Church" concept? Frankly, I believe it is time for all Christians to look again at the *ecclesia* of the New Testament, and see it in a more scriptural and simple light. Hopefully the pages of this journal will encourage efforts in this direction.

I agree that many Christians do have a few chinks in their concept of both the body of Christ and local churches as well, and have tried to address many of those chinks in this volume. It is apparent from Embrey's indiscriminate use of individual Christians, local churches and the universal church that he and Holt have quite a few chinks themselves!

Holt's "Fellowships" or "Forums"

Holt Understands Collective Action

The reader needs to understand that Holt's disciples get together from time to time in a national forum or fellowship, or a regional forum or fellowship, to worship, study, and pray together. There is an announced agenda of speakers, who speak on assigned subjects. While I don't understand these forums or fellowships to be local churches, they do illustrate that Holt understands the concept of collective action of Christians, unless you want to call it an *ekklesia*!

For example, in "A Great Time in the Lord," Vol. II, No. 6, p. 19, Holt says: "There was an agenda for each day." About next year, he says, "It will not be open to the public because the number of attendees is limited." Concerning the June, 1988 Forum/Fellowship, in the article entitled "June 1988 Get-together of Saints," *Vol. III,* No. 2, p. 18) Holt says: "The get-together is not for our antagonists, ...the specific subjects/studies have not yet been finalized..., The place has not yet been finalized, ...We hope we can have another one of that type even with a much larger group." Surely, we can see that these are all expressions of collective will, action, and subjection to one another. These forum/fellowships are not just Christians who happened to be in the same time in the same town, in the same hotel, listening to assigned speakers speak on assigned subjects!

In an article entitled "1988 Truth and Freedom Forum/Fellowship," (*Vol. III,* No. 3, p. 10), Holt calls this meeting a fellowship, but in "Great Success—1989 Truth and Freedom Forum," *The Examiner, IV,* No. 5, September, 1989, p. 2, Holt says:

> Moreover, the people involved with the Forum did not constitute a FELLOWSHIP. (Charles A. Holt, "Great Success—1989 Truth and Freedom Forum," *The Examiner, IV,* No. 5, September 1989, p. 2.)

I disagree. There was collective will, action, subjection to one another, and temporarily, at least, recognition of group entity. This constitutes fellowship, and at the time, Holt even called it fellowship. It's just possible he has a few chinks in his concept of "forum/fellowships."

Still concerning the 1988 Truth and Freedom Forum/Fellowship, Holt says:

> Those in charge have scheduled me for the first discussion session...You must register to attend!...It is not a place for any antagonist nor a time for debate or controversy.

All these are expressions of collective will, action, and subjection to one another. These are not just many Christians who happen to meet at the feed store by chance!

Holt Later Attempts to Deny Collective Action

In "Great Success—1989 Truth and Freedom Forum", *The Examiner, IV*, No. 5, p. 2, Holt says:

> There is no teaching, position, or doctrine to which all must or do subscribe. (Charles Holt, "Great Success—1989 Truth and Freedom Forum," *The Examiner, IV*, No. 5, p. 2.)

Clearly, one position to which all who attend must subscribe is "it is not a place for any antagonist nor a time for debate or controversy."

Holt also says:

> Yes, we do things in an organized, orderly fashion, but we are not "members of" nor do we "belong to" any organization that directs or controls our views or activities in serving the Lord. (Charles Holt, "Great Success—1989 Truth and Freedom Forum," *The Examiner, IV*, No. 5, p. 2.)

No direction nor control of activities? Who can believe it? Somebody in charge scheduled the speakers, subjects, time, place, and date. Somebody decided that it was no place for their antagonists. Yet Holt says:

> I repeat, there is no person, organization or institution to rule and control. (Charles Holt, "Great Success—1989 Truth and Freedom Forum," *The Examiner, IV*, No. 5, p. 3.)

And again,

> On Sunday morning the entire meeting centered around the Lord's Supper. You would just have to be a part of it to really understand and appreciate this very moving time. It lasted almost two hours! RICK ROBERTS coordinated this time together. (Charles Holt, "Great Suc-

> cess—1989 Truth and Freedom Forum," *The Examiner, IV*, No. 5, p. 4.)

Of course, I have no problem with Christians meeting to study and pray together. Christians did that in the Bible, as we have amply seen. They had collective will, action, entity, and subjection to one another while they did so. I do have a number of problems with someone who claims that collective action in local *ekklesias* is unscriptural, then expects anyone to believe these forum/fellowships just happen!

Holt Doesn't Understand What a Denomination Is

One of Holt's great problems is not just that he recklessly confuses individual Christians, local groups of Christians, and the universal *ekklesia*, but he also confuses a local group of Christians with a denomination. In all his denunciation of denominationalism, he doesn't know what a denomination is.

For example, Holt sometimes asserts that a local church is equivalent to a denomination:

> Let me repeat what I have tried to emphasize several times in this journal. There is not one essential requirement for having a denomination that the local C of C does not have! If so, name it. I said, "essential" to being a denomination. (Charles A. Holt, "What Do We Do If There Is No Local Church Institution," *The Examiner, III*, No. 3, May, 1988, p. 3.)

I can name one essential requirement for having a denomination that a local church does not have: *collective action of congregations*. Many in churches of Christ, the author included, have opposed denominationalism without knowing exactly what a denomination is. Sometimes we oppose denominational creeds, and so we should. We should despise the barriers denominational creeds erect between believers in Christ and the hindrances they impose to independent study of scripture. Sometimes we oppose the division they bring to the cause of Christ, and so we should. But denominationalism is much more than this.

We read of instances where a single local church acted in the New Testament. For example, in I Cor. 1.2, Paul spoke of the "church of God which is at Corinth," clearly speaking of a single local congregation. When Paul wrote Galatians, he addressed it "to the churches of Galatia," a plurality of churches, each acting independently. After the apostles died, man invented the idea of a plurality of congregations acting collectively. *A modern word describes this arrangement, although it isn't a Bible word. The word is "denomination".* This is precisely what a denomination is: a plurality of churches acting collectively. For example, the Methodist denomination consists of all the churches that function collectively in that denomination. The Episcopal denomination is a collection of local churches that function collectively to do the work of that denomination. On and on the list goes. Collective action of local churches is denominational action.

For an institution that has been among us for so long, it is surprising how little many of us have reflected on just what a denomination is. Even among those who oppose the division and unbelief that denominationalism produces few have stopped to analyze exactly what it is. Webster defines a denomination as "The name of a class of things, a class or kind (especially of units) having a specific name or value." Thus, we speak of currency consisting of several denominations: five dollar bills, tens, etc. Each denomination of money consists of a category of bills.

However, a denomination is more than something named. I have two children, both of whom we named, but I am not the father of two denominations.

Donald G. Tinder, in the *Evangelical Dictionary of Theology*, gives the following definition of a religious denomination:

> Denominations are associations of congregations—though sometimes it might be said that congregations are localized subdivisions of denominations—that have a common heritage. Moreover, a true denomination does not claim to be the only legitimate expression of the church. (Donald G. Tinder, *Evangelical Dictionary of*

Theology, Ed. Walter A. Elwell, [Grand Rapids: Baker Publishing House, 1984], p. 310.)

Consequently, a *denomination is a collective of congregations*. When congregations function as a unit, they function denominationally. Tinder admits our naivete about the rise of the denominational concept:

> Even though denominations within Protestantism have come to be the largest expression of organized Christianity beyond the level of the congregation, there has never been much theological reflection on denominationalism. A look at theological textbooks or church creeds confirms this. Probably the simplest explanation for this omission is that the Bible in no way envisages the organization of the church into denominations. (*Ibid., p.* 310.)

Now Holt asserts that a single church can be a denomination. No, it may have a denominational creed, it may be a part of a denomination, but by definition, it is impossible for *any single* congregation to be a denomination!

After saying that a single church of Christ is nothing but a denomination, then Holt says, about his own organization, Truth and Freedom Ministry, Inc.:

> The facts are, Biblically and according to civil law, that Truth and Freedom Ministry, Inc., and the local C of CC are equivalent human structures or organizations. (*Ibid.*)

Thus, if a local church of Christ is a denomination, so is Holt's organization! I don't believe it, but that is what he says!

Holt shows his confusion about denominationalism in "Questions and Answers," *The Examiner, IV*, No. 3, May, 1989, p. 30. He says:

> 1) What is a Lutheran Church? It is a church.
> 2) What is a Methodist Church? It is a church.
> 3) What is a Church of God? It is a church.

4) What is a Church of Christ? It is a church.

Commonality: Each one is a church!
Whatever No. 1 is, they all are! Each one is a denomination.

5) What is the name of the church in No. 4?

The name is: Church of Christ; and it is a church; therefore, Church of Christ church! It is a named or denominated Southside Church of Christ, for example. It is a denomination like all the others.

6) Whatever No. 1 is they all are.

To this we say:

1. A Lutheran Church is not a denomination. It is a local congregation affiliated with others under common oversight.

2. A Methodist Church is not a denomination. It is a local congregation affiliated with others under common oversight.

3. Holt says a Church of God is a denomination, but it may be a local church, as in I Cor. 1.2. The church in Corinth was not a denomination because it had no affiliation with other churches under common oversight. A Church of God may also be a local congregation affiliated with others under common oversight, i.e., part of the Church of God denomination.

4. Holt says a Church of Christ is a denomination. It is not a denomination either, since by definition, it is impossible for a single church to be a denomination. Denominations are associations of congregations. If this church of Christ has no affiliation with others under common oversight, it is not even part of a denomination, i.e., the church at Corinth.

5. What is the name of the church of Christ in No. 4? I don't know, it wasn't given.

Holt then assumes that anything denominated or named is a denomination. Holt has a name, thus, his own logic proves he is a denomination. If he denominated his children, they are denominations also. If his wife has a name, Holt married a denomination. If his car has a name, he drives a denomination. He denominated his organization, Truth and Freedom Ministry, therefore it is a denomination. This is all very heavy argumentation, but Holt doesn't know what a denomination is yet!

Conclusion

Local churches existed in the Bible, and do now. They were more than just saints who happened to be in the same locale. To this Embrey and Holt agree, at least sometimes. God desires local congregations to have collective entity, collective will, collective action, and subjection to one another. Holt and Embrey think such groups of Christians are fine, since (1) they believe brethren can decide to work together, (2) limit who will teach, (3) decide the subjects, (4) decide if they have a building, but just that they shouldn't be called "churches."

Appendix 9

The Body of Christ & the Lord's Supper:

How Denominational Concepts of Christ's Church Produce Erroneous Views of Communion

Christians worry about several controversial topics concerning the Lord's Supper. These topics concern (1) whether the fruit of the vine may be distributed in more than one container, (2) whether the unleavened bread may be in more than one piece, and (3) whether it is proper for local churches to have the Lord's Supper more than once on the first day of the week. While these topics may seem trivial to some, serious brethren whose allegiance to Christ and his teaching cannot be questioned, hold to both sides of these three issues.

Confessedly, while the author has studied all three of these controversies over his twenty-five years of preaching, they were not at the forefront of his study, nor were they his favorite subjects. When questions arose about them, he studied diligently the most powerful arguments of the strongest proponents of both sides, and acted according to his convictions in the matters.

However, in 1988, the author published the first edition of *Fellowship: With God and His People*, in which he explored denominational concepts of the body of Christ. After half a lifetime of opposition to denominationalism, he finally learned what a denomination was, and discovered that he had many denominational concepts himself. (Even if we're opposed to denominationalism, if we've got denominational concepts in our thinking, our actions will soon be denominational as well.) As the years have gone by since the publication of that book on fellowship, the author has seen innumerable applications of those denominational concepts, many times in areas of study surprisingly far from his original course of study. One such area is in these very matters of controversy surrounding the Lord's Supper. The author has been amazed at how simply ridding our thinking of denominational concepts vastly simplifies all three of these issues.

Part I: Erroneous Views of the Body of Christ

In Chapter 3, "The Relationship Between the Universal Church and Local Church," we noted that the universal church is not a collection of denominations, nor a collection of local churches (a denomination), but rather a collection of Christians. We saw there that a failure to understand this simple concept led to the Roman Catholic hierarchy, and later, the rise of the denominational concept in the Reformation Movement, and even in the American Restoration Movement, which was trying to escape the denominationalism they knew wasn't in the Bible. We've even seen the putting into practice of the concept in the sponsoring church concept in the churches of Christ and the Crossroads/Boston Movement.

One does not have to be much of a student of the history of similar endeavors, from the second century to the present one, to confidently know this movement is also doomed to produce even more coalitions of churches. This is not because of a lack of sincerity in those involved, but because they labor under a denominational concept of the body of Christ.

Part II: Erroneous Views of the Lord's Supper

The application of these basic principles on denominationalism to our present subject, the Lord's Supper, is that on every one of the three controversial questions we will address, a denominational view of the body of Christ is at the heart of the matter. If we view the body of Christ as a "church of churches," or a "body of bodies," we're bound to let that erroneous view of Christ's body drive us to erroneous views of the Lord's Supper, particularly the container question, the bread question, and the second offering of the Lord's Supper.

We begin by stipulating that we all should believe that: (1) There is one cup for one body, (2) there is one bread for one body, and (3) there is one communion for one body. However, serious questions remain for honest Bible students, like: (1) What is the body? (2) What is the cup? (3) What is the bread? and (4) What is the one communion?

Controversial Question Number One: One Cup for One Body

On the question of the container for the fruit of the vine, we all can say there is one cup for one body. However, when this statement is made, those who may use multiple containers think the statement means one element (the fruit of the vine) for the universal church, the body of Christ, while those who use only one container think the statement means only one container for one local church. (Note that these brethren really do not believe in one container, but rather one container per congregation!)

We attempt to settle this issue by examining whether a local church is ever referred to as a body of Christ. Of course, I've thought in those terms for years myself, and many of my brethren have too, but I now believe the body of bodies concept of Christ's body is just as wrong (and denominational) as the church of churches concept. We now show that a local church isn't a body in I Cor. 12.27, one of the most tempting passages for us to use.

In I Cor. 12.27, Paul says, "Now ye are the body of Christ, and severally members thereof."

Is the term "body" here referring to the universal church, or to a local church? To see, let's merely see how the word body is used elsewhere in the New Testament. In Eph. 4.4, Paul says, "There is one body." Is there just one universal church, or just one local church? Of course, there is not just one local church. In I Cor. 12.20, Paul says, "There are many gifts but one body." Is this one body just one universal church, or just one local church? Again, there is not just one local church. In Eph. 1.23, when Paul says, "The church is his body, the fulness of Christ." The universal church is his body, not a local church. In Eph. 2.16, Paul teaches that Gentiles and Jews are reconciled to God "in one body," which again must be the universal body of believers. Likewise, in Col. 1.18, Paul says that Christ "is the head of the body, the church." This church must be the universal church, and cannot be a local church. In I Cor. 12.13, Paul says, "We were all baptized into the one body." We are not baptized into a local church, but into the universal church. Surely, we can see in all these passages that the body of Christ is referring to the universal church, of which there is only one, and cannot possibly refer to a local church, of which there are thousands.

To emphasize this point even further, we challenge the reader to find more than one body of Christ in the New Testament. Paul was not wrong when he said, "There is one body." Is that what we believe, or do we believe there are thousands of bodies and that the local church is a local body?

Similarly, did Paul say in I Cor. 12.13, "We were all baptized into many *bodies*"? In I Cor. 12.27, did he say, "Ye are the *bodies* of Christ"? In Eph. 1.23, did Paul refer to "the church which are his *bodies*"? In Eph. 2.16, did he say God reconciled Jew and Gentile "both in many *bodies*"? In Eph. 3.6, did Paul state that Christians are "fellow-members of the *bodies*"? In Eph. 4.4, did he say, "There are many *bodies*"? In Eph. 4.12, did he refer to "the building up of the *bodies*"? In Eph. 4.16, did Paul speak of "all the *bodies* fitly framed" and "the increase of the *bodies*"? Did Paul speak of Christ as "the savior of the *bodies*" in Eph. 5.23? Did he speak of Christians as "members of his *bodies*" in Eph. 5.30, or of Christ as "the head of the *bodies*, the churches" in Col.

**The Body of Christ:
A Local Body or Universal Church?**

	Local	Univ.
Rom. 12.5 - "We who are many are one body in Christ"		**X**
I Cor. 10.17 - "we who are many are one body"	**?**	**X**
I Cor. 12.13 - "all baptized into one body"		**X**
I Cor. 12.27 - "ye are the body of Christ"	**?**	**X**
Eph. 1.23 - "the church which is his body"		**X**
Eph. 2.16 - "reconcile them both in one body"		**X**
Eph. 3.6 - "fellow-members of the body"		**X**
Eph. 4.4 - "there is one body"		**X**
Eph. 4.12 - "unto the building up of the body"	**?**	**X**
Eph. 4.16 - "all the body fitly framed"	**?**	**X**
- "increase of the body"	**?**	**X**
Eph. 5.23 - "the savior of the body"		**X**
Eph. 5.30 - "we are members of his body"		**X**
Col. 1.18 - "the head of the body, the church"		**X**
Col. 1.24 - "his body's sake, which is the church"		**X**

***Never Said:
"Bodies" or "A Body"***

Figure 15

1.18, or of Christ's "*bodies'* sake, which are the churches" in Col. 1.24? In all these passages, we can see that never did the writers in the New Testament refer to the body of Christ in the plural. The body of Christ always refers to the universal church, and never a local church or churches.

Figure 15 illustrates this point even further. It gives every passage speaking of the body of Christ, and indicates whether the term body is used of a local church, or the universal church. As the Xs indicate, every single one of these passages can be understood as speaking of the universal church, and several of them (indicated by ?s) may be thought to refer to local churches.

However, when we realize that there is only one body, and that no writer by inspiration ever spoke of "bodies" or "a body" in reference to the body of Christ, we cannot imitate the language of the New Testament by speaking of local churches as bodies of Christ. The New Testament spoke of but one body of Christ, and that body was always the universal church, and never a local one. In I Cor. 12.27, when Paul says, "Ye are the body of Christ," he uses the term "body" like he does everywhere else, not of a local church, but of the universal church.

We now notice the positive teaching of I Cor. 12.27. If this verse is not referring to the local church at Corinth as the body of Christ, what is the teaching of the passage? Most of us realize the church of Christ is spoken of as his bride, his kingdom, and God's family. If Paul had told these same Christians, "Ye are the bride of Christ," his point would not have been that each congregation is a bride, and that Christ has a bride in every city, perhaps more than one in some cities! His point would have been that the universal church, all Christians of all places and all times, should be pure as a bride, whether all the Christians to whom he referred to were in the same congregation or not.

Likewise, had Paul told the Corinthians "Ye are the family of Christ," he wouldn't have implied that each congregation is a family, but that all Christians everywhere and of all times comprise one family, and that they ought to conduct themselves toward each other as family members, whether they are in the same local church or not. Had he said, "Ye are the kingdom of Christ," he wouldn't have been teaching that every local church is a local kingdom, but that all Christians are in the one universal kingdom of Christ. If we can understand those figures, then we can understand that Paul uses the figure of the body to point out that the universal church, all Christians everywhere, ought to function like a body. This is true of Christians, whether they are in the same congregation or not. The essential point of Paul's teaching concerning spiritual gifts in I Corinthians 12 is that Christians should use their gifts for the benefit of all the members of the body of Christ, whether they were members of the same local church or not.

We can drive this point home even further by asking, if we can understand that all Christians everywhere are not in separate kingdoms, but one kingdom, and that we are not in separate families of God, but one family, and that we as Christians are not in separate brides, but one bride, then why can't we understand that we are not in separate bodies, but the one universal body or church of Christ? Of course, we can understand the body of Christ in this sense, and it is the only sense we can understand the concept of the body of Christ. Paul agrees when he says, "There is one body" (Eph. 4.4), that "We are members of his body" (Eph. 5.30), and "The body is one and hath many members, and all the members of the body, being many, are one body" (I Cor. 12.12). We had just as well teach there are many universal churches or many Gods, as teach that there are many bodies of Christ.

We now emphasize a major point of agreement. We all agree that there is one cup for the one body, but what is the cup? Again, we agree that the term "cup" sometimes means *a drinking vessel*, and sometimes the term refers metonymically to *the liquid contained in a drinking vessel.* We all use this figure of speech every day. Metonymy is "A figure by which one name is used instead of another." (E. W. Bullinger, *Figures of Speech Used in the Bible* [Grand Rapids, MI: Baker Book House, 1898], p. 538.) If we speak of a lady eating ice cream and we say, "She ate the whole carton," we realize she didn't literally eat the cardboard box the dessert came in, but all the ice cream in the carton. If one were to ask, "Out of how many containers did she eat it?" we would have no idea. She might have eaten it out of the box itself, or perhaps a dish, or perhaps more than one dish. The fact that she ate the whole carton simply doesn't tell us.

If we speak of someone eating cereal, I might say, "I could eat the whole box." Again, I'm not going to eat any of the cardboard box, but that which is contained within the box. If I do eat the whole box, out of how many containers did I eat it? You have no idea whether I ate it out of the cardboard container itself, out of a cereal bowl, or out of several cereal bowls. The figure of speech simply doesn't tell you.

If we speak of someone eating olives, and we say, "She ate the whole jar," we're speaking of the quantity eaten, not how they were eaten, whether directly from the glass container, or out of a bowl, or perhaps several bowls over several hours or days.

As a matter of fact, the term "cup" may be used metonymically even when no container is present, as in Mt. 20.22, where Jesus spoke of the cup of suffering which he was to drink, speaking of his crucifixion. There is no literal container in this passage at all.

Likewise, the term "cup" may refer to a plurality of containers. When a mother says, "I raised my babies on the bottle." Should we immediately assume she used only one container? If she tells us her husband is "on the bottle," should we assume all his drinking was out of one container?

These are points of illustration to show how a container may be used for its contents, or for the contents of many containers. However, whether we understand the figure of metonymy or not, *if we have a nondenominational view of the body of Christ, we can understand this: If the body of Christ is the universal church, as we believe it is, then it's impossible for the term "cup" in the Lord's Supper to refer to the container!* The body of Christ—the universal church—never did, doesn't now, and never will, use only one container for the fruit of the vine! One who teaches that the cup is the container teaches a doctrine that is impossible for one to obey! Those who proclaim this doctrine do not believe in one cup for one body, but one cup for one congregation, because they believe the universal church, the body of Christ, is composed of local churches, a thoroughgoing denominational view of the body of Christ.

Notice Paul's language concerning the cup in I Cor. 10.16:

> The cup of blessing which we bless…

Who is the "we" in this passage? In the previous verse, Paul says, "I speak as to wise men, judge ye what I say." The "I" refers to Paul in Ephesus, the "ye" refers to the Christians in Corinth. At the beginning of the letter, (I Cor. 1.2), Paul addresses the letter "with all that call upon the name in every place," referring to Christians everywhere. Thus, when Paul refers to "the cup of blessing which we bless," he refers to himself, the Corinthians, and all Christians everywhere. Now, did all those Christians use the same container for the Lord's Supper? Did Paul use it first in Ephesus, sail across to Corinth and let them use it in Corinth, and then they passed it on to all other Christians? Obviously, the "cup of blessing" refers not to the container, but to its contents, the fruit of the vine, which was, and is, used throughout the universal church.

In conclusion on the container question, we present a simple argument. If those who argue that the cup must be a single container (per congregation), none of us can practice what they teach if the one body is the universal church.

Controversial Question Number Two: One Bread for One Body

In I Cor. 11.23–29, Paul writes:

> For I received of the Lord that which also I delivered unto you, that the Lord Jesus in the night in which he was betrayed took bread: and when he had given thanks, he brake it and said, This is my BODY, which is for you: this do in remembrance of me. In like manner also the cup after supper, saying, This cup is the new covenant in my blood: this do, as often as ye drink it, in remembrance of me. For as often as ye eat this bread, and drink the cup, ye proclaim the Lord's death till he come. Wherefore whosoever shall eat the bread or drink the cup of the Lord in an unworthy manner, shall be guilty of the BODY and the blood of the Lord. But let a man prove himself, and so let him eat of the bread, and drink of the cup. For he that eateth and drinketh, eateth and drinketh judgment unto himself, if he discern not the BODY [emphasis mine—SGD].

The word "bread" is from the Greek *arton*, which may correctly be translated either bread or loaf. Understanding this, some brethren argue that there is to be one piece for one body; thus, the unleavened bread should not be broken during the observance of the Lord's Supper. This sounds reasonable, to be sure. Why not, in deference to the sincere convictions of such Christians, refrain from breaking the bread?

In addition, we all agree that there is one bread for the one body. Likewise, we all agree that sometimes the word *arton* here means loaf, and at other times it means bread. But again, let's not let a denominational view of the body of Christ determine our thinking here, for if the body of Christ is the universal church, it is utterly impossible for *arton* here to be the loaf! Even those brethren who believe there should be one piece or one loaf for one body don't practice it: they use one loaf per congregation, not one loaf for the body of Christ. They're viewing the body of Christ as composed of all the local bodies, a completely denominational view of the church for which Christ died. The practice of these brethren isn't wrong—a congregation can use one piece of bread if it so desires—their preaching is impossible to obey! The body of Christ never did use one piece of bread, still doesn't, and never will. The brethren who defend this doctrine don't use one piece of bread for the body of Christ, still don't, and never will.

On the other hand, *arton* can also mean bread. The one bread is unleavened bread, not any other type of bread. The one body, the universal church, has always used one bread. To illustrate the word being used this way, notice Jesus' language in Jn. 6.31:

> Our fathers did eat manna in the desert; as it is written, He gave them bread (*arton*) from heaven to eat.

I affirm that the Jews coming out of Egyptian bondage ate one bread, that is, manna, to the exclusion of all others (at least as far as this statement is concerned), but they didn't all eat of one piece, for in Ex. 16.12-14, we read where Moses said at the time:

> In the morning you shall be filled with bread (*arton* in the Greek Old Testament) behold, upon the face of the wilderness there lay a small round thing, as small as the hoar frost on the ground.

Thus, the congregation of Israel, God's universal church in the Mosaic period, all partook of one bread, no matter how many pieces they used! The same is true of God's universal church during Christ's rule: all partake of one bread, unleavened bread, regardless of how many Christians in how many congregational assemblies partake of that one bread.

Controversial Question Number Three: One Communion for One Body

The third doctrinal question concerning the body of Christ and the Lord's Supper is based on a similar vein of thinking as the previous two. Brethren who take the position that a second offering of the Lord's Supper is unscriptural make three basic arguments:

> 1. A local congregation that offers the Lord's Supper more than once on the first day of the week is violating scripture, "for Paul taught that the observance was to be partaken of by the entire body."
>
> 2. There is no example of a church in the New Testament offering the Lord's Supper more than once on the first day of the week.
>
> 3. The second offering of the Lord's Supper leads to its abuse by brethren.

Concerning the first argument, a representative sample of such teaching may be taken from the writing of a dedicated Christian by the name of Bill Shamblin, who has worked tirelessly in the Southern California area for decades, and whose teaching on this subject has traveled extensively throughout the West coast of the United States. The author knows brother Shamblin, appreciates him exceedingly highly in love for his work's sake, and has studied with him extensively on this subject. Over the years, brother Shamblin has published a booklet titled, *The Segmental Observance of the Lord's Supper*, in which he earnestly sets forth his position. A representative sample of quotations from his booklet, which demonstrate his line of thinking, follow:

> The Apostle Paul calls the local church or congregation of the church, The Body of Christ, I Cor. 12.27. (William E. Shamblin, *The Segmental Observance of the Lord's Supper* [Port Hueneme, CA: published by William E. Shamblin, n.d.], p. 3.)

> Since the congregation is the body of Christ, Christ is observing the Lord's Supper when his body, the congregation, observes it. (Shamblin, *The Segmental Observance of the Lord's Supper*, p. 6.)

> There can be no joint participation unless his body (the whole congregation) is participating. (Shamblin, *The Segmental Observance of the Lord's Supper*, p. 6.)

> Paul warned to be very careful not to eat and drink damnation to yourself by eating separate from and failing to discern the Lord's body. (Shamblin, *The Segmental Observance of the Lord's Supper*, p. 16.)

> Jesus eats and drinks only when the church eats and drinks as his body. Since an individual member or segmental part of a congregation is not the body, then such cannot eat and drink as the body, and under such circumstances. Christ is not eating and drinking, for it is not his body eating and drinking. Now if Christ is not eating and drinking, he is not jointly participating, hence there is no communion with Christ, and it is therefore not the Lord's Supper. That's why the Corinthians were not eating the Lord's Supper, because they were not eating together as the body of Christ. (Shamblin, *The Segmental Observance of the Lord's Supper*, p. 18.)

As the reader can plainly see, the basis of brother Shamblin's whole line of argument is that the local church is the body of Christ, something we've seen that the Bible nowhere teaches, and is the basis of denominational concepts of the body of Christ. Let's just take the above quotations and make some brief comments about each one:

> The Apostle Paul calls the local church or congregation of the church, The Body of Christ, I Cor. 12.27. (Shamblin, *The Segmental Observance of the Lord's Supper*, p. 3.)

Response: This statement is never proved, it's just assumed and asserted. Paul did say in Eph. 1.22, "There is one body," and he also spoke of a plurality of churches of Christ in Rom. 16.16 when he said to the Romans, "The churches of Christ salute you." If there is but one body, but there are many local churches, it is impossible that the one body is a local church, but rather it must be the universal church. Likewise, "congregation of the church" is denominational lingo, as well. As we've already seen, both the universal church and every local church is composed of Christians, not churches. It's proper to speak of congregations of the Lutheran denomination, or congregations of the Methodist denomination, for so they are. When we speak of congregations making up the Lord's church in its universal sense, we betray our denominational thinking of the body of Christ.

> Since the congregation is the body of Christ, Christ is observing the Lord's Supper when his body, the congregation, observes it. (Shamblin, *The Segmental Observance of the Lord's Supper*, p. 6.)

Response: Shamblin now builds on his previous assumption, which is a false foundation. Note here, that if the body of Christ is the universal church, and the universal church has never partaken of the Lord's Supper simultaneously, Shamblin's argument makes it impossible that the body of Christ has ever partaken of the Lord's Supper with Christ! Who can believe it? Either Paul and Jesus are confused, or Shamblin confuses the body of Christ with a denomination.

> There can be no joint participation unless his body (the whole congregation) is participating. (Shamblin, *The Segmental Observance of the Lord's Supper*, p. 6.)

Response: Again, if the body of Christ is the universal church, according to Shamblin's argument, the universal church has never participated in the Lord's Supper, including the Apostle Paul, nor Shamblin himself.

> Paul warned to be very careful not to eat and drink damnation to yourself by eating separate from and failing to discern the Lord's body. (Shamblin, *The Segmental Observance of the Lord's Supper*, p. 16.)

Response: Here is an indication of the seriousness of Shamblin's doctrine: If the body of Christ is the universal church, all Christians of all time, and of all places have never done anything but eat and drink damnation unto themselves!

> Jesus eats and drinks only when the church eats and drinks as his body. Since an individual member or segmental part of a congregation is not the body, then such cannot eat and drink as the body, and under such circumstances, Christ is not eating and drinking, for it is not his body eating and drinking. Now if Christ is not eating and drinking, he's not jointly participating, hence there is no communion with Christ, and it is therefore not the Lord's Supper. That's why the Corinthians were not eating the Lord's Supper, because they were not eating together as the body of Christ. (Shamblin, *The Segmental Observance of the Lord's Supper*, p. 18.)

Response: As before, Shamblin bases his argument on an erroneous denominational concept that the body of Christ is composed of all the congregations, and that each congregation is a local body. If Paul is correct and there is one body, then according to Shamblin, since the body has never partaken of the Lord's Supper simultaneously, Christ has never participated in the Lord's Supper with his body, and there never has been any communion with Christ.

I don't believe that brother Shamblin believes any of these conclusions that the basis of his doctrine drives him to, but they are clearly the result of the consequence of his denominational view of the body of Christ. In short, the Apostle Paul taught, "There is one body." Bill Shamblin teaches there are thousands.

Brother Shamblin closes his argumentation by using the following illustration:

> For instance, if a congregation assembled to break bread, and a family of disciples living five miles from the meeting place was unable to attend, they would obviously not be together with the disciples in that bread-breaking service. But suppose they broke bread at a later meeting of the congregation that day (usually the evening service) at which time another family of disciples who lived five miles in the opposite direction were unable to attend. Now here are disciples breaking bread in the same congregation on the first day of the week who are not within five miles of each other all day. This practice provides for a segment or part of the church to worship separate from the body; hence, without joint participation or communion with the body. (Shamblin, *The Segmental Observance of the Lord's Supper*, p. 9.)

Response: On the surface, this may sound logical, but if the Apostle Paul is correct when he says there is one body, and that body is the universal church, then according to Shamblin's statement, the body has never jointly partaken of the Lord's Supper! Although our partaking the Lord's Supper is to be done in the assembly of a local church, and the two families in Shamblin's illustration should (and probably do) desire to partake when all of them are present, Shamblin's enthusiasm to have them to do so results in the concept that there never has been in all history and in all locales any joint participation or communion with the body. Can we believe it?

For example, in I Cor. 10.16-17, Paul said concerning himself (in Ephesus at the time) and the Corinthians:

> The cup of blessing which we [Christians in Ephesus with Paul, Christians in Corinth, and Christians in all the world—SGD] bless, is it not a communion of the blood of Christ? The bread which we [Christians in Ephesus

> with Paul, Christians in Corinth, and Christians in all the world—SGD] break, is it not a communion of the body of Christ? Seeing that we, who are many [Christians in Ephesus, Christians in Corinth, and Christians in all the world—SGD] are one bread, one body, for all partake of the one bread.

Surely, we can see that Paul here speaks of the universal body of Christ partaking of the Lord's Supper, not a local body, the classic denominational concept. To use Shamblin's language, *since Paul and the Corinthians were not within five miles of each other most Sundays, they didn't have joint participation or communion most Sundays!*

Is There a Bible Example of a Second Offering of the Lord's Supper?

I freely agree there are no examples of a second offering of the Lord's Supper, just like brother Shamblin knows there are no examples of "the second assembly" for preaching itself! Shamblin preaches in second assemblies, the congregations with whom he labors have them, and yet they know there is no example of such in the entire New Testament. Likewise, they have no example of second assemblies to pray, or sing, or contribute to their local treasury, or even of a second assembly of any kind. Similarly, there are no examples of congregation-owned meeting houses, baptisteries in meeting houses, or preaching on radio and television, yet these brethren participate in all these things. If these brethren don't think seriously enough of this argument to use it consistently, why should anyone else take it seriously at all?

Positive Argument for Second Offering of the Lord's Supper

Lest someone think we can have second assemblies and permit Christians to partake of the Lord's Supper in those assemblies without scriptural authority, we give a positive basis for a Christian to partake of the Lord's Supper in a second assembly. In I Cor. 11.24-25, Paul quoted Jesus saying:

> And when he had given thanks, he brake it, and said, This is my body, which is for you; this do in remembrance of me. In like manner also the cup after supper, saying, This cup is the new covenant in my blood: this do, as often as ye drink it, in remembrance of me.

When Jesus said "this do," *what* were Christians to do? They were to eat and drink. *When* were they to do it? Those who reject multiple offerings of the Lord's Supper agree it was on the first day of the week. *Where* were they to do it? Again, those who reject multiple offerings of the Lord's Supper agree it was in an assembly of a local church. *Who* was to do it? Individual Christians. When Christians partake at a second offering of the Lord's Supper, they are those who are to partake, doing what Jesus said they were to do, where Paul said to do it, when Paul said to do it, and the whole body never partakes simultaneously because the whole body, the universal church, never has.

The Second Offering of the Lord's Supper Leads to Abuse by Brethren

The third major argument used by those opposed to the second offering of the Lord's Supper is that of abuse. "If we permit people to partake of the Lord's Supper at more than one time on the first day of the week, they will deliberately forsake assembling with other Christians when they shouldn't, and partake of the Lord's Supper at another time."

Thus, the doctrine is now pressed into service to prevent people from sinning. How many doctrines have been invented for this very purpose: to prevent people from sinning. The Pharisees of Jesus' time were experts at this. To prevent people from working on the sabbath, the Pharisees, who nobly wanted people to obey God's law carefully, godlessly invented traditions to keep people from sinning—traditions that even God himself hadn't authorized. Someone rightly said that the Pharisees were like lawyers, and you know how lawyers are: they build high fences of protection around laws they want people to obey, and build loopholes around the laws they don't have such an interest in. Those of us with a conservative attitude toward scriptural authority must be careful not to be like the Pharisees, by making laws where God made none.

Of course, none of us want people to sin, but even if people do abuse local assemblies because of the second offering of the Lord's Supper, is that justification for denying something authorized? If men abuse the eldership, does that mean we shouldn't have elders? When Bible classes are abused, should we abandon them? When preachers are abusive, should we stop men from preaching? When tracts are abused, should we cease their use? When people abuse confession of sin, should we outlaw confession? If those who are opposed to the second offering of the Lord's Supper don't think enough of the abuse argument to use it consistently, why should the rest of us?

Summary

In closing this brief study, we summarize our main points:

1. The body of Christ is the universal church, made up of all Christians worldwide; it is not a local congregation.

2. The body of Christ has never used one container for the fruit of the vine, but has always used one element, the fruit of the vine, to show Christ's blood.

3. The body of Christ has never used one piece of bread, but has always used one element, unleavened bread, to show Christ's body.

4. The body of Christ has never partaken of the Lord's Supper in one assembly, but when Christians do what Jesus and Paul said, in an assembly of Christians, "then we, who are many, are one body," partake in a communion of the body and blood of Christ.

Appendix 10

Corporate Documents of the Gospel Guardian Foundation

In Chapter 3, "The Relationship of the Universal Church and the Local Church," we traced the history of the denominational concept of the body of Christ from Roman Catholic hierarchy through the churches of Christ. We established that this was true even of champions who were fighting institutionalism (more correctly denominationalism). For the sake of preserving the historical record for posterity, we include here photographic reproductions of the Articles of Amendment to the Articles of Incorporation of Gospel Guardian Foundation, dated September 1, 1958. Signatories to this document were Roy E. Cogdill, Yater Tant, James W. Adams, Harry Pickup, Jr., Osby Weaver, Fred A. Hutson, and Troy C. Irwin.

ARTICLES OF AMENDMENT

TO THE

ARTICLES OF INCORPORATION

OF

GOSPEL GUARDIAN FOUNDATION

(formerly known as Gospel Guardian Company, Inc.)

Pursuant to the provisions of the Revised Civil Statutes of the State of Texas, the undersigned corporation adopts the following Articles of Amendment to its Articles of Incorporation:

ARTICLE ONE. An amendment to the Articles of Incorporation was adopted by the shareholders of the corporation changing the name of the corporation from Gospel Guardian Company, Inc. to Gospel Guardian Foundation. The amendment alters or changes Article One of the original articles of incorporation and Article One is hereby amended to read as follows:

"ARTICLE ONE. The name of the corporation is Gospel Guardian Foundation."

ARTICLE TWO. Article Two of the original articles of incorporation shall be amended to read as follows:

"ARTICLE TWO. The purpose for which it is formed is to support a religious, charitable and educational undertaking as authorized by Subdivision 105, Article 1302, of the Texas Revised Civil Statutes of 1925, to wit: To promote New Testament Christianity by various means, including the publication of papers and tracts pertaining only to and in support of religion, setting forth the tenets of the Churches of Christ, and to make available to the Churches of Christ everywhere religious literature with which to dissiminate New Testament teachings, and to promote other activities pertaining to and encouraging religious activities, and to do such other acts as will promote an active interest, love and respect for religion, and particularly New Testament teachings; to receive, hold, manage, administer and expend property and funds for charitable and eleemosynary purposes, including the assistance and support of charitable and eleemosynary institutions, associations and undertakings; to take property and funds by will, gift or otherwise, and to hold such funds under a legal charitable trust for religious or educational purposes, providing, however, that this foundation shall not have the power to hold or take property or funds for any purpose other than a religious, charitable or eleemosynary one; to borrow money, with or without security, and to issue promissory notes and other evidences of indebtedness, pledges, mortgages and other instruments of hypothecation; to adopt by-laws prescribing the duties of the officers and agents of the corporation, the details of its organization and time and manner of its meetings, and any and all details incident to its organization and the efficient conduct and management of its affairs, and to do any and all things necessary to carry out the general purpose for which this corporation is organized."

"The purposes of this corporation are and shall be substantially the same as they were upon the date the charter was originally granted."

ARTICLE SEVEN. The following article should be added o the original articles of incorporation:

"ARTICLE SEVEN. The property of this corporation now owned or hereafter acquired is irrevocably dedicated to religious, charitable, educational and eleemosynary purposes, and upon the liquidation, dissolution or abandonment of same, will not enure to the benefit of any private person but shall be transferred, assigned, set over and distributed to such fund, foundation or corporation organized and operated for religious, charitable or eleemosynary purposes of the type and purposes of this charitable corporation. In the event that no such type of organization can be found or agreed upon, then all of said funds shall be turned over to a school or college operated by the members of the Churches of Christ, to be determined by the remaining trustees. Provided, however, that said fund, foundation or corporation shall be exempt from taxation within the meaning of the revenue laws of the United States of America which may be in force at said time. The activities of this corporation shall at no time include the carrying on of propaganda or otherwise attempting to enforce legislation as prohibited by paragraph 170(c) of the Internal Revenue Code, and no part of the net earnings shall enure to the benefit of any private shareholder or individual, and there will be no participation in or intervention in, including the publication and distributing of statements, any political campaign on behalf of any candidate for public office. Any publication shall be restricted to publications of a religious nature and will not include publications or printing of a kind ordinarily carried on for profit."

Dated September 1, 1958.

(CORPORATE SEAL)

GOSPEL GUARDIAN FOUNDATION

Roy E. Cogdill
Roy E. Cogdill

Yater Tant
Yater Tant

James W. Adams
James W. Adams

Harry W. Pickup, Jr.
Harry W. Pickup

H. Osby Weaver
H. Osby Weaver

Fred A. Hutson
Fred A. Hutson

Troy C. Irvin
Troy C. Irvin

The above and foregoing constitutes all of the present officers, directors, trustees and members of Gospel Guardian Foundation at the time of the making of this affidavit.

Roy E. Cogdill
President

STATE OF TEXAS }
COUNTY OF DALLAS }

I, a Notary Public, do hereby certify that on this 1st day of September, 1958, personally appeared before me Roy E. Cogdill, Yater Tant, James W. Adams, Harry Pickup, Jr., H. Osby Weaver, Fred A. Hutson and Troy C. Irvin, who declared that they are the President and all of the trustees and members of the corporation executing the foregoing document, and being first duly sworn, acknowledged that they signed the foregoing document in the capacity therein set forth and declared the statements therein contained are true; and further state that a meeting of all of the trustees and members of this organization was held in Lufkin, Texas on or about the 15th day of July, 1958 with more than 80 per cent of the members and trustees of this organization affirmatively voting in favor of the above and foregoing charter amendment. That this instrument is signed by by the President who is also a member of the Board of Trustees and who has signed in behalf of said organization.

IN WITNESS WHEREOF, I have hereunto set my hand and seal the day and year before written.

[signature]
Notary Public In and for Dallas County, Texas

Bibliography

American Christian Review. Edited by Ben Franklin.

American Standard Bible. Nashville, TN: Thomas Nelson & Sons, 1901.

Ayrinhac. *Legislation on the Sacraments*. Cited by O. C. Lambert. *Catholicism Against Itself*, Vol. II. Winfield, AL: O. C. Lambert, Publisher, 1966.

Banowsky, William S. *The Mirror of a Movement, The Restoration Movement Through the Viewpoint of the Abilene Christian College Lectureships*. Dallas, TX: Christian Publishing Co., 1965.

Barnett, Maurice. *The Discipling Movement*. Phoenix, AZ: Maurice Barnett, publisher, 1987.

Beasley-Murray, G. R. *Baptism in the New Testament*. Grand Rapids: Wm. B. Eerdmans Publishing Co., 1962.

Benedict, David. *Fifty Years Among the Baptists*. Glen Rose, TX: Newman & Collins, 1913.

Biblical Discipleship Quarterly. Cited by Maurice Barnett. *The Discipling Movement*. Phoenix, AZ: Maurice Barnett, publisher, 1987.

Bingham, Joseph. *The Antiquities of the Christian Church*, II. London: Reeves & Turner, 1878.

Boles, H. Leo. *Gospel Advocate* (November 10, 1932).

Brewer, G. C. *Autobiography of G. C. Brewer*. Murfresboro, TN: DeHoff Publications, 1957.

Brightwell, W. E. *Gospel Advocate* (December 20, 1034).

Bullinger, E. W. *Figures of Speech Used in the Bible*. Grand Rapids, MI: Baker Book House, 1898.

Calvin, John. *Commentary on Ps. 33 and on I Sam. 18.1-9*. Cited by M. C. Kurfees. *Instrumental Music in the Worship*. Nashville, TN: Gospel Advocate Co., 1969.

Campbell, Alexander. *Millennial Harbinger* (1834, 1853). Reprinted Rosemead, CA: The Old Paths Book Club, 1950.

Catholic Encyclopedia, Vol X. Edited by Charles G. Herbermann. New York: The Encyclopedia Press, Inc., 1911.

Christopher, Hiram. *American Christian Review* (July 2, 1867).

Clarke, Adam. *Commentary,* IV. Nashville, TN: Abingdon Press. n.d.

Cogdill-Woods Debate. Lufkin, TX: The Gospel Guardian Company, 1958.

Darwin, Francis. *Life and Letters of Charles Darwin*, Vol. I. New York: D. Appleton and Co., 1898.

Dawson, Samuel G. *Christians, Churches, and Controversy: Navigating Doctrinal & Personal Controversy.* Amarillo, TX: Gospel Themes Press, 2003.

Dawson, Samuel G. *Denominational Doctrines: Explained, Examined, Exposed.* Sumner, WA: Gospel Themes Press, 1990.

Dawson, Samuel G. *Formality vs. Humanity: When God Despises Scriptural Worship.* Amarillo, TX: Gospel Themes Press, 1997.

Dawson, Samuel G. *Marriage, Divorce, & Remarriage: The Uniform Teaching of Moses, Jesus, & Paul.* Amarillo, TX: Gospel Themes Press, 2002.

DeHoff, George W. *Sermons on First Corinthians.* Murfreesboro, TN: The Christian Press, 1947.

Discipline of the Free Methodist Church. North Chili, NY: B. T. Roberts, Publisher, 1887.

Discipline of the Methodist Church. Edited by Emory Stevens Bucke. Nashville, TN: The Methodist Publishing House, 1960.

"Divine Property?" *Newsweek Magazine* (July 5, 1971).

Embrey, Gaylon. "Starting a Church." *The Examiner* (March 1986). Reprinted in Vol. III, No. 1.

Evangelical Dictionary of Theology. Edited by Walter A. Elwell. Grand Rapids: Baker Publishing House, 1984.

Fisher, George Park. *History of Christian Church.* New York: Charles Scribner's Sons, 1827.

Fitz Gibbons, Gerald H. *Spiritual First Aid Procedures.* Cited by O. C. Lambert. *Catholicism Against Itself,* Vol. II. Winfield, AL: O. C. Lambert, Publisher, 1966.

Garrett, Leroy. *The Stone-Campbell Movement, An Anecdotal History of Three Churches.* Joplin, MO: College Press Publishing Co., 1981.

Girardeau, John L. *Instrumental Music in the Public Worship of the Church.* Richmond, VA: Whittet & Shepperson, Printers, 1888.

Hawley, Monroe. *Redigging the Wells.* Abilene, TX: Quality Publications, 1976.

Hiscox, Edward T., D. D. *The Standard Manual for Baptist Churches.* Philadelphia: American Baptist Publication Society, 1890.

Holt, Charles A. "A Great Time in the Lord." *The Examiner* (Vol. II, No. 6).

Holt, Charles A. "Great Success—1989 Truth and Freedom Forum." *The Examiner* (September 1989).

Holt, Charles A. "June 1988 Get-together of Saints." *The Examiner* (Vol. III, No. 2).

Holt, Charles A. "1988 Truth and Freedom Forum/Fellowship." *The Examiner* (Vol. III, No. 3).

Holt, Charles A. "The Myth of the CHURCH of the Bible." *The Examiner* (November 1987).

Holt, Charles A. "What Do We Do If There Is No Local Church Institution?" *The Examiner* (May 1988).

Humble, Bill J. *Alexander Campbell and Controversy*. Rosemead, CA: Old Paths Book Club, 1952.

Jone-Adelman. *Moral Theology*. Cited by O. C. Lambert. *Catholicism Against Itself,* Vol. II. Winfield, AL: O. C. Lambert, Publisher, 1966.

Kerr, Hugh Thomson. *A Compend of Luther's Theology*. Philadelphia: The Westminster Press, 1943. Cited by Lewis W. Spitz, Ph.D. *Our Church and Others*. Saint Louis, MO: Concordia Publishing House, 1969.

Ketcherside, W. Carl. *Mission Messenger*. St. Louis, MO: W. Carl Ketcherside, publisher.

Ketcherside, W. Carl. *The Twisted Scriptures*. Reprint edition. Swengal, PA: Reiner Publications, 1965.

Lambert, O. C. *Catholicism Against Itself,* Vol. II. Winfield, AL: O. C. Lambert, Publisher, 1966.

Lenski, R. C. H. *The Interpretation of St. Paul's First and Second Epistles to the Corinthians*. Minneapolis, MN: Augsburg Publishing House, 1937.

Lipscomb, David. *Gospel Advocate* (1890, 1906). Nashville, TN: Gospel Advocate Publishing Company.

Lipscomb, David. *Gospel Advocate* (1890, 1910). Cited by Herbert E. Winkler. *Congregational Cooperation of the Churches of Christ.* Self-published, 1961.

Lipscomb, David. *Gospel Advocate* (December 3, 1931). Nashville, TN: Gospel Advocate Publishing Company, 1890, 1906.

Make Sure of All Things. Brooklyn: Watch Tower Bible & Tract Society, revised 1957.

McGarvey, J. W. *Biblical Criticism*. Cincinnati, OH: Standard Publishing Company, 1910.

McKean, Kip. *Bulletin of the Boston Church of Christ* (August 16, 1987). Boston, MA.

McNabb, Talmadge F. "The Church with the Right Name." *Sentinel of Truth* (October 1968). Cited by Monroe Hawley. *Redigging the Wells*. Abilene, TX: Quality Publications, 1976.

Memphis Meeting with the Representatives of the Herald of Truth, September 10, 1973. Memphis, TN: Getwell Church of Christ, 1973.

Menninger, Dr. Karl. Cited by Ann Landers. *Seattle Post-Intelligencer* (October 24, 1986).

Milligan, Robert. *Scheme of Redemption*. Nashville, TN: Gospel Advocate Co., 1868.

Monroy, Juan. "Cuban Personality Converted to Christ." *Restoration* (October 1971).

Monroy, Juan. "Let's Pray for Paul VI." *Restoration* (April 1972).

Mosheim, John Lawrence. *Ecclesiastical History,* I. Rosemead, CA: Old Paths Book Club, 1959.

Munnell,Thomas. *Lard's Quarterly* (January 1865). Lexington, KY: Moses Lard.

New American Standard Bible. LaHabra, CA: Lockman Foundation, 1971.

Packer, J. I. *Fundamentalism and the Word of God.* Grand Rapids, MI: William B. Eerdmans Publishing Co., 1958.

Pierce, James. *A Vindication of the Dissenters.* Cited by John L. Girardeau. *Instrumental Music in the Public Worship of the Church.* Richmond, VA: Whittet & Shepperson, Printers, 1888.

Questions on the Confession of Faith and Form of Government of the Presbyterian Church in the United States of America. Philadelphia: Presbyterian Board of Publications, 1842.

Quizzes on Hospital Ethics. Cited by O. C. Lambert. *Catholicism Against Itself,* Vol. II. Winfield, AL: O. C. Lambert, Publisher, 1966.

Restoration. Abilene, TX: Herald of Truth, Fifth and Highland Church of Christ.

Robertson, A. T. *Word Pictures in the New Testament.* Nashville, TN: Broadman Press, 1931.

Rumble. *Quizzes on Hospital Ethics*. Cited by O. C. Lambert. Winfield, AL: O. C. Lambert, Publisher, 1966.

Schaff, Philip. *History of the Christian Church.* New York: Charles Scribner's Sons, 1887.

Sentry Magazine, XIII, No. 4. Edited by Floyd Chappelear. Centreville, VA.

Shamblin, William E. *The Segmental Observance of the Lord's Supper.* Port Hueneme, CA: William E. Shamblin, Publisher, n.d.

Smith, Charles. *Oliphant-Smith Debate*. Nashville, TN: Gospel Advocate Company, 1952.

Spitz, Lewis W., Ph.D. *Our Church and Others*. Saint Louis, MO: Concordia Publishing House, 1969.

Spurgeon, Charles. *Spurgeon Memorial Library,* Vol. I. n.d.

Srygley, F. B. *Gospel Advocate* (December 3, 1931).

Srygley, F. B. *Gospel Advocate* (November 1, 1934). Cited in *The Willis-Inman Debate.* Louisville, KY: Truth Magazine, 1968.

Stevens, Eldred. *Contending for the Faith.* Birmingham, AL.

"That the Brethren May Know." Abilene, TX: Fifth and Highland Church of Christ, n.d. Cited in *The Cogdill-Woods Debate.* Lufkin, TX: Gospel Guardian Company, 1957.

Thayer, Joseph Henry. *Greek-English Lexicon of the New Testament.* Grand Rapids, MI: Zondervan Publishing House, 1889.

The Truth that Leads to Eternal Life. Brooklyn: Watch Tower Bible & Tract Society of New York, Inc., 1968.

Tinder, Donald G. *Evangelical Dictionary of Theology.* Editor Walter A. Elwell. Grand Rapids: Baker Publishing House, 1984.

Totty, W. L. *Contending for the Faith* (August 1973).

Totty, W. L. *Contending for the Faith* (May 1979).

Turner, Robert F. "The Schools and Denominationalism." *The Preceptor* (June 1962).

Wallace, Foy E., Jr. *Gospel Advocate* (May 14, 1931).

Ward. *The Priestly Vocation.* Cited by O. C. Lambert. *Catholicism Against Itself,* Vol. II. Winfield, AL: O. C. Lambert, Publisher, 1966.

Webster's New World Dictionary. Second College Edition. New York: The World Publishing Company, 1970.

Wesley, John. *Universal Knowledge, A Dictionary and Encyclopedia of Arts, Sciences, History, Biography, Law, Literature, Religions, Nations, Races, Customs, and Institutions.* Edited by Edward A. Pace. New York: Universal Knowledge Foundation, 1927.

West, Earl. *Search for the Ancient Order,* II. Indianapolis, IN: Religious Book Service, 1950.

Williams, Charles B. *New Testament in the Language of the People.* Chicago: Moody Press, 1966.

Willis, Wayne. "The Plight of the Church of Christ Liberal." *Mission* (June 1973). Cited by Monroe Hawley. *Redigging the Wells.* Abilene, TX: Quality Publications, 1976.

Willis-Inman Debate. Louisville, KY: Truth Magazine, 1968.

Winkler, Herbert E. *Congregational Cooperation of the Churches of Christ.* Self-published, 1961.

Woods, Guy N. *Annual Lesson Commentary*. Nashville, TN: Gospel Advocate Publishing Company, 1946.

Scripture Index

John

Acts

Romans

I Corinthians

II Corinthians

Galatians

Ephesians

Philippians

Colossians

I Thessalonians

II Thessalonians

I Timothy

II Timothy

Titus

Philemon

Hebrews

James

I Peter

II Peter

I John

II John

III John

Jude

Revelation

Topical Index

V

W

Denominational Doctrines:
Explained, Examined, Exposed

Samuel G. Dawson

384 pages

This Book Will Help You Explore
These Controversial Topics:

Jehovah's Witnesses—Are They Really?
Was Jesus a Created Being?
Modern-Day Tongue-Speaking—Is It from God?
I Corinthians 14 & the Charismatic Movement
Matthew 24 & Prophetic Speculation
Revelation 20 & Premillennialism
The Indwelling of the Holy Spirit
Are Babies Born Totally Depraved?
Is Anyone Unconditionally Elected to Be Saved?
May a Christian So Sin as to Be Lost?
Should Christians Keep the Sabbath?
Answering Sabbatarian Arguments
Was Joseph Smith a Prophet of God?
Theistic Evolution
How to Be Just a Christian
Arguments Against Baptism Answered

Ideal for: Individual Study, Preaching,
Elders, Adult Classes,
Personal Evangelism, New Converts, Gifts

Christians, Churches, & Controversy:
Navigating Doctrinal & Personal Clashes

Samuel G. Dawson

216 pages with comprehensive indexes

An eighteenth century Scottish poet wrote concerning war: "Rash, fruitless war, from wanton glory waged, is only splendid murder."

An older preacher used this quotation when he wrote concerning a particularly brutal doctrinal attack on another elderly preacher by a group of younger, treacherous preachers. While many controversies among Christians and churches aren't this vicious, many Christians and congregations simply don't know how to navigate personal and doctrinal clashes, and thus, do more harm than good. Such situations expose some noble and naïve souls to some pretty treacherous Christians. Yet, many Christians consent to much worse than Saul did at Stephen's stoning while "consenting to his death" by just holding the coats of the stone-throwers. Most members, whose jobs aren't even on the line, refuse to ratchet up their courage to be bothered by congregational problems and decisions. They may just want difficulties handled by the congregational leaders so they can avoid being involved. Consequently, many Christians go blithely on, consenting through ignorance to mistreatment of others that goes on behind the scenes.

This book is not for you if:

You're not a serious student of the Bible
Your concept of Bible study is listening to your teacher go through a quarterly class book
Your concept of being a Christian consists mainly of "going to church"
If you depend on the preacher to do your studying for you
You're in a denomination where all the thinking is done at the top
If you're an elder who is afraid for the congregation to study controversial subjects

Ideal for: Individual Study, Preaching, Elders,
Adult Classes, Personal Evangelism, New Converts, Gifts

Samuel G. Dawson

A physics and mathematics graduate from Texas Tech University, Samuel G. Dawson did research in celestial mechanics and intercontinental missile guidance in the aerospace industry before preparing to preach the gospel of Christ. In twenty-two years of public teaching, he did extensive live call-in radio work daily for eight years and participated in a number of religious debates. Sam's scientific background has given him a logical and thorough approach to the scriptures and a reputation for making Bible students re-think teaching they've taken for granted.

Over one hundred thousand cassettes of his classes and sermons have been distributed across the nation. His most popular ones are now available in cassette albums: *Marriage, Divorce, & Remarriage* demonstrates how Moses, Jesus, and Paul all taught the same thing about this controversial subject. It deals frankly with issues confronting many Christians today and the people they are trying to teach. Sam recently put this material in book form. *The Teaching of Jesus* shows how many people take Jesus' teaching out of the context of the people he preached to and misapply it to our day. *How to Study the Bible* teaches dedicated Bible students how to study from choosing a dependable translation to rules for interpretation to solving difficulties in the Bible.

Sam drew on decades of experience working with local congregations to write *Fellowship: With God and His People (The Way of Christ Without Denominationalism)* and *Denominational Doctrines: Explained, Examined, Exposed.* He co-authored a *Handbook of Religious Quotations* and has written numerous tracts.